THE MARSH OF GOLD

Pasternak's Writings on Inspiration and Creation

D0792623

Studies in Russian and Slavic Literatures, Cultures and History

Series Editor: Lazar Fleishman

ACADEMIC
STUDIES
PRESS

The Marsh of Gold

Pasternak's Writings on Inspiration and Creation

Texts by **Boris Pasternak,**
selected, translated, edited, introduced
and provided with commentaries and notes

by ANGELA LIVINGSTONE

Boston
2010

On the cover: Leonid Pasternak. Portrait of his son Boris (a fragment).
Around 1917

Copyright © 2010 Academic Studies Press
All rights reserved

ISBN 978-1-936235-07-0 (paperback)

Book design by Yuri Alexandrov

Published by Academic Studies Press in 2010
28 Montfern Avenue
Brighton, MA 02135, USA
press@academicstudiespress.com
www.academicstudiespress.com

Contents

I
EARLY PROSE
(1910–1919)

II
A SAFE-CONDUCT
or "THE PRESERVATION CERTIFICATE"
(1928–1931)

III
FIFTEEN POEMS
(1912–1931)

PREFACE

Boris Pasternak, 1890–1960, thought and wrote all his life about the nature of poetic creation and what is traditionally called inspiration; few have pondered these matters so intently or described them so illuminatingly. This book presents his major writings on these subjects. The translated texts are accompanied by an Introduction, discursive Commentaries and an essay on *Doctor Zhivago*.

Much of the book is based on my *Pasternak on Art and Creativity* (C.U.P. 1985). At all points, however, it differs from it. Looking back at that earlier book, I realized it needed not only thorough revision of the translations but also radical re-writing of the Commentaries in view of the important studies of Pasternak appearing over the last two decades and my own somewhat changed and expanded perception of his thought.

So this is a new book, with a new title. While many of the texts by Pasternak are the same ones as in the earlier book, with the autobiographical *A Safe-Conduct* still central among them, all translations have been thoroughly revised; moreover, no excerpts from *Doctor Zhivago* are included but twenty-four new texts have been added—nine prose pieces and fifteen poems. All the Commentaries are written afresh. The Introduction and the final Essay on *Zhivago* are also wholly new.

While the book is designed primarily for English-readers, references are given to numerous Russian works, in the hope that Russian-readers and people studying Russian will also use it.

ACKNOWLEDGMENTS

Above all, I wish to thank Evgeny Borisovich Pasternak and Elena Vladimirovna Pasternak for innumerable instances of help received from them over the years, and for all their kind encouragement of my work. My profound gratitude goes to them for their lifelong dedication to preserving, introducing and publishing Pasternak's prose and poetry, and especially for the recent superb edition of his Complete Works in Eleven Volumes with its full and excellent annotations.

My warmest thanks are due to Lazar Fleishman for his support of this project; I am extremely grateful to him, moreover, for reading much of the typescript and responding with invaluable criticisms.

Discussion of many of Pasternak's ideas with Fiona Björling has been an important spur to my work on this book. Susan Biver, Fiona Björling and Kay Stevenson have read and commented on lengthy portions of the typescript, for which I am deeply grateful to them. I wish also to thank Leon Burnett, Herbie Butterfield, Diane Fahey and Philip Terry for their responses to parts of the book in progress. For elucidation of certain Russian words I thank Anna Chernova and Natalia Gogolitsyna; for skilled assistance with the computer I thank Stephen Doubtfire and Kristin Hutchinson.

A grant from the British Academy enabled me to attend the Conference on Pasternak organized by Perm University in July 2006, at which I was able to develop ideas relevant to this book. A great deal of the new translation for it was done at the peaceful and stimulating Baltic Centre for Writers and Translators in Visby, Gotland in the spring of 2005. My thanks to the Inter-Library-Loan section of the University of Essex Albert Sloman Library for finding and obtaining so many books for me, and to my own Department of Literature, Film and Theatre Studies for giving me—despite my retirement—abundant space, technology and personal support.

I gratefully acknowledge permission from the publishers of Berkeley Slavic Specialties to re-publish my translation of Pasternak's essay on Kleist and part of my commentary on it, both first published by them in *A Century's Perspective*, 2006; also permission from Stanford University Press to reprint (in shortened form) the article "How to Translate the Title *Okhrannaia gramota*" and to use parts of "Re-reading *Okhrannaia gramota*: Pasternak's Use of Visuality and his

Conception of Inspiration", both published in *Eternity's Hostage*, 2006. I thank also Michael Schmidt of Carcanet Press Ltd for the right to quote Donald Davie's translation of Anna Akhmatova's poem "Boris Pasternak" as published in Davie and Livingstone, eds, *Pasternak*, London, 1969.

My translations of "Ordering a Drama" (*Zakaz dramy*) and "[On the Threshold of Inspiration]" (*Prezhde vsego . . .*) were first published in *PN Review* 5, 4 (1978). Translations of "To Anna Akhmatova", "To Marina Tsvetaeva" and, in earlier form, "February" and "Again Chopin . . ." were first published in *European Voices: Modern Poetry in Translation*, 18, edited by Daniel Weissbort in 2001. My earlier translation of *A Safe-Conduct* (*Okhrannaia gramota*) appeared in Pasternak, *Collected Short Prose*, edited by Christopher Barnes in 1977; the present translation of it is a much-revised version of the one included in my *Pasternak on Art and Creativity*.

NOTE ON TRANSLITERATION AND DATES

I have used the Library of Congress system of transliteration of Cyrillic, in which problematic vowels are represented as follows: **я** as **ia**; **ю** as **iu**; **e**, **ё** and **э** all as **e**; **и** and **й** as **i**; **ы** as **y**, and hard and soft signs are both represented by the sign **'**. Except in Russian-language contexts, Russian names already familiar in an English spelling are spelt in the familiar way (thus: Gogol, Gorky, Mandelstam, Mayakovsky, Scriabin, Tchaikovsky, Tolstoy), the surname-ending "-skii" is represented as "-sky", the name Aleksandr becomes Alexander, an adjectival name of a street or square is given in the masculine form, Tsentrifuga is written Centrifuga. For names of persons and places, the soft sign has been transliterated only in the Notes and Bibliography and in Russian-language contexts.

Dates accord with British usage, thus 1.2.1930 means February 1st, 1930.

ABBREVIATIONS

PSS is used throughout as an abbreviation of the title of the new and authoritative collection of Pasternak's complete works, namely:

Pasternak, Boris. *Polnoe sobranie sochinenii s prilozheniiami, v odinnadtsati tomakh* [Complete Collected Works with appendices, in Eleven Volumes]. Chief editor: D.V. Tevekelian. Compiled and provided with commentaries by E.B. Pasternak and E.V. Pasternak. Introduction by Lazar Fleishman. Moscow: Slovo, 2003–05.

Reference to particular pages in its eleven volumes is done on the following model: PSS, 10, 22 for *Polnoe sobranie sochinenii*, volume 10, page twenty-two.

Titles of two works by Pasternak frequently mentioned in the present volume are sometimes abbreviated as follows: *A Safe-Conduct* as *S-C*; *Doctor Zhivago* as *DrZh*. Parts and chapters of these works are referred to as follows: *S-C* 2,17 for *A Safe-Conduct*, part two, chapter seventeen; *DrZh* 14,9 for *Doctor Zhivago*, part fourteen, chapter nine.

An asterisk following a shortened title means that the full title will be found in the Bibliography.

A BRIEF CHRONOLOGY

Pasternak's life and major publications (poetry unless otherwise stated)	Other significant events
	1880 Birth of Blok.
	1881 Death of Dostoevsky.
	1889 Birth of Akhmatova.
1890 Born in Moscow. (Brother and two sisters born 1893, 1900, 1902.)	
	1891 Birth of Mandelstam.
	1892 Birth of Tsvetaeva.
	1893 Birth of Mayakovsky.
1900 Meets Rilke on a train journey.	
1903 Meets Scriabin, begins six-year study of music. Thrown by a horse, breaks his leg—"getting out of two future wars in one evening".	
	1904 Russia defeated in war with Japan.
	1905 Year of revolutionary uprisings and changes.
1906 A year in Germany with his family.	
1908 Enters Moscow University.	
1909 Decides against a career in music; becomes student of philosophy. As pianist, joins "Serdarda", group of young poets, artists, musicians.	
	1910 Death of Tolstoy.
	1911 Assassination of Prime Minister Stolypin.
1912 Summer semester at University of Marburg under Hermann Cohen. Decides against a career in philosophy. Visits Italy.	1912 Acmeism and futurism replace symbolism as main poetic movements.
1913 Graduates from university. Gives lecture "Symbolism and Immortality".	1913 Belyi, *Petersburg*. Mandelstam, *Stone*.
1914 As member of moderate futurist group "Centrifuga", meets Mayakovsky. *Twin in the Clouds*.	
1914–16 Works as tutor, then in management of chemical factories in the Urals.	1914–18 World War I.
	1916 Mayakovsky, A *Cloud in Trousers*.
1917 Returns to Moscow at the February revolution. *Above the Barriers*.	1917 February and October revolutions.
1918 Works as librarian in People's Commissariat of Education.	1918 Blok, *The Twelve*.

Pasternak's life and major publications (poetry unless otherwise stated)	Other significant events
	1918–20 Civil War.
1921 Parents and sisters emigrate.	1921 Death of Blok.
	1921 Execution of poet Gumilev.
1922 Marries artist Evgeniia Lur'e; seven months with her in Germany. *My Sister Life*.	1922 Mandelstam, *Tristia*; Eliot, *The Waste Land*; Joyce, *Ulysses*; Rilke, *Duino Elegies*.
1923 Joins neo-futurist group "Lef". Living poorly but now a well-known poet. Birth of son Evgenii. *Themes and Variations*.	
1924 Works briefly in library of People's Commissariat for Foreign Affairs.	1924 Death of Lenin (January); beginning of Stalin's rise to power.
1925 *Aerial Ways* (four stories: "The Mark of Apelles", "Letters from Tula", "Childhood of Liuvers", "Aerial Ways"); *The Year Nineteen Hundred and Five*.	1925 Resolution on Literature published by Communist Party. Suicide of poet Esenin.
1926 *Lieutenant Schmidt*.	1926 Babel, *Red Cavalry*. Death of Rilke in Switzerland.
1928 *Lofty Malady*.	1928 Start of first Five-Year Plan for collectivization of agriculture and for intensive industrialization.
1929 *A Tale* (prose).	
1930 Separates from first wife; marries Zinaida Neigaus. Official journey to the Urals.	1930 Suicide of Mayakovsky.
1931 Criticised by RAPP. To Georgia with Zinaida. Again to the Urals. *A Safe-Conduct* (prose); *Spektorsky*.	
1932 Adds idiosyncratic postscript to collective letter from writers to Stalin on death of his wife. Working on translations; no further original work until 1940.	1932 Union of Soviet Writers founded; all other literary groups disbanded.
1934 Telephoned by Stalin. Speaks at Writers' Union congress.	1934 First congress of Soviet Writers' Union. Arrest of Mandelstam.
1935 Insomnia, depression. Obliged to attend Congress of Writers in Defence of Culture, in Paris.	
1936 Is allotted a dacha in Peredelkino (near Moscow). Refuses to sign letter condemning generals accused of conspiracy.	1936–38 Years of state terror: show trials and executions.
	1937 Arrest and execution of poet Tabidze, suicide of poet Yashvili (Pasternak's friends). Death of Mandelstam in a prison camp.
1938 Birth of son Leonid.	
1939 Death of mother in London.	
1940 Translates *Hamlet*.	
1941 Evacuated to Chistopol in the Urals. Translating Shakespeare's tragedies.	1941–3 Blockade of Leningrad by the Germans.
1943 Visits the war front. *On Early Trains*.	1943 Battle of Stalingrad.

Pasternak's life and major publications (poetry unless otherwise stated)	Other significant events
1945 Death of father in Oxford. *Earth's Expanse*. Starts writing the novel *Doctor Zhivago*.	1945 Soviet troops enter Berlin; end of World War II.
1946 Refuses to condemn Akhmatova and Zoshchenko; is attacked by Fadeev, Secretary of Writers' Union; meanwhile, has a growing reputation abroad. Love relationship with Olga Ivinskaia.	1946–51 "Zhdanov" repression in the arts.
1947–49 Further attacks on him by the Writers' Union.	
1947–51 Translates Goethe's *Faust*, I and II.	
1949 Supports family of Ivinskaia, imprisoned because of him (released in 1953). *William Shakespeare in Boris Pasternak's Translation*.	
1952 Heart attack, three months in hospital.	
	1953 Death of Stalin.
1956 *Novyi mir* rejects *Doctor Zhivago*. Contract with State Publishing House for an abridged version; agreement with Italian publisher Feltrinelli.	1956 Khrushchev denounces Stalin at Twentieth Congress of the Communist Party. "Thaw" in literature. Suicide of Fadeev.
1957 Months in hospital. Publication of *Zhivago* forbidden in Soviet Union; Feltrinelli publishes it in Italian. *Doctor Zhivago*.	
1958 Awarded the Nobel Prize for Literature; *Zhivago* translated and published in many countries; press campaign against him in USSR; expelled from the Writers' Union; forced to renounce the Prize. *Autobiographical Sketch* (prose, published abroad).	
1959 *When the Weather Clears* (published abroad). Feltrinelli publishes *Doctor Zhivago* in Russian.	
1960 Dies, in Moscow; thousands attend his funeral in Peredelkino. *The Blind Beauty* (incomplete play, published abroad).	
	1966 Death of Akhmatova. Bulgakov, *The Master and Margarita*.
1970 Award of the Nobel Prize to Solzhenitsyn.	
1974 Expulsion of Solzhenitsyn from the Soviet Union.	
	1985 Gorbachev becomes First Secretary of the Communist Party.
1988 *Doctor Zhivago* serialized in *Novyi mir*.	
1989 *Collected Works of Boris Pasternak in Five Volumes*, Moscow, 1989–92.	
2003 *Complete Works in Eleven Volumes*, Moscow, 2003-5	

NOTE ON PASTERNAK'S CONNECTIONS WITH LITERARY GROUPS

Symbolism was the dominant movement in Russian poetry during the first decade of the twentieth century. Pasternak read the work of the symbolists with warm interest, especially that of Blok and Belyi. By 1912 two other major poetic movements were dominant. One was acmeism, which was represented by Gumilev, Gorodetsky, early Akhmatova and Mandelstam, and which flourished as a formal movement until 1914; it replaced the symbolists' musical suggestiveness with an architectural precision, and the symbolists' yearning for "other worlds" with "a respect for the four dimensions of this world". The other movement was futurism, which counted Mayakovsky, Khlebnikov, Kruchenykh, Kamensky, and David and Nikolai Burliuk among its members. Anti-mystical, anti-aestheticist, anti-traditional, the futurists cultivated modernity, virility, bold compound rhyme, word-invention. Their 1912 manifesto, "A Slap in the Face of Public Taste", contained such advice as "Throw Pushkin, Tolstoy, etc, overboard . . . "

Pasternak's professional literary début was with the symbolist-oriented "*Lirika*" group; this was reconstituted early in 1914 as the "innovatory" futurist group, "Centrifuga", led by Sergei Bobrov (1889–1971) and rivalling the more extreme "cubo-futurist" group of which Mayakovsky was a member. Centrifuga differed from cubo-futurism in its far more respectful attitude towards the literary tradition. (See Lazar Fleishman, "Pasternak i predrevoliutsionnyi futurizm".*)

Pasternak was not at ease in inter-group arguments or when under pressure to identify himself with group doctrine. *A Safe-Conduct* contains sharp words about the feuding among rival literary groups (see S-C 3,2), but in 1918 he was already writing: "Symbolist, Acmeist, Futurist? What murderous jargon! Clearly aesthetics is a science which classifies air balloons according to where and how the holes are placed in them that prevent them from flying." "Some Propositions"). All the same, out of admiration for Mayakovsky he remained close to futurism, and became a member of the post-revolutionary neo-futurist group "Lef". The history of Lef has been called a "fascinating story of attempts to create an avant-garde art and literature based on, and helpful to, Communism", as well as "the story of fierce literary battles and defense against the attacks of the orthodox proletarians and other groups." (Vladimir Markov, *Russian Futurism*, London, 1969, p. 381). Pasternak left "Novyi Lef" (as it was called in its revived form) in 1927, saying he was repelled by its "excessive sovietism, i.e. depressing servility, i.e. tendency to riotous behaviour with an official mandate for riotous behaviour in its pocket" (quoted by Fleishman in *Pasternak v dvadtsatye gody*, 82. *)

All literary groups were dissolved in 1932 with the formation of the monolithic Union of Soviet Writers, of which Pasternak, like every writer who wished to publish, became a member. In 1934 he was elected to the board of that union. According to its statutes, drawn up in 1934, "socialist realism is the basic method of Soviet literature and literary criticism. It demands from the artist a truthful, historically concrete representation of reality in its revolutionary development. Moreover, the truthfulness and historical concreteness of the artistic representation of reality must be linked with the task of ideological transformation and education of the workers in the spirit of socialism." (Quoted from Abram Tertz, "On Socialist Realism", translated by G. Dennis, 1960, p. 24.) Pasternak said very little about this conception but often expressed his strong dislike of slogans and prescriptive statements. At the end of 1957 he told visitors from the West (Gerd Ruge, *Pasternak. Eine Bildbiographie*. München: Kindler Verlag, 1958): "No, I did not become a socialist realist. But I did become a realist. For which I am thankful."

The Marsh of Gold

*Pasternak's Writings
on Inspiration
and Creation*

INTRODUCTION

When Boris Pasternak, as a young student, went to Venice in 1912 it was to look for a "marsh of gold, one of the primal pools" of creativity. He had just begun "fundamentally" writing poetry. Years later he wrote that "what is clearest, most memorable and important about art is its coming into being, and the world's best works of art, while telling of very diverse matters, are really telling about their birth". A great deal of what he wrote does indeed seem prompted by a desire to find precise words for what is conventionally called "inspiration".

Pasternak travelled to Venice from Marburg, the German university town where he had gone from Moscow for a summer semester of philosophy. He had chosen that university because of the high value its scholars gave to authenticity and because of their characteristic quest for origins, for "how science thinks at the hot beginnings and sources of world-important discoveries". Pasternak was drawn to origins not as causes of subsequent phenomena, and not as past moments one yearns to return to, but as occasions for knowing and celebrating the force with which something that might never have been comes into being. One of his fictional characters, speaking about art, speaks "as though someone were alternately showing him the earth and hiding it in his sleeve, and he understood living beauty as the ultimate difference between existence and non-existence".[1] Such an extreme and difficult stance of wonder is present throughout Pasternak's work; the attempt to give an account of it is basic to his few pieces of theoretical and autobiographical prose.

2

The present book brings together a selection of Pasternak's writings on artistic inspiration, art's origin in life. Most are prose texts, varying in length from a couple of pages to the ninety-page autobiographical work *A Safe-Conduct*, which is without doubt the most important of all he wrote on this subject. But he was primarily a poet and, since many of his poems contain something like definitions of themselves, fifteen poems are also included in this book. The book's five parts are arranged chronologically, Parts I to IV consisting of a text or texts translated into English and followed by a Commentary.

Part I offers nine of his writings from the period 1910 to 1919. Three of these were published soon after being written: an article from 1916 (a rare participation in literary polemics), one story ("Letters from Tula") and the group of statements entitled "Some Propositions" which, though written last in this early period, is placed first because it so strongly expresses Pasternak's main feeling about art and his resistance to the literary debates going on around him. The six other pieces in Part I were not published in his lifetime nor meant to be. The two long fragments from 1910 ("Reliquimini" and "Ordering a Drama"), perhaps startling at first with their excited impressionist style and their trying out of strange ideas, belong to his first attempts to pin down in words the sensation of being inspired to create something; two difficult pieces, the unfinished essay on Kleist and the 1913 lecture-synopsis, reward sympathetic reading; the two other jottings, from 1912 and 1913, are fascinating records of the poet's unusual way of thinking and perceiving. These six little-known pieces give valuable glimpses of the turbulent mind of someone finding his way into poetry after an adolescence spent first in music and then in philosophy.

Other early fictional works, though not represented in this volume, are also discussed in the Commentary to Part I in so far as they deal with art and artists.

A reader new to Pasternak would do well, however, to start with Part II, which presents the unconventional autobiography *A Safe-Conduct*, written 1928–30 and published 1931, the best known of Pasternak's work except for *Doctor Zhivago*. An exact translation of its title would be "A (or The) Preservation Certificate", which I am introducing as a sub-title. My Commentary concentrates on the four chapters which set out a theory of art in relatively defining terms, and on the relation of two other poets, Rilke and Mayakovsky, to that theory. But really the whole of *A Safe-Conduct* is about the events, impressions and thoughts which led to a life in poetry.

The fifteen poems, with their Russian originals but with minimal commentary, constitute Part III. They form a supplement to I and II, as they cover the same years and resemble the early prose texts in their fervently precise style.

The 1930s and '40s were a time of unprecedented interference in literature by the ruling Communist Party and of damaging pressures from Party-influenced critics and editors. It was a time in which Pasternak, producing less of his own work, devoted himself largely to translation, including that of eight plays by Shakespeare and both parts of Goethe's *Faust*, as well as numerous lyric poems from several languages. Part IV presents some of his articles and speeches from this period, in the hope of showing his attempts to sustain and communicate his unchanged concern with inspiration and originality, in circumstances now hostile to such thoughts. The Commentary includes discussion of his response to the Communist Party's subtly oppressive 1925 decree, its first statement about literature. It also includes discussion of his intervention in the "anti-formalist campaign" of 1936.

Part V is an essay on *Doctor Zhivago*, differing from I to IV in that no text by Pasternak is presented. His one novel (written 1946–55, published abroad in 1958) is well enough known. Longish passages from it are quoted, however, to show the very much wider meaning he gave to art and inspiration as his views evolved.

3

Pasternak himself indicated some biographical origins of his conception of art. He recalls being woken one night, at four years old, by music: his mother (a concert pianist) was playing a trio with two friends and he was frightened by the sound of the stringed instruments which was "like real calls for help and news of a disaster coming in from outside through the window".[2] He was to think of that moment as the transition from unconscious infancy to consciousness; a transition, then, through art, the first conscious meaning of which was cries for help. He also recalls later in his childhood watching his father (a well-known artist) packing up the illustrations he had drawn for Tolstoy's novel *Resurrection;* the novel was being serialized, so there was a race against time and a uniformed railwayman would come right into their kitchen for the drawings. Pasternak recalls the details: joiner's glue boiling, the drawings being hurriedly wiped and glued, the sealed parcels speedily handed over.

If a sense of art as a mysterious response to external need began with a crying violin and the creative life of his mother, the association of art's production with excited speed began with his observation of the artistic work of his father.

These two motifs recur repeatedly. The sense of need appears, for example, in the extraordinary image of a truncated trochee, in the fragment "On the Threshold of Inspiration". Without art, everything is like a halved trochaic foot at the end of a line of verse, that is to say a stressed syllable demanding an unstressed one to follow it. The longed-for lightness of the unstressed is not a mere question of versification: the lighter syllable is the "feminine" element completing an otherwise incomplete reality. Elsewhere this is reversed and the creative impulse becomes a response to women's suffering, as in the glimpse of ill-treated "amazons" in the first part of *A Safe-Conduct* and, much later, in *Doctor Zhivago,* in Iurii's first glimpse of Lara in a scene which seems to be "calling for help"—the very same phrase is used as about the violin in the infancy episode.

Meanwhile, the packing up of paintings in the kitchen becomes a metaphor for writing; rapidly pressed-in contents of a parcel represent the compressed content of a poem. Such an image appears at the end of "Ordering a Drama", and is elaborated in "The Black Goblet".

The two recalled experiences—external need, internal speed—are combined in the *S-C* narrative of the birth of poetry in the poet's life (1,6). There, a force of feeling is said to be racing the sun, but it is only in the compassionate look back at things left behind and needing to be included that "that which is called inspiration" occurs. Nothing is more typical of the youthful Pasternak than this exhilaration in fast movement, interrupted by distress on account of everything that is unexhilarated, this hint of a breathlessly performed rescue, wild armfuls of transformed—transferred—objects.

4

Pasternak's adolescence was devoted not to poetry but to music. Another childhood recollection records the origin of his study of music. Going out one day from the family dacha, he found himself enchanted by sounds filling the woodlands; the new neighbour playing the piano turned out to be Alexander Scriabin, the composer; Scriabin became his hero and he resolved to become a composer himself. That winter, when Scriabin, by then a friend of his parents, had set off from their house for a long stay abroad and Pasternak's mother began playing one of Scriabin's pieces, the thirteen-year-old Boris—"as soon as the first sixteen bars had formed themselves into a sentence full of an astounded readiness unrewardable by anything on earth"—rushed hatless and coatless outdoors to try to bring the composer back. "Astounded readiness", "unrewardability"—concepts equally applicable to his own adoration of Scriabin—express not mere passive openness but the heady refusal of closure which would always characterize art for him. It is the subject of his fragmentary essay, "Heinrich von Kleist".

After six years of studying to be a composer, and despite the fact that "more than anything in the world /he/ loved music, and more than anyone in music—Scriabin", despite also the fact that Scriabin himself had praised the then nineteen-year-old's piano compositions, saying he had much more than a mere gift and could "say something of his own in music", he quite suddenly gave it all up. Later he said that a musical career would have been a constriction, but he also said, later still, that giving it up had been a "direct amputation, the removal of the most living part of /his/ existence"; he remained tortured by a "burning need for a composer's biography."[3]

From music he plunged into philosophy, no less ardently, and again successfully, being encouraged by the famous Marburg philosopher Hermann Cohen to make a career as a philosopher. Then, just as he had abandoned music at the moment when the highest authority assured him of his exceptional talent for it, he did the same with philosophy: merely brought his studies to their conclusion and made a wholly fresh start, this time in poetry.

The switch from philosophy to poetry is explored in the incomplete "Kleist" essay as an escape from intellectual system into the freedom of the unsystematic. Little is said about this in *A Safe-Conduct*, nor is there much in that work about the switch from music to poetry except that "fifteen years of abstinence from words, which had been sacrificed to sounds, meant being doomed to originality, the way certain kinds of maiming doom a person to acrobatics". That he had a permanent limp after a fall from a horse makes the analogy a poignant one, and its ironic modesty stands in curious relation to the speed and power evoked only three paragraphs later in the poetry-initiating race against the sun. But several notebook-writings from shortly after the break with music reflect the pain of it. In "Ordering a Drama", all of life is seen chasing after music "as if music had arrived in the town and had put up somewhere and everyone were fighting their way toward music as if to a hotel with a celebrity . . . , where to find music, where is it staying, *haven't you seen music*". Meanwhile it is interesting to note that in the same work the music teacher is named "Shestikrylov", which means "Six-Winged" and undoubtedly refers to the seraph in Pushkin's 1826 poem "The Prophet": the seraph meets a wanderer in the wilderness and makes him a poet by giving him fiery speech and preternatural senses. So was music, after all, the angel who set the poet on the right path? Two years later, in "On the Threshold of Inspiration", an urban winter day is still felt to be leaning "like a plank, towards music" and, soon after that, music is referred to in the lecture-synopsis "Symbolism and Immortality" in terms that suggest it was indeed the motivating angel. The poet is "symbolized by rhythm", and rhythm is "music's sole symbol". Then one of the clauses runs: "Inspiration is the syntax of poetry", and syntax is "concrete in alliteration"; one may surmise that alliteration and syntax, rather than, say, metaphors or ironies, are chosen to represent inspiration here because these forms—repeated sounds, organized phrases—are fundamental to music too. Indirectly, the chief power in poetry is identified as a musical power, not at all in the sense of the mystical melodiousness beloved by the symbolists, but as organization and rhythmic pattern. The overwhelming importance Pasternak always gives to the felt force of inspiration may well be due to his having first met it in the more immediately stirring medium of music. It therefore seems appropriate to include in this book one of his (rather few) poems about music, "Again Chopin . . . "

5

When the infant was woken by the piano trio, he found "the whole range of vision flooded with music". When the teenager heard a symphony in the forest he felt the sounds were as much *in* the forest as were light and shadow, twigs and birds. In both memories the visible is saturated with the audible, the tangible with the intangible, matter itself seems penetrated by lyricism. In a similar way, a kind of drenching or invading of the real surroundings by feeling is central to the account of inspiration in *A Safe-Conduct* 2,7, Pasternak's most direct piece of theorising on this subject.

The feeling spoken of there is not one we all often have, nor is it one that appears as the subject-matter of great drama: the real theme of *Romeo and Juliet*, says Pasternak, is not the passions portrayed in that play but the artistic power which created it. T.S. Eliot, too, said something like this when he wrote: "The episode of Paolo and Francesca employs a definite emotion, but the intensity of the poetry is something quite different from whatever intensity in the supposed emotion it may give the impression of . . . " and: "The difference between art and the event is always absolute".[4]

The elusive experience of a feeling which is more properly called a "power", and its need for symbol, for allegorical language, since it cannot be named literally, are the main elements in Pasternak's short theoretical statement in *A Safe-Conduct*, 2,7. Only in *Doctor Zhivago* does that power (sometimes called a "feeling") exchange its elusiveness for a different kind of mysteriousness, one that may also be called "religious".

6

Traditional ideas of inspiration correspond to the "breathing in" implicit in the word—the invoked Muse, God as inspirer of the Bible, Nature's influence, the wind on the cliffs at Duino—but considerable emphasis usually falls on the poet himself, the one breathed into by the external agent.

Pasternak not only renounced the "romantic manner" (as he declared in *A Safe-Conduct* and described in "Letters from Tula"), he also tacitly renounced romantic and ancient conceptions of inspiration as breathed by some higher or vaster being into the poet. He describes a different movement, that of a power striking outward into the surrounding world, which wants it and is changed by receiving it. Since an alternative name for the power is "feeling", it would seem to come from the poet. Yet he so consistently avoids saying "*my* feeling" and so regularly withdraws attention from the person of the poet that the event could appear to take place outside, the poet merely joining in. Strength, power, force, even energy—all these words have been used to translate the Russian word "*sila*", a word Pasternak uses as often as Wordsworth mentions "power" in his investigation into the origin of poetry in life, *The Prelude*. But when, noting sounds of earth and winds, Wordsworth states "Thence did I drink the visionary power", he expresses the romantic view which Pasternak rejects. Both the stress on "me" and the notion of "drinking" (drawing something in from outside) are absent from his view of the matter. The person is scarcely present in the event, or ceases to be as the event proceeds. Again there is a coincidence with Eliot who writes (in the essay already quoted) that the "progress of an artist is a continual *extinction of personality.*"

Inspiration, for Pasternak, happens as much to a place as to a person; it takes place. In 1910, when he was twenty and just starting to be a poet, he wrote a long, meditative letter to his cousin Olga Freidenberg which shows something of the origin of this thought. He reminds her of a sensation they had shared on an evening walk together: they had felt that their surroundings were, somehow, strangely "approaching". Or—"impending": the verb *"nastupat'"* is used here idiosyncratically. It means "to begin", with a connotation of "impend" or "be imminent", and is normally translated "approach" when the subject of the verb is, say, evening or autumn or the new year. Here, though, it is the physical surroundings that are said to "begin" or "approach", or even "become". He writes: "I knew that you . . . were feeling the *approach* of the surroundings, something even more agitating than beauty; and that welling over in you was a devotion, almost dedication, to the tread of that approach [imminence]; which we so briefly call lyricism—when one feels that one is oneself approaching [imminent] . . . " From the very beginning of his life as a poet, Pasternak experienced lyrical inspiration as a definite event, as something happening, and happening not primarily in the person but outside and all around him, characterised by a movement of its own; in the quoted letter he mentions its (almost animate) "tread". And it is "even more agitating than beauty": one commentator has pointed out, with citation of this passage, that the concept of beauty, so important in traditional aesthetics, is not important in Pasternak's theory, but yields its usual centrality to the concept of power (*sila*).[5]

A sense of the person as less important than the place, and the whole of the place as changed by an approaching "power", is felt by Pasternak not only in the case of inspiration but also in the case of love. In his youth the awareness of a power (or "feeling") more outside than within him led to intently focused ideas about art (the main subject of the present book); in his later years the same awareness is likely to be expressed as characterising the experience of love. Thus in *Doctor Zhivago* we read that Iurii and Lara loved each other not because they were "consumed by passion, as people wrongly say", but "because everything around them wanted this". Earth, sky, clouds and trees all wanted it, we read, and then, with only the word "perhaps" to modify the extraordinary statement: "Their love was a pleasure to the surrounding /strangers, distances and rooms/ perhaps *even more than it was to themselves*." (*DrZh* 15,15, my italics—A.L.)[6]

Pasternak does not speculate as to how the inspirational power is generated, but it is evidently neither divine nor an emanation from nature. *Somehow* subjective being ceases to adhere to the writer and becomes the "free subjectivity" of a place and its objects. Thus in "Reliquimini" the features of the town square grow animate, while the poet drops to the ground in sympathy with them; in "Ordering a Drama" the very furniture is about to dance; in "Symbolism and Immortality" poetry is called "madness without a madman"; in "Letters from Tula" a shift towards creativity begins with the words "there will no longer be a poet". By the same token, a poet cannot have a biography, and a work of art is not attachable to the ostensible author. Pasternak relates how he once tried to explain to someone who hoped to be a writer that "what creates a writer and a text is a third dimension—a depth that raises, vertically above the page, whatever is said or shown, and—more important—separates the book from the author."[7]

Disappearance or separation of the poet from the poetic process has featured prominently in literary-theoretical discussion in the twentieth century; Pasternak's experience corresponds to some of the ideas put forward, while also greatly differing. Maurice Blanchot's belief, for instance, that in the writing process a moment comes "which annuls the author" recalls Pasternak's conception of it, while the sheer fervour of Blanchot's concern with the "origin" of a work is comparable to Pasternak's. Blanchot, however, puts the "emergent work" and "the space of composition", as well as a kind of "nowhere",[8] at the centre of the event, whereas Pasternak invariably invokes "reality", not with mimesis in mind but with a conviction that the whole of reality is transformed by the poetic force. Such emphasis on the whole surroundings is related to the device of metonymy (imagery based on the proximity of things to each other, rather than on their similarity) which has often been seen as typical of his work, a device which he himself once called a preference for "contiguity" over metaphor (see end of "Black Goblet" commentary). Whatever is there, spatially or temporally contiguous, is the real entirety which inspiration shifts.

It should also be said that in all Pasternak's writing about the origin of poetry there is a spirit of affirmation and delight which leaves no room for any nothingness or for, say, Blanchot's belief that the writer desires to reach the "point which *cannot be reached* and yet is the only one which is worth reaching" (my italics—A.L.)[9] For Pasternak the elusiveness of the creative moment does not mean a failure to capture it. "I love—and perhaps this is my only love—", he wrote, "life's truth in the form it naturally takes for a single moment at the very crater-edge of artistic forms, to disappear the next moment into them."[10] Even his 1935 speech, made when he was in the grip of chronic insomnia, illness and depression, stated that poetry would "always remain an organic function of human happiness".

7

None of Pasternak's contemporaries thought about art quite as he did. In the severe conditions of later Soviet intellectual life, his views seemed to many dangerously eccentric or wrong. But even in the 1920s and earlier, when his experience of poetry was to some extent shared by equally gifted fellow poets, his view of art still stood out as strongly distinctive. Closest to him was Marina Tsvetaeva, with whom, after her emigration, he conducted an intense correspondence, much of it concerned with the nature of creativity. Tsvetaeva shared his sense of inspiration's tremendous rapidity and of its being a response to a need in the external world; in fact she went further than he did, saying it is a reflex before thought, even before feeling, the deepest and fastest (as by electric current) spearing of the whole being by a given phenomenon, and the simultaneous, almost preceding it, answer to it . . . Command for an answer given by the phenomenon itself. Command? Yes, if S.O.S. is a command (the most unrepulsable of all).[11]

Tsvetaeva is just as concerned as he is with trying to define genius, inspiration and art, and she too writes of an indefinable force. But she calls that force "elemental", a word Pasternak does not use, and for her it comes *upon* and into the poet, as in the more traditional theories.

He has strangely little in common with his other great post-symbolist contemporary, Osip Mandelstam. "Strangely", because Mandelstam-the-acmeist's conception of the "enormously compressed reality" in a poem bears a similarity to Pasternak's imagery of speed and packing: Mandelstam writes that, like a mathematician easily "squaring some ten-figure number", a poet quietly "raises a phenomenon to the tenth degree". His anti-symbolist delight, moreover, in actual existence and identity ("A = A: what a splendid poetic theme!") is also a Pasternakian delight.[12] But his admiration for perfect construction (in fugues, in cathedrals) and for the solid tension of "the word as such" is quite unlike Pasternak's ravishment by nature's moods and changes, and where for Mandelstam creation is linked to recollection and to rediscovery of one's place in a classical pattern, Pasternak finds the world's phenomena repeatedly unprecedented.

As for Vladimir Mayakovsky, whom Pasternak once felt he was so like that he had radically to redefine himself, comparison again leads to contrast. The two poets may coincide in thinking art a product of everyday reality, but their views of that reality differ. Pasternak discerns in reality a need to be saved by art, as well as a model for art to copy, while Mayakovsky discerns social commands and sees poetry's task as active engagement with them;[13] his verse thus flourishes on the rhythm of decisions and challenges rather than sensations and impressions. In an essay on the two of them, Tsvetaeva constructed a series of antitheses, such as: "Pasternak—absorption, Mayakovsky—projection"; "Pasternak—magic, Mayakovsky—broadest daylight"; "Mayakovsky—a poet with a theme, Pasternak—a poet without a theme; the *theme* is: poet."[14]

8

If all things can be set in motion, and if world and art link up like a single disyllabic word, then everything necessary for transformation is present and no invented beings or imaginary worlds, no *realiora*, are required. Dislike of invention is something Pasternak often expressed, from the time when he told himself to "stop using these dreams as fuel" ("Ordering a Drama"), through the explicit break with "romanticism", to his saying a year before his death:

"I have never liked or understood (and don't believe in the existence of) the fantastic, the romantic, in itself, as an independent domain, the strangeness of Hoffmann, for example, or Carlo Gozzi." This continues: "For me, art is an obsession, the artist is someone possessed, seized, by *reality* and carried away by everyday existence . . . "[15] Czesław Miłosz aptly summed him up as "a man spellbound by reality".[16]

Whenever Pasternak praised a work of art he called it "realistic". Naturally, this did not mean it was based on an "undertaking to look all the relevant facts of a situation in the face" or that it was an attempt "to give an illusion of reflecting life as it seems to the common reader"—not, anyway, if "relevant" and "common" imply something already known;[17] he meant that the work conscientiously conveyed a new experience. The "nymphs and salamanders" he objects to in Chopin criticism, the symbolist cosmogonies he is sarcastic about in *Doctor Zhivago,* are not matters of experience, and their would-be amazingness obscures the actual amazingness of reality. He would have said, with Wallace Stevens, "The world is the only thing fit to think about."[18] Of course it is possible that he placed so much emphasis on "realism"—which he did most strongly from the 1930s on—as a response to the uncomprehending attacks then being made on him as a writer supposedly concerned with unreal matters (although his "realism" was very far from the "socialist realism" imposed upon writers from the 1930s onward). This, though, would explain only the insistence, not the view itself.

Concern for the real brings with it a concern for precision and fidelity. It also brings a concern for content. Although what seemed to demand most attention from his early readers was the power of his language—the vigorous, colloquial syntax and sometimes difficult imagery—Pasternak always stressed the primacy of content, and scorned preoccupation with form. Each of his poems, he said, began from a desire for it to contain one whole individual thing, whether it was February, or a certain railway station, or the soul accepting danger like a pear falling from its tree. The poet is urged on by the real thing needing to be packed and conveyed. Accordingly, he was (after 1916) reluctant to discuss literary periods and movements, or genres, styles and poetic devices; this is made very clear in "Some Propositions".

9

In seeking words for the force (or: power, energy, strength, *sila*) which he has encountered, Pasternak often seems to be trying out a number of appellations. In "The Black Goblet" he elevates the concept of originality to an "independent postulate", an "integral principle". Writing to Tsvetaeva in 1926 he experiments with "identity", along with "objectivity", in an attempt to define the sensation of that force: he says that reading a poem of hers has made him long to do nothing else but "write endlessly about art, about genius, about the revelation of objectivity—which has never yet been properly discussed by anyone, the gift of identity with the world." Uncertain of his chosen word, he goes on: "With this term I am designating an elusive, rare, magical feeling known to you in the highest degree . . . ", and then: "as you read, try the word on, call to mind what you yourself have felt, help me."[19]

It is remarkable that he felt he was talking about something "never yet properly discussed by anyone"—something neglected, then, by Plato, by Longinus, by the German Romantic thinkers so well known to him, and by the Russian contemporaries of his youth with their many discussions of art and inspiration. But also remarkable is his begging his addressee to "try the word on". Rather than insist on his preferred word, he wants her to know what feeling he is using it to mean, and to find her own word for that feeling. Words we propose for the nature of the real are provisional, he seems to say; use what name you like so long as you convey the thing meant. This position is often encountered in his remarks about art. Thus Chopin's *études* teach "history, or the structure of the universe, or anything whatever . . . ", and (in *Zhivago*) the dynamic cohering of human lives could be called "Kingdom of God" or "history" or "something else". This is not to say that language cannot cope: just the contrary. It is remote from Tiutchev's "A thought once uttered is a lie", or Schiller's "Should the soul *speak,* then, alas! it's no longer the *soul* that speaks."[20] For Pasternak, all uttered thoughts can be true, and the soul can speak even if it is called something else.

He has been described as a latter-day anti-nominalist—that is, one who believes that abstractions correspond to realities.[21] He does indeed seek to evoke dynamic realities corresponding to such words as "epoch" or "power" or "life". The word "art", too, corresponds, for him, to something irreducibly real, for it is "not the name of a category, not an aspect of form, but a hidden mysterious *part of the content.* When a *grain* of this force enters into the composition of some more complex mixture, it turns out to be the essence" (*DrZh* 9,4). His poems will often combine something concrete with something abstract, as if that too were concrete; a season, a situation or a city can mix with the particulars it consists of or contains. A "year of war" combines with spokes of rocking-chairs, "to cross a road" is "to step on the universe", a century crashes down onto a named quarter of a city. Definite mixes with diffuse; scrutinised particular with conventional generality. The preoccupation is finely embodied in the opening lines of "In Reisner's Memory": "Larisa, now is when I shall regret / That I'm not death, am nought compared with it. / I would have found out how, without glue, / A living story holds to the fragments of days."[22] Abstractions are somehow in the world.

But Pasternak must also be called a nominalist, in that for him names are *only* names and one abstract word can be replaced by another when both seek to name the same thing. Feelings, forces and essences need not be named conclusively, and it may be better if they are not. In the poem "Let's drop words" he imagines someone asking who it is that ordains the details the world is made of, and he answers, as if with an evasive smile: "the god of details". Nor does it matter, in that poem, whether names have been found for life's biggest mysteries—whether, say, "the riddle of the grave" has been solved: the only thing that matters is that "life is detailed". In a similar assertion William Blake, objecting to Joshua Reynolds' calling the minuteness of beautiful forms their weakness, declared (*c.* 1808): "Minuteness is their whole Beauty".[23]

Pleasure in the freedom and mutability of language lasted for Pasternak all his life. *A Safe-Conduct* states, in a wonderfully offhand quasi-definition, that art "is the interchangeability of images". In a poem of around the same time he wrote: "Call it what you like, but the forest covering everything ran like a narrative . . . "[24] This "call it what you like" comes up again and again in many forms. Even when speaking to the Board of the Soviet Writers' Union in 1936, Pasternak declared: "You see, comrades, I am deeply indifferent as to the separate components of any integral form, so long as it is primal and genuine." The same "call it what you like" underlies the world-view set out in *Doctor Zhivago*, his one novel and the most important to him of all his writings.

I

EARLY PROSE

SOME PROPOSITIONS*

1

When I talk about mysticism or painting or the theatre, I talk in the peaceable, unconstrained way in which any freely thinking amateur discusses things. When the talk turns to literature I remember a book and I lose my ability to reason. I have to be shaken and brought by force, as though from a swoon, out of a physical condition of dream about the book, and only then, very reluctantly and overcoming a slight revulsion, will I join in a conversation on some other literary topic, where what is being talked about is not a book but something else, no matter what: public readings, say, or poets, or poetic movements, or the new writing, and so on.

But never, not for anything, will I move uncompelled, of my own free will, out of the world of what I care about into that world of amateur carefreeness.

2

Contemporary trends of thought have imagined art to be a fountain, whereas it is a sponge.

They have decided that art ought to gush forth, whereas it should absorb and become saturated. They think it can be broken down into means of depiction, whereas it is composed of organs of perception.

Its proper task is to be always among the spectators and to look more purely, receptively and faithfully than all others; but in our day it has come to know powder and the make-up room and it displays itself from a stage; as though there were two kinds of art in the world, and one of them, having the other in reserve, can permit itself the luxury of self-distortion, which is equivalent to suicide. It shows itself off, whereas it ought to be sunk in obscurity at the back of the gallery, scarcely aware that its hat is aflame on its head[1] or that, despite its hiding away in a corner, it is stricken with translucence and phosphorescence as with a disease.

---

* *Neskol'ko polozhenii*. PSS, 5, 23–27. Written 1918–19. First published in *Sovremennik* 1 (Moscow, 1922). Originally intended as introduction to a projected book, *Kvintessentsiia* (*Quintessentia*), containing "Articles about the Human Being". In the manuscript each passage had a title; for description of the manuscript see Lazar Fleishman, "Neizvestnyi avtograf Borisa Pasternaka" in *Materialy XXVI nauchnoi studencheskoi konferentsii*, Tartu, 1971.

3

A book is a cubic piece of burning, smoking conscience—and nothing else. Mating calls are the care nature takes to preserve the feathered species, her vernal ringing in the ears. A book is like a wood-grouse[2] at its mating-ground. Deafened with itself, listening spellbound to itself, it hears nobody and nothing. Without it, the spiritual genus would have had no continuation. It would have become extinct. Monkeys had no book.

It was written. It grew, became intelligent, saw something of the world, and now it has grown up and it is this. It is not to blame for the fact that we can see right through it. Such is the arrangement of the spiritual universe.[3]

Yet only recently people thought the scenes in a book were dramatisations. This is an error. Why would it want them? They forgot that the only thing in our power is to know how not to distort the voice of life which sounds within us.

Inability to find and tell the truth is a deficiency which cannot be covered up by any amount of ability to tell untruths.

A book is a living being. It is fully conscious and in its right mind: its pictures and scenes are what it has brought from the past, has kept in its memory and is not willing to forget.

4

Life has not just begun. Art was never at a beginning. It was always constantly present before it began to form.

It is infinite. And here, in this moment, beyond me and in me, it is such that—as if from an assembly hall[4] suddenly flung open—I am bathed in its swift, fresh ubiquity and sempiternity, as if the moment were being led up to swear an oath of allegiance.

No genuine book has a first page. Like the rustling of a forest, it is born God knows where, and it grows and rolls, awaking arcane wilds of the forest, until suddenly, in the darkest, most awe-striking, panicking moment, it rolls to its end and begins to speak with all tree-tops at once.

5

Where is a miracle? It is in the fact that there once lived on earth a seventeen-year-old girl called Mary Stuart,[5] and one October day, at her little window, outside which the Puritans were whooping, she wrote a French poem that ended with these words:

Car mon pis et mon mieux
Sont les plus déserts lieux.[6]

Secondly, it is in the fact that once, in his youth, at a window, outside which October was carousing and raging, the English poet Charles Algernon Swinburne finished his "Chastelard"[7] in which the quiet plaint of Mary's five stanzas had swelled up as the uncanny droning of five tragic acts.

Thirdly, finally, it is in the fact that when once, some five years ago, a translator glanced through the window, he could not tell which was the more surprising.

Whether it was the way the Elabuga blizzard knew Scots and was still distressed about the seventeen-year-old girl, as of yore; or the way the girl and the English poet, her sorrower, were able to talk to him so well, so intimately well, in Russian, about what still disturbed them both just as before and had never stopped haunting them.

What does this mean?—the translator asked himself. What's going on there? Why is it so quiet (and yet so snowstormy!) over there today? One would think that what we are sending should make them bleed profusely. Yet over there they are smiling.

That is where the miracle is. In the unity and identity of the lives of these three and of a whole host of others (bystanders and eye-witnesses of three epochs, personages in a biography, readers) in the real-life October of who knows what year, which is droning and growing blind and hoarse out there beyond the window, beneath the mountain, in . . . art.

That's where it is.

6

There exist misunderstandings. They have to be avoided. There is room here for a tribute to boredom. A writer, people say, a poet . . .

Aesthetics does not exist. It seems to me aesthetics does not exist as a punishment for the way it lies, pardons, indulges, condescends. For the way it knows nothing about the human being and yet spins its yarns about specialisms. Portraitist, landscapist, genre painter, still-life painter? Symbolist, acmeist, futurist? What murderous jargon!

Clearly, this is a science which classifies air balloons according to where and how the holes are placed in them that prevent them from flying.

Inseparable from each other, poetry and prose are two poles.

Through its inborn faculty of hearing, poetry seeks the melody of nature amid the noise of the dictionary, then, picking it out like picking out a tune, it gives itself up to improvisation on that theme. Through its scent, according to its spirituality, prose seeks and finds the human being in the category of speech, and if the age is deprived of him it recreates him from memory and secretly sets him down somewhere, to pretend later on, for the good of mankind, that it found him amid the contemporary world.

These principles do not exist in isolation.

As it fantasises, poetry comes across nature. The real, living world is the only project of the imagination which has once succeeded and which still goes on being endlessly successful. Look at it continuing, moment after moment a success. It is still real, still deep, utterly absorbing. It is not something you are disappointed in next morning. It serves the poet as example, even more than as a sitter or a model.

7

It is madness to put your trust in common sense. It is madness to have doubts about it. It is madness to look ahead. It is madness to live without looking.

But at times to roll back your eyes and to sense, with rapidly rising blood-temperature, how—stroke upon stroke, recalling convulsions of lightnings on dusty ceilings and plaster casts—there begins to delve and drum at your consciousness the reflected wall-painting of some unearthly, rushing past, eternally vernal thunderstorm: this is *pure* madness, this is in any case the purest madness!

It is natural to strive for purity.

Thus we go up close to the pure essence of poetry. It is disturbing, like the ominous turning of ten windmills at the edge of a bare field in a black and hungry year.

[RELIQUIMINI]*

It's growing dark. How many roofs and spires! And all of them, catching and tearing, have bent the sky down like a misty bush, then let it go, and it's risen up and is shivering, shivering with the tautness of tiny accumulated stars.

But it is not yet black, it's a straw-pale sky drawn on fading parchment, and whenever an illuminated advertisement is placed in the distance it doesn't rouse or cut into the dark but is itself lulled and wan like smoky sunburnt leather. And now, down below, the blossoming black darkness and the hats and the breathings of ovals around eyes and oaks, and various inexplicable posings and slidings, all are being knotted and tied together in big moist glistening excited bunches; the street will fasten one of these bunches, now here now there, with the thorn of a gas-lamp, and tie it to the next one, so that these drooping

---

* Untitled. PSS, 3, 420–429 (listed there by reference to its opening words: "*Uzhe temneet. Skol'ko krysh i shpitsei!*"). Written 1910. First published by Anna Ljunggren in *Juvenilia Borisa Pasternaka. Shest' fragmentov o Relikvimini* (Stockholm, 1984).

throngs and bunches are moving, moving, like posies pinned on by the street-lamps. Glimmering drawing-rooms come together with a tongue-tied whisper of curtains, while, in the damp flushed shop-windows below, unbridled crockery and copper in music-shops, melodious fainting book-bindings, and even toys—dolls and stoves—and even, even the desolate unalive window-panes of technical offices have flung themselves after the street with exultant sensuality, and in mirror-like apartments the doubles of the street, its rubbed-out drafts, run out to a meeting with it. Its reflections float like spirits in these cubic flasks of windows; and wherever the lamps are not lit remnants of half-brewed greenish-pink sky float fragrantly in the lawyers' flasks in front of the town square, together with petals of the monument and its admirers.

There a whole small volume of maple leaves has flown to pieces, like sadness or a briefly written story, over the meek washed asphalt. Some way further off, a girl has bought a cupful of maize from a little old woman stiff with cold, and the pavement has flooded with pigeons.

Here's evening, the air like a denuded avenue, buildings casting down their eyes, the girl with pigeons and the wind that has conquered everything and turned everything into weather-vanes and index fingers; and the entire dusk is like an immense rusty weather-vane beginning to groan, and like the pointing melancholy of coast-lines. At this moment, through shifting crowds and horse-cabs, someone cuts across the square in my direction, walking straight ahead without deviating, and passing the monument to the great man;[8] he must want his manner of walking to make up for a great deal, it is so unnatural and joyfully frenzied. Here he comes, here he comes, almost breaking into a run—and now something strange happens: he throws himself down with a diving movement under the feet of some passing students and drops to the pavement with all its commotion of tossed up maple stubs; he takes a small pencil from his right-hand pocket and with an ecstatic movement raises it above the muttering leaves and the buzzing circlet of the gas-light's reflection, as if about to write something on the asphalt. It is so close to the scattered maize that the old woman thinks he is stealing and she starts to swear, shouting fragments of abuse into the lonely, desolate, fallen air; while the girl runs off and the pigeons shatter the quietness, taking it apart in tiny bits, and the students seize the surprising fellow powerfully by the elbows—they are medics and they think he is suffering from epilepsy.

Now pedlars come running towards one another with empty trays, while in the cold gloom church-bells burst out in finely shredded chimes which try to cover the pavement and road with tin. They are dishevelled by side-streets. I too approach. The fellow is standing up now and, unable to form a sentence, is trying incoherently to prove that he's quite all right, he just lost a button; he has large eyes and a tie like a black flood; good Lord, it's Reliquimini, I used to go to secondary school with him and he was so good at writing my essays . . .

Soon he and I are standing beside the monument to the great man, carriages are flying in the air, the crowd is being stitched and unstitched by tiny claws of light.

Here is our conversation.

"Tell me, Reliquimini, are you quite well?"

"Yes, yes, thank you, but goodbye, I've got an appointment."

"Wait, look here, we use *ty* to each other; what is the meaning of your behaviour over there on the asphalt?"[9]

"Oh, I beg you not to mention that . . . "

"For one thing, we use *ty*, and for another, listen . . . "

At this moment a slender lady comes out from behind the shadow of the great man, walks past and looks round haughtily in our direction; her chin is chiselled like the statue's, and the chin and lips are holding back all the enraptured frenzy of her figure and eyes, she is so . . .

"Well, go on . . . "

"Look, Reliquimini, we used to be friends—well, if you don't want to, goodbye." (I feel hurt and I want to go away.)

Then he says: "You know, I am the son of an artist, oh dear, that's not what I meant to say; yes, over there on the asphalt, it's ridiculous now. But just look around, how this square has tilted and has finally scooped and scooped the sky with its branches. And, you know, in the sky cracked stars are diluted, dissolved as if in blue egg-white, they quiver like embryos in the stirred-up puddles of the sky. And it's dusk here, look, by the monument and on the square, streaks of dusk, and look, faraway phosphorescent carriages flicker, like striking a match, when brakes go on and carriages start up again.

"Just look at this chaos of shadows and silhouette-patches, all this buzzing and flowing thaw of blackened colours feathered with soot, look at them, and: there's the horizon, naked and eternal, and the verticals of buildings, naked and regal, and here's the square for you, bitterly compressed pure angles, and look, far far away over there, past the stand selling grapes, there's my friend Mozart, and now he's stopped in front of the carts—wait . . . " Here he had to pause because men were driving iron girders past, lashing the road with a lazy, deafening din; I really did see Mozart standing there, he let the carts go banging past, then started walking on, cutting a direct, level path through the darting people.

"So look at the lines of the roofs and porches and you'll see—no, you'll feel, in such a way that your knees suddenly start to shake—the difference between the first and the second; or rather you'll immediately see whole parishes, frenziedly growing and dying away—parishes of colours and shadows praying to lines, to outlines and to edges, those bright inexorable gods; heroic lines, heroic outlines—it's these the colours deify as they melt in fanatic rapture. Look, they're descending from every possible side, scourging themselves and sobbing and laughing and blowing their noses, to lay themselves down in the liberated lines of their pure God."

"My friend, I don't understand a thing, but I see that you are in a state of excitement. I wouldn't have put my questions to you except that I wanted to know the reason for that incident on the pavement."

"Yes, yes, on the pavement . . . God is an outline, a fence. God is a limit for the god-creators, a limit to prayer, oh it's so hard for us just now . . . There are some who have a god, an archaic eternal outline to archaic eternal prayers; perhaps those prayers were once like colours tossing about without forms, and they found their outlined reservoir, their form: they are strange to us, those people, big and small at once; they have a god because they have no prayer and they have no prayer because they have a god. God may be old; but a prayer should be always springing up; if a prayer is not a fleeting glimpse, a flashing patch of light, will a god be its focus? Oh, excuse me, Koinonievich,[10] I'll be back in a moment, there's someone I know, I'll go and say hallo and bring him back here . . . "

And off he went, as directly as ever, not making a turn towards his acquaintance, who was buying dahlias from a small boy, or maybe not dahlias but it *is* autumn now; he switched the dahlias to his left hand and started shaking Reliquimini's fingers, then put an arm round his neck and began to kiss him. The dahlias must have tickled Reliquimini's neck with their coldness, but at this moment two or three silent couples got up from the benches and walked away arm in arm. Really, how sad; what is he saying, this eccentric fellow; it's some kind of neopythagoreanism,[11] and those couples have gone so we can sit down for a while. And now a wind coming from various angles, collapsing like a seamstress after work, began creeping out through the yellow birch leaves, and the leaves crept together, a pond was in store for them, and in the pond the urban street was rowing whole towns of little, inarticulate lights. And the leaves went creeping all round the pond, glancing, peering, scarcely stirring, sniffing at the earth.

Meanwhile over there, walking along with Reliquimini, his acquaintance is making gestures with the dahlias, probably as thoughts arise in his mind, and he keeps smelling them, burying himself in them, perhaps chewing or smoking them like tobacco, and he slows down his pace when Reliquimini speaks, leaning his head to one side and making circles with his right arm like an orchestra-conductor or a discus-thrower. So there they are, walking along, and there's the creeping damp of thousands of [gas-lamp] extinguishers; and the gas mantles of the damp, incited by foliage, begin blowing the puddles with their lights and reflections; and a chiming of church-bells rolls once again through autumn; it's as if the sky were being carried across the road and it got dropped and smashed, splashing out a shrill wet sediment; puddles and gutters are already immersed, and—mist; this means Reliquimini has gone down a blind alley. No doubt he'd say brightness is also a god since it repeats things and encloses them in a shape, while mist is the ecstasy of the praying multitudes who have not found a god; may the devil understand this Reliquimini. And now—here he is himself, and his acquaintance is finishing a sentence: " . . . that's why I said it is a grief we share."

Then he presents himself to me, looking into my eyes with an unnatural directness and a sort of heartfelt conviction, leaning forward significantly . . .

"Makedonsky, yes, yes, Alexander of Macedon[12]—same name as that other, insurance company for insuring against damage to timber huts . . ."—and seeing that his witticism has failed he knits his classical brows and says impetuously: "Tell me . . .", then, as if with an inward struggle, he soundlessly continues the intonation of this "Tell me", scrutinizes the dahlias in his fist, knocking one unfortunate little leaf into place with his stick; then raises the stick, puts it under his arm, hands me the dahlias, leans forward, lights a cigarette and, with the shaven seriousness and profundity that come from having a cigarette between one's lips, he repeats: "Tell me . . . you saw him in that idiotic pose . . ." and he laughs a forced laugh. I feel I am being mocked and I want to leave and, as if guessing my thoughts, Reliquimini says:

"Sasha, you ought to explain this to him—and afterwards to me . . . " and we walk towards the benches through the mildewed air and the benches gape in the mist like toothless gums, as if the quietened square contains some sort of cold astonishment and the monument is only getting ready to sing of it; altogether it looks as if we are being dreamt by the objects. And altogether there's this bald, bald square with only individual leafless branches protruding, fingered by the cold. We sat down, Makedonsky, Reliquimini and I: Makedonsky—flat, smoothed out, Reliquimini in relief and unnaturally close, both of them resembling a wax seal dripped onto layers of mist and printed off, it was so thick.

Now Reliquimini takes his neighbour's stick and he drills at the sand, setting his feet apart. He has leant over and he speaks quietly.[13] "So, there was truth and untruth, and grief and happiness, and that feeling a child has when life is a plasma floating in itself and the one you deify is its cage: that's when life belongs to the one with the capital letter; and then your painful over-full readiness to have the outlines of a god, for you are endowed with the sense of a great limit, endowed with God, and indeed they do say that he suffered and is therefore yours—these are the unattainable outlines of your love.

"That was in childhood, a time when the facts of life are still full, full rituals; then there is an object for your feeling, your rapture and sadness, as if you consisted of swaying colours which have a god, their outline. Recall your childhood and it will seem to you that the excitements and facts which you experienced like a brush dipped in wondrous life are a drawing set you as a task . . . But this is so boring, I don't want to talk about it, but I've broken down; do understand that it is possible to get so drawn in to a certain sphere that all aspects of life are experienced within it and in its language."

"Tell me," I ask, "—see, I am asking you to address me as *ty*—all this may be related to romanticism, which wanted aesthetics to be the basis of everything; maybe you want . . . "

"Of course," he interrupts, "it is related to romanticism. But do people understand it? Perhaps they think all the torches of life, kindled by individual dramas of good and evil, happiness and unhappiness, truth and falsehood, once they're immersed in the aesthetic as if in a well, die out, and there remain only the splashing and rippling of beauty and ugliness. Oh no, people who say this have not felt all that soft quiet torment. The incendiaries of life never become any fewer; they approach the aesthetic with their torches and blow up that well, if it is not empty and if it's full of explosive aesthetic breath."

At this moment Makedonsky points to the remains of the bouquet—you see, he is so highly strung that while listening he was plucking at it. And Reliquimini suddenly starts lamenting: "What am I saying this for? Why do I say all this to you? See, I am an artist and I can't bear it when I see a poem of lines and outlines around me: a sort of flowing lyricism aches and aches inside me then, for I see the pure clarified family of the heroic, it needs worship and I want to summon a whole parish of worshippers, ecstatic colours, to these lines, for the lines, as I told you, are worshipped by colours gone crazy. Or—the other way round, which happens more often or even always—I see a whole pilgrimage which overthrows, vanquishes, inundates and drowns in its prayer the outlived outlines, and cannot drown them in anything bigger, but in the evenings even the external outline—God, the horizon—even the horizon is weathered away in the evenings like an edge of sandstone or like the skirt of a garment which smoulders and is burnt through by big ashily burning-out long cigarette-ends; the evening streets—they are stubbed out against the horizon. Yes and just imagine all that religious revolution of the dusk, when even the lines which have restrained day's fanaticism cease to be edges, when even the god-created lines break into pieces, multiply and bend and they themselves suddenly begin to float, to go down on their knees and want to tell some kind of rosary, press towards an altar, beat against the altar-rail, and now everything you see swells like a kind of spiritual highwater and there you are, it's twilight, a great steppeland of nomads that has risen up, a campaign of ghosts, spots, clumps, which embrace and weep and scourge themselves—and it's a kind of sorrow belonging to that godlessness when, Sasha don't interrupt, when there are whole squares full of singers but there is not the one who can be put in the vocative case, because all lines, oh dear this is boring you, all lines, vocative cases of colours, have bowed over, stopped being themselves, become an impetus, and there are no pure chiselled hands to accept the reciprocal frenzy."

"Ah, that was well said, Reliquimini," says Makedonsky, "that's what god-lessness is, it's a path with nobody coming towards you."

But I ask, bewildered: "Surely there's either God or there isn't, and after all God is not a line, and look, in all this chaos of twilight a god could be manifest as the unity of the twilight, and what has God got to do with it, anyway?"

"Again you're not understanding me. I don't feel a need for God in life, in morality or in matters of truth, although even there I understand him as a great outline, a contour within which your joys and sorrows circulate, as well as all this wealth of relations and feelings, the colourful blood of life. But we, artists, have a different blood-circulation; to us, if we are utterly, utterly pure, comes life which has forgotten itself, the world which feels it is not itself. What does that mean—'not itself'? It means: no longer subordinated to itself but seeking subordination, it means there was a subordination of colours to forms, of visible images to silence, subordination of characters to their relationships. You see, love was the frame in which life suffered; life always worships rapturously, and the frame of worship is God, and life had various contours, sketchings, outlines, and these are the lines, the laws, everyday life, the crossings of feelings between people. And such a twilight happens in life too, when all that's linear—meaning higher, subordinating and holy—itself wants lines above itself, around itself, because it itself is yearning—I have got distracted, you know, what I mean is this: façades start swaying, separate houses sway, the horizon breathes and at any moment it will start to pulsate—which means that life was once framed and the frames were immutable, immobile, but they too have got infected with life and have become life, und man muss die Götter, die Liebe, alle Rahmen, die Leben geworden, umrahmen . . . "[14] For some reason he gave a shout in a moist, breaking sort of voice; then, still more quietly: "And see, the lyric poet, who doesn't understand all this so rationally, feels for the twilight, and what is creativity if not compassion for the twilight? And the artist comes rushing and, with a sort of inspired miming, shows you that all the sacred cages have begun to rot, and he begs: enclose the twilight with God, for the forms have split, they have become a content, and for this the contents suffer pain. Look—life has flooded fate, and fate as chance is floating, floating—give fate a new fate, give fate a channel. Well, these are thoughts, this is consciousness, but there is also unmediated feeling and it leads to reflexes: I was just walking along and it was twilight.

"Twilight, do you understand that twilight is a thousandfold homeless agitation that has missed the path and lost itself; and the lyric poet has got to find places for twilight, and suddenly the maple leaves on the asphalt swarm and swarm like a multitude of twilights, and the asphalt is such a great distance, and there needs to be a colourless, tightening outline for the sake of which they would tremble and burn, and that's when I flung myself down headlong, to draw a god around the leaves, an outline for the blotches, peace to the frenzy."

So that was the sort of conversation we had: it was becoming boring and suddenly Makedonsky jumps up. "I ought to have been at my fiancée's long ago. Let's go together, Reliquimini, and you too"—he turns to me. I decline, and I go away, taking my leave. For the rest, let the facts speak.

Reliquimini and Makedonsky walk to the little road where the tram passes. It is not a lively line, and it has bumpy tram-cars of an old-fashioned kind. A noise begins booming and singing in the distance, and a minute later, far off, a spectre, swollen in the mist, turns the corner into the lane; it has a decayed red lamp like a single tooth; it comes rolling up and the roadway gleams. Reliquimini and Makedonsky get in.

"What are you doing now, Reliquimini?"

"I'm breaking down, and you, Makedonsky?"

"I'm going to my fiancée with you."

At the next stop, four very big students wearing overcoats get in, stooping; the tram sets off, they sway, they clutch at the backs of the seats and at one another, and the seat-backs break off, but the conductor just stands there on his two feet.

ORDERING A DRAMA*

Undialogical dramas and undramatic dialogues
First non-act

In the blurred window seethe the wintry twilight outlines of the boulevard, filtered through thin curtains. On the boulevard, bedecked with worsted branches, are weak lamps not properly brewed as yet, like swellings in the mist, pale because it isn't yet quite dark; there is a grey, cold sky like an arithmetic chart; and on it plaintive little lines of smoke from chimneys being crossed out by slate-crayons.

At the beginning of the act, outside the window is the quiet empty hunger of the twilight. Towards the end, when it is getting dark and the window-panes are being served with hoarfrost, while the yellow and violet street of shops is being poured into wedge-shaped crystal services, when, down below, the arched lamps gasp for breath, then into frosty crockery flows shaded blue-grey winter, then winter deeply and evenly blows at the frame. It blows noise and roofs and stars. It blows the starting-up of sledge-runners, tinkling bells, horns of motors; and all this noise is dressed in fur-coats, in furs; the noise plays hide-and-seek

* *Zakaz dramy.* PSS, 3, 457–466. Written 1910. First published in *Pamiatniki kul'tury* (Moscow, 1977).

with the room; then again winter blows a starry ash, a sky of grey crumbs and the thin black plates of sky in yards. But down below the lamps must be bursting again in the shops, exploding upwards like coloured inkwells and rinsing with coloured ink the light snow crumbled at the tiny window; dear, wounded snow which someone's cupped palm outside the winter-casement has abandoned like a baby. Later, towards the end of the act, when the shops are being shut and it's dark, in the big white snow-entangled boulevard there are little scraps and stitches of unfinished passers-by.

Then the ripe, paraffiny pomegranate-grains of the street-lamps are ringed with a misty, dirtily steamy juice, greenish or blackened with yellowness; they are encrusted like burdock seeds with dry branches and an intertwining of twigs, and you can't tear them off from the smoothed, swollen boulevard, they have stuck so fast!

It is dark. Over there in the distance, the livelier streets spurt now and then like struck matches, with their starting-up and their luminescent flaring—little hyphens of noise. While there, down below, the cars breaking in close to the pavement, fall like pieces of burning paper into a dark well. Then the blizzard, like something dropped, smashes against the frame and spills itself in a thick hissing scalding substance to weep and hum through a long-drawn hysterics of sorrow that is bursting its way through. Meanwhile, in generous girlish manner, it draws off the swept-up threads of snow that have risen in the air, and the smoke from chimneys, and twists them off to the side, and with this silk, borne widely sideways, it embroiders the darkness in the frame.

A room is the radiantly patterned and painted sensitivity of objects. Without any mysticism: the things in the room (like children gifted with attention, who experience a speaker by subjecting themselves to the movements of his head and the play of his mouth)—the things in the room have secretly and openly yielded themselves to the influence of winter that overhangs from the window. They shimmer with street and sky, palpably and impalpably.

But they are more than children. Here's this wintry room, which the lamp checks through like a proof-copy, and from behind the lamp the dusk peers in and offers various advice; the paraffin lamp, narrative under its crimson lampshade, puts hundreds of quaint corrections on furniture and corners; it takes a liking to the tapestry that droops with a grey depth and is overgrown with Persian beasts, and how indistinctly it singles that out, like some sad confused monologue; the dusk likes it too and looks it over once more; but why has the lamp crossed out the cupboard? And two gaslight paths creep from the seethed curtains to rescue the cupboard. In the middle of the room a whole handful of marvels: a small table with pencils on it and music manuscript paper:

a grand-piano, open and dusty; and to the left, by the wall, bad engravings to Lafontaine fables, some sort of pencilled foxes.

This is the composer's room, the music teacher's. There is one small point, just an observation, which must go into the scenario. In the consciousness three elements are sewn together with strong surgical thread, the kind that grows in. Music, a neighbourless land into which you fall and fall amid sounds. Candles, rounding up the room of wallpaper, portraits, twilight and tapestries, like a turbid, turbid flood; candles that let down the furniture like undone hair; in a word, this whole room, uplifted by the bathing candles, the room, the world of objects, this is the second element—a world of great and fragile realness—this is what meets you when you stand up after music. And the third is over there at the window: flakes of street, flakes of wintry sky, flakes of street-lamps, flakes of fur-coats, flakes of raised horse-cabs, flakes of skirts and muffs along half-frozen gutters, flakes of light flying like split coloured alum, flakes of children and shopping and nannies and windows of shops, all these things that have started running to catch up with music.

Oh this big life, life which is milliards of living specks tossed upward and chased down there aslant by a dense black darkness bending over roofs, a black winter sky shaking with snowflakes, like the palm of a hand reaching down to the pavement and roadway and raking in the street. The third element: crumbled and various life in its merry chase after music which is hiding. As if music had arrived in the town and put up somewhere, and everyone were fighting their way towards music as if to a hotel with a celebrity; they keep on throwing themselves about, and whatever slides and rolls and meets and parts and shudders from the dealt-out snowy sky is agitated by this search for music. And you cannot hear, outside the window, covered as if with tears for a long time now, you cannot hear how these fragments are being blown by the all-fusing, merry and ill, belated question of the snowy street: where to find music, where is it staying: *haven't you seen music.*

Thus. Three groups. First: past, reality as a great immobile legend of wood and cloth, objects in need, twilight in need, like a church parish that has grown stale from waiting. And lyricism, music, this is the second. Lyricism, pure, naked, and lifted up; lyricism which will never atone either for the dusk that has come to beg forgiveness or for the things in need of lyricism. The first is—reality without movement, the second—movement without reality. And the third: the music down there in the snowflakes, the music of people going in and out of their homes, in brief the street's music, which so strangely, strangely, seeks its own self; the movement of reality which tosses about and desponds and stretches at times, because it is reality, and reality is eternally *in need;* and look, there is music in fur-coats and music in smiles, but smiles and declarations are like soap bubbles blown by life into spaces all scratched by the freezing cold, and the shop-windows thaw, and the carriages flying through ashy air thaw against small unseen walls of rapture, of love who is passing by as a pedestrian. This chase of music after itself, isn't this life altogether?

So life is the third element. And the composer Shestikrylov,[15] who gave lessons in the winter twilight, the composer Shestikrylov, who was waited for by his pupils in the salon a long, long time, after which they would meet him in the entrance-hall where above the shelves with the musical scores on them, dusty and worthless, the gas-jet like a snug butterfly buzzed so nasally. They always took Shestikrylov's fur-coat from him and the layers of heaped-up snow on its collar were like narrowing eyes and like lips being licked, in the hall where the snug gas-butterfly hotly buzzed. The composer Shestikrylov was the surgical thread for the stitching up of the world-order that had been operated on. First the dear, perhaps dearest of *all*, inanimate world, the motley, coloured neediness of objects, life without life; and second—pure music, the duty of an inconceivable something to become reality and life, a sort of great singing eternal duty, like the remainder left after the third thing, after life, which also fulfils its duty of course but doesn't notice itself, merely offers itself as a caryatid for unrealised lyricism.

These three layers were being sewn together by the life of the composer, so that one whole should result; and according to which layer he was piercing, the composer Shestikrylov would at one moment be fretting and worrying, feeling the inanimate weight of guilt and need, while at the next, uplifted, he would gaze around: "Where are the kneelers?" But most often of all, most often of all, life was being stitched and embroidered by means of the composer, and together with it he would fling himself into the search for himself. There seemed to be in his soul a high-up weeping little casement, and outside it, many floors below, his life was flinging itself, harrowed and smithereened, black and white with blotches of brimful electric prices, searching for that very casement which was flying after it into the snowy night. All too often he forgot he had taken himself along with him once for all. But is it possible to bear this in mind eternally?

Well? There is a stage, then, and upon it, embroidered by human emotion as if in satin-stitch, the hidings and seekings of music.

Now I shall unobtrusively tell a small truth; a drama has been promised, and like all dramas it begins with a scenario, a description of objects. This is so life-like, after all, for is not the setting out of furniture in life the beginning of a drama? A room with objects—isn't this an order for a drama? I myself have never found anything else possible than to live amongst objects; like everyone else I live on the basis of the inanimate; and if someone were to ask me suddenly and severely: "Upon what basis do you live. . .?"

Oh, then I would point to recollection, and I don't know whether he would believe that the past is an inanimate object, and childhood too is something inanimate, that is, demanding.

Here is the scenario: twilight in the composer's apartment—and either there is no meaning in it or else it's to be followed by a drama. This is how it was in life too—there stood the inanimate principles, demanding to be set in motion, and people would start off here at a run, and some of them, the ones who always thought further than others, and more quickly became unrecognisable to their acquaintances, they endured this delicious suffering: to work, to think upon the inanimate. And grew conscious of it.

Subsequently life would knock at their door. They would open. And life, who had lost her way, would ask: "Does life live here?" [16] They would stare in amazement at this guest who was looking for herself in someone else's apartment, but they understood that her loneliness was hard to bear; so then they would settle the world of colours, objects, people, events, this whole complex world of contents, settle it down in their home and try to amuse it. And they would either tell reality a hundred personal trifles about herself, or else they would take her onto their lap and rock her to sleep with verses; so that by the time she left she would have forgotten herself completely, completely lost herself.

Later, they became artists. They were more attentive; approaching something which to the mass of people seemed inanimate, they would say: "We see your need, we see how inanimate and ornamental you are, you memories of ours; and we shall mourn and wring our hands for you."

How a drama is put together in life; how, unable to bear the inanimate pleas any longer, one moves the chairs and armchairs back, to dance and dance—this is what I want to convey here. And how, in the dance, life is sharpened to a sharp, sharp point. Oh what clean straight lines fate can draw with this agitation! How, in the dance, there's a desire to reach the unconscious; and maybe the furniture in its loose covers is ready to think that once it too sprang forth as a dancing soul and fell down as inanimate past. Then like ears of ripe barley the candle-flame is carved into the black bloated window-panes, and the panes in the frame seem dilated horse-black nostrils.

Meanwhile, the town has yawned with a sort of stony emptiness as on the evening before a holiday. And suddenly this on-the-eve yawn, this huge square of paving-stones, is cleft by the bow-shaped stroke of a bell, like a whip with a humming tip, and after it, crumbly, the black earthen avalanche of deep-voiced churchbells, and all this is upon the earth, it's here, where we are; and dances too are upon the earth, and Reliquimini, and Angelika, they too are upon the earth, and not once have they had to go to hell or to heaven in order to experience an encounter with hell or with heaven. So, it is all the sad drama of happiness.

If someone could be found who would draw a curtain across this stage with its furnishing of twilight; and who, furthermore, would find it interesting to raise this curtain once a week, on the deserted windy days of holiday when the asphalt stretches and crawls up to the first floors of shops, for are not asphalts and lowered steel shutters one and the same thing on holidays . . . ?—then flags hurry the dried secret snow; and shrunken snow, withered in the solid cold, drags itself down the pavement, inviting various half-frozen bits of paper to follow it. So, on such days, when house-fronts, gleaming with woven drawing-rooms, meet in the dusk at advertisement columns, while the asphalts, those temple-bones of the migraine-paved square—the asphalts grow inexorably, and the sky too, loaded with unfallen collected snows, is made up to look like an empty grey square of closed shops and vein-blue flags; on these days when the sky is made up as empty subsided pavements, perhaps that person I want so much will be interested in raising the curtain.

And now let's suppose he's been found. He is thin, but only up to the limit where it begins to be unacceptable for a decent person; he could have been painted by Holbein, for example. At any rate, when he moves off to pull the cord hanging from the edge of the inanimate, it turns out that his face has been assembled from the simplest and purest anatomical alphabet. Evidently, he is one of those who go from the simple to the simple with a complex gait. Now he is raising the curtain; he'll find there, as at the beginning of every drama, a man's solitude. Here, on our stage, the man is Reliquimini, who is sitting on the window-sill watching how the opposite pavement, composed of bakeries, pharmacies and coachmen's yards, floats up to the seaweeds of the boulevard; all have gas-lit windows like protruding eyes, all are swallowing shredded winter widely and lazily, and are blowing warm steam-bubbles; and it's not at all because, a few blocks away, from behind the roofs, attics are raking out like stokers the brick heat of the theatre wall, and not at all because the façade is that of the Aquarium, it's not at all because of this that Reliquimini is about to compare the turbid black-green darkness to an aquarium. And a flock of voracious shops is being fed from above with snowflakes. Reliquimini is waiting for the teacher; he wants to show him his recent compositions.

Ah, *pardon* . . . in my brochure of existence the days of creation have been shuffled too fast. Excuse me, I cannot remember except out loud. I can't do it silently, I'm sorry; silently I can only forget. And so . . . in the beginning was created the furniture, and then the word which had created it began to find the supplication of the inanimate unbearable, and it sent the musician Reliquimini among the furniture, as heroes used to be sent among the people; this musician was to arrive with a large country Bible, but solely for the sake of the inanimate. And now he was falling asleep. But as his day was all built-up with the inanimate world, his sleep too was a tangle of swaying exhausted objects.

In one dream the furthest veneer of this world came off (it must have been a hot convulsive dream that wouldn't fit into the room): and the rural musician, rubbing his eyes, kissing the matting in a delirium, heard the thousands of creeping and twisting, old and young but motley-hungry materials say, perhaps once in their lifetime, that *that,* the piece which had come off, that one in the corner, furthest away from the prettily-tiled and heated dream, do you see, do you see, they mooed to the waking man, it, the veneer, is dancing, it has returned to the dance, and we've been wanting to meet you, you ranged us along the walls and you whirled around, and you played on the Bechstein so as to whirl your way one day to the furniture and the material, but you too have been sleeping and you know—well, we think you such a comic fellow, you warmed everything up with your dream as hotly as if you were expecting someone to come from outside, from the snowflakes and frost, as if you were expecting your sister, or the postman who would say to you: "No, Reliquimini, I know the world better than you, and I make bold to assure you there is no such sister in all the world, here is your impatience and expectation back again, all covered with writing, you can heat the flat with this bundle." And maybe you would say to him "Be quiet! isn't it twenty degrees below zero in here? And am I not dreaming fathoms and fathoms of dreams; aren't they fuel? do they smoke? aren't they fuel? And must I—oh Lord, oh Lord—must I burn my impatience and expectation as well?!"

But it happened otherwise. Oh, how enriched you are today, rural musician who almost punched the postman; you can stop dancing, and you don't even need to play on the Bechstein, and—above all—stop using these dreams as fuel. Look, the window-panes are holding a service, and the mercury columns have risen on tiptoe like naughty children preparing to wail. In a moment you'll put out the lights and sit down, for look, there's enough light from the winter; and wait, well, you can strum a few chords into the half-dark if you really must. And with the soft pedal? Well, all right. Oh, how enriched you are today. Wait. Don't dance. Someone is dancing from us to you. The heating has been done. The veneer has torn off . . . it dances away . . . and there is Angelika.

Voila! Hylozoism![17] Or the creation of Eve from a rib snapped in sleep. Yes, it is all splendid, but this whole dramatic scheme about Reliquimini and Angelika and the million necessary and unnecessary known and unknown "bestmen" of their lives—as if a wedding were going on—all this is not worth a farthing if one highly important matter is missed out.

A few moments before my Holbeinesque Schleiermacher curtain-trader pulls the string,[18] the piano-tuner's dull monotonous octaves, fifths and fourths are heard off-stage, the sort that only happen in winter, walled up by a heated twilit wall: the tuner's torture-chamber. This is essential. For this rite is enacted in life, too, in the same sequence. There he is, tightly holding a couple of sounds in his teeth, beginning to strike one note, like a nail, dully and long. And isn't this what people do when they want to put love in tune; don't they nail it down? No, positively everything ends and begins with nails, if we follow the motto: *Alles sei wohltemporirt.*[19] And don't we receive what arrives nailed-down and nail it down again when we send it away?

HEINRICH VON KLEIST. ON ASCETICISM IN CULTURE*

(1)

A northerner finds himself in Odessa, where he spent several moments of his childhood—a place of character with characterful people and relationships.[20]

And what happens to the misty Odessa of his past is what happens to any portion of reality brought into his life as a *res nullius,* a piece of sheer life untouched by the everyday: it grows in him aesthetically, it is reborn into culture in his recollection, it becomes in his past what it would have become in his dramas, had he been a poet, in the references never made in his silent illustrations of theory, had he been a systematic student of rebirths—had he been a philosopher. Turning more and more into a symbol, it migrates through his life's ages.

Many years later, this northerner is once again on the road to Odessa. His childhood is now so far away that he already knows what it wants from him; he thinks, too, that his path is a path to the renewal of that ghostly theme which has developed through dreamings. Next, perhaps, immediate life disappears in the form of a question. And perhaps our very possession of it as the past is already akin to an answer; and of course an idea born out of that life—whether it is a scientific, an ethical or, ultimately, an aesthetic idea—is a response to this embodied question of the past.

If it is so, then our traveller from the North brings an answer to the past's errant symbol, to the street full of structures which are going stale and in whose span is suspended a harbour of reddish, rusty ships with a powerless evening sea settled down beyond them.

The answer: his own clarified awareness of a culture that can be created for their sake, for the sake of life.

When he arrives, he stumbles upon an unforeseen collision between what can be created and what can be put into practice, between reality and value.

When he resorts to the sole form in which all our immediate answers to nature are given, namely that of replacing this impossible dialogue by an exchange of

---

* *G. fon Kleist. Ob asketike v kul'ture.* PSS, 5, 294–303. Written 1911. First published, with omissions, in Boris Pasternak, *Sobranie sochinenii v piati tomakh,* edited by A.A. Voznesensky, D.S. Likhachev, D.F. Mamleev and E.B. Pasternak. (Moscow: Khudozhestvennaia literatura, 1991). I have divided it into numbered sections.—A.L.

thoughts with the people around him—when he addresses people—he sees that here people skim, but do not possess, culture; that here everything rests at the stage of the natural, whether unhappy or happy. He seeks reasons for this and in his search he suddenly discovers the concept of asceticism in culture, and notices its absence in the southern witnesses of southern nature and life. When he talks to them about this, they do not understand him.

Then he decides to write about it and suddenly remembers how near is the centenary of the death of one of the greatest ascetics of creativity, one whose suicide proceeded from his peculiar worship of life.

He decides to entitle his laconic experiment: "Heinrich von Kleist. On Asceticism in Culture."[21]

(2)

I wanted to write about Kleist in October in Moscow, my birthplace. Not only because the date of the article would have been the month of the centenary. But the first snow would have just appeared. At zero temperature, straight after the first sudden whiteness allotted to space amid the rest of the sky's dirty darkness, a fitful thaw would have been beginning; houses, porches, shreds of road, umbrellas of passers-by, animals, some faster, others dragging, would have begun to look black, and these warm breaking-through blotches would have grown and spread and, overtaking one another, would have gone over to the sky until the black street made its appearance in the familiar sweat of October rains.

Then, as I leafed through Kleist, I would have been surprised by the sudden darkness of a new snowfall. Through the window the crumbled town would have been visible, and a sky of countless snowflakes would have been on its way; the whole of it coming down slowly, heavily and obliquely onto the roofs, from left to right. Then everything would have been going quiet and the earth would have become burdened with vivid, wheel-scourged suburbs. And again there would have begun the chase of thawing black structures and people.

That is why I wanted to write about him in October. My readers would have had a winter like this as their neighbour. The town would have tossed about in front of them between the snow and the black sky, it would have come running up and gone rolling away, while the just-beginning winter would have weaned them from their usual story of events. They would have experienced that story creatively, that is to say ascetically—in the form of renewed instances of the unexpected, in the form of renunciations of the given. If they had then looked into the biography of Kleist the martyr, they would have read there what should indeed be read: the history of a man, a very great artist, who did not live but was constantly beginning, whose inner world was the constantly sudden coming of severe weather.[22]

This is how I would have needed October: as an assistant. Or rather: beneath the incipient winter of 1911—the way one puts a caption beneath an illustration to a novel—I would have put: the death of Kleist.[23]

(3)

I do not always think of that October in Moscow. Sometimes I go out to the sea or to a fountain where the black night of the steppe is so colourfully garnished beyond the lights. Then from inexplicable habit I think about creativity here in the South. Perhaps not even about its artists—I do not know them. But about what the people of the South want from their artists, and want from themselves in so far as creativity calls them.

Then I am obliged to think about the radical methodological delusion on which all southern aesthetic and ethical constructions are based, so typical and so incurably wrong. Again Kleist comes to mind—now, though, not as a prototype for my October article but in the form of a reference. In the face of flat squinting naturalism, which attacks culture because it lacks that lyrical running start which would have transposed the nature it possesses into the symbolic sphere of culture—in the face of this, the revival of Kleist's name has a special, almost educational, significance. This is a small excavation, and as such it is already a small Renaissance, or the seed of one. And if it is a renaissance—of realism as a tonality and solely within the pattern of culture as a whole—then its task is, on the other hand, to stop the mouth of one rather persistent impostor, the sham realism of the South—that is, simply, naturalism, which is inconsistent because it comes along to a general debate about culture just when, in denial of culture, it declares from the outset that it is denying itself the right to speak. Or can we have wholly forgotten that speech *is* culture?

Kleist is a realist, one bold enough even for our time. Does that mean he is an amoralist?

Kleist is a realist. Does that mean he is an opponent of culture?

And finally, descending from the ethical plane to the aesthetic: Kleist, tormented by his schemes, is tormented—by life; for his schemes are condensed and compressed life.

(4)

In his life Kleist's profile is at first that of a suicide. Only later does the poet in him acquire a distinct outline. This new transmutation is so sudden that one inclines to think of it as just a new name, not touching the essence of the matter. Probably he was a poet in the sense that he was constantly going away. In his cult of these continual breaks with the natural, in this peculiar asceticism which has no pure definite aim and therefore represents the asceticism of creativity, in this constant torture, he discovered the guiding thread of lyricism: beauty.

It led him to death. Or rather: he always found his inspiration in the ascetic act, in the break with the natural, in covering a greater or lesser stretch of the path to death. It was on this path that he became a poet. Realistically—from within—he mastered the meaning of the beautiful. He had endured too many of the world's valedictions and had come back too often; each time he set off he looked back.

It is easy enough to call his life-story a story of digressions from his vocation. That is to overlook the main thing. Digression was his vocation, a heavy, painful and finally funereal one. In fulfilling this vocation, he left us several undying dramas and tales, as well as his unfinished Kant and several fruitless notebooks from the mathematical college, also a patriotic newspaper not approved by the liberal ministry. Most likely at the very beginning of his development, while still in the military sphere, he had turned to self-education in that half-sleep which usually accompanies steps of this kind, suggested as they are by the trend of the majority or the spirit of the age. Or perhaps that feeling—so familiar to everyone—of worthlessness or guiltiness before those who are prominent in areas which for some reason have remained inaccessible to us—perhaps this pushed him to break with the career of his youth and resume his education.

By "science" the German culture of his time meant philosophy, and philosophy became Kleist's new exercise. We say "exercise", taking into account the awkwardness, and a certain inappropriateness, of this expression. Later we shall give a justification of it. For the moment let us remember the Greek origin of the word asceticism.[24]

When a romantic or a symbolist approaches philosophy, or indeed when any artist does who will later either abandon it when called away to the traditional feat of creativity, or else will experience in it a bitter crisis if he does not yet possess the name of his gift but still sees only one side of it, the side which gives him the right to be called an idealist and an agent of culture; when an artist joins a school of philosophy, it turns out that in the preliminary, dialectical stage he is a philosopher in a larger sense than is anyone else, for his innate and fundamental melody is that of giving up the immediacy of intuition;—this negative great poet of the systematics of being finds a real inspired performer in the genuine poet. The culture of asceticism finds an ascetic in the man of creativity. An extreme one. Extreme, because we shall see how this peculiar person will estrange the whole of being, around himself and in himself; even those portions of it, or only those, beyond which the idea that possesses them through this estrangement cannot reach. The single final stage of a pure process. And now we shall see that, in his practice, the artist will set free whole regions of past happening, which will become no one's, estranged for the sake of culture—for the idea of culture, which renounces the natural; he will leave them to be an emblem of culture-as-custom, an infinitely musical—because practical—emblem; to be an emblem of culture in the sense of a period of time, a self-renewing principle, a rhythmic asceticism. I imagine Kleist almost mad from his own attentiveness and ascetic diligence, I imagine him at his genuinely philosophical moments, going deep into the unities which have been set in the tissue of nature for the sake of a system of truth in it; these feats of logical purification he must have experienced as a profound inhalation, full of tension and leading to a great great sigh; and he probably experienced, too, these methodological unities as a linearly, radially concentrated form of separation— and, sensing what orderless Heraclitean *khroos*[25] of the irrational he had forsaken in this voluntary exile of consciousness, he felt yearning, the methodological yearning[26] of creativity, while postponing his return.

So, he "studied philosophy". And, as the biographers tell us, exhausted himself on the wrong path, forfeiting living time and living strengths. *Is that so?* Oh no: more and more often he loathed his work and felt his unfitness for it. Kleist is not yet an artist; but the future artist is already Kleist, already a finished personality in him. And this Kleist is a semi-dialectician as every artist is; he takes to pieces that which, all around him, has been given the wrong shape, that which all around him is neither eternal nor chaotic but only customary and has become by now natural and moral in everyday life, almost naturalistic— *not* aesthetic or cultural. He takes it to pieces, following his inspiration, which suddenly experiences reality as matter whose appearance can be expressed by the phrase "on the eve . . ." "On the eve of culture", its systematic thinker, its philosopher or its worker, will add; and the scholar will then complete the dialectical estrangement which the artist, too, accomplishes, in a place where that estrangement is hopeless—or rather, is full of hope, for the unities culture creates do not meet the semi-dialectical artist halfway, and he hasn't any of his own, except just one: that is, that he stages "culture" the way life is presented on the lyrical stage, that he enacts the general drama ("Culture") of life's negative running start—the overthrowing of naturalism: the drama of asceticism. That he is its *dramatis persona*, the ascetic.

(5)

An artist bears witness to everything as if it were new and primordial. Primordial but not unique—primordial as something that is brought to the threshold of culture—something full of longing for an idea, full of readiness for the eternal. We are not joking or playing with words. But we are ready to acknowledge paths of genuine creativity only in culture's logical and ethical direction—for these are paths of achievement which are ideal to the very end. While the practice of what we call creativity—its practice—is a ritual of renewed beginnings[27] in which the destiny of culture sounds incommensurably more loudly than in the enterprise of the physicist or the legislator. It sounds out heroically in the form we call the idea of the beautiful; the idea of the beautiful is the idea of culture in its opposite, which is left to nature.

But this is all there is to say about what an artist gives; this alone is his task; only in this confession of idealism which is eternally coming to a stop, does its dramatism show itself; in this uncompletedness there is not only a negative side—impossibility, transcendentality, nonsensicality. There is no ending, it is the never-beginning of a synthesis—positive through and through—this is what art is—the drama of culture—estrangement as such, estrangement without any established ownership of a right.

An artist does not create culture. He is busy with exercises—he is the ascetic of culture, of culture-in-general, of a possible culture; only rarely is he at the threshold of our, given, culture—usually the place he occupies with his great act points to the irrational possibility of a system—intelligible as an idea, as the idea of a possibility, intelligible on the ascetic threshold, and impossible to fulfil, to create.

The preliminary stage of philosophising, the stage of estrangements, renunciations of the natural—how germane this must be to the artist! But the artist's idealism is the idealism of the preliminary stage; where the philosopher matures into a systematic thinker or, pursuing one of the branches of a system, becomes a scholar, at this point the artist diverges from him, for *his* idealism is a game, not a system, it is symbolical, not real. The possibility that an idea may be transcendental, not the transcendentality of its possibility.

Hence Kleist's disappointment, his disappointment as a theoretician.

This is not all there is to say about his life. When we turn to the immediate life we meet in it Kleist the extreme pedant, carried away . . .

Kleist's life is not for those who like colourful little pictures. If anyone reassures us by saying: "Yes, we know, it's the life of a typical descendant of the already moribund blue-blooded German nobility", we shall hear even in this an excess of warmth and we'll hurry to obliterate it. Kleist starts off with a military man's life, then comes that of the philistine moralist, then suddenly, all at once like Minerva, the muse bursts in, crazy with realism, she lives along with the philistine, until suddenly there appears the suicide—who was there from the very beginning, whom we hadn't noticed, who had lived within the philistine as the genius of asceticism, and who, finally, swallows up all the others and whirls away for ever in the form—we have said this before—of the demon of asceticism.

The hussar leaning his elbow on clavichords in the evenings, listening to some dilettante comrade in a circle of girl-cousins and garrison-authorities' daughters, all of a sudden throws himself into learning; his subjects are, or are very close to, logic of pure cognition, mathematics, mathematical natural science—yes, all this at once. After that, astonishingly resolute, he perceives his destiny to lie in the career of a scholar.

We shall understand Kleist if we take his life as a story about the fanaticism of the project whereby a woman becomes a warrior. Thus we shall grasp the meaning, the significance, of his death. And we shall pay our debt to history if we detach the *idea* concealed in his fate from that fate itself, and find in it the eternal motive of his canonised death.

Suicide and motive. These concepts are so strongly combined it seems strange that acts of suicide have not turned up among logicians.

About Kleist's death it can be said that, all in all, he shot himself. Then we'll ask ourselves for the reason and we'll find one. But it could be said differently: Kleist merely put an end to himself. Then we do not need to look for a motive. Then merely "suicide"—as the final affirmative link in a tragedy, a link freely added by the killer himself to the one general harmony of fate—could serve as the motive for a second suicide, if such a thing were possible.

(6)

If Kleist had belonged to the circle of the Romantics, he would have written something which he might have entitled "Towards the Idea of Universal Playing". But then he would not have died. Then he would not have ended as such a demanding enigma for us, his posterity. Nowadays his festively furnished suicide,[28] to which he invited a random person, a girl he was merely *acquainted* with, as one might invite someone to an urgent walk which is called for by some sudden, as yet unrealisable, idea [or project, *zamysel*], so as to get away from its attack if only while walking, to get away from it dramatically, in a ludic act: in the play-walking of someone being pursued by an idea [*zamysel*] among play-forests which the north has set up in its distant places, and the distances are playing just as sorrowful an autumnal game as he is, that of being pursued by an idea; as one might invite another person in order to make the playing complete, for without the other, without a participant, the wandering of the pursued one would be a personal and fortuitous event, dumb and unrelated to language; whereas what is happening is that an *idea* has driven him out of doors, an idea which wants to be for the whole world, and not just experienced but *meaningful*; for the idea itself is playing: and for this to be so one needs the presence, at least, of another person in whose pure, interpreting attention meaningful eternity is enacted.[29]

Are not these words the words of logos, of the scheme; is not this its demand: "For where two or three are gathered together in my name, there am I in the midst of them"?[30] Thus the idea plays through its actors, its ascetics. Thus Kleist invited someone to die with him.

Nowadays we would hear in *such* a suicide something which Henriette Vogel probably did not hear, and we would reinstate a confession which Kleist himself probably did not make. But history, after all, has got to be created. For history is a continual repayment from those indebted to the past. Every reign mints its gold coins afresh. At the moment it is the reign of Symbolism and a reborn transcendental idealism. It is in their units that we shall pay our debt to Autumn 1811.

[ON THE THRESHOLD OF INSPIRATION]*

Above all I want to speak about the way the past sometimes appears on the threshold of inspiration.[31] When it's holiday time with the shops all closed and the servants gone away and people have vanished into houses of friends, the grey sky starts at the very asphalt; no umbrellas, hats or shop-windows full of vegetables would launch it so loftily and ceremonially. A painter chancing to be in the street at this moment will notice how the sky is scantily, brokenly tracked by the damp yellow autumn wind. From this dark sludge of maples and aspens left in the sky he will sense the fluent step of autumn. Then he'll look round and see how seldom the town on holiday without any people, hazy and faintly cracked by rains, touches the earth.

That's the painter. What a musician experiences, given this unpeopled vacation of streets, will be in the winter. It will be this. The winter day will slant from all the carriages and signboards, copying them sideways in cursive script, at an angle, with dry prickly pellets of sleet. Everything will freeze together from the sloping lines. This acute-angled dusk, frozenly sticking onto dawn, which lags not a pace behind the winter day, and onto evening—and evening is like a low ceiling; evening, from morning on, stops you standing up straight: straighten up and you'll bump against evening, so you walk hunched all day; this oblique and leaning day is like a plank, such a day is laid down towards music, towards the multitude of fur-coats, tickets and twenty-copeck coins and ladies arriving late.

And you force your way through a dark-blue fence of exhalations, stars, frost, darkness, squealings, freezing muzzles wrapped in sacking, separate halves of moustaches, letters of the alphabet, street-lamps, eyes that cannot be paired up, and snowflakes, through a tundra of dark-blue manes and dark-blue alleys after sudden lakes of flame at café doorways.

These are hints of that unattractive quality of past, which sometimes overtakes us; hints of it. But it is not enough, and even while we are undergoing it we are given something more. I have always experienced past as the stressed

---

* Untitled. PSS, 3, 510–512 (listed there by reference to its opening words, "*Prezhde vsego mne khochetsia govorit' o toi byli . . .* "). Written 1912. First published in *Pamiatniki kul'tury* (Moscow, 1977).

syllable in the final foot of a line of verse which is to have a feminine ending. Reality gave only the heavy syllable, the first half of the foot; a kind of melodic meaningfulness demanded the second half—evening, twilight—in which past, or its bandages, would weaken. (Bandages fastened onto past, which is sick, by the hand of culture that heals: the hand of scientific and moral creativity.)

And see: the thirst for something unstressed, unstressed eternally, something that cannot begin, for all past, even its twilight, is without exception stressed, it's all one single masculine ending, blunt, stopped short, which is sometimes sung for us only because we feel "this isn't the final syllable." For the element of dream is *disyllabic,* while past *(byl')* is truncated, senseless, irrational, it trembles half-way through a word.

Love, for life breaks off at love. At love, life unfolds itself . . . Love, a break, without hands, my life has someone's supple distant hands, so new I have to watch them all the time, which is why I suffer from insomnia.

But love is schematic, it is concerned only with the formal dynamics of this edge, only with an almost *a priori* correlation; with the way the scale pan carrying stressed past, that heavy pan, goes up, away, outbalanced by the pan of chaos.

Thirst for the unstressed, this *apeiron*[32] of song, not the *apeiron* which anticipates Pythagoreanism, perfection of the theoretical and ethical spheres— they end with a heavy stroke, they are masculine creative elements—but the one which follows Orphism, an element eternally on the eve. Past (strange word— of masculine gender)[33] is always imbued with a thirst for unstressed chaos, a yearning will to be feminine, whenever it's on the threshold of inspiration.

SYMBOLISM AND IMMORTALITY [SYNOPSIS OF A LECTURE]*

(1) The feeling of immortality accompanies experience when we teach ourselves to see subjectivity not as something belonging to personality but as a property of quality in general. Subjectivity is a category sign of quality; in it is expressed the logical impermeability of quality considered independently.

(2) Qualities are enveloped by consciousness which liberates them from connection with personal life, returns them to their immemorial subjectivity and is itself imbued with this tendency. Immortality takes possession of the contents of the soul. Such a phase is the aesthetic phase. In pure form this is what symbolism teaches. Living contents are led not to time but to a unity of meaning.

---

* *Simvolizm i bessmertie.* PSS, 5, 318–19. Synopsis of a lecture given in 1913. First published by Lazar Fleishman in *Stat'i o Pasternake* (Bremen, 1975). I have numbered the paragraphs—A.L.

(3) A poet dedicates the visual wealth of his life to timeless meaning. A living soul estranged from personality in favour of free subjectivity is immortality. Thus immortality is the Poet; and a poet is never a being, but is the condition for quality.

(4) Poetry is madness without a madman. Madness is natural immortality; poetry is the immortality allowed by culture.

(5) The meaning of music's one symbol—rhythm—is found in poetry. The content of poetry is the poet as immortality. Rhythm symbolises the poet.

(6) Theatre and quality. The concept of a statement as a phenomenon on the level of immortality, as distinct from an appearance. A word is a spiritual formation, visual and sensual in the sense of a statement. Word and poet.

(7) The perception and inspiration of creation.

(8) Inspiration is the syntax of poetry, it is concrete—incidentally—in alliteration.

(9) The reality accessible to personality is permeated with the quest for the free subjectivity belonging to quality. Signs of this quest, issuing from reality itself and concentrated in it, are perceived by the poet as the signs of reality itself. The poet submits to the tendency of the quest, imitates it, and conducts himself like the objects around him. People call this: being observant and drawing from nature.

(10) Symbolism thinks through to the end this tendency within what is experienced and builds its system in accordance with it. Therefore, as a system only, symbolism is completely realistic. However, the very analysis of the tendencies concealed within reality gives this system a religious character. Symbolism attains realism in religion. Does symbolism remain art?

[END OF A DECADE]*

Just now I was sitting by the opened window, waiting. During those minutes a whole strange decade of my life came to an end. I cannot avoid this laughable phrase: the decade of my—"activity as a composer".[34] And what a good thing that this anniversary fell at night-time. Nothing prevents me spending a while pondering it.

I am sorry for the thirteen-year-old boy with his sixth of August accident.[35] There he lies, as if today, in a fresh plaster cast that has not yet set, and through his delirium go the syncopated ternary rhythms of gallop and fall. Rhythm,

---

* Untitled. PSS, 5, 319–21 (listed by its opening words, "*Seichas ia sidel u raskrytogo okna . . .* ") Written 1913. First published in *Voprosy literatury* 9 (Moscow, 1972).

henceforth, will be an event for him, and, conversely, events will become rhythms; while melody, key and harmony will be the surroundings and substance of the event. Only the previous day, as I recall, I had no conception of the taste of creativity. Works of art simply existed as suggested states which left one nothing to do but experience them in one's own being. But the moment of waking up in orthopaedic trammels brought something new: an ability to deal with something uninvited, to make oneself the beginning of what until then had come without a beginning and, when first discovered, had already been standing there, like nature. I think of that boy and how cruelly I treated him.[36] Why didn't I warn him at the time; perhaps he would have avoided me, perhaps he and I would not have met and I would not have razed him to the ground.

Why be sorry for him? Believe it—he was lucky. And then—he is wholly in the past, in that warm, eternally green zone of consciousness, that Riviera of time, as befits a sick person.

I am sorry for myself now. After all, I too could reproach him for many things. He does not pay me with reciprocation. Here am I, completely given over to him—to the inclemency of his 1903 autumn—and his first encounter with music manuscript paper is dear to me.

But he sinks in his own twilight and doesn't know me; he does not even allow the thought that there exists a twenty-three-year-old-himself, only asks for his pillow to be set straight and tries to go to sleep.

Thanks to him, I am losing my equilibrium.—Everything is on his side, and in me something gives way and snaps off.

This is how we spend the present evening: he—with a broken leg, I with a break in my soul and a thickened heel—ten years lie between us.

I shall interrupt my recollections here. One must go out with something, after all, into the insistently rising dawn; one must have something ready for tomorrow.

Then, involuntarily, I ask myself: what is it, on the whole, that this being needs?

Oh, how useful is a falling-off of creativity![37] Like a hungry servant's imagination, this condition can embrace and express in one short line the entire essence of its absent master.[38]

Mentally it sets before itself, one after another, several temptations which are denied to it, in order to reject them instantly as misleading definitions of its true desire. At first it seems that the highest enjoyment, once apprehended, would drown your thirst in slaking it. But, supposing that could happen, imagining it having happened, you notice that the enjoyment does not cover your desire, whose food is creation; the desire remains above it, unslaked, like a lofty promontory appearing above a flood. Perhaps, if it is not noted for sensuality, your desire is for action. But even though you anticipate the very highest point in the category of action, that extreme active effort still spreads out like the same old indifferent lowness, not equal to the desire (as I said before) or to the enjoyment.

Suppositions multiply, one after the other, and all are as insubstantial as the first two, until you make your way through to a strange unaccustomed shaft of light, so simple and unforeseen that you cannot name it with your complex words.

To become a source of enjoyment, even of an enjoyment of such nature and dimensions that, when it is addressed to a human being, it presupposes no human being at all but a kind of "all-four-directions" taking-in of the enjoyment; to send out a wave of such enjoyment and (thanks to its peculiarity) to feel it, from oneself, in someone else; to send out, so as to receive in one's neighbour: this is the ring of creativity—integral, closed and returning to itself.

If sensuality in general is a stratum that welds together two quantities lying at its two sides, then the sensuality of art is the welding of a complete hoop.

THE BLACK GOBLET*

1

It is a quarter of a century now since, looking out wet-nurses for us somewhere beyond the Armoury, near the Kremlin, on the Embankment of all antiquities, or packing us into our cradles, us children lulled by the sweetness of infancy, you weren't afraid to tell us the rules for doing the fastest possible packing at any given moment, at the very first signal for assembly.

We grew up on the amazing mobility of your immoveables: the sobbing of your itinerant reality droned as it flew back from the hoar-frosted window-panes of the nursery and buzzed as it singed them a menacing yellow. And from the very beginning you told us the secret of the paths of communication and the secrets of all collisions, removing them one by one behind the little window of magic lanterns. Compressing the signboards, crumpling the fragments of horse-drawn trams and houses doomed for demolition, folding and pleating the gardens and allotments—you overloaded the sky to the utmost limits. Your travelling-horizon frightened us by the amount it could hold. And many a time we shuddered at the sight of the cracked splitting-open sky; we grew obsessed by its gross-weight of storm-cloud and by the variable outline of the tender net-weight of the heavens. You brought up a generation of packers. You began sending for experienced teachers from abroad: *des symbolistes pour emballer la globe comblée dans les vallées bleues des symboles.*[39] And opened your own school.

---

* *Chernyi bokal.* PSS, 5, 12–16. Begun 1913 (see PSS, 5, 515–16). First published in *Tsentrifuga* 2 (Moscow, 1916).

You, impressionists, taught us to roll up the versts, to make a neat row of the evenings, to lower the fragile products of whims into the cottonwool of twilights. And more, you instructed us in reading and writing, so that, in the proper place and at the appointed hour, we should be able to write the much-promising inscription: *this side up*. So now, thanks to you, we've been tracing on our hearts for who knows how many years the sign of the black goblet: *Handle with care!* Thereupon, by common consent and by mutual agreement, we received, as first graduates of your school of removals men, the honorary nickname of futurists.

With this meaningful nickname you tried, for the first time in your school's whole existence, to give sense to the hitherto aimless art of skilled apprentices and declining masters. In the work of the futurist the model manoeuvre of idle impressionism becomes for the first time a matter of vital necessity, the porter fastens the badge of the future to his coat, the traveller's route is made clear to him. Even more: by bestowing the name futurist on its heir, symbolism tacitly ordains a ferryman by trade to be the first settler of the century's chosen possibilities. Meanwhile, it is not because we are stopped short by circumspection but because we are prompted by the demon of accuracy that we now make a twofold amendment.

2

One must be seriously ticklish for the current theory of futurism in its popular form to have an effect. "The rhythm of life abducted in a taxi, the rhythm of creation lodged in technological enterprises . . ."[40] "Excuse me, but what is all this leading to? Is this where contemporary art begins?"—Why yes, that's just how some ape which had changed unrecognizably from one day to the next would explain its new tricks—as a hitherto absent representative of the non-cloven-footed arriving in the menagerie. Just like that. But apes need no justification. And in any case even Aristotle's mimesis cannot serve as a speech of justification in defence of the ape.

The art of impressionism—the art of the thrifty handling of space and time—is the art of packing; the main feature of impressionism is that of getting ready for a journey, and futurism is for the first time a clear instance of actual packing in the shortest possible time. The haste that is natural to it is as remote from the unaccustomed speed of a Mercedes as it is from the slowness of Narzes' travels.[41] In general, movements at all the observable speeds are but one of the many and varied attributes of the whole item of goods destined for this packing. And, finally, this haste has not the slightest connection with the mystical haste of the mystics' perennially approaching—at any time, even hourly—*deadlines* and opening paths. By the way, this is the second of the amendments we were prompted to make by the demon of accuracy. The first, however, still waits to be dealt with.

This haste is none other than the urgency of our appointment; at every step, every day, every hour, art receives from the age an immutable, flattering, responsible, extremely important and urgent appointment. Where the ape of art sees in *lim t* = 0 a formula for the cinematic instant,[42] the visitor to the menagerie perceives just the opposite limit. Allow, then, the impressionism in futurism's core metaphor to be an impressionism of the eternal. Transformation of the temporal into the eternal by means of the limitational instant—this is the true meaning of the futurist abbreviations.

The symbolists displayed to us, in symbols, models of all possible *coffres volants*.[43] Content, impressionistically packed away in landscapes, actual and fictitious, in stories, real (thus criminal) and imaginary (thus brain-puzzling); in myths and in metaphors: this content became the live adventuristic contents of a unique *coffre volant*—that of the futurist.

The soul of the futurist, a packer with a special sort of mentality, is realistically proclaimed by him in the metaphor of the absolutism of the lyrical; it is the only acceptable form of *coffre volant*. The hearts of the symbolists smashed against symbols, the hearts of the impressionists haunted the thresholds of the lyrical and surrendered to the lyrical their whipped-up hearts. But only with the heart of lyricism does the heart of the futurist, this apriorist of lyricism, begin to beat. True lyricism was always of this sort, this is truly the *a priori* condition for the possibility of the subjective.

The subjective originality of the futurist is not at all the subjectivity of the individual. His subjectivity is to be understood as a category of Lyricism itself—of the Original in the ideal sense. Incidentally, it would be desirable to supplement the Dictionary of Abstractions with the latter term. Then we could stop resorting to the ambiguous word "subjectivity". Then, on all those occasions when aestheticians start talking about "Platonic-Schopenhauerian" ideas, about archetypes or about the ideal, we would put in our fine little word.

The Original is the integral principle of originality (logically proportionate to the concepts *V, d* etc) and nothing more. Not a word about anamnesis or premature models! Such is the independent postulate of the category of originality—inherent in Lyricism itself.[44]

First of all, then, the muscles of the futurist abridgements are not in the least akin to the musculature of contemporary reality. What look like futurism's neural techniques speak rather of the nervosity of the assault on reality carried out by Lyricism. Eternity is, perhaps, the most dangerous of rebels. Its deeds are violent, insistent, lightning-quick.

3

Further, not the angel of modesty but the demon of accuracy extorts a second confession from us: *is* the Futurist the settler of the Future, of the new, the unknown?

A confused tone, blessed on its way by the symbolists, has been introduced in recent literature, a tone of most profoundly serious promises about things lying outside lyric poetry. These promises were no sooner pronounced than everyone forgot them: benefactors as well as benefacted. They were never kept because their profundity exceeded all the bounds of feasibility in three dimensions.

No forces will make us set to work, even in words, on the . . . preparation of tomorrow's history assignment. Still less will we dare attempt such a deed of our own free will! What we see in art is a distinctive kind of *extemporale* whose sole aim is that it should be executed brilliantly.

Amid the objects accessible to the unarmed eye there has now arisen to the eye of the armed the spectre of History, terrible if only because its visibility is unusual and contradicts its nature.

We do not wish to lull our consciousness with piteous and nebulous gene-ralisations. We must not be deceived: reality is disintegrating. As it disintegrates, it gathers at two opposite poles: Lyricism and History. Both are equally *a priori* and absolute.

Battalions of heroes, does everyone nowadays honour in you a battalion of seers, does everyone know that the dazzling sheaves of the "latest news" are the sheaves of that destructive pull with which the magnetic field of the heroic deed is fraught—the field of battle: the field of the invasion of History into Life. Heroes of its dread *a priori*! The inhuman lies at the base of your humanity. Life and death, rapture and suffering—these false propensities of the person— are rejected. Heroes of renunciation, in your splendorous unanimity, you have acknowledged these conditions as the chiaroscuro of history itself and have hearkened to its shattering inspiration.

Are we to play the hypocrite to the seers? No, nothing will persuade us to insult them with an unpermitted approach. Not even if it's with an exactitude down to one-hundred-millionth, an exactitude permitted to any one of us, in our hundred-million fatherland.

Not the shade of timidity, but the demon of accuracy, prompted us to make this confession.

Years passed, each stagnating in turn, as if by habit. Was it from absent-mindedness? Who knew their face, and, as for them, did they distinguish anyone's face?

And now, at the end of one of them, reckoned the 1914th, you daredevils, you alone and no one else, have roused them with an unprecedented clamour. In fire and smoke he has appeared to you, and to you alone, the demon of time. You and you alone will put him into a new bondage. We, though, shall not touch the age, as indeed we have never touched it. But between us and you, you soldiers of absolute history, there are millions who admire mutual approaches. They'll settle the new era which you will have won back in battle, but—family men or bachelors, people falling in love or divorcing—they will wish to accomplish this new removal with all the mystery of egoism and in all life's magnificence.

And now, tell me: how can we do without the solitary packers, the packers who have their own special kind of mentality and whose every thought has always been directed to the sole question: how should life be folded up so that it can be transported by the heart of the lyric poet, that repository of transferred meaning with its sign of the black goblet and the inscription: *With care. This side up.*

LETTERS FROM TULA*

I

Outside in the open, larks were pouring forth their song, and in the train from Moscow the gasping sun was being carried along on a great many striped seats. It was setting. A bridge with the inscription "Upa"[45] floated past a hundred small windows at the very moment when the fireman, flying ahead of the carriages, on the tender, discovered in the noise of his hair and the excited freshness of evening, to one side of the tracks, the town racing to meet the train.

There, at that same moment, people were greeting one another in the streets and saying "A good evening to you". Some of them added: "Have you come from there?" "Going there", a few replied. "Too late", they rejoined, "it's finished."

"Tula, the tenth.

So you've changed over, as we arranged with the conductor. The General who gave up his seat has just bowed to me on his way to the bar, as though I were a close acquaintance. The next train to Moscow is at three in the morning. He was saying goodbye and leaving. The porter is opening doors for him. Out there, cab-drivers are making a noise. From afar, like sparrows. Dearest, my seeing you off like this was madness. Separation is ten times harder now. There's somewhere for imagination to start from. It will grind me down. There's a horse-tram approaching, they're changing the horses. I'll ride in and look at the town. Oh this melancholy! I'll beat it down, I'll blunt its fury with poems."

"Tula. Alas, there is no halfway. Either leave at the second bell or else set off together on the journey, all the way to the grave. Listen, it will be getting light by the time I've done the whole journey in reverse, the same journey in all its details, even the most trivial. They will be subtle forms of refined torture now.

What grief, to be born a poet! What a torturer—imagination! The sun is in the beer. It's sunk to the bottom of the bottle. Across the table—some sort of

---

* *Pis'ma iz Tuly.* PSS, 3, 26–33. Written April 1918. First published 1922 in *Shipovnik* 1 (Moscow, 1922).

agriculturalist. His face is brown. He's stirring his coffee with a green hand. Oh, my dear, all around me are strangers. There was one witness—he's gone (the General). There is another—world-wide—not acknowledged. Nonentities! For they think it's their own sun they are gulping with milk from saucers. They don't think it's in yours, in ours, that flies get stuck and kitchen boys' saucepans clatter and Seltzer water gushes and silver roubles click on the marble like the clicking of a tongue. I shall go and look at the town. It has remained to one side. There is a horse-tram, but it isn't worth it; I'm told it's a walk of forty minutes or so. I found the receipt, you were right. I'll hardly have time tomorrow, I'll need a good sleep. Day after tomorrow. Don't worry—a pawnshop, it can wait. Oh, writing is sheer torment. But I haven't the strength to leave you."

Five hours passed. There was an extraordinary silence. One could no longer see where was grass and where coal. A star was flickering. There was not a single living soul now at the water tower. In a rotting hollow in a swamp of moss lay black water. In the water—the trembling reflection of a small birch tree. The tree was feverish. But that was very far away. Very, very far away. Except for the birch tree, not a soul on the road.

There was an extraordinary silence. Unbreathing boilers and carriages lay on the flat earth, like conglomerations of low clouds on windless nights. Had it not been April, summer lightnings would have been playing. But the sky was restless. Touched by transparency as though by an illness, faintly pierced from within by spring, it was restless. The last Tula horse-tram had arrived from the town. Folding backs of benches were banging. Last to get out was a man with letters protruding from the wide pockets of his wide coat. The others went into the waiting room, towards a group of highly strange young people noisily eating their supper at the far end. This man stayed outside the building, looking for the green post-box. But it was impossible to say where was grass, where coal, and when a weary pair dragged a shaft across turf, digging out a path with a harrow, no dust could be seen and only the lantern by the horse-yard gave a dim notion of it. The night made a long guttural sound—and everything went quiet. This was very, very far away, beyond the horizon.

"Tula, the tenth (crossed out), the eleventh, one o'clock in the night.

Dearest, have a look in the text-book. You've got Kliuchevsky, I put it in your suitcase myself.[46] Don't know how to begin. So far I understand nothing. It's so strange—and dreadful. While I write to you, everything is carrying on as it has to at the other end of the table. They are being geniuses, holding forth in speeches, lobbing words to each other, flinging napkins theatrically onto the table after wiping their clean-shaven mouths. I haven't said who they are. The worst kind of bohemianism (carefully crossed out). A film company from Moscow. They have been doing "Time of Troubles" in the Kremlin and in places with ramparts.[47]

See what Kliuchevsky says. I haven't read him but he must include the episode about Peter and Bolotnikov.[48] That is what has brought them to the Upa. I've heard that they staged it to the letter and filmed it from the other bank. Now they've got the seventeenth century stuffed in their suitcases, and everything else is slumped over a dirty table. The Polish women are terrible, the minor nobility still worse. Oh my dear friend! I feel sick. This is an exhibition of the ideals of the age. The fumes they give off are my own, our shared fumes. A miasma of ignorance and the most unlikeable insolence. It is myself. Dearest, I have posted you two letters. I can't remember them! Here is the vocabulary of these (crossed out, not replaced by anything). Here's their vocabulary: genius, poet, ennui, verses, untalented, philistine, tragic, woman, I and she. Dreadful to see one's own features on strangers. It's a caricature of (gap, not filled).

Two o'clock. My heart's faith is stronger than ever, I swear to you there will come a time—no, let me tell it as from this moment. Night, torment me, torment me, it isn't enough yet; sear me through and through, burn clearly and luminously, tearing your way through—forgotten, wrathful, fiery word "conscience". (A line is drawn under this word, partly going through the paper.) Burn, frenzied tongue of oil which has lit up half the night.

A new style of living has come into fashion, which means there are no positions on earth where a human being can warm his soul at the fire of shame; everywhere shame has got damp and won't burn. Lies, and the confusion of licence. For thirty years all the exceptional people, old and young, have been living like this, letting shame get drenched; and now this style has spread to the world in general, to people who aren't heard of. For the first time, the first time since distant childhood, I am burning" (all this is crossed out).

A fresh attempt. The letter remains unposted.

"How to describe it? I must start at the end. Otherwise it won't work. Here goes then, and if you don't mind I'll use the third person. Did I tell you about the man strolling past the luggage counter? Well, I'll tell you. The poet, who will henceforth put this word in quotation marks until it is purified by fire, the "poet" observes himself in the outrageous behaviour of the actors, in the disgrace which exposes his comrades and his age. Is he just trying to be interesting? No. They confirm his identity with them, it is no delusion. They get up and come over to him. "Colleague, can you change a three-rouble note?" He dispels the error. Actors are not the only ones who shave. Here's change for three roubles. He gets rid of the actor. But it is not just a question of shaving. "Colleague", this riff-raff said. Yes. He is right. This is evidence from a witness for the prosecution. At that moment something new happens, something which is really nothing but in its way gives a jolt to all that has been done and felt in the waiting room up to now.

The "poet" at last recognises the man who was strolling past the luggage counter. He has seen that face before. The man is from these parts. He saw him once, more than once, in the course of a single day, at various times, in various places. It was when a special train was being made up at Astapovo,[49] with a goods truck to carry the coffin, and when crowds of unknown people were travelling off in different directions from the station and in various trains which circled and cut across each other all day long because of unforeseen problems at the confused junction where four tracks came together, ran apart and crossed as they returned.

And now a sudden consideration bears down upon everything that has happened to the "poet" in the waiting room; as if with a lever it turns the stage round—the consideration that—this is Tula! This night is a night in Tula. A night in places belonging to Tolstoy's biography.[50] Is it any wonder that the magnetic needles start dancing in this place? The incident shares the nature of the location. It is happening on the *territory of conscience,* on its gravitational ore-bearing sector. There will no longer be "a poet". He swears to you. He swears to you that one day when he sees "The Time of Troubles" on the screen (for it will be shown one day), the scene on the Upa will find him utterly lonely—unless actors have improved by then and, after spending a whole day stamping about on the mined territory of the spirit, dreamers of all persuasions remain intact in their ignorance and bluster.

While these lines were being written, small low-level lights for the sleepers came out of the trackman's hut and wandered over the tracks. Whistles began to sound. Cast iron woke up, cries came from chains being knocked about. Carriages were very quietly sliding past the platform. They had been sliding past for a long time and there was no end to them. Behind them something that breathed heavily was approaching and growing, something unknown, nocturnal. Arriving, joint by joint, behind the locomotive was a sudden cleansing of the tracks, the unexpected appearance of night within the range of the empty platform, the coming of silence over the whole breadth of signal posts and stars—an onset of rural peacefulness. That moment was the thing snorting at the tail of the goods train, bending under the low awning, nearing and sliding.

While these lines were being written, the mixed train for Elets began to be shunted together.

The man who had been writing went out on the platform. Night lay on the entire expanse of damp Russian conscience. Lanterns illumined it. Goods trucks with winnowing machines under tarpaulin moved over it slowly, bending the rails. It was trampled by shadows and deafened by tufts of steam like small cockerels breaking loose from the valves. The writing man skirted the station. He went out, beyond its façade.

Nothing changed on the whole space of conscience while these lines were being written. From it came a wafting of putrefaction and clay. Far, far away, from its opposite edge, a small birch tree glimmered and, like a dropped ear-ring, a hollow was outlined in a swamp. Stripes of light, tearing from the waiting room to the outside, fell onto the horse-tram floor, under the benches. These stripes ran riot. A banging of beer, madness and stench was falling under the benches after them. And when the station windows died down, a crunching and snorting could still be heard somewhere nearby. The writing man walked up and down. He thought of many things. He thought about his art and how he was to find the right path. He forgot who he had been travelling with, had seen off, and had been writing to. He assumed that everything would begin when he stopped hearing himself and a complete physical silence entered his soul. Not the Ibsen kind, but *acoustic*.

He thought these things. A shiver ran over his body. The east was turning grey, and onto the entire face of conscience, still plunged in deep night, a quick, perplexed dew was dropping. Time to think of a ticket. Cocks sang and the ticket office was coming to life.

II

Only then did an exceedingly strange old man finally go to bed in his hotel room in Posolsky Street. While letters were being written at the station, the room had been shaking from small light footsteps and his candle in the window had caught whispers interrupted by frequent silences. It was not the old man's voice, yet there was not a soul in the room besides him. All this was surprising and strange.

The old man had had an extraordinary day. He had left the meadow sorrowfully on hearing that it was not really a play but was as yet a free fantasy, to become a play only when shown at "The Magic". At first, when he saw the nobles and the commanders heaving about on the other bank and the common people bringing captives and knocking their hats off into the nettles, when he saw the Poles trying to cling to broom bushes at the edge of the ravine, and saw their hatchets which didn't gleam in the sun or make a ringing sound, the old man had begun burrowing through his own repertoire. He could not find any such chronicle in it. He decided it was from something earlier—Ozerov or Sumarokov.[51] Then someone pointed out the camera-man to him and, by mentioning "The Magic", an institution he hated with all his heart, reminded him that he was old and alone and that times had changed. He went away, depressed.

Walking along in his old nankeen trousers, he thought of how there was no one in the world now to call him Savvushka.[52] It was a holiday. The day was warming itself on dropped sunflower seeds.

Rude, loud voices spat novelty at him. Up on high the moon was melting and crumbly as a cottage loaf. The sky seemed cold, astonished by distance. Voices were greasy from stuff eaten and drunk. Even the drowsy echo across the river was soaked in saffron mushroom, rye gingerbread, lard and vodka. There were crowds on some of the streets. Crude frills gave women and their dresses a peculiar speckled look.

Tall weeds kept up with the strollers, just behind them. Dust was rising, sticking eyes together and obscuring the burdock which beat smokily against wattle fencing and clung to clothes. The old man's stick seemed part of his sclerosis. Convulsively and with a gout-sufferer's solidity, he leaned on this prolongation of his gnarled veins.

All day he had had the sensation of being in a terribly noisy market-place. It was because of the spectacle he had seen. It had failed to satisfy his need for tragic human speech. This silent omission rang in the old man's ears.

All day he had walked about feeling ill from not hearing a single pentameter from the other shore.

And when night came, he sat down at his table, leant his head on his hand and began thinking. He decided it was his death. This mental confusion was so unlike the bitterness and smoothness of his recent years. He resolved to take his medal out of the cupboard and warn someone, if only the concierge, it didn't matter who—yet still he remained sitting there, waiting for all this perhaps to pass off.

The horse-tram trotted by with a metallic ringing. It was the last one for the station.

About half an hour passed. A star shone. Apart from that—not a soul any-where. It was late. The candle burned, chilled and shivered. The softened outline of the book-case rippled in four black streams. Just then the night made a long guttural sound. Very far away. In the street someone banged a door and began talking in quiet excitement, as is appropriate on a spring night with not a soul around and only in one room at the top of a hotel a light and an open window.

The old man stood up. Transformed. He had found it at last. Her and himself. Something was helping him. And he threw himself into aiding these hints, so as not to miss them both, so they should not slip away, so as to get into them and become completely still. He reached the door in a few strides, half-shutting his eyes and gesturing with one arm, covering his chin with the other. He was remembering. Suddenly he straightened up and walked boldly backwards, with a stride that was not his own but someone else's. Apparently he was acting.

"Well now, it's a real snowstorm, Liubov Petrovna" he declaimed, and he cleared his throat and spat into a handkerchief; then again: "Well now, it's a real snowstorm, Liubov Petrovna," he declaimed, and did not cough and now the speech came out as it should.

He began shifting his hands and making movements in the air as if he had come in from bad weather and was unfastening his clothes, throwing off a fur coat. For a while he waited for a reply to come from behind the partition, then, as though not able to wait any longer, asked: "Aren't you at home, Liubov Petrovna?", still in the voice of somebody else, and shuddered when, as he expected, he heard—after two and a half decades—the merry, beloved reply beyond *that* partition: "I *am* at home!" And again, this time most credibly of all, creating an illusion that would have been the pride of certain fellow actors in the same position, he drawled out, as if tinkering with his tobacco, glancing sideways at the partition and now and then deranging his parts of speech: "M-m, I'm sorry, Liubov Petrovna,—but isn't Savva Ignatevich there?"

It was too much. He could see them both. Her and himself. The old man was stifled by soundless sobs. Hours passed. He wept and whispered. There was an extraordinary silence. And while the old man was shuddering and helplessly pressing his eyes and face with a handkerchief, and trembling, and kneading it, shaking his head and making brushing-away gestures like a person giggling so much that he chokes and is amazed at the fact that, God forgive him, he is still alive and has not exploded—at the railway they started to make up the mixed train for Eletsk.

For an hour he preserved his youth in tears as if in spirit, And when he had no more tears it all turned to nothing, flew away, disappeared. He immediately went dull and seemed to grow dusty. Then sighing, as if guilty, and yawning, he began to get ready for bed.

He too shaved his face, like everyone in the story. He too, like the main character, was looking for a physical silence. In the story he was the only one to find it, by making a stranger speak through his lips.

The train was on its way to Moscow and in it, carried on a great many sleeping bodies, was an enormous crimson sun. It had just made its appearance from behind a hill and was going upward.

Commentary on I
(EARLY PROSE)

The first group of texts is from the period 1910–19. In their different ways, all are meditations on art and inspiration.

"Some Propositions"

This group of seven short passages is placed first because it represents Pasternak's first really clear and authoritative-sounding statement of his ideas about art, "his first manifesto free from the influences of any literary groups".[53] When he speaks of art in general, it is usually literature that he has in mind.

Enclosing the seven passages with a letter to Tsvetaeva, in 1926, Pasternak wrote:

> Looking through some old rubbish, I found in a 1922 collection two pages for which I would go through fire and water[54] . . . Read them without haste and do not be misled by the form: they are not aphorisms but genuine convictions, perhaps even thoughts. I wrote them in 1919. But because these ideas are inseparable from me rather than gravitating towards a reader (sponge and fountain), there is an averted head and an oblique elbow to be sensed in the style, which may make it difficult.[55]

The *Propositions* have two main contents: criticism of contemporary talk about art, and assertions about what art really is. There is a strong moral orientation, not as regards ethical actions but in the insistence on the poet's responsibility to be truthful. Such truthfulness Pasternak will later call "realism". Its keyword, introduced without the least equivocation at the beginning of passage three (and a central motif in *Letters from Tula*, written the same year) is "conscience".

They start with confession of a withdrawal from the "carefree" self-confidence of other talkers about literature, and of love for "the book". This absorption in reading, or in remembering a book read, is balanced in passage three by a writer's, rather than a reader's, kind of book-absorption. The image there is a powerful one: a book in process is like a wood-grouse (or capercaillie) in its mating season, so absorbed in performing its courtship ritual that it is deaf to everything else and can easily be killed by the hunter. Pasternak does not spell out the vulnerability but it is present in the image of this bird. When Mandelstam, in 1923, praised the world-oblivious, work-absorbed quality of Pasternak's verse, he recalled this very passage: "Pasternak's poetry is simply birds' mating-calls, a wood-grouse in its mating season, a nightingale in the spring . . . At present we have no poetry healthier than this." Tsvetaeva wrote similarly of absorption in composition: "To hear correctly is my concern. I have no other . . . " and: "I write for the work itself . . . Have I time for others, or for myself?"[56]

While in the first passage it is from a position of personal pain that Pasternak rejects the world of careless amateur talk about literature, in the second there is as much authority as anguish in his criticism of contemporary poetic movements such as futurism which want art to "gush forth"; instead it should absorb its surroundings like a sponge (an image used also in the poem *Spring*). Those contemporary movements fail to realize that true art results from sensitive perception. As he said earlier, in a letter: "One could throw away everything, and theory above all, of course, and keep just one thing: sensitive impressionability and obedience to the impressions received. This is how art begins."[57] Futurists and other avant-garde artists seek the easy success of public readings and flamboyant behaviour (as in "Letters from Tula"), whereas, he thinks, art should stay hidden, even if "stricken with phosphorescence".

In passage six there are sharp remarks about the tendency of avant-garde poets to congregate under appellations ending in "-ism", and about discussions under the heading of "aesthetics", a science which "classifies air balloons according to where and how the holes are placed in them that prevent them from flying." Forty years later Pasternak will still write of his horror of people who prefer gathering in "herds" to having individual opinions. The view of poetry and prose as two opposite yet inseparable poles is a direct dissension from the current theories of *Lef*; this too is something Pasternak held to and acted on throughout his writing life: though a poet, he wrote stories, and attempts at a novel, long before *Doctor Zhivago*.

The polemical or rejective remarks in "Some Propositions" are accompanied by restorative descriptions of what art is. These are strikingly original, whether the image is of hiding at the back of the theatre-gallery with hat on fire, or of the spellbound grouse, or of a fresh, new and "infinite" book, as responsible as the taking of an oath and mysterious as something growing from forest depths to an outburst of tree-tops. Amazement is fundamental. Pasternak is amazed by the phenomenon of a book, and by how artistic feeling is passed on from age to age.

Eleven years before the "Propositions", aged seventeen, he asked: "What is art if not philosophy that has passed into a state of ecstasy . . . ?"[58]—and the thoughtful last paragraph of passage six seems an enactment of this view: "The real, living world is the only project of the imagination which has once succeeded and still goes on being endlessly successful. Look at it continuing, moment after moment a success . ." These words could seem to foreshadow lines by Wallace Stevens: "The magnificent cause of being, / The imagination, the one reality / In this imagined world . . ", except that where Stevens' emphasis here is on the imagination, Pasternak's is on the world which the imagination has made and which can be pointed to.[59]

The climactic seventh passage is a direct, unpolemical account of being inspired. There is a state of possession, but emphasis on a possessed *person* is avoided: the rolled back eyes suggest loss of individuality, the temperature rise is impersonal, the event responded to is a nonhuman one. This is the transition into vision without a visionary, the "madness without a madman" to be mentioned in "Symbolism and Immortality".

In conclusion comes a sinister hint of danger which refers at once to the real and serious famine in Russia after the revolution and to something disturbing about poetry itself.

"[Reliquimini]" and "Ordering a Drama"

These two writings belong among the earliest pieces of Pasternak's prose to have survived. They were written in exercise books six or seven years before the *Propositions*, never intended for publication, and discovered only in 1967. Nearly fifty such "First Attempts" (*Pervye opyty*) have now been published in Volume Three of the *Complete Works of Boris Pasternak* (2003–5) edited by Evgeny and Elena Pasternak. The handwritten texts had gaps, unsorted-out alternatives and occasional indecipherable words. Other signs of their experimental nature are the thick mixture of metaphor and descriptive detail, and the erratic punctuation, some of which I have omitted or simplified. This odd, dense prose is rich in motifs characteristic of the poet's later work; here they occur in their intensest, primary form. It is clear from them that Pasternak was possessed by a single vision and was developing a single main cluster of images for it which would evolve and settle but not radically change.

These works are presented both as examples of what he was writing in the student years described in *A Safe-Conduct* and as brilliant pieces of prose in their own right. Art's origin is their thematic focus.

"[Reliquimini]"

The beginning suggests painting and one is reminded that Pasternak, son of an artist, spent his childhood surrounded by very fine contemporary paintings. The city in evening twilight with "breathings of ovals around eyes and oaks", "posings and slidings", "throngs and bunches", could bring to mind, say, Pissarro's

"Boulevard Montmartre: Night", along with other impressionist streets merging into rain or dusk. Into a scene which is not merely diffuse but almost *pointilliste* with its "tiny accumulated stars", "petals of the monument" and maize grains strides a poet, affirmative and frenzied, only to throw himself to the ground like a madman and try to draw with a pencil around scattered leaves. This fall of the poet is one of the series of fallings, faintings and collapses which accompany self-assertions of the "poet" throughout Pasternak's youthful work. It has been noted that "the concept of creation in the early Pasternak is inseparable from the concept of 'falling'".[60]

Reliquimini is the name Pasternak gave most often to the central poet-character of these early writings. It is also the name with which he signed his own earliest poems.[61] (See note on names, below.) Here, to his former school-friend, the narrator, Koinonievich, Reliquimini bursts out in ecstatic praise of the surrounding scene—so, of course, the introductory description was anomalously his, not Koinonievich's, the latter being set up as someone who, though intelligent and philosophical, cannot comprehend speeches of extreme rapture. Meanwhile Reliquimini's other friend, Makedonsky, who inhabits the same sphere of reference as himself, does not properly understand his speeches either, merely approving of their eccentricity; apparently he represents the histrionic type of artist of whom Pasternak will later be very critical. Reliquimini himself is a visionary, preoccupied by the need to find words for his vision.

The vision he wants to express is that, in the visible world of colours and lines, the colours have become a desperate "parish" of worshippers with no one to worship; searchers for gods. While the "gods" which can bring them peace and solace are the outlines, contours, frames for the colours' chaos. The two categories seem distinct until it turns out that lines themselves, once drawn, do not stay put; in the twilight's erasure of them, they too begin to need forms to hold them together; so *they* are now god-seekers. Having uttered all this, Reliquimini, driven by his thoughts to an extreme of excitement, starts shouting (for some reason in German) that the dissolving frames now need to be framed themselves; at this point, according to him, the saviour artist rushes in to frame them, for "what is creation if not compassion for the dusk?" His short German speech equates "gods", "love" and "frames", and identifies that which they dissolve back into as "life". Life, then, is another name for the desirous crowd of colours. I will attempt a sober summary of Reliquimini / Pasternak's thought. Life is chaotic, dynamic and in great need of being formed and shaped. Art gives it form and shape. But works of art themselves then become part of continuing life, part of the continuing potential content which is in need of form.

All this is Reliquimini's explanation to his rational friend of why he fell to the ground and tried to draw lines round a mass of leaves. Certainly, he was not trying to control them; rather (as three years later in "Symbolism and

Immortality") he was "submitting himself to the tendency of /their/ quest". Rather than asserting himself, the artist follows reality's own tendency towards becoming art.

Godlessness is a positive value in this "religious revolution of the dusk", as it implies process, movement and the impulse towards art. But Reliquimini is not advocating godlessness; he is a lover of the process of finding, losing and again seeking. Seeing lines, he is moved by lyricism to summon up the chaos of colours; seeing colours, he is moved by it to provide forms for them. At one point colours are called "content", and lines—"forms": the entire material scene is the potential substance of art.

Isaak Babel's short story entitled "Line and Colour" (1926) is similarly concerned with a polarity of outlines and colours, but uses it in a more familiar way, showing up the extent of Pasternak's idiosyncrasy.[62] In the Babel story, colours—lavish, a pleasure to the imagination—are what is seen by the short-sighted Romantic who rejects spectacles (namely by Alexander Kerensky, soon to become the ill-fated Prime Minister of 1917); while outlines—lucid and sharp—are what is seen by the fearless politician (Leon Trotsky) with glasses securely on his nose and no self-indulgence; Trotsky prevails (at least in the story) with a brief, "linear", one-word start to his speech: "Comrades!" Babel's focus is on individuals' vision, on who can see what, and on how we define our personality through our selected objects of sight. In "Reliquimini", seven years before the two categories were forced into life-and-death battle, Pasternak creates his own highly unusual dynamic from their polarity, with lines and colours conceived as autonomous, quasi-subjective essences. The poet's gaze is only a starting-point; the real "drama" (to anticipate the title of the next piece) takes place out there in the perceived world and has nothing to do with personality.

A "linear/non-linear" dichotomy recurs in several of Pasternak's published stories. In "The Mark (or: Line) of Apelles", the poet, challenged to express himself by drawing a line, instead seduces a beautiful woman; in "The Childhood of Liuvers", Zhenia is confused when her brother answers her question as to "what makes Asia *Asia*?" by saying people drew a line on the map; in "Aerial Ways", the straight-lined thoughts of Lenin and Liebknecht eventually lead to a bereaved mother fainting onto a floor heaped with rubbish. In each case something straight yields to something amorphous and elusive.

"Ordering a Drama"

Much of the description is again impressionistic, with pellets, crumbs, flakes, stitches and blots, chimes crumbling, asphalt crawling. As in "Reliquimini", it is Pasternak's own extreme *ostranenie*,[63] the "making strange" of reality in the very process of making it perceptible. Here, however, the description is of what is on either side of windows. Pasternak's characteristic window imagery first appears in these early notebooks.[64] Like a window, the poet stands transparently between outer and inner.

Again a place is the source of inspiration; a room is described in detail and presented as if it were self-evidently a demand for a drama. Drama is no longer a matter of interrelations between persons on a stage but is the stirring of things in a room into movement and action. Objects are full of longing, this time not for gods but for music, dance and drama. As if shy of mentioning an arcane truth never uttered before, Pasternak admits that he has "never found anything else possible than to live amongst objects, like everyone else I live on the basis of the inanimate . . . "; he wants to convey "how, unable to bear the pleas of the inanimate any longer . . . one moves chairs and armchairs back, to dance and dance". This is an advance sketch of the originating backward glance in *A Safe-Conduct* 1,6: inanimate things, longing to be animated, are what is looked back at, "what meets you when you stand up after music". Getting up from the piano, the composer looks round with altered eyes and cannot endure the exclusion of the room and its objects from his music.

"Ordering a Drama" sets out to construct something like a philosophical system. Three accounts are given of a division of reality into three categories. With a slight adjustment of their sequence in the first account, the categories can be named as (1) inanimate things, or fact, or "reality without movement"; (2) a lyrical or musical element, which is "movement without reality"; (3) "flakes"—meaning both the impressionistic view of the town full of people and the principle of life which stirs it, since "life" is also given as a name for the flakes. Not all of this is clear, but certain things are clear enough. It is clear that the life of a particular man is needed to combine the three categories. Here it is the composer Shestikrylov. Pasternak's repeated stress on art's arising from an artist's biography suggests this is something too surprising to be passed over lightly; indeed, Shestikrylov's life is surprisingly called a thread stitching the three categories of reality together like three layers of cloth. It is also the surgical thread sewing up the world-order which, for its cure, has been operated on. There is humour in this idea, as well as in that of the musician as a Messiah sent to save the drawing-room furniture. But it is also a perfectly serious first statement (to himself, in so far as he was not planning to publish it) of his conception of the artist as not at all an independent agent "but a component part of the elemental process of transforming reality into art, a means of uniting them".[65]

But the systematising breaks down, with music chasing music, the music in things chasing the music of the musician, the composer racing along looking for himself (a window looking for a window), and life looking for its or *her* self. This seems an alternative version (now in terms of human life) of the colours' urgent search for lines in "Reliquimini", the general need of potential content for form.

The final part of "Ordering a Drama" mentions the abandonment of features which Pasternak will later bundle into his conception of romanticism: everything easy and self-willed, such as a cultivated dreaminess, atmospheric piano-playing, deliberate dancing. Objects can "heat up" without our pretences, he believes, can shed their veneer (as they will most notably in the poem "Slanted Pictures") and dance *by themselves*. When feeling alters the surrounding reality, the artist has only to observe and copy.

Note on names in the early fiction

The surnames of Pasternak's characters are conspicuous and somewhat baffling. "Reliquimini", later appearing more correctly as "Relinquimini", is Latin for "you [plural] are left behind", and is usually understood as the poet's address to inanimate objects. This seems explained by the passage in *S-C* 1,6 (mentioned above and to be discussed later in this Commentary) where, looking at the things "left behind" by his ecstatic feeling, the poet becomes inspired. The name has also been understood as "you remain", another possible translation of the Latin verb, one which would stress less the origin of inspiration than its result—that is, less the objects' being left behind by the poet's feeling than their surviving (remaining) in the poem after he has been moved to include them.[66] Meanwhile, "Shestikrylov" means "with six wings" (as in Pushkin's "Prophet"; for this, see Introduction). Less clear is the possession of famous names by some characters, such as Alexander Makedonsky, otherwise known as Alexander of Macedon. This has been called a comic device to mark the experimental, non-serious nature of these writings; or a means of "/laying bare/ the conventional and artificial nature of the reality depicted"; or a deployment of irony against the Nietzschean "understanding of a genius as a necessarily strong and powerful person able to rise above ordinary human morality"—thus Makedonsky nervously plucks to pieces a bunch of dahlias, which in Russian are "*georginy*" and symbolise heroism by their reference to Saint George the Victorious (an explanation which does not cover all examples.)[67] I speculate that, in view of Pasternak's belief (later quite explicit) that *every* human being is capable of genius, the liberal distribution of names of the famous among the actually not-famous-at-all may be a pointer to this capability in them.

"Heinrich von Kleist. On Asceticism in Culture"

This essay is a product of Pasternak's time as a student of philosophy, when he was doubting his aptitude for that subject and thinking hard about the difference between a philosopher and a poet. It is a difficult piece of writing, in some places almost impenetrable, because it is unfinished or because he was writing it for himself rather than for readers. Although its subject is someone else, he tacitly explores in it the change from philosopher to poet which he foresaw would take place in himself. Its relevance to Pasternak's own biography has been explored by Lazar Fleishman.[68] Here we are concerned with its ideas about the nature of a poet and the origin of poetry in life.

In Odessa Pasternak confirmed his long-held view that there can be no culture without asceticism. What led to the making of culture? He sensed an answer to this question in that very break in his studies towards which he was moving. For this reason Kleist, a great writer whose life was all fractures and discontinuities and who, moreover, had studied and abandoned philosophy, was important to him.

In using the word "asceticism" Pasternak is thinking of its Greek meaning, "exercise", and has in mind the rigorous exercising of a mental or physical ability, involving an abstinence not especially monastic or even especially spiritual but something else—an abstaining from, and freeing oneself from, what is natural for the sake of "culture" which (he considers) does not come about naturally. The words *uprazhnenie* (exercise) and *praktika* (practice) are almost synonymous here with "culture" and "artistic creation."

Unlike the lives of the relaxed, nature-following southerners, Kleist's life followed, Pasternak notes, a path of painful departures and renunciations. But what looked like "digressions from his vocation" were not that at all: "digression *was* his vocation". In his shifts of direction Kleist was exercising a refusal of stasis, an openness to life, which also characterise artistic work. Although not all Kleist's life-changes went, in fact, in the direction of artistic creation, Pasternak writes as if breaking with the past is itself a creative act. "/Kleist/ was a poet", he writes, "probably in the sense that he was constantly going away". And "creativity—its practice—is a ritual of renewed beginnings".

Part two unexpectedly describes snowy autumnal weather. Kleist committed suicide in the autumn of 1811; Pasternak was writing in the summer of 1911. Had he been writing in October, he muses, he would have been looking out at fitful snowfalls and thaws, sudden darkenings and quietenings, a chase of strange black figures through changed streets. His readers would then have experienced his essay on Kleist "creatively, that is to say ascetically". Feeling the shifting weather, they would have been freed from expecting the expectable and from holding on to easy, natural ideas. Such feeling would have been close enough to Kleist's (he doubtless means) for them to sympathise with Kleist's unharmonious temperament and paradoxical behaviour.

In Part three, he makes clear (or almost clear) that his purpose is "educational": he hopes to turn minds away from their accustomed naturalism, meaning from that which is not ascetic, not lyrical, not dynamic. He wants to turn them instead towards "realism". This word too has its Pasternakian meaning: "realistically" is equated (in Part four of the essay) with "from within" and implies the realisation

61

in art of something which has been genuinely experienced as part of one's inner life. Kleist is realistic in that he writes boldly, directly and with difficulty of what reality, for him, is. (Three decades later, in the essay on Chopin, even music is called "realistic" and Chopin is praised for a similar ascetic choice of the difficult.)

Kleist and Pasternak both studied philosophy. A poet studying philosophy feels at first at home in it because a beginning philosopher, like a beginning poet, is engaged in exercising his renunciation of intuition, his abandonment of nature. But the future poet will not go on with philosophy as he does not wish to be a "systematic" thinker. What matters to him is the thought of the *"possibility"* of system; the whole adventure is the possibility of conceiving of an ultimate synthesis, *not* its once-for-all achievement. Pasternak's celebration of unfinishedness, probably supported by his study of Kant's aesthetics, is as strongly felt and argued (though less systematically!) as Bakhtin's.

In Part four he calls the creative person an extreme ascetic because such a person will, in his work, "alienate (or: estrange) the whole of being", will "set free whole regions of the past". "Set free", it seems, means: free them from being anyone's property, the property of anyone's everyday life. Instead, those regions will become "no one's" (*oni stanut nich'imi*). Past happenings, which have become fitted into our fixed view of things so that we feel we possess them, are "liberated" in a work of art from that fixed view. It is for the sake of culture that the artist thus estranges what is, liberates what was. For "estrangement" Pasternak is not using the term *ostranenie*, later so strongly associated with Shklovsky, but *otchuzhdenie*, closer to "making alien" than "making strange". But there are resemblances to formalist theory. The artist unmasks what has been covered up by convention, "takes to pieces that which has been given the wrong shape all around him and is neither eternal nor chaotic but only customary".

Two major statements about art and culture are made here. One is that in art there cannot be any ending or rounding-off; an artist cannot have the satisfaction a philosopher might have who at last completes his system and sets down his logical conclusion. Art *is*, and the "drama of culture" *is*, to quote Pasternak's tremendously powerful and original phrase, the "never-beginning of a synthesis" (or, to translate it more exactly, the "non-approach of a synthesis"). In an oddly stammering paragraph, he describes this as absolutely positive (*nenastuplenie sinteza—splosh' polozhitel'no*).

The other statement, more implicit, is that a "synthesis" would be equivalent to establishing ownership, whereas art is by definition that which is not owned; it makes all its material into something owned by no one. The constant theme in Pasternak's work of the unimportance of the poet or artist as person—as someone to whom it *could* all belong?—is related to this idea of the non-possessedness of art, its non-fixity in any person. A year before the Kleist essay, trying to describe the distinct and specific experience of the approach of "lyricism", he used similar terms to those we find here. "It seems to me that the purpose of similes is to liberate objects from belonging to the interests of life or science /and/ make them into free qualities . . . " [69]

In the interpretation of Kleist's extraordinary suicide as a kind of drama, Pasternak's quotation from Saint Matthew appears to ascribe a kind of sanctity to his own drama of the "never-beginning synthesis".

In 1941, he wrote a second essay on Kleist as introductory note to his own translations of Kleist's work. This essay is almost entirely biographical and of minor interest for his own development or ideas.[70]

"[On the Threshold of Inspiration]"

Thoughts about art emerge from the description of a town with the writer (or painter) *in* it. The opening concept is *byl'* (быль), unfortunately an untranslatable word. It has been translated as "fact", "true story", "that which really happened". Its emphasis is on actual as distinct from imaginary happenings. Pasternak generally means by it everything that has happened in the past and grown fixed, as distinct from the mobile present. In "Ordering a Drama" he offers a marvellously quaint definition of this word, very much in the light of his own conception of the world's need for art: *byl'*—"past, reality as a great immobile legend of wood and cloth, objects in need, twilight in need, like a church parish that has grown stale from waiting", and wonders a page or so later whether anyone would believe that "the past is an inanimate object, and childhood too is inanimate, that is, demanding." It becomes clear towards the end of "On the Threshold" that a monosyllable is required and I have rendered it as "the past", or "past" without a definite article, hesitantly rejecting "the lived" and "the been" (the latter near-perfect, were it not for "bean"). "Past" is certainly better than "fact" (as I translated it in 1985) but is still, alas, inadequate to the richly suggestive, laconic Russian *byl'*.[71]

For the heaviness of *byl'*, the factual and artless, the having-happened (and therefore immobile and in need of movement), Pasternak uses an odd but powerful metaphor which he was never to use again. This image is discussed in the Introduction: neatly indicating both the incompleteness and the realness of *byl'*, seen as *half* of the whole truth, he compares it to a trochaic word broken off in the middle at the end of a line of verse. Longing for the feminine connects this versificatory analogy with Pasternak's lifelong theme of compassion for women.

"Symbolism and Immortality"

This is no more than the synopsis of a talk, the full text of which is not extant. The talk was given in 1913 in Moscow to a group called "Circle for Study of Problems of Aesthetic Culture and Symbolism in Art". Forty-three years after giving the talk, and a year before his death, Pasternak wrote a summary of its content as he remembered it; this is in his second autobiographical memoir, *People and Propositions*. Reading the 1913 synopsis, one is hard put to it to guess how each point might have been developed. Unfortunately, the later summary, though clear in itself, helps only slightly with this question.

The synopsis, like any set of notes prepared for an immediate lecture, is not fully accessible to anyone other than the lecturer. In order to understand it as far as possible, I have numbered the paragraphs and shall refer to them by number.

The ideas expressed here are closely related to those in *A Safe-Conduct* and, in a different form, in *Doctor Zhivago*. Paragraph 1 introduces the idea that it is possible to conceive of a subjectivity which belongs not to a person but to "quality" in general. This "free subjectivity" underlies much of what Pasternak wrote about creativity. In the present volume, it is discussed by him in the 1911 Kleist essay, variously used in some of the poems about poetry, and alluded to in a somewhat opaque passage in *The Black Goblet* which at least makes it reassuringly clear that the label "subjectivity" is inadequate.

"Subjectivity", then, ceasing to be the property of the artist as a person, becomes the property of "quality"—that is to say, of the perceived quality of the surrounding world. This strange thought becomes easier if we bear in mind that Pasternak is speaking of the world of sensation, rather than the world as it (presumably) is in itself, and if, instead of supposing him to mean that material things can become subjectively conscious (though often enough his formulations do suggest that), one reads into these assertions something like "as if" or "seemingly". (As John MacKinnon sensibly notes, "objects, after all, do not by themselves yelp and yearn . . . ")[72] This reading is supported by such phrases as *"consciousness* [my italics—A.L.] frees qualities from . . . personal life" (paragraph 2) and "perceived by the poet" (paragraph 9); it is supported, above all, by paragraph 10 where "reality" is equated with "what is experienced" (or "that which has been experienced", or "that which has been lived through" [*perezhitoe*]). This equation is given no special foregrounding (at least not in the synopsis): to Pasternak the identity of the two concepts seems clear and obvious. That is to say: the "world" is the world of our experience, of our perception and feeling. Instead of "subjectivity becomes the property of all qualities" we could therefore read, without losing anything, "subjectivity is *felt to be* the property of all qualities". I lose the sensation of being "me", the poet might say retrospectively, and instead it is as if everything else begins to manifest its self, *its* "me". By consistently omitting the "as if", however, Pasternak emphasizes, not that reality is merely our experience, but that experience *is* the reality.

The high value given to suspension of personality does not, of course, mean that Pasternak's many other, positive, statements about personality are invalid or inconsistent (for example, at the end of *A Safe-Conduct* 1,2, and in the 1934 speech, and in much of *Doctor Zhivago*); it means only that in the act of artistic creation personality is temporarily given up, sacrificed.

Paragraph 2 says that artistic consciousness liberates qualities (things as perceptions, sensations) from their link with personal life, that is, from their usefulness to us, and returns them to some "immemorial" condition of subjectivity which they have lost and which (to look ahead to paragraph 9) they have been searching for. The image of such a search underlies many of Pasternak's other writings. As we have seen, a sense that all reality is searching or yearning for something fills the poet's wild pronouncements in "Reliquimini"; and in "Ordering a Drama" life comes knocking at the artist's door searching "for itself"; in *S-C* 1,6 the poet speaks of hearing the sound made by objects in their yearning to be gathered up into the artistic event.

Paragraph 9: to meet reality's need, a poet, has only to submit and "conduct himself like the objects around him"; by letting go of his ego-centred, object-using personality he will come to feel—or to find—that subjectivity has been restored to the objects and there is no fundamental difference between himself and them. This recalls the moment in "Reliquimini" where "altogether it looks as if we are being dreamt by the objects", and in the 1917 poem "Stifling Night" (*Dushnaia noch'*) the poet overhears twigs and wind arguing with each other "about me (*pro menia*!)!"[73] In each case, objects become subjects, the poet their object.

Why such difficult concepts? Pasternak was writing for listeners who had spent some three years studying problems of symbolism and to whom his philosophical terms would not be daunting. But he may show awareness of the difficulty of his language when he notes that "people call this being observant and drawing from nature". He knows the phenomenon is normally described more simply, but also knows that conventional terms such as "being observant . . . " fail to convey what is vital in the nearly inconceivable experience he is concerned with.

To go back to paragraphs 3 and 4: these speak of immortality. What is immortal is not the human being as such but human creativity—in other words, that arising of "free subjectivity" in the creative event. But how does immortality come into it? Pasternak is not interested in immortality in the sense of individuals living for ever. This notion he dispatches both in a jotting of 1911 which says there can be nothing more foolish than the notion of a continuation of life after death[74] and in *Zhivago* 3,3 where Iurii speaks to the mortally ill Anna Gromeko about the absurdity of individual resurrection. What does interest him is the "timeless meaning" to which the poet is dedicated, that (sense of a) disappearance of time when the "living soul" is "estranged from personality" in favour of "free subjectivity" (paragraph 3). This is confirmed in paragraph 4, which states that in the creative process madness is present although no mad person is present.

Why is madness mentioned? The traditional association of genius with madness is not irrelevant, but may it not also be that Pasternak is looking at the actual components of the Russian word for "madness"? In paragraph four the Russian word usually translated as "madness" contains no element meaning "mad" but translates literally as "without mind" (without-mind-ness [*bez-um-ie*]). Mind (if it can be equated with personality) is what is left behind in the creative act, so a "without-mind" condition can be understood as equivalent to the separation (or estrangement, or liberation) of subjectivity from me-the-individual-poet. *Bezumie* and *bessmertie* (without-death-ness) thus point to the same condition; "madness is natural immortality". Not that we should cultivate insanity so as to live for ever, but that when mind/personality is suspended a timeless dimension is entered. Persons die, the poet as person will die, but the inspired and creative state escapes time and death.

The very much later summary of the remembered lecture in *People and Propositions* makes the whole thing appear much more accessible, yet it is so far from explaining the points listed in the synopsis that it almost seems to be about a different talk altogether.

> Once in late autumn I gave a talk . . . with the title "Symbolism and Immortality". Some /listeners/ sat on the ground floor, some listened from above, lying on the intermediate floor and thrusting their heads over its edge.
> The talk was based on a thought about the subjectivity of our perceptions—on the fact that there is something else there corresponding to the sounds and the colours we perceive in nature: an objective vibration of sound waves and light waves. I developed the idea that this subjectivity is not the special property of any individual but is a generic, supra-personal quality, it is the subjectivity of the human world, of humankind. I suggested that from every person who dies there remains a portion of the undying generic subjectivity which was contained in him during his life and through which he participates in the history of human existence. My main purpose was to put forward the proposal that perhaps this maximally subjective and universally human corner or lot of the soul was art's immemorial area of activity and its chief content. And, further, that although the artist is of course mortal like everybody else, the happiness of existence which he has felt is immortal and can be felt through his works by others centuries after him, in a certain approximation to the personal and bodily form of his original sensations.
> The paper was entitled "Symbolism and Immortality" because it affirmed the symbolical and conventional nature of every work of art, in that most general sense in which we can speak of the symbolics of algebra.[75]

It is characteristic of the later Pasternak that he writes more simply and in terms applicable to people generally, not just to poets. His long-ago idea of a universally shared subjectivity is now re-cast as the idea of a condition shared not with the "qualities", the experienced signs of the surrounding "reality", but with "humankind"; and "free subjectivity" now appears to be something no less necessary, natural and understandable than the way we interpret variations in wavelengths of electromagnetic radiation as colours, and compressions and rarefactions of air molecules as sounds. Just as we experience the world as coloured and sounding, so (the older Pasternak seems to be implying) we may—through paintings, music and poetry—experience it as changed by artistic inspiration, can apprehend what the poet felt, and can participate in the accompanying experience of deathlessness.

"[End of a Decade]"

The recurrent motif of the "falling" poet may in part derive from Pasternak's physical fall from a horse at the age of thirteen. In the present piece he recalls that incident and summarizes the period of his adolescence when, perhaps partly prompted by the fall, he was working towards having "a composer's biography". The painful absoluteness of his giving up music at the age of nineteen is reflected here in his conceiving of two quite separate people: himself as thirteen-year-old-beginning-musician and himself as twenty-three-year-old-beginning-poet.

With the statement that he is interrupting his recollections, the fluent and accessible style changes to one less easy to follow, with no allowances made for some future general reader. I will attempt a partial paraphrase. In the uncreative period which followed his leaving university in summer 1913—that is, at the time of writing this very piece in his notebook—Pasternak felt like a servant whose master, namely creativity, had gone away, leaving him both unfed and (hungrily) enabled to perceive and define that master. He calls to mind things he needs, and rejects them as not answering the central need: to imagine the torrential slaking of his thirst for some lower enjoyment (*naslazhdenie*), is to realise that even then the main thirst will remain. Giving up any hope of slaking a thirst, and indeed giving up this metaphor, he unexpectedly moves on to something which seems new and simple—an idea of producing enjoyment for others so great that it will go far beyond individuals and be universal ("all-four-directions"). For this he devises an image of a completely joined-up, welded hoop. Ordinary sensuality may join two beings together, but the sensuality of art rolls round the universe and comes back without a break to the artist.

It is interesting to find that something like a ubiquitously rolling "wave of enjoyment" itself comes back forty or so years later in *Doctor Zhivago* (5,7): "Delight in life, like a quiet wind, was moving in a broad wave, not choosing its direction, over earth and town, through walls and fences, through timber and flesh, enveloping everything on its path."

"The Black Goblet"

The rhetorically clever and self-conscious style of this more public essay, written and published as part of the literary debate Pasternak was involved in before he distanced himself from conflicting groups, is very different from the unemphatically sparkling and only incidentally obscure manner of the early fiction. The essay itself comes close at times to being an instance of the art that has no other task than "to be executed brilliantly", and part of its interest lies in its exemplifying its own central image of packing.

Addressing representatives of dominant trends in the painting and poetry of his youth—impressionists and, along with them, symbolists (the first symbolists and also the first futurists were called impressionists)—Pasternak says it was from them that the following generation of writers, he and fellow futurists of the "Centrifuga" group, learnt how to "pack" reality into art. The teachers sometimes got too much of it in and "overloaded the sky"—that is, with mysticism—but *content* is established as the virtue of poetry, and fast packing as a poet's best skill. Futurists, says Pasternak, are the first to succeed at what their predecessors were trying to do. He depicts them stowing fragile things into their hearts, for curiously enough it is futurists' hearts, rather than their poems, that are compared to packing-cases marked with the sign of the black goblet to keep them upright.

Section one expresses gratitude, then, to the previous generation of poets, and confidence in his own group's achievement. The second and third sections qualify praise of futurists by two "amendments". The second section explains (this is the first amendment) that the idea of speed in packing does *not* refer to the popular notion of futurism, promoted by Shershenevich and the Italian Marinetti, as worship of technology and fast cars, and does not mean the subject-matter of poems is to be speed. That popular version is "ape-talk". What speed means to Pasternak is by contrast the "thrifty" handling of space and time, an inner urgency conveyed to the things depicted, whatever they might be. Nor has this urgency anything to do with another kind of haste, that of the mystics, probably meaning the second generation of Russian symbolists who invoked a transcendental realm and expected imminent apocalypse. His urgency is that of the artist who incessantly finds himself given a real task by the age he lives in.

Instead of reducing time to the almost-nothing of the "cinematic instant", the group Pasternak supports transforms time into eternity, so much so that he names his kind of futurism "impressionism of the eternal". This then is the essential lyricism. While the symbolists valued symbols, Pasternak's futurist values the lyrical itself. Lyricism is now set up as an autonomous principle. It is, alternatively, named "originality", and, making (rather obscurely) the same sort of allusion to science and mathematics as he is later to make in *A Safe-*

Conduct, Pasternak remarks that the concept "original" could stand alongside "integral", "differential" and "other words ending in '-al'", as a basic function of exact thinking, objective and accurate like mathematical concepts. If those words could be used, he says, the word "subjectivity" could become redundant, which would be an advantage since what is meant by it here is *not,* as might be thought, the subjectivity of the individual but the "free subjectivity" he spoke of in "Symbolism and Immortality".

The second "amendment" (in section three) shows that Pasternak's futurism also excludes writers (Mayakovsky among them) who argue that poetry should be committed to current political questions and help "prepare tomorrow's history assignment"—as if for a lesson. No contempt for history is implied; the point is only that the two modes should keep separate from each other. History and lyricism are opposite poles, equally valid and *a priori,* never to meet unless conceivably in mutual admiration. (They remain essential categories of Pasternak's thinking right up to *Zhivago,* where the lyrical Zhivago confronts the historical Strelnikov.) People who make history have a different task from the poet's, yet they too could be called a kind of "seer", since they go close up to, and *see,* the "spectre of History". The spectre is terrible and inhuman ("reality is disintegrating") and their job is to control it. Doing so, they conquer a new piece of history, like a piece of land, for folk to move into and live in humanly.

Surely there must be irony in the rhetorical gesturing of the paragraph starting "Battalions of heroes . . . "? But it does seem that in Pasternak's view the men of history are heroic and visionary. He will depict them in later works with an uncanny alien sympathy—thus there is the military officer, Lemokh, in "The Tale", who is all "masculine spirit of fact", and, later, Strelnikov. Their work is vital, but the lyric poet's task is vital too. He has to pack the most valuable and delicate aspects of present life into his black-gobleted heart, to transfer them into the newly conquered territory—the future—for the sake of all.

Four main assertions, overtly about futurist poetry but also about poetry altogether (as Pasternak conceived it), can be derived from this essay: (1) that it is the opposite of history—of political, military, or other practical, action; (2) that it attends to the "eternal" quality of the present moment, a task requiring the utmost rapidity, economy and care; (3) that it depends on originality, which is conceived as an autonomous principle and force; and (4) that it is urgently needed.

"The Black Goblet" was Pasternak's second published article. It was preceded by one published in 1914 as "The Wassermann Reaction" (the title being a medical term for a method of diagnosing syphilis). This is not included in the present book because it refers so closely to a polemic Pasternak was involved in briefly and reluctantly and because, with the exception of one paragraph, it does not shed more light on his idea of poetry. It has two purposes: to attack Vadim Shershenevich, a futurist poet who wrote with his eye on the market, and to distinguish "false" futurism (Shershenevich's sort) from "genuine" futurism (exemplified by Velimir Khlebnikov). Towards the end of the article comes, still in the polemical context, an interesting statement about poetry:

> The fact of similarity, more rarely an associative link through similarity and never through contiguity—is the origin of Shershenevich's metaphors. Yet only phenomena of contiguity have that compulsoriness and spiritual drama that can be justified metaphorically.[76]

This distinction between, on the one hand, metaphor based on contiguity— that is, on things being together in space or time or, as Michel Aucouturier says, in the "immediate subjective association of two impressions experienced together", and, on the other hand, metaphor based on mere similarity between things or ideas, has been taken up by Roman Jakobson and, after him, by a number of scholars, who find Pasternak's own verse characterised by metonymy, that is by selection of images according to their contiguity rather than their similarity. Olga Hughes writes that, in the paragraph quoted from "The Wassermann Reaction"—

> Pasternak, without naming it, describes metonymy and explains his predilection for metonymic expression . . . A poet who resorts to similarity as the basis for constructing his tropes tosses the keys into the hands of "the amateurs from the crowd" . . . For /Pasternak/ it is the "morbid necessity" of bringing together dissimilar but proximate objects that gives life to an image.[77]

"Letters from Tula"

The first part of this story is not about inspiration as such but about the shamefulness of its looking like, or even being like, imitations of itself. All Pasternak's struggle against the romantic "manner" is sketched out here.

A poet sitting in a station waiting-room encounters his unwitting, carefree imitators. These "bohemian" play-actors and show-offs are the types berated in the second of "Some Propositions". There is nothing humorous about his dislike of them; Fleishman has noted how this story differs from the rest of Pasternak's early work in respect of its moralising tone. Pasternak hated the "cabaret aspect of Mayakovsky's futurism" which seemed doubly unacceptable during a revolution, "which should be the time of a radical moral renewal of the human spirit".[78] The "bohemians" in the story are not poets, however, but film actors, and it must be relevant that in March/April 1918, when Pasternak was writing this story, Mayakovsky and his fellow-futurists, Burliuk and Kamensky, were taking part in the making of a film.[79]

The lone poet suffers a crisis of conscience and self-blame. Rather like Thomas Mann's poet-hero Tonio Kröger who senses an awful rightness in being mistaken for a thief and arrested, or like Rilke's Malte Laurids Brigge, terrified of being taken for a Parisian tramp yet feeling he *is* one, Pasternak's hero senses that the actors do represent himself, if in exaggerated form. Then he remembers that he is in Tula, a town associated with Tolstoy, and Tolstoy was at once an artist of genius and a great conscience-driven moralist. This connection helps him consider that art has not merely to be the opposite of gaudy, brash and conceited but has to be so rigorously the opposite of those qualities that the person of the artist will virtually vanish. He needs to attain "a complete physical silence". What does this mean? A condition, it seems, in which he will not hear himself nor, presumably, see himself; nor will he *be* heard or seen. The fictional poet resolves to be the opposite of the film actors—not listened to or, as far as he can tell, looked at. Part one of the story is thus an expansion of the last sentence in the second "Proposition" which hides art "at the back of the gallery".

The narrative now leaps to a successful realisation of the deeply ashamed poet's ideal, for Part two depicts an artist who *is* hidden "at the back of the gallery", unseen and without fame. His non-theatricality is emphasised by his being, not an unlooked-at writer but (oxymoronically) an unlooked-at theatre actor, a former actor of tragic drama who acts out one of his roles without audience or stage. He is, moreover, a person one would hardly want to look at in any case: old, sclerotic, bitter, ready to die. But the reader, his paradoxical watcher, now sees art separating itself from all personal ugliness, anger, age, illness, mortality, if only for a moment. Afterwards the artist becomes a mere person again, "dull", sobbing and going drearily to bed. "He too . . . was looking for a physical silence. In the story he was the only one to find it by making a stranger speak through his lips." There is no contradiction in his finding silence through speaking; it is the artist as biographical man who falls silent.

Thus Part one leads to a longing for the "eternity" Pasternak ascribes to art and Part two gives a demonstration of it. Although the old man will soon be dead, his briefly perfect non-play-acting acting-of-a-play will not.

The atmosphere of "Letters from Tula" is charged with the hiss and rumble of steam trains; its teaching is hidden under, as well as conveyed by, the movement of trains. The trains underline the evocation of Tolstoy, who died (in 1910) at a railway station, with huge crowds of mourners arriving by railway.[80] One sentence about the trains particularly recalls an example of great art. After the words "the carriages had been sliding past for a long time and there was no end to them", we read (to use Pasternak's word order): "Behind them was growing the approach of something heavily breathing, unknown, nocturnal". Reading this sentence, we are likely to recall the slow approach of the train under which Anna Karenina throws herself, while the word "something" echoes Tolstoy's "something huge, inexorable knocked into her head".[81] What the "something" brings for Anna is, of course, death, but Pasternak's "something" brings an unexpected vision of what the track will be like when the train has passed: cleansed, silent and peaceful. As "silent" is the main word he is going to associate in this story with honest and genuine art—not only in the poet's longing for a real "acoustic" silence but also in the twice-occurring sentence "There was an extraordinary silence"—the suggestion is that, through Tula, Tolstoy's own honesty is reaching the anguished poet as well as the aged actor.

Pasternak's anxiety about art is twofold. Wholehearted devotion to art may damagingly ignore the rest of the world. But art practised with anything less than wholehearted devotion brings it close to fake or second-rate versions of itself: its own inescapable element of posing assimilates it to other kinds of posing. The intense to-and-fro of his engagement with this theme is seen in "The Mark of Apelles" (briefly discussed below) which is about a posing that begins wilful and inventive but ends genuine, while "Letters from Tula" refers to the false posturing with which we are publicly surrounded and which can only be overcome by full-hearted, solitary drama.

The solution to both anxieties is that the artist must conceal his private self and work with tireless vigilance at being genuine. From now on, this thought never left Pasternak, as can be seen from poems as late as those in *When the Weather Clears* which advise the artist: "don't sleep, don't sleep".[82]

Other early fiction

Almost all of Pasternak's fictional prose writing has to do with the nature and origin of art. Between 1918 and 1929 he published five stories: "The Mark of Apelles" (1918), "Letters from Tula" (1922), "The Childhood of Liuvers" (1922), "Aerial Ways" (1924) and "The Tale" (1929). The subject of three of these ("Apelles", "Tula", "Tale") is an artist's experience. That of "Liuvers" is a young girl's experiences told in a way that suggests analogy with the artist's. Leaving out "Aerial Ways", which is concerned with human fate more generally, I will note points in these works that are relevant to the theme of art and inspiration, as well as points from the unfinished "History of a Counter-Octave" (1916–17), rejected by the author but saved from becoming stove-fuel and published in 1974.[83]

The plot of "Mark of Apelles" is a curious jest. A poet called Relinquimini (the name now spelt according to the Latin) challenges a poet called Heinrich Heine (not the German poet) to speak of love with a laconicism equal to that shown by the Greek painter Apelles who expressed his own unique quality by drawing a single line on a wall. To meet the challenge, Heine travels to the town mentioned in his challenger's love-poems, Ferrara, leaving a message to ensure he will be hastily pursued. Thus he forces himself into the utmost concentration and brevity in the trick he undertakes in Ferrara; he announces that he has found some of Relinquimini's manuscripts. Just as he expects, a beautiful woman arrives at his hotel, asking for the (non-existent) papers; he speaks to her in fantastic, tragical ways, at once ludicrously histrionic and so soberly aware of playing a role that he moves—one is persuaded—beyond the role and over into real feeling. (Similarly in *A Safe-Conduct* Mayakovsky will be said to be playing a role with such abandon that it seems more natural than any naturalness.) She falls in love with him, their conversation becomes an embrace. Heine has created a love-experience out of nothing, and his Apelles mark is accomplished when the mystified, fascinated lady defines him: "You're a sort of extraordinary child. No, that's not the word—you're a poet."

If this is taken as a paradigm of poetic creation, then poetry involves both conscious pretence and an incomparable naturalness, while its lexical abundance turns out to be laconic. It also involves headlong speed, risk, irresponsible reliance on chance, readiness for the unknown; and it occurs on the closest possible border with actual life.

In this story, wordy praise of laconicism introduces a discussion of "simple" and "complex" which echoes a lapidary sentence in "Ordering a Drama": "Evidently he is one of those who go from the simple to the simple with a complex gait." This points forward to Pasternak's conversation with Scriabin in *A Safe-Conduct* and to his conception of great art as an intense and rapid sketch.

"History of a Counter-Octave" deals with moral implications of the artist's self-absorption. An inspired organist is described as ecstatically improvising, very much in the manner of the wood-grouse at its mating-ground in "Some Propositions", for "every force that gives itself up to rapid unplanned growth at last reaches a limit where, looking all round, it no longer sees anybody in its vicinity". His absorption in art causes the death of his child, who has wandered in among the heavy machinery of the old church-organ; later he is shocked to find himself stroking the child's body in octaves.

The sentence just quoted describes the absorption which *precedes* the inspirational "backward glance": this artist looking round is unseeing and is not yet disturbed by his own indifference to the rest of reality. But although the hideous consequence suggests castigation, the matter is not clear-cut. It is asserted that he knows something uniquely valuable through his ecstasy, something he would otherwise never have known: "the organist shuddered from a feeling that is known only to the artist—he shuddered from the similarity existing at this moment between himself and the cantilena, from the dim surmise that it knew him no less than he knew it." Even if this is the germ of the concept of "identity" between the artist and the work of art which Pasternak was to develop in *A Safe-Conduct*, it would seem he could not as yet balance the claims of the moral and the aesthetic, and the story was discarded, perhaps for this reason. Christopher Barnes, however, sees more firmly in this story the unequivocally "anti-romantic message, condemning dramatic self-display by the literary artist . . . which is also found in 'Mark of Apelles' and 'Letters from Tula'". [84]

Art is "organs of perception", says Pasternak in "Some Propositions". Sense-perception is one of the links between his meditations on art and "The Childhood of Liuvers", which presents a growing girl through her sensations, perceptions and emotions.

"At no point is it said . . . that she is like a poet. Nevertheless the comparison between adolescent child and poet lies just beneath the surface owing to the lack of a clear dividing line between her own point of view and that of her narrator." [85] So how is Zhenia like a poet? A theme of putting names to places and sensations runs through this story. While her brother reads maps and memorises place-names, Zhenia instinctively resists grasping the names before she has seen and experienced the places. On the train journey to Asian Russia her mind is an excited silence into which unknown places crash and hurtle, to be named only afterwards: awed by the mysterious forest-landscape resembling " an enormous green-yellow storm-cloud", she at last asks: "Is this the Urals?" as if the name grew organically out of that sight. While her friend learns sexual words from books and schoolgirl talk, Zhenia knows nothing until she perceives the quality of pregnancy in her mother and in a serving-woman, only then learning words for it. After geographical and sexual understandings comes another kind, a moral one. Here, too, she goes through a process of first perceiving and feeling and only secondly naming. Her incommensurate grief and self-blame when a stranger is killed by her parents' horse are due to the fact (not guessed by her watchful tutor) that the man who has died is a "third person, completely indifferent, without a name or with a random one", entering her life for the first time. Only after the chaos of sensations and feelings does an abstraction—"Thou shalt not kill"—become meaningful to her, in her own formulation: "You who are particular and living shall not do to *this /other who is/ misty and general* what you do not wish for your particular living self."

Zhenia's understanding, arising directly from perceptions and impressions, is contrasted with the experience of those for whom conventional definitions arrive first and inhibit intensity of perception. So the story is an exploration of a kind of not-knowing, or of not knowing too soon, and it could be said that

Zhenia is like the Pasternakian poet for whom the world is seen and felt, again and again, without a name and as if for the first time. It thus anticipates the much later, definitional statement: "We try to name it. The result is art."

Several basic facts about Seriozha, hero of "The Tale", are from Pasternak's own life: Jewish, a poet, finishing university in 1913, employed for a while as tutor in a wealthy household in the Urals. His thoughts and feelings are also Pasternak's own. Seriozha thinks back to his tutoring months and recalls that what led him towards being a writer was a combination of pity with the hope of acquiring great wealth which he would distribute among distressed women; for he wanted to imitate "the event in Galilee" and "renew the universe".

The story chiefly concerns a young writer beginning to write, and it contains a powerful account of inspiration, as part of Seriozha's reminiscing about the summer before the war. The account has three stages; the theme of the first is perception, of the second—speed, of the third—absorption. First, while he is still wondering how to obtain the millions he desires

> there suddenly flew by a moment of such acute perceptibility that, forgetting everything, he froze to the spot, just as he was, and listened, distraughtly alert. But there was nothing to listen to. Only the room flooded with sunshine seemed to him barer and more spacious than usual. He could have gone back to his interrupted preoccupation. But he could not . . .

Just as suddenly, he remembers that he recently promised to write a tale.

The second stage is when his search for the woman he is fond of, Anna, turns into a fast run, up and down stairs and along corridors; the fast movement is then reflected in his thought (when he has found her and impetuously proposed marriage) that the actual places in the surrounding world have begun to move: "Oh, how glad he was that all these Sokolniki and Tverskie-Iamskie [places where he has been with her or with other women] and the days and nights of the last two weeks had not remained standing still but had at last started moving!" That something has changed is confirmed by Anna who (like Camilla, in "Apelles", defining "Heine" with: "You're a child, no, a poet") tells Seriozha: "There is something wrong with you . . . You must put yourself in order".

They arrange a walk but instead (this is the third stage) Seriozha sits down, *forgets* her and starts to write the tale. Coming to his room, she sees only the back of a man writing at his desk. Moved by compassion to write for a compassionate purpose a story about compassion, he is so immersed in writing it that he forgets to attend to the woman he has just—out of compassion—asked to marry him. Art's moral paradox, exemplified here, is very like the situation Pasternak imagines in the already quoted letter to Tsvetaeva where he stops himself mentioning the poem of hers which has thrilled him: " . . . not another word about /it/, otherwise

I'll have to abandon you, abandon my work, abandon my family and, sitting with my back to all of you, write endlessly about art . . . "[86]

The tale Seriozha writes is about a man who achieves what he himself wishes to achieve, by offering himself, body and soul, for sale to the highest bidder, with the proviso that he should be able to distribute among women the wealth he will have obtained. He performs on stage as musician and poet to the audience of bidders. In a new treatment of the theme of artist as actor, the stage performance is no longer a search for self-definition or for lonely honesty, but a sacrifice and readiness for martyrdom.

Motivation by compassion, and the transformation of art's posing into total self-giving, are two of the main thoughts in "The Tale". But it also yields a wealth of other formulations about artistic creation, some more metaphysical than ethical. "In places Seriozha put down words which did not exist /and/ left them temporarily on the paper so that later they could guide him . . . into spoken language formed by the *inter-relation of rapture with everyday life* . . . " (My italics—A.L.) The performance of the self-auctioner in the tale within the tale gives rise to further telling expressions: his images are "examples of complete and arrow-like submission to the earth", and (as in the piece quoted at the beginning of the Introduction):

How strangely this man seemed to experience everything. As if someone were alternately showing him the earth, then hiding it in his sleeve, and he interpreted living beauty as the ultimate distinction between existence and non-existence. What was new about him was that he held on to this difference, which was not thinkable for longer than a moment, and raised it into a permanent sign of poetry.

II

A SAFE-CONDUCT*
or "THE PRESERVATION CERTIFICATE"[1]

* *Okhrannaia gramota*. PSS, 3, 148–238.
Part One was first published in *Zvezda* 8 (Moscow, 1929); parts Two and Three in *Krasnaia nov'* 4 and 5/6 (Moscow, 1931). A separate edition was published in Leningrad in 1931, with alterations. For more on publication of this work see PSS, 3, 551.

PART ONE

1

One hot summer morning in the year 1900 an express train is leaving Kursk station. Just before its departure someone[2] comes up to the window from outside, wearing a black Tyrolean cloak. With him is a tall woman.[3] Probably his mother or older sister. They talk to my father about something in which they are all equally initiated, but while the woman exchanges fragmentary words with my mother in Russian, the unknown man speaks only in German. Although I know the language perfectly, I have never heard it spoken as he speaks it. For this reason, on the crowded platform between two ringings of the bell, the foreign man seems to me a silhouette among bodies, a fiction in the thick of the unfictitious.

During the journey, nearer to Tula,[4] the two of them appear again in our compartment. They say the express is not scheduled to stop at Kozlovka zaseka[5] and they are not sure the guard will tell the driver in time to make a halt at the Tolstoys'. I gather from the rest of the conversation that they are going to see Sofia Andreevna,[6] as she travels to Moscow for the concerts and was at our house not long ago, whereas that infinitely important something, symbolised by the letters Ct. L. N.,[7] which plays a hidden but puzzlingly smoky role in our family, yields to no embodiment. It has been seen too early in infancy. Its hoariness, later renewed in drawings done by my father,[8] Repin[9] and others, has long been assigned by my childish imagination to a different old man, one I saw more often and probably at a later date: Nikolai Nikolaevich Ge.[10]

Then they say goodbye and go to their own carriage. A little further on, the flying embankment is sharply braked. There is a flashing of birch-trees. Down the whole length of the track, coupling-plates snort and collide. A cumulous sky tears loose with relief out of a whirl of singing sand. Spreading low to the ground as though dancing the *russkaia*,[11] an empty carriage and pair makes a half-turn out of a copse and comes flitting up to the two who have left the train. The silence of a railway halt that knows nothing of us is momentarily disturbing, like a shot. The train will not wait here. They wave goodbye with handkerchiefs. We wave back. We can just see them being helped in by the coachman. Now he has handed the rug to the lady and has half stood up, red-sleeved, to arrange his sash and gather the long skirts of his coat beneath him.

In a second he will be off. At this moment a curve in the line picks us up and, slowly turning like a page that's been read, the railway halt disappears from sight. Face and incident are forgotten, it would seem, for ever.

2

Three years go by, outdoors it is winter. Dusk and fur coats have shortened the street by a third. Along it fly the noiseless cubes of carriages and lamps. An end is put to the inheriting of proprieties, interrupted more than once already. They are washed away by the wave of a more powerful kind of succession—that of faces.

I shall not describe in detail what preceded this. How nature was revealed to the ten-year-old in a sensation recalling Gumilev's "Sixth Sense".[12] How his first passion, in response to the intent five-petalled stare of the plant, was botany. How the names found in the handbook brought peace to the sweet-scented pupils of eyes that were straining unquestioningly toward Linnaeus, as though from obscurity to glory.[13]

How in the spring of 1901 a company of Dahomey horsewomen was put on show in the Zoological Garden. How the first sense of woman was linked for me with the sense of a naked formation, closed ranks of anguish, a tropical parade to the sound of a drum. How I became the slave of forms earlier than I ought because, in them, I had seen too early the form of slaves. How, in the summer of 1903, in Obolenskoe, where the Scriabins were our neighbours, a girl brought up in a family we knew, who lived beyond the Protva, was almost drowned while bathing. How the student who jumped in to save her perished, and then she herself went mad after several attempts at suicide from the same cliff. How later, when I had broken my leg, getting out of two future wars in one evening, and was lying motionless in the plaster, the house of these friends the other side of the river was on fire, and the shrill alarm-bell of the village shook in delirium, crazed as a village idiot. How the slant-angled glow kept pounding and stretching itself like a launched kite, then suddenly curled the splints of its framework into a tube and dived head-over-heels into pie-soft layers of crimson-grey smoke.

How, as he galloped that night with a doctor from Maloiaroslavets, my father's hair turned grey at the sight of the wreathed reflection that rose like a cloud two versts away over the forest road, convincing him that what was burning was the woman he loved, with three children and a hundred-pound weight of plaster that could not be lifted without risk of a permanent crippling.

I shall not describe this, the reader will do it for me. He likes plots and horrors and regards history as a story with never-ending sequels. It is not known whether he wants it to have a rational ending. The places he likes are those beyond which his walks have not extended. He is wholly immersed in forewords and introductions, while for me life has revealed itself only at the point where he is inclined to sum things up. To say nothing of the fact that history's inner articulation is thrust on my mind in an image of inevitable death, I have come fully alive, even in life itself, only on those occasions when the tedious cooking of the ingredients was finished and, having dined from the whole, a feeling equipped with all conceivable spaciousness tore itself loose to freedom.

And so it is winter outdoors, the street is chopped a third shorter by dusk and all day long it is full of errand-running. A whirl of street-lamps chases after it, lagging behind in a whirl of snowflakes. On my way home from school the snow-covered name of Scriabin skips down from a poster onto my back.[14] I carry it home on the flap of my satchel, water flows from it onto the window-sill. This adoration attacks me more cruelly and undisguisedly than any fever. Whenever I see him I turn pale, then immediately blush because of that very pallor. If he speaks to me, I lose all power of thought and hear myself answer something off the point while everyone laughs, though *what* I say I do not hear. I know he guesses everything, yet not once has he come to my aid. It means he does not spare me, and this is just that unshared, unrequited feeling I thirst for. This alone—and the fiercer it is, the more surely—protects me from the ravaging effect of his indescribable music.

Before leaving for Italy, he drops in on us to say goodbye. He plays— this cannot be put into words—has supper with us, talks philosophy, chats unaffectedly, makes jokes. The whole time it seems to me he is suffering an agony of boredom. The moment of leave-taking comes. Good wishes resound. Like a clot of blood mine, too, drops into the general heap of farewells. All this is said on the move, and the exclamations, crowding in the doorway, gradually cross into the entrance hall. Here everything is repeated with a recapitulating jerkiness and the hook of a collar that for a long time won't go into its tightly sewn loop. The door bangs, the key turns twice. Passing the grand piano, which with all the hinged radiance of its music-rest still speaks of his playing, my mother sits down to look through the *études* he has left, and no sooner have the first sixteen bars formed themselves into a sentence full of a kind of astounded readiness, unrewardable by anything on earth, than—coatless and bareheaded—I am racing downstairs and along Miasnitsky Street in the night, to bring him back or set eyes on him once more.

This has been experienced by everyone. To all of us tradition has appeared, to all it has promised a face, to all, in different ways, it has kept its promise. We have all become people solely in the measure in which we have loved people and have had the opportunity to love. Never, under cover of its nickname, "milieu", has tradition been satisfied with the compound image made for it, but has always detailed to us one or other of its most decided exceptions. Why then have the majority departed in the shape of an acceptable, merely tolerable, commonness? Rather than a face, they preferred facelessness, being frightened of the sacrifices tradition demands from childhood. To love selflessly and unreservedly, with a strength equal to the square of the distance—this is the task of our hearts while we are children.

3

Of course I did not catch up with him, nor did I really think of doing so. We met six years later, on his return from abroad. This period coincided fully with my adolescent years. And everyone knows the vastness of adolescence. However many decades come flying in for us afterwards, they are powerless to fill this hangar, to which they come for memories, day and night, separately or in a bevy, like trainee aircraft coming in for fuel. In other words, these years in our life constitute a part that exceeds the whole, and Faust, who lived them twice, lived something essentially unimaginable, to be measured only by a mathematical paradox.

He arrived, and immediately rehearsals of *L'Extase* began.[15] How I should like to exchange this name, which smacks of a taut soap-wrapping, for something more suitable! The rehearsals were in the mornings. The way to them lay in soupy darkness, along Furkasovsky Lane and Kuznetsky Bridge Street, both sunk in icy pulp. Along the sleepy road, the hanging clappers of belfries were plunged in mist. On each belfry a solitary bell gave out a single boom. The others stayed unanimously silent with all the abstinence of Lenten copper.[16] At the exit from Gazetny Street, Nikitsky Square was whipping egg with cognac in the crossroads' resonant whirlpool. Wailing iron of sleigh-runners drove into puddles, flintstone clicked beneath the concert-goers' canes. At such hours the Conservatoire resembled a circus at the time of its morning clean-out. The amphitheatre cages were empty. The stalls were slowly filling. Barely driven with sticks into its winter quarters, the music kept slapping its paw out over the wooden panelling of the organ. All of a sudden the public began to arrive in a steady stream, as if a city were being left to the enemy. The music was let loose. Colourful, countlessly breaking and multiplying with lightning speed, it scattered in leaps across the platform. They would set it in order, it would speed with feverish haste towards harmony, then suddenly attaining an unprecedentedly unified thunder, it would break off with all the bass whirlwind sounding, go dead still and line up along the footlights.

This was the first settlement of man in worlds opened up by Wagner for invented beings and mastodons. On this site an uninvented, lyrical dwelling was being erected, materially equal to the whole universe which had been ground down to make its bricks. Above the wattle fence of the symphony blazed the sun of Van Gogh. Its window-sills were covered with the dusty archives of Chopin.

The inhabitants did not poke their noses in this dust, but with their whole way of being they fulfilled the finest behests of their forerunner.

I could not hear it without tears. It was engraved in my memory before it lay on the zinc plates of the first proofs. There was nothing unexpected in this. The hand which wrote it had lain on me six years earlier with no less weight.

What else were all those years but further transformations of the living imprint, left to the whim of growth? It is not surprising that in the symphony I met an enviably happy coeval whose vicinity could not help telling upon my friends and family, upon my work and my whole daily life. And this is how it told.

More than anything in the world I loved music, and, in music, more than anyone else, Scriabin. I had begun to babble in music not long before my first acquaintance with him. By the time of his return, I was the pupil of a certain composer who is alive and prospering to this day.[17] The one thing I had still to learn was orchestration. Various things were said, but what counts is that, even had the opposite been said, I could not have imagined my life outside music.

But I did not have absolute pitch. This is the name of the ability to recognise the pitch of any note sounded at random. My lack of this quality which had nothing to do with musical talent in general, but which was fully possessed by my mother, gave me no peace. Had music been my true career, as it seemed to outsiders, I would not have cared about absolute pitch. I knew that outstanding composers of my time did not have it, and that both Wagner and Tchaikovsky were thought perhaps to have lacked it. But to me music was a cult, the destructive point, that is, where gathered everything most superstitious and self-abnegating in me, therefore whenever my will grew wings at some evening inspiration I hastened to humble it in the morning by recalling, again and again, the defect I have mentioned.

All the same, I had written several serious pieces.[18] Now I was to show them to my idol. A meeting was arranged, which was quite natural in view of the acquaintance between our households, but which I apprehended with my usual extremeness. Under any circumstances this step would have seemed to me importunate and in the present case it grew, in my eyes, to something like blasphemy. And when the appointed day came and I was on my way to Glazovsky Street where Scriabin was temporarily living, I was not so much taking him my compositions as a love which for a long time now had been too big to express, and my apologies for the imagined tactlessness of which I felt myself to be the involuntary cause. These feelings were now being tossed and squeezed by an overcrowded No. 4, carrying them inexorably toward their formidably nearing goal, along the tawny Arbat[19] which was being dragged towards Smolensky Lane by shaggy, sweaty raven-black horses and pedestrians, all up to their knees in water.

4

I appreciated then how well schooled our facial muscles are. With my throat tightened from agitation, I mumbled something with a parched tongue, slaking my answers with frequent gulps of tea so as not to choke or commit some other blunder.

The skin twitched over my jawbone and the bumps of my forehead, I jerked my eyebrows, nodded and smiled, and each time I touched the wrinkles of this mimicry, ticklish and sticky as spiderweb, at the bridge of my nose, I found in my hand a convulsively clutched handkerchief repeatedly wiping large drops of sweat from my brow. Behind my head, and tied up by curtains, spring was drifting smokily the whole length of the road. While in front of me, between my hosts who were trying to draw me out of my difficulty with a redoubled loquacity, tea was breathing in cups, a samovar, pierced with an arrow of steam, was hissing and sunshine was billowing, hazy from water and manure. Smoke from a cigar-end, fibrous as a tortoiseshell comb, stretched from the ashtray up to the light and, reaching it, crawled satedly sideways along it, as if along a piece of cloth. I don't know why but this spinning of dazzled air, steaming waffles, smoking sugar, and silver burning like paper increased my nervousness unbearably. It subsided when I went over into the salon and found myself at the piano.

I played the first piece still in a state of agitation; the second, almost in control of it; the third, surrendering to the pressure of the new and unforeseen. My glance happened to fall on my listener.

Following the gradual progress of the performance, he had raised first his head and then his eyebrows, and finally, beaming, stood up himself and, accompanying the changes in the melody with elusive changes in his smile, he floated towards me along its rhythmic perspective. He liked all of it. I quickly finished. At once he began assuring me that it was absurd to talk of mere musical gifts when there was something incomparably greater here and I had the ability to say something of my own in music. Referring to the passages that had just flashed by, he sat down at the piano to repeat one that had attracted him the most. It was a complex phrase and I did not expect him to reproduce it exactly, but something else happened that was unexpected: he repeated it in a different key, and the deficiency that had tormented me all these years splashed out from beneath his hands as his own.

I gave a start, and, again preferring the vicissitudes of guesswork to the eloquence of fact, I made a double plan. If to my confession he should object, "But Boria, I haven't got it either", then—all right, it would mean I was not imposing myself on music, but music was meant as my destiny. But should his answer be about Wagner and Tchaikovsky and piano-tuners and so on—but already I was approaching the alarming subject, and, interrupted in mid-question, was already swallowing down the answer: "Absolute pitch? After all I've said to you? What about Wagner? What about Tchaikovsky? And the hundreds of piano-tuners who have it . . . "

We were walking up and down the salon. He kept putting his hand on my shoulder or taking me by the arm. He spoke of the harmfulness of improvisation, of when and why and how one should write. As models of the simplicity one should always aspire to, he mentioned his new sonatas, notorious for their difficulty. Examples of a reprehensible complexity he took from the most banal of parlour songs. I was not disturbed by the paradox in this comparison. I agreed that facelessness was more complex than having a face; that a wasteful prolixity seemed accessible because it had no content; that because we are corrupted by empty clichés we think—when after long desuetude we come across something unprecedentedly rich in content—that *that* is mere formal pretentiousness. Imperceptibly he went on to more definite exhortations. He inquired as to my education, and, learning that I had chosen the Law Faculty because it was easy, advised me to transfer without delay to the philosophy section of the Historical and Philological Faculty—which in fact I did the next day. And while he talked I thought over what had happened. I did not go back on my bargain with fate. I remembered the sorry issue of my coin-tossing. Was my god dethroned by this chance event? Not in the least—it raised him from his previous loftiness to a new height. Why had he refused me the most simple answer I had so longed for? That was his secret. Some time, when it would be too late, he would present me with the omitted confession. How had he overcome his own doubts in his youth? That too was his secret and that was what raised him to a new height. But the room had long been in darkness, the lamps were lit in the street outside, it was time to leave.

As I said goodbye, I didn't know how to thank him. Something was mounting up in me. Something was tearing and trying to get free. Something was weeping, something was exulting.

The very first stream of coolness in the street gave off a sense of houses and distances. The whole multitude of them rose to the sky, lifted up from the cobbles by the single-heartedness of the Moscow night. I thought of my parents and the questions they were impatiently preparing to ask me. Whatever way I told it, my news could have only the most joyful meaning. And only now, for the first time, yielding to the logic of the tale I was to tell, did I consider the happy events of the day as fact. In such guise they did not belong to me. They became reality only when destined for others. However exciting the news I was taking home, my soul was unquiet. And yet there was a sensation more and more resembling happiness in my awareness that this very sadness was something I would never be able to pour into anyone else's ear, and that, like my future, it would stay below in the street, along with all my Moscow, mine at this moment as never before. I walked down side-streets, crossing over more often than I needed to. Entirely without my knowledge a world was melting and cracking in me which, just the day before, had seemed inborn for ever. I walked on, quickening my step at every turning, not knowing that that night I was already breaking with music.

Greece had an excellent understanding of the different ages of life. She took care not to mix them up. She knew how to think of childhood in an enclosed autonomous way, as the main nucleus of integration. How greatly she possessed this ability can be seen in the myth of Ganymede[20] and many other such myths. Similar views formed part of her conception of the demi-god and the hero. In the Greek view, a certain portion of risk and tragedy has to be gathered sufficiently early into a single handful, clearly visible at a glance. The foundations of certain parts of the building, and in their midst the fundamental arch of fatality, must be laid at once, at the very beginning, in the interest of its future good proportions. And finally, perhaps in some memorable analogy, death too has to be lived through.

This is why antiquity, with its art of genius, always unexpected and enthralling as a fairy tale, knew nothing of romanticism.

Brought up on a rigorous demand such as would never be repeated—the superhumanity of deeds and tasks—it knew absolutely nothing of superhumanity as personal affect. It was insured against this by the way it prescribed for childhood the entire dose of the extraordinary that is contained in the world. And when, after taking it, a person entered gigantic reality with gigantic strides, both his gait and his surroundings were accounted ordinary.

5

One evening not long after that, as I was setting out for a meeting of Serdarda, a drunken fellowship founded by a dozen poets, musicians and artists, I remembered I had promised Iulian Anisimov, who had previously read excellent translations of Dehmel, that I would bring him another German poet, the one I preferred to all his contemporaries.[21] And again, as more than once before, the volume *Mir zur Feier*[22] found itself in my hands during my most difficult time, and went off through the slush toward wood-built Razguliai,[23] to the damp interlacing there of olden times, heredity and youthful promises, to be stupefied by rooks in the attic under the poplars and to return home with a new friendship—that is, with a flair for one more door in the town, where as yet there were but few. But it's time I told how this volume came my way.

What happened was that six years earlier, in the December dusk I have twice started describing here, together with the noiseless street, ambushed everywhere by mysterious grimaces of snowflakes, I too was shuffling about on my knees, helping my mother set my father's bookshelves in order. The printed entrails, already wiped with a rag and shoved on all four sides into a rough pile, were being replaced in straight rows on the disembowelled shelves, when suddenly out of one of the heaps, an especially wobbly and disobedient one, there fell a small book with a faded grey cover. It was wholly by chance that I did not push it back but picked it up from the floor and later took it to my room. A long time passed and I came to love this book—as well as another which soon joined it and which the same hand had dedicated to my father. But even more time passed before I realised that their author, Rainer Maria Rilke, must have been that very same German whom once, one summer long ago, we had left in mid-journey on the rotating section of a forgotten railway-halt in a forest. I ran to my father to check my guess and he confirmed it, wondering why it should excite me so much.[24]

I am not writing my own biography. I turn to it when someone else's demands this. Along with its principal character, I consider that only a hero deserves an actual life-story, while the history of a poet is wholly untellable in this form. It would have to be assembled from inessentials that spoke of concessions to pity and compulsion. A poet voluntarily gives his whole life such a steep slope that it cannot exist in the vertical line of biography where we expect to meet it. It cannot be found under his name and has to be sought under someone else's, in the biographical columns of his successors. The more a productive individuality is enclosed in itself, the more collective—without any allegory—is its story. The realm of the subconscious in a genius submits to no measurement. It consists of everything that happens to his readers and that he does not know. I am not presenting my reminiscences to the memory of Rilke. On the contrary, I myself received them from him as a gift.

6*

Although my story has inclined this way, I have not asked what music is or what leads up to it. I haven't done so, not only because I woke up one night in my third year of life to find the whole range of vision drenched with it for more than fifteen years ahead, so that I had no occasion to experience its problematics, but also because it now ceases to bear on our theme. The same question, however, in relation to art in general, art as such—in other words, in relation to poetry—cannot be passed over. I shall not answer it theoretically nor in sufficiently general form, but much of what I am going to relate will be an answer to it, the answer I can give for myself and for my poet.

---

* An asterisk to a chapter number indicates that the chapter is discussed in the Commentary.

The sun used to rise behind the Post Office, slip down Kiselnyi Lane and set over the Neglinka.[25] After gilding our half of the house, it would make its way after lunch into the dining-room and kitchen. Our apartment was government property and its rooms were adapted from classrooms. I was studying at the university. I was reading Hegel and Kant. It was the sort of time when at every meeting with friends gulfs would open up and first one of us, then another, would come forward with some newly manifested revelation.

Often we got each other up, deep in the night. The reason always seemed urgent. The one who was woken was ashamed of his sleep, as of an accidentally exposed weakness. To the fright of the house's unfortunate inhabitants, who were all regarded as nonentities, we would instantly set off—as if making for an adjoining room—to Sokolniki and the Iaroslavl railway crossing.[26] I was friends with a girl from a wealthy family. It was obvious to everyone that I loved her. She took part in these walks only in the abstract, on the lips of those more used to sleeplessness and better adapted to it. I was giving a few meagrely paid lessons so as not to take money from my father. In the summers, when my family went away, I would stay on in the town at my own expense. An illusion of independence was obtained through such moderation in food that on top of everything else there was hunger, which conclusively transformed night into day in the empty apartment. Music, to which I was still only postponing my farewell, was already becoming interwoven with literature. The depth and charm of Belyi and Blok could not help being revealed to me.[27] Their influence was combined in a singular way with a force that surpassed mere ignorance. Fifteen years of abstinence from words, which had been sacrificed to sounds, meant being doomed to originality, the way certain kinds of maiming doom a person to acrobatics. I and some of my acquaintances had connections with Musaget.[28] From others I learned of the existence of Marburg. Kant and Hegel were replaced by Cohen, Natorp and Plato.[29]

I am characterising my life of those years with a deliberate randomness. I could multiply these signs or exchange them for others. However, the ones I have given are enough for my purpose. Using them to estimate, as on a sketch made for calculations, what reality was for me at that time, I shall now ask myself where, and by virtue of what, was poetry being born from it. I shall not have to ponder the answer long. This is the one feeling my memory has preserved in all its freshness.

It was born from the irregularities in these ranks of things, from the differences in their speed, from the way the more sluggish of them lagged behind and heaped up in the rear, on the deep horizon of memory.

Love sped along most impetuously of all. Sometimes it would find itself at the head of nature and overtake the sun. But as this happened only rarely it can be said that that which gilded one side of the house and began to bronze the other, that which washed weather away with weather and turned the heavy winch of the four seasons, moved forward with a constant superiority, nearly always competing with love. While the remaining ranks dragged along behind at various distances. I often heard the hiss of a yearning that had not begun with me. Trying to catch up with me from behind, it provoked fear and pity. It issued from the point at which everyday life had been torn away, and it either threatened to put brakes on reality or begged to be joined to the living air which in the meantime had got a long way ahead. What is called inspiration consisted in this backward glance. The most turgid, uncreative parts of existence called for a special vividness because of the distance to which they had rolled away. Inanimate objects acted still more strongly. They were models for a still life, a form especially beloved of artists. Piling up in the furthest distance of the living universe, and being in a state of immobility, they provided the fullest possible idea of its moving entirety, as any limit does which seems to us a contrast. Their location marked a frontier beyond which astonishment and pity had nothing to do. There science was at work, seeking out the atomic foundations of reality.

But since there was no second universe from which one might have lifted reality out of the first, taking it by its tops as though by the hair, the manipulations it itself called for required that a depiction of it be made, as in algebra which, in respect of magnitude, is constrained by a similar singleness of plane. But this depicting always seemed to me a way out of the difficulty and not a goal in itself. The goal I always saw as transferring the thing depicted from cold axles to hot ones, in setting the outlived in motion, to pursue and catch up with life. This is how I reasoned at that time, and it is not very different from how I think now. We depict people in order to cast weather upon them. Weather—or nature,[30] which is the same thing—we depict in order to cast our passion upon it. We drag the everyday into prose for the sake of poetry. We draw prose into poetry for the sake of music. This, in the broadest sense of the word, is what I called art, set by the clock of the living race, which beats in generations.

This is why the sensation of a town never corresponded to the place in it where my life was lived. An inward pressure always flung it back into the depth of the perspective I have described. There clouds puffed and kicked their heels, and the mingled smoke of innumerable stoves thrust through the crowd of them and hung athwart the sky. There, in lines, as if along embankments, collapsing houses plunged their porches into snow. There the frail squalor of destitution was fingered by soft guitar twangings of drunkenness. And large, stately ladies, hard-boiled from the bottle and red in the face, emerged with their swaying husbands into the nightly tide of cabs, as if from the feverish uproar of tubs into the birch-twig cool of a bathhouse anteroom. There people poisoned themselves and got burned down, threw acid at marriage-breakers, drove to their weddings in satin and pawned their furs. There the varnished grins of a way of life that was cracking apart exchanged winks on the quiet, and, as they waited for my lesson, my alumni, school pupils repeating the year, would sit down and set out their textbooks, their faces painted saffron-bright with unintelligence. There too, with its hundred auditoriums, the grey-green, much-littered university ebbed and flowed with sound.

Sliding the glass of their spectacles along the glass of their pocket watches, the professors would raise their heads to address the galleries and vaults. Heads of students came away from their jackets and hung on long cords, pairing off in even numbers with the green lampshades.

During these visits to the city, where I arrived each day as if from another, my heartbeat invariably speeded up. If I had gone to a doctor then, he would have assumed I had malaria. But these attacks of chronic impatience could not be cured by quinine. This strange perspiring was caused by the stubborn crudeness of those worlds, their turgid obviousness, which nothing from within spent to its advantage. They lived and moved as if striking attitudes. The antenna of a mass predestination rose up mentally in the midst of them, uniting them into a kind of colony. Just at the base of this imagined post came the attack of fever. It was generated by currents sent by the mast to the opposite pole. Conversing with the distant mast of genius, it summoned some new Balzac from those regions into its own small settlement. But one had only to move a short way from the fatal rod for immediate tranquillity to set in.

I was not feverish, for example, at Savin's lectures, because this professor was not cut out to be a type. He lectured with real talent, which grew in proportion as his subject grew. Time did not take offence at him. It did not tear away from his assertions, leap into ventilators or fling itself headlong toward the doors. It did not blow the smoke back into the flues or dart off the roof to catch hold of the hook of a tram sweeping away into the snowstorm. No, it plunged head and ears into medieval England or the Robespierre Convention, pulling us in with it and, along with us, everything we could imagine alive beyond the high university windows fashioned at the very cornices.[31]

I also stayed healthy in a room in some cheap furnished lodgings where, with several other students, I was study-leader for a group of grown-up pupils. Here nobody shone with talents. It was quite enough that instructors and instructed, expecting no legacy from anywhere, joined in a common effort to shift themselves from the standstill life was preparing to nail them to. Like their teachers, among whom were some who had stayed on at the university, they were untypical of their professions. Clerks and office workers, labourers, domestic servants, postmen—they came here so that one day they might become something else.

I was not feverish in their active midst and, in rare harmony with myself, I often turned off from there into a nearby side-street, where whole guilds of flower-sellers lived in one of the courtyard buildings of the Zlatoustinsky monastery. It was here that small boys came to load themselves with all the flora of the Riviera, before going to peddle it on the Petrovka.[32] Peasant wholesalers ordered the flowers from Nice and these treasures could be got from them on the spot for a mere trifle. I was especially drawn to them at the turn of the academic year when the bright March twilight, realising one fine evening that studies had been going on without lamps for some time, took to coming into the dirty lodgings more and more often and was soon not even being left behind on the hotel porch after the lessons were over. The street broke its habit of covering its head with a low kerchief of winter night and suddenly seemed to rise up at the porch from under the earth with a kind of dried fairy tale on its scarcely stirring lips. Spring air shuffled jerkily over the hardy cobbles. The outlines of the street, as if a live skin were drawn tightly over them, shivered a chilly shiver, tired of waiting for the first star, whose appearance the insatiable, fabulously leisurely sky kept tediously putting off.

The fetid gallery was packed to the ceiling with empty wicker boxes which had foreign stamps under their sonorous Italian postmarks. In reply to the felted grunt of the door, a cloud of paunchy steam would billow outside, as if to relieve itself, and in the very steam one could guess at something unspeakably exciting. Directly opposite the vestibule, in the depth of the gradually sloping chamber, youthful pedlars crowded at a small fortified window, taking the counted goods and stuffing them into their baskets. There too, at the broad table, the proprietor's sons were silently slicing open new parcels just brought from the Customs. Bent open in two like a book, the orange lining laid bare the fresh core of the wicker box. Serried tangles of chilled violets were lifted out all in one piece like dark blue layers of dried Malaga raisins. They filled the room—a sort of janitor's lodge—with such a stupefying fragrance that even the columns of early evening dusk and the shadows layered all over the floor seemed cut out from a damp, dark-lilac turf.

But the real miracles were to come. The owner would go through to the very end of the yard, unbolt one of the doors of the stone shed and raise a trapdoor by its ring, and in that moment the tale of Ali Baba and the forty thieves would come true in all its dazzling splendour. On the floor of the dry cellar burned four turnip-shaped globe lightnings[33] explosively, like suns; and hot sheaves of peonies, yellow daisies, tulips and anemones, sorted according to colour and kind, raged in enormous tubs, rivalling the lamps. They breathed and swayed and seemed to be vying with one another. A dusty sweetness of mimosa was washed away by a wave of bright scent that came pouring with unexpected force, a watery scent threaded with liquid needles of aniseed. It was the scent of daffodils, vivid as a sweet brandy diluted to pure whiteness. Yet even now all this jealous storm was conquered by the black cockades of the violets. Secretive and half-insane, like pupils of eyes without whites, they hypnotised you by their indifference. Their sweet, uncoughed breath filled the broad frame of the trapdoor from the bottom of the cellar. They coated your chest with a woody pleurisy. This scent kept recalling something, then slipping away, leaving the mind fooled. It seemed the idea of the earth which persuaded them to return each year had been made up by the months of spring on the pattern of this scent, and somewhere near at hand lay the sources of Greek beliefs about Demeter.

7

Then, and much later, I regarded my attempts at poetry as an unfortunate weakness and expected no good from them. Even then there was one person, Sergei Durylin,[34] who supported me with his approval. This was due to his uniquely responsive nature. From my other friends, who had seen me practically getting on my feet as a musician, I took pains to hide these signs of a new immaturity.

On the other hand I was studying philosophy with a fundamental enthusiasm, for I felt that the rudiments of a future application to something lay somewhere in its vicinity. The range of topics lectured on to our group was as far removed from the ideal as was the method of teaching them. It was a curious jumble of antiquated metaphysics and unfledged enlightenmentism. For the sake of agreement, the two tendencies gave up the last remnants of any meaning they might still have had if they had been taken separately. The history of philosophy was becoming a literary dabbling in dogmatics, and psychology was degenerating into a frivolous pamphleteering nonsense.

Young lecturers like Shpet, Samsonov and Kubitsky were not able to alter this process.[35] Yet even the older professors were not so very much to blame. They were bound by the obligation, already making itself felt, for lectures to be popular to the point of spelling out every word. Although the participants were not quite aware of it, precisely at that time the campaign for the eradication of illiteracy had begun.[36] Students with grounding in their subject tried to work on their own and grew increasingly attached to the exemplary university library. Sympathies were divided among three names. A large group was excited by Bergson. Adherents of Göttingen Husserlianism found support in Shpet. Followers of the Marburg school had no one to guide them and, left to their own resources, they were united by the chance ramifications of a personal tradition that had started as far back as Sergei Nikolaevich Trubetskoi.[37]

A remarkable phenomenon in this circle was the young Samarin.[38] A direct scion of the best Russian past, and linked moreover by various gradations of kinship to the history of the very building on the corners of Nikitsky Square,[39] he would put in an appearance about twice a term at some seminar or other, like a cut-off son turning up in the parental apartment at the hour when the family was assembled for dinner. The seminar-leader would stop reading and would wait while the lanky eccentric, embarrassed by the silence he had caused and was himself prolonging by selecting a seat, clambered up the creaky boards to the farthest bench of the plank-built amphitheatre. But the moment discussion of the paper began, all that crashing and creaking that had just been dragged so laboriously up to the place under the ceiling would come down again in renewed, unrecognisable form. Samarin would seize on the speaker's first slip of the tongue and hurl down some extemporisation from Hegel or Cohen, rolling it down, like a ball going over the rib-like ledges of an enormous store of boxes. He would get excited and swallow his words, and he spoke with a voice innately loud, sustained on that level note which is adopted as one's own from childhood to the grave and is always the same, knowing neither whisper nor shout and which, along with the throaty "r"-sound inseparable from it, instantly betrays breeding. I lost sight of him later but was involuntarily reminded of him when I re-read Tolstoy and came across him again in Nekhliudov.[40]

8

The summer coffee-house on the Tverskoi Boulevard had no name of its own but everyone called it the *Café grec*. It was not closed during the winter and its function then became a strange enigma. Once, by chance, without having arranged it, Loks,[41] Samarin and I met in this bare pavilion. We were the only visitors it had had, not only that evening but perhaps for the whole of the past season. It was the turning-point towards warm weather; there was a wafting of spring. Scarcely had Samarin arrived and sat down with us than he began philosophising, arming himself with a dry biscuit and using it, like a choirmaster's tuning fork, to beat out the logical articulations of his speech. A piece of Hegelian infinity stretched across the pavilion, composed of alternating affirmations and negations. Probably I told him what subject I had chosen for my doctoral thesis, and at that he leapt from Leibniz[42] and mathematical infinity to the dialectical kind. Suddenly he started talking about Marburg. This was the first account I had heard of the town itself rather than of the school. Later I was to realise that there was no other way to talk of its antiquity and poetry, but at that moment his enamoured description, accompanied by the rattling of the ventilation fan, was for me a new experience. Samarin abruptly recollected that he had only come in for a moment and not to philosophise over coffee, startled up the café-owner who was nodding in a corner behind his newspaper and, learning that the telephone was out of order, burst out of the ice-covered starling-house even more noisily than he had burst into it. Soon we, too, got up. The weather had changed. A wind had risen and begun lashing down a February sleet. It laid itself on the earth in regular windings like a figure eight. There was something nautical in its frenzied looping. This was how hawsers and nets were piled up in wavy layers, stroke upon stroke. On the way, Loks kept starting on his favourite theme of Stendhal, but I stayed silent, greatly helped in this by the blizzard. I could not forget what I had heard, and I grieved for the little town which I thought I was no more likely to see than my own ears.

That was in February, and one morning in April my mother announced that by collecting her earnings and economising on the housekeeping she had saved two hundred roubles, which she was giving to me with the advice to travel abroad. Neither my joy nor the complete unexpectedness of the gift can be described, nor how undeserved it was. No small amount of strumming on the piano had had to be endured to make up such a sum. But I had not the strength to refuse. There was no need to choose a route. In those days, European universities were constantly informed of one another. That very day I began hurrying to and from the administrative offices and, together with a small number of documents, I brought certain treasures away from Mokhovoi Street. These were detailed lists of lecture courses scheduled for the summer term of 1912, printed in Marburg two weeks earlier. I studied this prospectus, pencil in hand, and could not part with it whether walking along or standing at the grids of office counters. My absorption reeked of happiness a mile away and by infecting secretaries and clerks with it I speeded up unawares the already straightforward procedures.

My programme was naturally a Spartan one. Third-class travel, and abroad even fourth if necessary, the slowest trains, a room in some small village outside the town, bread and sausage and tea. My mother's self-sacrifice bound me to a tenfold avarice and I wanted to get to Italy as well on her money. Besides this, I knew that a very perceptible sum would be swallowed up by the university entrance fee and the fees for particular seminars and courses. But even if I had had ten times the money, I would not, as I was then, have retreated from this programme. I don't know how I would have disposed of the remainder but nothing in the world would have moved me into the second class or tempted me to leave my trace on a restaurant table-cloth. Tolerance towards comforts, and the need to be comfortable, appeared in me only in the post-war period. That period set up such obstacles to the world which allowed nothing decorative or indulgent into my room that for a while my whole character could not help changing too.

9

At home the snow was still melting and the sky was floating out onto the water in pieces from under the crust of ice like a transfer image sliding out from its tracing paper, but all over Poland the apple trees were in warm blossom and the land sped from morning to night and from west to east in a summery sleeplessness like some Romance part of the Slavonic design.

Berlin seemed to me a city of youths who, just the day before, had received broadswords and helmets, canes and pipes, real bicycles and frock-coats like the grown-ups' ones. I came upon them as they were making their first appearance, not yet used to the change, each of them pluming himself on what had yesterday fallen to his lot. On one of the most excellent streets, I was hailed from a bookshop window by Natorp's manual of logic, and I went in to buy it with the sensation that next day I would see the author himself. In forty-eight hours of travel I had already spent one sleepless night on German territory, and now a second lay ahead of me.

Only in Russia have folding bunks been introduced in third-class carriages, abroad you have to pay for the cheapness of the transport by nodding all night long, four in a row, on a deep-seated bench divided up by arm-rests. Although this time both benches in the compartment were at my disposal, I did not feel like sleeping. Only now and then, at long intervals, single passengers, mostly students, came in to stay for a station or two, then, silently bowing, sank into the warm unknown of night. At each replacement of them, sleeping towns came rolling in beneath the platform roofs. For the first time the immemorial Middle Ages were revealed to me. Their authenticity was fresh and terrifying, like everything that is original. Clanking the familiar names like naked steel, the journey took them out, one after the other, from descriptions I had read, as if from dusty scabbards manufactured by the historians.

Flying up to them, the train stretched out in a chain-mail wonder of ten riveted carriages. The leather casing of the carriage joints swelled and sagged like blacksmith's bellows. Beer, blotched by the lights of the station, sparkled clearly in tall, clean glasses. Emptied luggage carts moved off smoothly down the stone platforms on thick, stone-like rollers. Under the vaults of colossal landing-stages the torsos of short-snouted engines sweated. They seemed to have been carried up to that height by some prank played by the low wheels when they came to an unexpected halt while fully wound up.

Towards the unpeopled concrete its six-hundred-years-old forefathers drew from all sides. Quartered by a slanting trellis of beams, the walls unsmoothed their drowsy decoration. Pageboys crowded on them, knights, maidens and ginger-bearded ogres, and the chequered lathing of the lattice-work was repeated as an ornamental design in the grid-like visors of the helmets, the slits of the ballooning sleeves and the criss-cross lacing of the bodices. Houses stepped almost up to the lowered window. Completely stunned, I leaned on its broad rib and spellbound myself by whispering over and over again a short, now old-fashioned, exclamation of rapture. But it was still dark, and the leaping paws of the wild vine were a scarcely visible black against the stucco. And when the hurricane struck anew, redolent of coal and dew and roses, and I was suddenly spattered by a fistful of sparks from the hands of the night flying past in a passion, I quickly raised the window and began thinking about the unforeseeable events of the next day. But I must say at least something of where I was going, and why.

A creation of the genius Cohen—its way paved by his predecessor in the chair, Friedrich Albert Lange,[43] well known in our country for his *History of Materialism*—the Marburg school of thought won me over by two peculiarities. First, it was original: it dug everything over to the very foundations and built on a clear space. It did not join in the lazy routine of all conceivable "isms" which always cling to the tenth-hand omniscience so remunerative to them, are always ignorant and always, for one reason or another, are afraid of re-examining in the open air the culture of the ages. Not being subjected to terminological inertia, the Marburg school turned to the primary sources— the authentic signatures left by thought in the history of knowledge. If popular philosophy speaks of what one or another writer thinks, and popular psychology of how the average man thinks, if formal logic teaches you how to think in the baker's shop so as not to get the wrong change, the Marburg school was interested in how science itself thinks in its twenty-five centuries of uninterrupted authorship, at the hot beginnings and sources of world-important discoveries. With such a disposition, authorised as it were by history itself, philosophy grew young and clever again beyond all recognition, changing from a problematic discipline into a primordial discipline about problems, which is what it ought to be.

The second peculiarity of the Marburg school proceeded directly from the first and consisted in a scrupulous and exacting attitude towards the heritage of history. Quite alien to this school was the abominably condescending attitude that sees the past as a kind of poor-house where a band of old men in chlamys and sandals or periwigs and camisoles gabble some impenetrable stuff of their own, excused by the vagaries of the Corinthian order, the Gothic, the Baroque, or some other architectural style. For this school the homogeneity of the structure of knowledge was a principle of the same kind as the anatomical identity of historical man. In Marburg they knew history to perfection and never tired of pulling treasure after treasure out of the archives of the Italian Renaissance, French or Scottish rationalism and other schools that have been insufficiently studied. In Marburg they looked at history through both Hegelian eyes, that is with the generalising of genius and at the same time within the strict boundaries of commonsense probability. Thus this school did not speak, for example, of the stages of the world spirit but spoke, let's suppose, of the postal correspondence of the Bernoulli family,[44] knowing as it did so that every thought, however distant in time, when it is caught on the spot and in action, must be fully receptive to our logical commentary. If this is not so, it loses its immediate interest for us and falls into the province of the archaeologist, the historian of costumes, manners, literatures, socio-political trends and so forth.

These two features, autonomy and historicism, say nothing of the content of Cohen's system, but I did not intend to speak about its essence and would not have undertaken to do so. Nonetheless these two things explain its attractiveness. They speak of its originality, that is of the living place it occupies in a living tradition for one part of the contemporary consciousness.

As a particle of that consciousness, I was speeding to the centre of attraction. The train was crossing the Harz mountains. In the smoky morning, leaping forth from the forest, thousand-year-old Goslar went flashing by like a medieval coal-miner. Some time later Göttingen rushed past. The names of the towns grew louder and louder. Most of them the train flung out of its path in full flight without a nod. I found the names of these spinning-tops on the map as they rolled away. Ancient details rose up around some of them, to be drawn into their vortex like astral rings and satellites. Sometimes the horizon widened as in "The Terrible Vengeance" and, smoking simultaneously in several orbits, the earth, all separate townlets and castles, began to have the agitating quality of a night sky.[45]

10

During the two years preceding this journey, the word Marburg never left my lips. The town was mentioned in every secondary-school textbook in the chapters on the Reformation. Even for children a small book about Elizabeth of Hungary, who was buried in the town at the beginning of the thirteenth century, had been published by Mediator. Any biography of Giordano Bruno, listing the towns where he lectured on his fatal journey from London to his native country, mentioned Marburg as one of them. And yet in Moscow, un-likely as it may seem, I did not once realise that the Marburg of these references was identical with that for whose sake I gnawed away at derivative and differential tables and jumped from MacLaurin to Maxwell, who was definitely beyond me. It was not until I had walked past the old post station and the "Hotel zum Ritter", clutching my suitcase, that this identity faced me for the first time.[46]

I stood with my head thrown back, gasping. Above me towered a dizzy slope on which in three tiers stood the stone maquettes of the university, the Rathaus and the eight-hundred-years-old castle. After ten steps I no longer knew where I was. I recalled that I had left my connection with the rest of the world in the carriage of the train, and now it could not be retrieved any more than the hooks, luggage-rack or ashtrays. Clouds stood idly above the tower clock.

To them the place seemed familiar. But even they did not explain anything. Evidently they were the watchmen of this nest and never went away from it. A midday silence reigned. It communed with the silence of the plain that spread below. Between them they seemed to sum up my stupefaction. The upper one exchanged languorous winnowings of lilac with the lower. Birds chirruped, as if waiting for something. I scarcely noticed any people. The motionless contours of roofs were curious to see how all this would end.

Streets stuck to the steep slopes like Gothic dwarfs. They were arranged one below the other, the cellars of the one gazing over the attics of the next. Their narrow gorges were crowded with miracles of the box-building craft. The storeys of the houses, widening out upward, rested on protruding beams and, almost touching roofs, reached out hands to one another over the roadway. There were no pavements. In some roads it was impossible for two people to pass.

Suddenly I realised that Lomonosov's five years of trudging over these same cobbles must have been preceded by a day when he entered this town for the first time with a letter for Leibniz's disciple Christian Wolff, and when he did not yet know anyone here.[47] It is not enough to say that the town had remained unaltered since that day. One must understand that in those days too it may have been just as unexpectedly tiny and ancient. And one could turn one's head and experience the shock of exactly repeating a bodily movement from terribly far away. Scattered at one's feet with its whole blue-grey swarm of slate roofs, the town, just as in Lomonosov's time, resembled a flock of doves bewitched in mid-swoop towards a moved feeding-rack. I shivered as I celebrated the two-hundredth anniversary of someone else's neck muscles. Then I came to myself, saw that a stage-setting had become actuality and set off to look for the cheap hotel recommended by Samarin.

PART TWO

1

I took a room at the edge of the town. It was in one of the last houses along the Giessen road. At this spot the chestnut trees planted along it, shoulder to shoulder as if by command, wheeled about to the right, the whole column of them. The highway glanced back one last time at the sullen hill with the small ancient town, and disappeared behind the forest.

The room had a dismal little balcony looking out on the next-door kitchen garden. The carriage of an old Marburg horse-tram stood there, taken off its axles and turned into a hen coop.

The room was let by an old woman, a civil servant's widow. She lived with her daughter on her meagre widow's pension. Mother and daughter were as alike as two peas. As always happens when women are afflicted with goitre, they kept catching my glance which was furtively directed at their collars. At such moments I was calling to mind those children's balloons that are gathered into an ear-like tip at one end and tied tightly. Maybe they guessed this.

Through their eyes, which I wished I could let a little air out of by placing my palm on their throats, an ancient Prussian pietism gazed at the world.

Their type, however, was uncharacteristic of this part of Germany. Here another type prevailed, the Middle German, and into nature herself crept the first inklings of a South and a West, the existence of Switzerland and France. Thus, in the presence of her leafy surmises, green at the window, it was most fitting to be leafing through French volumes of Leibniz and Descartes.

Beyond the fields which advanced on the ingenious hen-house, the village of Ockershausen could be seen. This was a long encampment of long barns, long carts and massive shire horses. From there another road trailed along the horizon. As it entered the town it was christened the Barfüsserstrasse. "Barefoots" was what Franciscan monks were called in the Middle Ages.

This must have been the very road by which winter arrived here each year, for if one looked in that direction from the balcony many things appropriate to winter could be imagined. Hans Sachs. The Thirty Years' War. The sleepy, unexciting nature of historical calamity when it is measured not in hours but in decades. Winters, winters, winters and then, when the century had lapsed, a century as deserted as an ogre's yawn, the first arising of new settlements under the vagrant skies, somewhere in the distance of the run-wild Harz, with names as black as the sites of fires—Elend, Sorge and other such names.[48]

At the back, away from the house, flowed the River Lahn, crumpling beneath itself bushes and reflections. The railway line stretched beyond it. In the evenings, into the muffled snorting of the spirit-lamp in the kitchen there would burst the accelerated jingling of a mechanical bell, to whose sound the railway swing-beam would come down by itself. Then a man in uniform would loom up in the dark at the crossing and sprinkle it quickly from a watering can in anticipation of dust, and that very second the train would rush by, convulsively flinging itself up and down and in all directions at once. Sheaves of its thrumming light dropped into my landlady's saucepans. And the milk always got burnt.

Down onto the fluvial oil of the Lahn slid a star or two. In Ockershausen the cattle just driven in were bellowing. Marburg was flashing operatically on the top of the hill. If the Brothers Grimm could have come here once more, as they did a hundred years ago, to study law with the celebrated lawyer Savigny, they would have gone away once again as collectors of fairy tales. Making sure I had the front-door key on me, I set off for the town.[49]

The old-established citizens were already asleep. Only students crossed my path. They all looked as if they were performing in Wagner's *Meistersinger*. The houses, which had seemed a stage-set even in daytime, were pressing still more closely together. The hanging lamps that were strung across the roadway from one wall to the other had no space in which to let themselves go. Their light crashed down with all its might onto sounds. With lily-shaped patches it drenched the noise of receding heels and the explosions of loud German speech. As if the electricity knew the legend about this place.

Long, long ago, some half a thousand years before Lomonosov, when the year one thousand two hundred and thirty was a new year upon earth, just an ordinary year, a living historical person came down these slopes from Marburg castle: Elizabeth of Hungary.

This is so far away that, if imagination ever reaches it, a snowstorm will arise of its own accord at the point of its arrival. It will come about from a process of cooling, by the law of the vanquishing of the unattainable. There, night will set in, the mountains will be clothed in forest, in the forests wild beasts will appear. While human ways and customs will be covered with a crust of ice.

The future saint, canonised three years after her death, had a tyrant for her confessor, that is, a man without imagination. This sober, practical man perceived that the torments imposed on her at confession brought her to a state of rapture. Looking for tortures that would be a real suffering to her, he forbade her to help the poor and the sick. Here legend takes over from history. It says she had not the strength for this. It says that, to whiten the sin of disobedience, a whirlwind of snow screened her with its body on her way down to the lower town, transforming the bread into flowers for the length of her nocturnal journeys.

Thus nature sometimes has to deviate from her laws when a convinced fanatic insists too much on the fulfilment of his own. It does not matter that here the voice of natural law is clothed in the form of a miracle. Such is the criterion of authenticity in a religious epoch.

We have our own, but nature will always be our defender against casuistry.

Flying downhill, the street grew more and more twisted and narrow the nearer it came to the university. In one of the house-fronts, baked in the cinders of the centuries like a potato, was a glass door. It opened into a corridor that led out on to one of the precipitous northern slopes. There was a terrace there, set with little tables and flooded with electric light. The terrace hung above the lowland that once gave so much disquiet to the countess of that land. Since then the town which had become established along the path of her nightly excursions had set firm on the height in the shape it had taken by the middle of the sixteenth century. But the lowland that had harassed her spiritual peace, the lowland that had made her break the rule, the lowland set astir by miracles as before, walked fully in step with the times.

A night dampness wafted from it. Iron rumbled on it sleeplessly and sidings slithered back and forth, now flowing together, now apart. Something noisy was falling and lifting at every moment. Till morning the watery thunder of the dam sustained at one pitch the deafening note it had taken up in the evening. The slashing squeal of the sawmill joined in with the oxen in the slaughterhouse at an interval of a third. Something kept bursting and lighting up, letting out steam and toppling over. Something kept fidgeting and veiling itself with coloured smoke.

The café was frequented chiefly by philosophers. Others had their own cafés. On the terrace sat G- and L-,[50] and Germans who subsequently obtained Chairs in their own country and abroad. Among the Danes, the English women, the Japanese and all those who had come together here from every corner of the world to hear Cohen, a familiar, excitedly melodious voice could now be heard. It was the voice of an advocate from Barcelona, a pupil of Stammler, active in the recent Spanish revolution and now in the second year of continuing his education here—he was declaiming Verlaine to his acquaintances.[51]

Already I knew a number of people in Marburg and was not shy of anyone. Already my tongue had run away with me into two promises and I was anxiously preparing for the days when I would be examined on Leibniz by Hartmann and on one of the parts of the *Critique of Practical Reason* by the head of the school.[52] Already the image of the latter, which for a long time had been a matter of guesswork and had proved to be terribly inadequate at first acquaintance, had become my property, that is it had begun to have an existence of its own within me, altering according to whether it plunged to the bottom of my disinterested enthusiasm or floated up to the surface when with the delirious ambition of the novice I tried to guess if I should ever be noticed by him and invited to one of his Sunday dinners. This was something that immediately raised a person in the local esteem, for it marked the beginning of a new philosophical career.

Already I had confirmed, through him, my sense of how a great inner world can be dramatised when presented by a great man. Already I knew how the shock-headed, bespectacled old man would raise his head and take a step backward as he told of the Greek conception of immortality, and would sweep his arm through the air in the direction of the Marburg fire station as he interpreted the image of the Elysian fields. Already I knew how, on another occasion, he would stealthily creep up on pre-Kantian metaphysics, and would croon away, pretending to woo it, then suddenly utter a raucous bark and give it a terrible scolding with quotations from Hume. How, afterwards, following a fit of coughing and a lengthy pause, he would drawl forth, exhausted and peaceable: "Und nun, meine Herren. . .", which meant he had finished telling the century off, the performance was over, and it was possible to move on to the subject of the course.

Meanwhile, almost no one was left on the terrace. Its electric lights were being switched off. Morning was being revealed. We looked down over the rails and found that the nocturnal lowland had completely vanished. The panorama that had taken its place knew nothing of its precursor in the night.

2

About that time the V- sisters came to Marburg.[53] They belonged to a wealthy family. In Moscow, while I was still at grammar school, I had been friends with the elder girl and had given her occasional lessons in goodness knows what. Or rather, the family had paid me to hold discussions with her on the most unforeseen topics.

But in the spring of 1908 our school-leaving dates coincided and, while preparing myself for the examinations, I undertook at the same time to coach the elder V- girl for them.

The majority of my exam questions were on matters I had thoughtlessly neglected when they were being gone through in class. I had not enough nights to get these subjects up. Nevertheless, off and on, heedless of the hour and oftenest of all at break of day, I would hurry round to V- for the study of subjects that invariably differed from my own because naturally enough the order of the exams in our different schools failed to coincide. Owing to this muddle my position was even more complicated. I didn't notice it. My feeling for V- was not new and I had known about it since I was fourteen.

She was a charming, pretty girl, excellently brought up, and spoiled from infancy by an old Frenchwoman who worshipped her. This old lady knew better than I did that the geometry I was bringing into the house for her favourite at such unearthly hours was more Abelardian than Euclidean.[54] And, cheerfully underlining her own shrewdness, she never absented herself from our lessons. I was secretly thankful for her interference. In her presence my feeling could remain inviolate. I did not judge it and could not be judged by it. I was eighteen. In any case my temperament and upbringing prevented me giving rein to my feelings, nor would I have had the boldness to do so.

It was the time of year when people dissolve paint in little pots of boiling water, and gardens left to their own devices warm themselves idly in the sunshine, cluttered with snow thrown down from everywhere. They are filled to the brink with a bright, quiet water. And overboard, on the other sides of the fences, gardeners, rooks and bell-towers stand in columns along the horizon, exchanging two or three words a day in loud remarks heard right across the town. Against the frame of the ventilation-pane rubs a damp, grey, woolly sky. It is full of undeparted night. It keeps its silence for hours on end, silence, silence, then, all of a sudden, it rolls into the room the rounded rumble of a cartwheel. The rumble stops as abruptly as if this were a game of "magic stick" and the cart had nothing else to do than jump from the roadway in through the window. [55] And now it was no longer "he". And the idle silence was still more mysterious, pouring like spring-water into the hole hewn out by the sound.

I don't know why all this has impressed itself on me in the image of a school blackboard with the chalk not rubbed off properly. Oh, if we had been stopped at that point and the blackboard wiped to a gleaming wetness, and if, instead of theorems about isometric pyramids, we had had expounded to us in copperplate, with careful pressures of the chalk, just what lay ahead of us both. Oh, how stupefied we should have been!

But where does this notion come from, and why does it occur to me here?

Because it was spring, which had completed in rough its eviction of the cold half-year, and all round on the earth, like mirrors not hung up, lakes and puddles were lying face-upward telling how the insanely spacious world had been cleaned and the premises were ready to be let again. Because at that time, to the first who wished for it, it was given to re-embrace and re-live all the life there is upon earth. Because I loved V-.[56]

Because the very *perceptibility* of the present is itself already the future, and the future of the human being is love.

3*

But there exists in the world a so-called elevated attitude towards women. I shall say a little about this. There is the boundless sphere of phenomena which provoke suicides in adolescence. There is the sphere of mistakes made by the infantile imagination, of childish perversions and youthful starvations, the sphere of Kreutzer sonatas and of sonatas written against Kreutzer sonatas.[57] I was in that sphere once and stayed in it a shamefully long time. What *is* it, though?

It tears you to pieces and nothing ever comes of it but harm. Yet there will never be a liberation from it. All those who enter history as human beings will always go through it, for these sonatas, which are the threshold to the only complete moral freedom, are written not by Tolstoys and Wedekinds but—through their hands—by nature herself.[58] And only in their mutual contradictoriness lies the fullness of her purpose.

Having founded matter upon resistance and divided fact from illusion by a dam called love, nature is concerned for the dam's stability, that is for the world's entirety. Here is the point where she goes crazy and starts her morbid exaggerations. It can truly be said that here, at every step, she turns a fly into an elephant.[59]

But excuse me, she makes real elephants too, does she not? It is said to be her main business. Or is that mere talk? Well, what about the history of species? And the history of human names? And the place where she makes them is actually here, in these sluiced-off sections of living evolution, at the dams where her agitated imagination has such free play!

So may it not be said that the very reason we exaggerate in childhood and our imaginations grow disordered is that then we are flies and nature is making elephants of us?

Holding to the philosophy that only the *almost impossible* is real, she has made feeling extremely difficult for everything that lives. She has made it difficult for the animal in one way, for the plant in another. The way she has made it difficult for us shows her breathtakingly high opinion of the human being. She has made it difficult for us not through any sort of mechanical wiles but through what she considers has absolute power for us. She has made it difficult for us through that sense of our fly-like vulgarity which seizes each of us, and the more strongly the further we are from the fly. This is stated with genius by Hans Christian Andersen in his "Ugly Duckling".

All literature about sex and the very word "sex" smack of an intolerable vulgarity and in this lies their purpose. It is solely through this repulsiveness that they are useful to nature, because her contact with us is founded precisely on the fear of vulgarity, and anything not vulgar would fail to strengthen her means of control.

Whatever material our thoughts might supply in this connection, the *fate* of that material is in her hands. And by means of the instinct that she has allocated to us from her own entirety, nature always arranges that material in such a way that all the pedagogues' efforts to make it easier to be natural invariably make it more difficult, and *this is just how it should be*.

This is needed, so that feeling itself should have something to overcome. If not this panic, then another. And it makes no difference *what* filth or nonsense the barrier is composed of. The movement that leads to conception is the purest thing known to the universe. And this purity alone, which has triumphed so many times in the course of the centuries, would be enough to make everything that is not it seem by contrast fathomlessly dirty.[60]

And there is art. Art is concerned not with man but with the image of man. And the image of man, it turns out, is bigger than man. It can be engendered only in motion, and even then not in just any motion. It can be engendered only in the transition from fly to elephant.

What does an honest man do when he speaks *only* the truth? While he is telling the truth, time goes by; in that time, life moves on ahead. His truth has dropped behind, it deceives. So *must* man do the speaking, everywhere and always?

Now in art his mouth is stopped. In art, man falls silent and the image begins to speak. And it turns out that *only* the image can keep up with the progress of nature.

In Russian *vrat'* [to tell lies] means "to say more than is necessary" rather than "to deceive". [61] It is in this sense that art "tells lies". Its image embraces life and does not seek a spectator. Its truths are not depictive but are capable of eternal development.

Art, as it speaks about love through the centuries, is the *only* thing that does *not* put itself at the disposal of the instinct for strengthening the means of impeding feeling. After taking the hurdle of a new spiritual development, a generation preserves the lyric truth and does not reject it, so that from a very big distance one could imagine mankind to be gradually composing itself from the generations in the person of lyric truth.

All this is extraordinary. All this is breathtakingly difficult.

Taste teaches morality, but power teaches taste.

4

The sisters were spending the summer in Belgium. They heard from someone that I was in Marburg. Around the same time they were called to a family gathering in Berlin. They decided to look me up on their way there.

They put up at the best hotel in the little town, in its most ancient quarter. The three days I spent constantly in their company were as unlike my usual life as holidays are unlike workdays. I was endlessly telling them something or other, and was intoxicated by their laughter and by signs of understanding from others who chanced to be around. I took them to places. Both were seen with me at lectures in the university. And so the day of their departure came.

The evening before it, the waiter said to me, as he laid the table for supper, "Das ist wohl Ihr Henkersmahl, nicht wahr?"—that is: "Eat for the last time, it's the gallows for you tomorrow, isn't it?"

In the morning I entered their hotel and ran into the younger sister in the corridor. She looked at me, and, realising something, stepped back without a greeting and shut herself in her room. I went on to the elder sister and in dreadful agitation I said that it could not go on like this any longer and that I begged her to decide my fate. There was nothing new in this except for my insistence upon it. She got up from her chair and backed away from the explicitness of my agitation, which seemed to be advancing upon her. As she reached the wall she suddenly remembered that there existed a means of putting a stop to all this at one blow—and refused me. Soon a noise started up in the corridor. A trunk was being dragged from the neighbouring room. Then came a knock at our door. I hurriedly composed myself. It was time to leave for the station. It was a five-minute walk there.

Once there, the ability to say goodbye abandoned me completely. Just as I realised that I had said goodbye only to the younger sister and had not even begun to say it to the elder, the smoothly gliding express from Frankfurt loomed up at the platform. In virtually a single movement it swiftly gathered up its passengers and swiftly took off. I ran alongside the train, took an extra run at the end of the platform, and jumped up onto the step of the carriage. The heavy door was not slammed shut. A furious conductor barred my way, at the same time holding me by the shoulder so that I should not be so shamed by his remonstrations that—who knows?—I would decide to sacrifice my life. My travellers ran out onto the landing from their compartment. They thrust banknotes at the conductor to rescue me and purchase a ticket. He gave way to mercy and I followed the sisters into the compartment. We sped to Berlin. The fairy-tale holiday went on, scarcely interrupted and tenfold enhanced by the frenzy of movement and a blissful headache from what had just been experienced.

I had leapt onto the moving train solely in order to say goodbye, but again I forgot to say it, and again remembered only when it was too late. I had still not come to my senses when day was gone and evening had come and, pressing us to the ground, the roof of the Berlin station platform was moving up over us with its resonant breathing. The sisters were being met. It was not desirable for them to be seen with me in my disorderly state of emotion. They persuaded me that our farewells had been made and I alone had not noticed. I sank into the crowd, which was gripped by the gas-like roaring of the station.

It was night, a thin rain was drizzling down. I had nothing to do in Berlin. The next train in the direction I needed left in the morning. I could easily have waited at the station for it. But I felt it was impossible to stay among people. My face was jerking and twitching, tears kept coming to my eyes. My thirst for a final and utterly devastating farewell was still unquenched. It was like the need for a great cadenza, which shakes an aching music to its roots so as to remove the whole of it at once with the single pull of its final chord. But this relief was denied me.

It was night, a thin rain was drizzling down. The asphalt outside the station was as smoky as the platform, where the glass of the roofing swelled in its iron like a ball in a string net. The clicking sound interchanged by the streets was like the popping of carbon dioxide. Everything was wrapped in a quiet ferment of rain. Because what had happened was unforeseen, I had on me what I had had when I left home—no coat, no luggage, no documents. I was shown out of hotels at the first glance, with polite excuses about all the rooms being taken. At last I found a place where my travelling so light was no objection. It was the lowest kind of hotel. Alone in the room I sat down sideways on a chair that was standing by the window. Beside it was a table. I dropped my head onto it.

Why do I specify my posture so exactly? Because I spent the whole night in this posture. Now and then, as if at someone's touch, I raised my head and did something to the wall, which slanted widely away from me under the dark ceiling.

As if with a yardstick, I measured it from underneath with a fixed, unlooking stare. Then the sobbing started again. Again I sank my face in my hands.

I have specified the position of my body with such exactitude because this had been its position that morning on the footboard of the flying train, and it remembered it. It was the pose of a person who has fallen from something high that held and carried him for a long time, then let him go, and passed noisily over his head to vanish round a turning for ever.

At last I got to my feet. I looked round the room and flung a window open. Night had gone, the rain hung in a misty spray. It was impossible to say whether it was falling or had stopped. The room was paid for in advance. There was not a soul in the hall. I went away without telling anyone.

5

Only now did something leap to my eyes that had probably started before but had been constantly overshadowed by the proximity of what had happened and by the ugliness of a grown-up person crying.

I was surrounded by changed things.[62] Something not experienced before had crept into the essence of reality. The morning knew me by sight and made its appearance in order to be with me and *never* leave me.

The mist dispersed, promising a hot day. Little by little the town began to move. Carts, bicycles, vans and trains began sliding in all directions. Above them human plans and desires wreathed like invisible plumes. They spread like smoke and moved with the conciseness of familiar parables that are clear without explanation. Birds, houses and dogs, trees and horses, tulips and people had all become shorter and more abrupt than childhood had known them. The fresh laconicism of life revealed itself to me, crossed the road, took me by the hand and led me along the pavement. Less than ever did I deserve brotherhood with this vast summer sky. But there was no talk of that as yet. For the time being, all was forgiven me. Some time in the future I would have to repay the morning for its trust. And everything around was dizzily reliable, like a law that says one never stays indebted for *that* sort of loan.

I got a ticket without any trouble and took my place in the train. There was not long to wait until its departure. Then I was rolling along again from Berlin to Marburg, but now, unlike the first time, I was travelling by day, with a ticket, and was a completely different person. I travelled in comfort on the money borrowed from V-, and an image of my Marburg room kept appearing to my mind's eye.

Opposite me, with their backs to the direction of travel, there sat, swaying in a row and smoking: a man in a pince-nez that was watching its chance to slip off his nose into a newspaper placed close beneath it, a clerk from the Forestry Department with a game bag over his shoulder and a gun at the bottom of the luggage-rack, and another person, and another. They hampered me no more than the Marburg room I could see in my mind. My species of silence hypnotised them. From time to time I broke it on purpose to test its power over them. They understood it. It was travelling with me, I was its attendant and wore its uniform, which was familiar to everyone from his own experience and beloved of everyone. Had this not been so, my neighbours would certainly not have repaid me with their silent sympathy for the way I was courteously slighting them rather than associating with them and not so much sitting in the compartment as posing for it, though without actually posturing. In that compartment there was more kindness and dog-like sensitivity than there was cigar and engine smoke; ancient towns flew up to meet us, and the setting of my Marburg room kept becoming mentally visible to me. What was the reason for this?

About two weeks before the sisters' flying visit, a trifling thing had happened which at that time was far from unimportant to me. I had presented papers in both the seminars.[63] My papers were successful. They received approval.[64]

I was pressed to develop my points in more detail and put them forward before the end of the summer term. I had seized on this idea and begun working with redoubled zeal.

Yet from this very ardour an experienced observer would have diagnosed that I would never make a scholar. I *lived* the study of science more powerfully than is demanded by the subject. A kind of vegetable thinking dwelt in me. Its peculiarity was that any second-rate idea would unfold boundlessly in my interpretation of it and would start demanding sustenance and tending, so that when, under its influence, I turned to books, I was drawn to them not by pure interest in knowledge but by a wish to find literary references in support of my idea. Despite the fact that my work was being accomplished by means of logic, imagination, paper and ink, what I loved it for most was the way it was becoming overgrown, in the course of the writing, by an ever thicker ornamentation of juxtapositions and quotations from books. And because, with the limited time available, at a certain stage I had had to give up copying pieces out and instead started simply leaving the authors open at the pages I needed, a moment arrived when the theme of my work had materialised and could be surveyed by the naked eye from the doorway of my room. It stretched across the room in the likeness of a tree-fern heavily unfurling its coils on desk, divan and window-sill. To disarray these coils meant to disrupt the course of my argument, while to tidy them up completely was tantamount to burning a manuscript of which no fair copy had been made. With utmost strictness the landlady was forbidden to touch them. For some time the room had not been cleaned. And when on my journey I saw this room in my imagination, I was really seeing in the flesh my philosophy and its probable fate.

6

On arrival, I did not recognise Marburg. The hill had grown tall and gaunt, the town looked wasted and black.

The landlady opened the door to me. Looking me up and down, she requested me on future occasions of this kind to give advance notice either to her daughter or to herself. I said I had not been able to warn her because I had suddenly been obliged to go to Berlin very urgently, without coming home first. She looked at me still more mockingly. My sudden appearance from the other end of Germany, as lightly equipped as if from an evening walk, did not fit with her way of thinking at all. It seemed to her a clumsy fabrication. Shaking her head all the time, she handed me two letters. One was sealed, the other a local postcard. The sealed one was from my Petersburg cousin who was unexpectedly in Frankfurt.[65] She wrote to say she was on her way to Switzerland and would be in Frankfurt for three days. The postcard, a third of which was covered with a neat, characterless handwriting, was signed by another hand, only too familiar from the signatures to university notices: Cohen's. It contained an invitation to dinner the following Sunday.

Roughly the following conversation took place in German between myself and my landlady: "What day is it today?"—"Saturday."—"I won't be having any tea. And before I forget. I must go to Frankfurt tomorrow. Please wake me in time for the first train."—"But if I'm not mistaken, the Herr Geheimrat . . . "—"It's all right, I'll manage."—"But that's impossible. At the Herr Geheimrat's they sit down to table at twelve, and you'll . . . " But there was something improper in this solicitude about me. With an expressive glance at the old lady I went to my room.

I sat down on my bed, unable to collect my thoughts, but this lasted hardly more than a minute, after which, mastering a surge of useless regret, I went down to the kitchen and got a dust-pan and brush. I threw off my jacket, pushed up my sleeves and set to work dismantling the jointed plant. Half an hour later, the room was just as it had been the day I arrived, and even the books borrowed from the library did not disturb its orderliness. I had tied them up in four neat bundles so they would be handy when there was a chance to go to the library, and I kicked them right under the bed. At this moment the landlady knocked at my door. She had come to tell me the exact time of the departure of tomorrow's train, by the timetable. At the sight of the change that had taken place she froze to the spot, then suddenly, shaking her skirts, blouse and cap as if puffing out a ball of feathers, she floated towards me through the air, quivering and stiffened. She held out her hand and with wooden solemnity congratulated me on the completion of my difficult work. I did not feel like disappointing her a second time. I left her in her noble delusion.

Then I washed and went out on the balcony, wiping my face. Evening was coming. Rubbing my neck with a towel, I looked into the distance, at the road that joined Ockershausen and Marburg. I could no longer remember how I had gazed in that direction on the evening of my arrival. The end, the end! An end to philosophy, to any thought of it whatever.

Like my fellow-passengers on the train, it too would have to reckon with the fact that every love is a crossing over into a new faith.

7*

It is surprising that I did not go home straight away. The value of the town had lain in its school of philosophy. I no longer needed this. But it turned out to have another.

There exists a psychology of creation, the problems of poetics. Yet what is experienced most immediately in the whole of art is precisely its coming into being, and about this there is no need to make guesses.

We cease to recognise reality. It presents itself in some new category. This category seems to us to be its, not our, condition. Except for this condition everything in the world has been named. It alone is unnamed and new. We try to name it. The result is art.

What is clearest, most memorable and most important about art is its coming into being, and the world's best works of art, while telling of very diverse matters, are really telling about their birth. I first understood this in its whole magnitude in the period I am describing.

Although, all the while I was talking things through with V-, nothing happened that could have altered my situation, our talks were accompanied by much that was unexpected and which resembled happiness. I would despair, she would comfort me. But her mere touch was such bliss that it washed away with a wave of rejoicing the distinct bitterness of what I heard, which was not subject to repeal.

The day's circumstances were like a rapid, noisy rushing to and fro. We seemed to be continually flying full speed into darkness, then flying out again fast as an arrow without pause for breath. Thus, without once stopping to look round, we found ourselves, twenty or so times in the course of the day, in that crowded hold from where time's rowing galley is set in motion. This was none other than the grown-up world for which I had been jealous of V- since childhood, when I had loved her, a schoolgirl, in my schoolboy fashion.

Returning to Marburg, I found I had parted not from the girl I had known for the length of six years but from the woman I had seen a few moments after her refusal of me. My shoulders and hands were no longer my own. Like some one else's, they begged to leave me and enter the fetters by which a human being is chained to a common cause. For now even of her I could not think except in irons, I loved her only as someone in irons, only as a prisoner, only for the cold sweat in which beauty serves its time. Each thought of her instantly joined me to that choral collective which fills the world with a forest of inspired, rote-learned movements and is like battle, like forced labour, like medieval hell and like craftsmanship. I mean that which children do not know and which I shall call the sense of *the present*.

At the beginning of *A Safe-Conduct* I said that love sometimes outstripped the sun. I had in mind that patency of feeling which, every morning, outdistanced the whole of the surrounding world with the reliability of a piece of news just confirmed for the hundredth time. In comparison with this, even sunrise acquired the character of a town rumour still needing to be checked. In other words, I had in mind the patency of a power which outweighed the patency of light.

If I had the knowledge, ability and leisure and were now to decide to write a creative aesthetics, I would construct it upon two concepts—the concepts of power and of symbol. I would show that, as distinct from science, which takes nature in the section of a shaft of light, art is interested in life at the moment when the ray of power *is passing through it*. I would take the concept of power in the same very broad sense in which it is taken by theoretical physics, with the sole difference that it would be a question not of the principle of power but of its voice, its presence. I would explain that, in the context of self-awareness, power is called feeling.

When we imagine that in *Tristan, Romeo and Juliet* and other memorable works a powerful passion is portrayed, we underestimate their content. Their theme is wider than this powerful theme. Their theme is the theme of power.

It is from this theme that art is born. Art is more one-sided than people think. It cannot be directed at will, wherever you wish, like a telescope.[66] Focussed upon reality, which is being displaced by feeling, art is a record of this displacement. It copies it from nature. In what way is nature displaced? Details gain in sharpness, losing independence of meaning. Each one could be replaced by another. Any one of them is precious. Any one, chosen at random, will serve as witness of the state that envelops the whole of transposed reality.

When the signs of this condition are transferred onto paper, the characteristics of life become the characteristics of creation. The latter leap to the eye more sharply than the former. They have been better studied. There is a terminology for them. They are called devices.

As activity, art is realistic, and as fact it is symbolical. It is realistic in that it did not itself invent metaphor but found it in nature and faithfully reproduced it. The transferred sense similarly means nothing in individual examples, but refers to the general spirit of all art, in just the same way as the parts of displaced reality mean nothing if taken separately.

It is by the figure of its whole pull that art is symbolic. Its sole symbol is in the sharpness and non-obligatoriness of images, which characterise it *as a whole*. The interchangeability of images is the sign of the situation in which the parts of reality are mutually indifferent. The interchangeability of images—that is, art—is the symbol of power.

Properly, only power needs the language of material proofs. The other aspects of consciousness are durable without any signs. They have a direct path to the visual analogies of light: number, precise concept, idea. But there is nothing except the mobile language of images, that is, the language of accompanying signs, for power to express itself by, the fact of power, power which lasts only for the moment of its occurrence.

The direct speech of feeling is allegorical, and there is nothing by which it can be replaced.*

8

I went to visit my cousin in Frankfurt and my family who by then had arrived in Bavaria. My brother called on me, then my father did. But I noticed nothing of this. I had radically started writing poetry. Day and night, at any moment at all, I was writing about the sea, the dawn, the southern rain, the coal of the Harz.

Once I was especially carried away. It was one of those nights that just manage to get to the nearest fence and lean there over the earth, worn out and drunk with tiredness. Utter windlessness. The sole sign of life is this black profile of the sky leaning against the wattle fence, drained of strength. And one other. The strong scent of stocks and of flowering tobacco plants, which is the earth's reply to that exhaustion. What cannot the sky be compared to on such a night! The big stars are like a party, the Milky Way is like a large social gathering. But, even more, the chalky streakings across the diagonal expanses of space recall a bed of flowers at night. In it there are heliotropes and gilly-flowers. They have been watered in the evening and pushed sideways. Flowers and stars are so close together it seems the sky itself got under the watering-can and now the stars and the white-speckled grass cannot be disentangled.

I wrote with passionate absorption, and my desk was covered with a different dust than before. That previous, philosophical, dust had accumulated from an act of apostasy. I had trembled for the wholeness of my work. But it was

---

* For fear of misunderstandings, I will repeat: I am speaking not of the material content of art, not about the ways it can be filled, but about the meaning of it as a phenomenon, its place in life. Individual images are visual *per se*, and based on the analogy of light. The individual words of art, like all concepts, live by being known. But the word of art as a whole, which does not submit to quotation, consists in the movement of the allegory itself, and this word speaks symbolically of power. [Pasternak's footnote.]

from solidarity that I did not brush away the present dust, from sympathy with the gravel of the Giessen highway. And at the far end of the desk's oilcloth a long unwashed tea glass shone like a star in the sky.

Suddenly I got up, pierced by the sweat of this idiotic universal dissolving, and began pacing the room. "What a foul trick!" I thought. "Won't he remain a genius for me? Am I breaking with *him*? It's more than two weeks since his postcard came and I started this mean game of hide-and-seek with him. I must give him an explanation. But how can it be done?"

I remembered how pedantic and strict he was. "Was ist Apperzepzion?"[67]— he would ask a non-specialist at the examination, and when the latter translated it from Latin as *durchfassen* (to grasp through), his answer would ring out: "Nein, das heisst durchfallen, mein Herr" (No, sir, it means to fail [fall through]).

The classics were read in his seminars. He would interrupt the reading to ask what the author was driving at. One was expected to snap out the main idea, with a single noun, like a soldier. Not only vagueness was unendurable to him but so was an approximation to the truth instead of the truth itself.

He was somewhat deaf in the right ear. And it was on his right side that I sat when I had to analyse the passage set me from Kant. He let me get well under way and lose myself in the subject, then, when I was least expecting it, disconcerted me with his usual "Was meint der Alte?" (What does the old man mean?)

I do not recall what it was, but suppose on the multiplication table of ideas the right answer was the one to the question "What is five times five?" "Twenty-five", I replied. He frowned and waved his hand to one side. There followed a slight modification of my answer, which failed to satisfy him because of its timidity. Obviously, so long as he prodded into space and appealed to those who knew, my answer kept reappearing in increasingly complex variants. At least, though, we were talking about two and a half tens or, roughly, half a hundred divided by two. But the increasing clumsiness of the answers was the very thing that made him more and more irritated. Yet nobody dared repeat what I had said, after the look of disgust on his face. Then with a movement that seemed to say, "Up to you now, back rows!" he heaved over towards the others. And, in a merry clamour on all sides, calls of sixty-two, ninety-eight, and two hundred and fourteen were heard. He raised his hand, barely calming the storm of jubilant nonsense, and, turning towards me, quietly and drily repeated to me my own answer. There followed a new storm, in my defence. When he had grasped the whole situation, he took a good look at me, patted me on the shoulder, and asked where I came from and how many terms I had spent in Marburg. Then, snorting and frowning, he asked me to go on, repeating all the time, "Sehr recht, sehr richtig. Sie merken wohl? Ja, ja. Ach, ach, der Alte!" (Quite right, quite correct. You see? Aha, the good old fellow!) And I remember a great deal more.

Well, how does one approach such a person? What should I say to him? "Verse?" he would drawl. "Verse!" Had he not studied enough of human untalentedness and its subterfuges? "Verse."[68]

9

All this must have happened in July, as the lime trees were still in flower. The sun was forcing its way through the diamonds of their waxen blooms as if through pieces of kindling glass, and was scorching the dusty leaves with small black circles.

I had often walked past the exercise ground. At noon, dust moved above it like a steamroller and there was a dull noise of something shuddering and clanking. Soldiers were trained there, and during the drill hours sausage-shop boys with trays on their shoulders and schoolboys from the town used to linger in front of the Platz and stare. There was certainly something to look at. Scattered all over the field, spherical dummies like cockerels in sacks were jumping up and down in twos and pecking at each other. The soldiers were wearing quilted jackets and helmets of steel net. They were being taught fencing.

This spectacle was not new to me. During the summer I had looked my fill at it.

Yet on the morning after the night I have described, as I walked into town and was drawing level with the field, I suddenly remembered that less than an hour ago I had seen this field in a dream.

After a night of not deciding what to do about Cohen, I had gone to bed at dawn, slept through the morning and had the dream about the field just before waking. It was a dream of a future war, sufficient, as the mathematicians say—and necessary.

It has long been observed that, however much the regulations dinned into regiments and squadrons keep talking about war-time, the peace-time mind is unable to make the transition from premisses to conclusion. Every day, since no military formation could pass through the narrow streets of Marburg, the chasseurs, pale in their faded uniforms and up to their brows in dust, marched around the town by the road below. Yet the most one could call to mind at the sight of them was the stationers' shops where those same chasseurs were sold by the sheet, with a free pot of glue for every dozen bought.

It was different in a dream. There impressions were not limited by the needs of habit. There it was colours that moved and drew conclusions.

I dreamed of a deserted field and something told me it was Marburg under siege. Pale, lanky Nettelbecks[69] were going by in single file, pushing wheelbarrows. It was some dark hour of the daytime, a kind that does not happen in reality. The dream was in Frederick the Great style, with fortifications of earth and entrenchments. On the battery mounds the outlines of people with field glasses were just distinguishable. They were tangibly enveloped in a kind of silence that does not happen in reality. It pulsed in the air like a blizzard of loose earth, not just being there, but *taking place*. It seemed to be constantly being tossed up from spades. This was the saddest dream of all the dreams I have ever had. I probably wept in my sleep.

What had happened with V- had lodged deep in me. I had a healthy heart. It worked well. Working at night, it would pick up the most accidental and worthless of the day's impressions. And now it had latched onto the exercise ground, and a push from it was enough to set the mechanism of the training field in motion, and the dream itself, on its circular path, quietly chimed, "I am a dream about war".

I don't know why I was going into town, but I was going with such a weight in my soul that my very head seemed packed with earth for fortification purposes.

It was lunchtime. At this hour no one I knew was in the university. The seminar reading-room was empty. Individual houses of the town moved up towards it from below. The heat was pitiless. Here and there at window-sills, drowned people appeared with crumpled collars awry. The half dark of drawing-rooms rose beyond them like smoke. From within came haggard female martyrs, their housecoats looking boiled on their bosoms as if in laundry coppers. I turned towards home, deciding to go by the higher ground, where there were many shady villas under the castle wall.

Their gardens lay prostrate in the furnace of heat, and only the stalks of the roses, which seemed to have come straight from an anvil, stooped haughtily in the slow blue fire. I was musing about a little street that descended steeply behind one of those villas. There was shade there. I knew this. I resolved to turn off into it and have a short rest. What was my astonishment when in the same stupefaction in which I was preparing to settle myself in it, I saw Professor Hermann Cohen already there. He caught sight of me. The retreat was cut off.

My son is in his seventh year.[70] When he doesn't understand a French phrase but simply guesses its meaning from the situation in which it is spoken, he says, "I understand, not from the words but *because*." Full stop. Not because of this or that, but: I *understand* because.

I shall use his terminology and call the mind with which one *arrives* somewhere, as distinct from the mind one takes out riding for the exercise, the *because mind*.

This because mind was the kind Cohen had. Talking to him was quite frightening, going for a walk with him was a serious matter. Beside you, leaning on a stick and moving along with frequent stops, went the very spirit of mathematical physics, which had assembled its basic principles by way of a gait just like this, going step by step. In his roomy frock-coat and his soft hat, this university professor was filled, to a certain strength, with the precious essence that in former times had been bottled in the heads of the Galileos, Newtons, Leibnizes and Pascals.

He did not like talking while he walked but merely listened to his companions' chatter, which was always uneven because of the stepwise structure of the Marburg footpaths. He would stride, listen, suddenly stop, utter something caustic about what he had heard, then, pushing off from the pavement with his stick, would continue his procession up to the next aphoristic breathing-space.

And that was how our conversation went. Mention of my blunder only aggravated it—this he let me know in deadly wordless fashion, by not adding anything to the sarcastic silence of his stick propped on a stone. He inquired as to my plans. He did not approve of them. In his opinion I should stay on until the doctoral examination, take it, and only then return home to take the State examination, with the idea of coming back later to the West, perhaps, and settling there. I thanked him most fervently for this hospitality. But my gratitude told him far less than did my longing for Moscow. In the way I made him a present of it he rightly detected a certain insincerity and silliness, which offended him because, in view of life's enigmatic brevity, he could not bear enigmas that shortened it artificially. And, restraining his irritation, he descended slowly from slab to slab, waiting to see if this person would finally talk sense after such manifest and tiresome trivialities.

But how could I say to him that I was abandoning philosophy irrevocably, that I was going to finish my studies in Moscow like most people, just so as to get them finished, and that a later return to Marburg was not even in my mind? To him, whose final words before his retirement were about fidelity to a great philosophy and were uttered to the university in such tones that, along the benches where a number of young ladies were sitting, there was a flutter of pocket handkerchiefs.

10

At the beginning of August my family moved from Bavaria to Italy and invited me to Pisa. I had run out of funds; there was scarcely enough for my return to Moscow. One evening, no different, I imagined, from many more such evenings ahead of me, I was sitting with G-[71] on our time-honoured terrace, complaining of the sorry state of my finances. He talked it over. At various times he had had occasion to live in real penury, and it was precisely at those times that he had done a lot of roaming around the world. He had been to England and Italy and he knew ways of living on almost nothing while travelling. His idea was that I ought to get to Venice and Florence on the remainder of my money, then go on to my parents for a remedial feed and a fresh subsidy for the return trip, which might even be unnecessary if I were miserly enough with what I had left. He began putting figures down on paper that really did add up to a most modest total.

The head-waiter in the café was friendly with all of us. He knew the ins and outs of all our lives. When at the height of my examinations my brother had come to visit me and had begun to hinder my work during the day, this eccentric fellow discovered in him a rare gift for billiards and got him so interested in the game that he would go to him from morning on, to improve his play, leaving me my room for the whole day.

He took the liveliest interest in our discussion of the Italian plan. Though absenting himself every few moments, he kept coming back and, tapping with his pencil down G-'s estimate, he found even this insufficiently economical.

From one of his absences he hurried back with a thick reference book under his arm, placed on the table a tray bearing three glasses of strawberry punch and, ramming the book open, chased through the whole of it twice, from the beginning and from the end. Having found in the whirl of pages the one he was looking for, he announced that I had to leave that very night by the express departing at three-something a.m., in token of which he proposed that we should all have a drink with him to my journey.

I did not hesitate long. It's true, I thought, following the line of his reasoning. A formal discharge has been received from the university. All the marks of my written work are in order. It is now half past ten. It's no great sin to wake the landlady. There's plenty of time for packing. Right, I'm going.

He was as delighted as if it were he that was to see Basel next day. "Listen", he said, smacking his lips and collecting the empty glasses. "Let's take a good look at each other; that's a custom of ours. It might come in useful, you never can tell what the future holds." I laughed in answer and assured him that this was superfluous for I had done it long ago and would never forget him.

We said goodbye. I went out after G-, and the dim clinking of nickel-plated cutlery fell silent behind us, as it seemed to me then, forever.

Several hours later, having talked ourselves dry and stupefied ourselves with walking about the little town which quickly exhausted its small supply of streets, G- and I went down into the suburb adjoining the station. We were enveloped in mist. We stood in it motionless, like cattle at a watering-place, doggedly smoking with that wordless obtuseness that time and again puts cigarettes out.

Gradually day began to glimmer. Dew, like goose-flesh, tightened the kitchen-gardens. Out of the haze burst forth little beds of satiny seedlings. Suddenly, at this stage in the coming daylight, the town stood outlined, the whole of it at once, on its distinctive height. There, people were asleep. There churches, castle and university stood. But they were still merged with the grey sky like a shred of spiderweb on a damp mop. It even seemed to me that the town had scarcely taken shape before it began dissolving like the trace of a breath cut short a half-pace from a window. "Well, it's time!" said G-.

It was growing light. We walked quickly up and down the stone platform. Pieces of an approaching roar flew into our faces out of the mist, like stones. The train flew in, I embraced my friend and, flinging my suitcase up, leaped into the carriage. The flints of the concrete rolled away like a shriek, the train door clicked, I pressed myself against the window. The train was cutting off in the shape of an arc everything I had been living through and, sooner than I expected, the Lahn, the crossing, the highway and my recent home flashed past, tumbling one upon the other. I tore at the window to get it down. It wouldn't yield. Suddenly it went down by itself with a bang. I leaned out with all my might. The carriage was swaying on a headlong bend; there was nothing to be seen. Farewell philosophy, farewell youth, farewell Germany!

11

Six years passed. When everything had been forgotten. When the war had dragged by and come to an end and the revolution had broken out.

When space, previously the home of matter, had become gangrened with the untruths of life in the rear, and had moulted and grown holes of abstract non-existence. When we were debilitated by a tundra of wet and our soul was bordered by a drawn-out, tinkling State drizzle. When the water had begun to eat the bone and there was nothing to measure time with. When independence, already tasted, had had to be renounced and, at the powerful prompting of things, there came, long before old age, a fall into a new childhood. When I had fallen into it by moving into my parents' home at their request, as their first voluntary apartment-sharer[72]—one low second-storey dusk there crawled out of the darkness and over the snow, to resound in our apartment, a ringing of the telephone from outside time. "Who's there?" I asked. "G-", came the answer. I was not even surprised, it was so surprising. "Where are you?", I forced myself to say, from outside time. He replied. Another absurdity. The place was right next to us, across the courtyard. He was phoning from what had previously been a hotel and was now a Narkompros hostel.[73] A minute later, I was sitting in his room. His wife had not changed in the least. His children I had not known before.

But the unexpected thing was this. It turned out that he had lived on the earth all these years like everyone else, and—though abroad—had lived under the same gloomy war for the liberation of small nations. I learned he had recently come from London. And was either in the party or a fervent supporter of it. He had a job. With the government's move to Moscow, he had been transferred automatically along with the corresponding Narkompros department. This explained his being our neighbour. That was all there was to it.

And I had run to him as to a Marburger. Not, of course, in order to take up life afresh, with his help, from that far-off dawn when we stood in the darkness like cows at a cattle ford—a little more carefully this time, and if possible without a war. No, of course, not for that. But knowing in advance that such resumption is unthinkable, I had run to find out what made it unthinkable in my life. I had run to cast a glance at the colour of my hopeless position, its unfairly personal hue; for a universally shared hopelessness, even when accepted as fair along with everyone else, has no colour and can offer no hope of a way out.

So I had run to look at a living, personal hopelessness, awareness of which would have been a way out for me. But there was nothing to look at. This man could not help me. He was damaged by the damp even more than I was.

Later I had the good fortune to visit Marburg once more. I spent two days there in February 1923. I went there with my wife[74] but did not succeed in bringing it close to her. Thus I was guilty toward them both. But it was hard for me too. I had seen Germany before the war, and now I was seeing it after. What had happened in the world was presented to me in the most terrible foreshortening. It was the period of the occupation of the Ruhr. Germany was cold and starving, deceived about nothing and deceiving nobody, with her hand stretched out to the times like a beggar's (a gesture not her own at all), and the entire country was on crutches.

To my surprise I found my landlady alive. She and her daughter flung their arms up at the sight of me. Both were sitting in just the same places as eleven years ago, sewing, when I appeared. The room was to let. They unlocked it for me. I would not have recognised it but for the road from Ockershausen to Marburg. As before, this was visible from the window. And it was winter. The untidiness of the cold, empty room, the bare willows on the horizon, all this was unusual. The landscape that had once spent too much thought on the Thirty Years' War had ended by prophesying war for itself. Before leaving I went into a cake-shop and sent the two women a large walnut cake.

And now about Cohen. I could not see Cohen. Cohen was dead.

12

So—stations, stations, stations. Stations flying by to the rear of the train like stone moths.

In Basel there was a Sunday quietness, so that you could hear the swallows scraping the eaves with their wings as they flitted about. Glowing walls rolled upward like eyeballs under the slopes of tiled roofs, black as cherries. The whole town was narrowing them and opening them wide like eyelashes. And the same kiln heat that burned in the wild vines on the private houses burned in the ceramic gold of the Primitives in the clean, cool museum.

"Zwei francs vierzig centimes"—the peasant woman in the shop, in her Canton costume, pronounces with an astounding purity, but the place where the two pools of language merge is not here but is over to the right, past a low hanging roof and to the south of it across the free-spreading, hot federal azure, uphill all the way. Somewhere below St Gotthard and, they say, in the depths of night.[75]

And I slept through such a place, tired out by the nightly vigils of a two-day journey! The one night of my life when I ought not to have slept—almost a sort of "Simon, sleepest thou?"[76]—may I be forgiven. Still, there were moments when I did wake up and stand at the window, for disgracefully short minutes, "for their eyes were heavy". At those moments . . .

All around, the hubbub of a peasants' meeting—of peaks crowding together without motion. Aha, so whilst I was dozing and we were drilling our way screw-like from tunnel to tunnel, with whistle after whistle in the cold smoke, we were being surrounded by a breathing that exceeded the breathing we were born to by three thousand metres.

The dark was totally opaque, but echo filled it with a rotund sculpture of sounds. Chasms conversed unashamedly loudly, like old gossips washing the bones of the earth in their talk.[77] Everywhere, everywhere, everywhere, streams were prattling and rumouring and filtering. It was easy to guess how they were hung out over the steeps and were let down into the valley like twisted threads. While, from above, overhanging slopes jumped down onto the train, settled themselves on the carriage roofs and, with shouts to each other, dangling their feet, enjoyed a free ride.

But sleep overcame me and I kept falling into an impermissible slumber on the threshold of the snows, under the blind white Oedipal eyes of the Alps, on the peak of the demonic perfection of the planet. At the level of the kiss which it places here, upon its own shoulder, in love with itself, like Michelangelo's Night.[78]

When I woke, a pure Alpine morning was looking in through the windows. Some obstacle, a landslide or something, had brought the train to a halt. We were asked to cross to another train. We walked along the track of the mountain railway. The ribbon of the line went twisting through disconnected panoramas, as if the path were continually being pushed round a corner like something stolen. My luggage was carried by a barefoot Italian boy who exactly resembled the ones depicted on chocolate wrappings. Somewhere nearby, his flock was making its music. The jingling of the bells fell in lazy shakings, toward and away. Gadflies were sucking the music. Most likely its skin was twitching. There was a fragrance of camomile flowers, and, everywhere, invisibly slapping waters were idly pouring everywhere from hollow to hollow, not ceasing for an instant.

I soon felt the effect of not having slept enough. Though I spent half a day in Milan, I retained nothing of the city. Only the cathedral was dimly stamped on my mind as I walked through the town towards it, its face repeatedly changing according to which crossroads had the turn of revealing it. Like a melting glacier, it kept rising up against the deep-blue vertical of August heat and seemed to be feeding the numerous cafés of Milan with ice and water. When at last a rather small square set me at the cathedral's foot and I craned my neck to look up, it slid down into me with all its choir and the rustling of pilasters and turrets, like a cork of snow sliding down the jointed top of a drainpipe.

But I could hardly stand upright and the first thing I promised myself when I should get to Venice was to have a thoroughly good sleep.

13

When I came out of the station building with its provincial awning in a kind of Customs and Excise style, something smooth slid quietly up to my feet. Something malignantly dark, like slops, and touched by two or three sequins of stars. It was rising and falling almost imperceptibly and was like a painting, darkened with age, in a swaying frame. At first I did not grasp that this depiction of Venice was in fact Venice. That I was in it and this was not a dream.

The Canal by the station went away round a corner, like a blind gut, towards further wonders of this floating gallery upon a sewer. I hurried to the stopping-place of the cheap steamboats which here did the work of trams.

The steamer sweated and panted, wiped its nose and spluttered, and over the same unruffled surface along which it dragged its drowned moustaches the palaces of the Grand Canal floated in a semi-circle, gradually dropping behind us. Palaces are what they are called but they could be called fairy castles and still no words could give an idea of those carpets of coloured marble hung plumb down into the nocturnal lagoon as into the arena of a medieval tournament.

There exists a special Christmas-tree East, the East of the Pre-Raphaelites. There exists the image of a starry night, as in the legend of the adoration of the Magi. There exists an age-old Christmas carving: a gilded walnut, its surface splashed with blue candlewax. There exist the words halva and Chaldea, magicians and magnesium, India and indigo. With these belong the nocturnal colouring of Venice and her watery reflections.

As if to establish its gamut of nuts all the more firmly in the Russian ear, cries ring out on the motor-launch for the passengers' information: "Fondaco dei turchi! Fondaco dei tedeschi!"—as the boat draws in, first to one bank then to another.[79] But of course the names of the quarters have nothing to do with walnuts [funduki], but enshrine recollections of caravanserais once founded here by Turkish and German merchants.

I forget where exactly I saw my first gondola—in front of which one of these innumerable Vendraminos, Grimanis, Corneros, Foscaris and Loredanos,[80] that is—the first gondola to draw my attention. But it was certainly beyond the Rialto. Noiselessly it came out from a side-turning onto the canal, and, at right angles to our path, proceeded to moor at the nearest palace portal. It seemed to have been sent up from backyard to front porch on the rounded belly of the wave rolling slowly forth. Behind it a dark fissure remained, full of dead rats and capering melon peel. Before it a lunar desert streamed in a wide roadway of water. The gondola had a female hugeness, the way everything is huge that is perfect in form and incommensurable with the place its body occupies in space. Its bright crested halberd flew lightly along the sky, carried high by the wave's curving nape. And just as lightly the black silhouette of the gondolier sped among the stars. While the small cowl of the cabin kept vanishing, as if pressed down into the water at the saddle between stern and prow.

Even before coming here I had decided, from what G- had told me about Venice, that the best place to stay would be the quarter near the Academy. So this was where I left the boat. I do not remember whether I crossed the bridge onto the left bank or stayed on the right. I remember a tiny square. It was surrounded by palaces just like the ones on the canal, only greyer and sterner-looking. And their feet rested on solid ground.

The square was flooded with moonlight and in it people were standing or walking about or half-lying down. There were not many of them and they seemed to drape it with moving, slightly moving and unmoving figures. It was an unusually quiet evening. One couple caught my attention. Without turning to face each other, enjoying a shared silence, they were gazing intently into the distance of the opposite bank. Probably they were servants from a palazzo taking a rest. What first attracted me was the calm demeanour of the man-servant, his grizzled close-cut hair, the grey colour of his jacket. There was something un-Italian about these things. There was something northern in them. Then I saw his face. It seemed to me a face I had seen before, I just could not recall where.

I went up to him with my suitcase and expounded to him my concern for shelter, using a non-existent dialect which had formed in me after past attempts to read Dante in the original. He courteously heard me out, thought a little, and asked a question of the housemaid standing beside him. She shook her head negatively. He took out a watch with a lid, looked at the time, clicked it shut, replaced it in his waistcoat and, still thoughtful, with a nod of the head invited me to follow him. From the moonlight-flooded façade we turned a corner into complete darkness.

We walked down narrow stone streets no wider than apartment corridors. Now and again they lifted us up onto short bridges of humpback stone. There the dirty sleeves of the lagoon stretched out on either side, the water in it so densely packed it was like a Persian carpet rolled into a tube and forced with effort into the bottom of a crooked case.

People came towards us over the humped bridges, and the approach of a Venetian woman was heralded long before her appearance by the rapid clicking of her shoes on the stone tiles with which this quarter was paved.

High above us, laid sheer across the pitch-black cracks we were wandering through, shone a bright night sky, forever withdrawing itself. It seemed the down of a dandelion shedding its seeds was scattered all over the Milky Way and it was solely to let in a shaft or two of this moving light that the alleyways occasionally stepped apart to form squares and crossroads. And, surprised by my odd sense of knowing him, I talked away to my companion in the non-existent dialect, lurching from pitch-black to bright down and from down to pitch, while with his help I sought out the cheapest possible lodging.

But on the embankments, at the outlets to the open water, other colours reigned and the quietness gave way to commotion. Arriving and departing motor-launches were crowded with people, and the oil-black water burst in snowy spray like shattered marble, breaking to bits in the mortars of engines now hotly working, now stopping dead. And right next to its gurgling came the vivid hiss of burners in the fruit-merchants' stalls, where tongues were at work and fruits were bouncing and pounding about in absurd columns of a kind of half-cooked compôte.

In the scullery of one of the restaurants by the shore we received useful information. The address we were given sent us back to the start of our pilgrimage. We retraced our whole path in reverse as we walked towards it. So that by the time my guide installed me in one of the hotels near the Campo Morosini, I felt I had just traversed a distance equal to the starry sky of Venice, moving to meet its own contrary movement. If I had been asked then what Venice was—"Bright nights", I would have said, "and tiny squares and peaceful people who seem oddly familiar."

14

"Well, my old friend!" the landlord growled at me, loudly as if I were deaf. He was a sturdy man of some sixty years in a dirty unbuttoned shirt. "I'll fix you up like one of the family." Blood rose to his face, he eyed me with lowered head, and, putting his hands behind the buckles of his braces, he drummed with his fingers on his hairy chest. "Want some cold veal?" he bellowed, not softening his glance and deducing nothing from my reply.

He was, no doubt, a good-hearted fellow who, with his moustaches à la Radetzki, was pretending to be a fearsome monster.[81] He could remember Austrian rule and, as soon became apparent, spoke a little German. But to him this was chiefly the language of Dalmatian sergeant-majors and my fluent pronunciation led him to sad reflections on the decline of the German language since his soldiering days. Besides which he probably suffered from heartburn.

He raised himself up behind the counter as if he were standing on stirrups and bawled something out to someone in a murderous voice, then he came bouncing down into the little yard, where we became acquainted. Several small tables stood there, with dirty cloths on them. "Took a liking to you the moment you came in", he snarled at me with malicious glee and, gesturing to me to take a seat, he sank onto a chair himself two or three tables away. I was brought beer and meat.

The courtyard served as a dining-room. The hotel's guests, if it had any, must have had supper long ago and gone off to their rooms, and only in the very corner of that guzzling-rink one seedy little old man was sitting it out and making obsequious sounds of agreement each time the landlord turned to him.

I had already noticed a couple of times, as I tucked into the veal, how the moist, pink slices were strangely vanishing and reappearing on the plate. Evidently I was falling asleep. My eyelids were sticking together.

All of a sudden, as in a fairy-tale, there appeared at the table a dear little wizened old woman, whom the landlord briefly informed about his ferocious liking for me, straight after which I went up a narrow staircase with her somewhere, then, remaining alone, groped for the bed and lay down in it without another thought, having undressed in the dark.

I woke to a vivid, sunny morning from ten hours of headlong uninterrupted sleep. The fabulous was confirmed. I was in Venice. Tiny patches of reflected brightness swarming on the ceiling as in the cabin of a river steamboat told me that this was so and that now I would get up and run to look at it.

I examined the room where I was lying. On nails hammered into a painted partition hung skirts and blouses, a feather-duster on a ring, and a carpet-beater hooked to its nail by a loop. The window-sill was heaped with tins of ointment. There was a sweet-box with unrefined chalk in it.

Behind a curtain drawn across the whole width of the attic I could hear a shoe-brush knocking and rustling. It had been audible for a long time. They seemed to be cleaning the shoes for the whole hotel. Mixed with this noise was a woman's soft murmur and a child's whisper. In the murmuring woman I recognised my little old lady of the day before.

She was a distant relative of the landlord and worked for him as his housekeeper. He had given up her kennel of a room to me; but when I tried somehow to set this right, it was she who anxiously begged me not to interfere in their family affairs.

Stretching myself before getting dressed, I surveyed everything around me once again and suddenly the events of the previous day were illumined by a momentary gift of clarity. My yesterday's guide had reminded me of the head-waiter in Marburg, the very one who had hoped he might be of use to me again.

Probably a hint of imposition in his request had increased this resemblance still more. So that was the reason why I had instinctively preferred one person in the square to all the others.

The discovery did not surprise me. There is nothing miraculous in this sort of thing. Our most innocent hallos and goodbyes would have no meaning at all were time not threaded through with the unity of life's events, that is, with the criss-crossing effects of the trance of the everyday.

15

And so I too was touched by this happiness. I too had the fortune of discovering that one could go day after day to meet a piece of built-up space[82] as though it were a living personality.

From whichever side you approach the piazza, on every path to it the moment lies in wait when your breathing will quicken, your step will hasten and your feet begin carrying you towards it of their own accord. Whether from the Merceria or from the Telegraph, at a certain moment the road becomes the likeness of a portal, and the square, opening out its own broad-sketched universe, leads forth as to a reception—the Campanile, the Cathedral, the Doges' Palace and the three-sided gallery.

As you gradually grow attached to it, you come to have the sensation that Venice is a city inhabited by buildings—the four just mentioned, and several others of their kind. There is nothing figurative in this assertion. The word spoken in stone by the architects is so lofty that no rhetoric can reach up to it. Besides this, it is all overgrown, as if with seashells, with centuries of travellers' raptures. A growing admiration has forced the last trace of oratory out of Venice. No empty places have remained in the empty palaces. Everything is occupied by beauty.

When Englishmen, before getting into the gondola hired to take them to the station, linger one final moment on the piazzetta in poses that would be natural in a scene of farewell to a living person, you envy them the square the more keenly because, as is well known, no European culture has approached the Italian so closely as the English.

16

Once, beneath these same standard-bearing masts, thronged three centuries interlaced with the generations as with golden threads, magnificently woven into one another, and not far from the square slumbered the fleet of those centuries, a motionless thicket of ships. It seemed to continue the pattern of the city. Rigging thrust forth from behind garrets, galleys peeped through, movements were alike on dry land and on board the ships. On a moonlit night some three-decked vessel, standing across a street, would weld the whole street with the dead thunder of its onslaught arrested at full blast. And in that same funereal grandeur, frigates stood at anchor, picking out from beyond the port the quietest and deepest halls. For those times it was a very powerful fleet. Its numerical strength was amazing. In the fifteenth century it already numbered nearly three and a half thousand trading vessels alone, not counting the military ones; and seventy thousand seamen and shipworkers.

This fleet was the unfictitious reality of Venice, the prosaic underpinning of her fairy-tale quality. One might say, as a paradox, that its swaying tonnage constituted the city's *terra firma*, its landed stock, the subterrain of its commerce and prisons. Captive air pined in the snares of the rigging. The fleet was oppressive and wearisome. But, just as between a pair of communicating vessels, something responsive and redeeming rose from the shore on a level with its pressure. To understand this is to understand how art deceives its client.

The word "pantaloons" has a curious derivation. At one time, before its later meaning of "trousers", it meant a character in Italian comedy. But still earlier, in its original meaning, *pianta leone* expressed the idea of Venetian victoriousness and meant: the hoister of the lion (on the flag), that is—in other words—Venice-Victrix. There is even something about this in Byron, in *Childe Harold:*

> *Her very byword sprung from victory,*
> *The "Planter of the Lion", which through fire*
> *And blood she bore o'er subject earth and sea.*[83]

Concepts are reborn in remarkable ways. When we have grown accustomed to horrors, they become the foundations of good taste. Shall we some day understand how the guillotine could for a while be the model for a lady's brooch?

The emblem of the lion has figured in Venice in many different ways. Thus the hinged slot for secret denunciations on the stairway of the Censors, next to murals by Veronese and Tintoretto, was carved in the form of a lion's jaws. It is well known what terror this *bocca di leone*[84] inspired in people of that time, how it gradually became a sign of ill-breeding to mention the persons who had mysteriously disappeared into the exquisitely carved slot, in cases when the authorities themselves expressed no regret on their account.

When art raised palaces for enslavers, people trusted it. They thought it shared the general opinions and would share the general fate in the future. But this is just what did not happen. The language of the palaces turned out to be the language of oblivion and certainly not the pantaloon language mistakenly ascribed to them. The pantaloon purposes have disintegrated; the palaces have remained.

And Venetian painting has remained. From my childhood I was acquainted with the taste of its hot springs, through reproductions and in the museums' exported over-flow. But it was necessary to get to their birthplace to see—as distinct from particular pictures—painting itself, like a marsh of gold, like one of the primal pools of creativity.

17*

I looked at this spectacle more deeply and more diffusely than my present formulations of it will convey. I did not try to make conscious sense of what I saw in the way I am now interpreting it. But over the years the impressions have settled in me in this form by themselves, and in my condensed conclusion I shall not move away from the truth.

I saw which observation is the first to strike the pictorial instinct. How one suddenly understands what it is like for the visible when it begins to be seen. Once noticed, nature moves aside with the obedient spaciousness of a story and, in this condition, like someone asleep, is carried quietly onto the canvas. One has to see Carpaccio and Bellini to understand what is depiction.

I learned, further, what syncretism accompanies the flowering of craftsman-ship when the artist becomes one with the pictorial element and it becomes im-possible to say which of the three is most active upon the canvas and for whose benefit: the performer, the performed or the object of the performance. This confusion is what makes those misapprehensions possible by which the age, as it poses for the artist, is able to imagine it is raising him up to its own transitory greatness. One has to see Veronese and Titian to understand what is art.

Finally, although at the time I did not sufficiently value these impressions, I learned how little is needed for a genius to explode. All around are the lions' mouths which seem to be everywhere, thrusting into all intimacies, sniffing at everything—lions' jaws secretly swallowing one life after another in their dens. All around is the lions' roar of an imaginary immortality which is thinkable with-out laughter only because everything immortal is in its hands and is attached to its strong leonine lead. Everyone feels this, everyone endures it. To sense *only this* there is no need for genius: it is seen and endured by all. But if it is endured by everyone at once, that means there must be something in this menagerie that is sensed and seen by *no one*.

This is the drop that makes the genius's cup of endurance overflow. Who will believe it? The oneness of depiction, depicter and depicted object, or, more broadly,[85] indifference to the immediate truth: this is what puts him in a fury. As if a slap in the face were given to mankind in his person. And his canvases are invaded by a storm that purifies the chaos of craftsmanship with defining blows of passion. One has to see the Michelangelo of Venice—Tintoretto—to understand what is a genius, what is an artist.[86]

18

But I did not go into these subtleties then. Then, in Venice, and more strongly still in Florence, or, to be finally precise, in Moscow in the winters following my journey, other, more specific, thoughts entered my head.

The chief thing each person carries away from an encounter with Italian art is a sensation of the palpable unity of our culture, wherever he may have seen this and whatever name he may give it.

How much has been said, for instance, about the paganism of the humanists, and what different things have been said—that it is a legitimate tendency and that it is an illegitimate one. And indeed, the collision of the faith in resurrection with the age of the renaissance is an extraordinary phenomenon, central to the whole of European culture. Who has not also noticed the anachronism, often immoral, in the way canonical themes are treated in all these *Presentations, Ascensions, Weddings in Cana* and *Last Suppers,* with their *grand-monde* licentiousness and luxury?

It was in this very incongruity that the thousand-year-long peculiarity of our culture made itself known to me.

Italy crystallised for me what we unconsciously breathe in from infancy. Her painting itself finally accomplished for me the thought I had still to think about her, and while I went day after day from collection to collection, it flung at my feet a ready-made observation, thoroughly rendered down in pigment.

I understood, for instance, that the Bible is not so much a book with a stable text as the notebook of mankind, and that everything everlasting is like this. That it is alive not when it is compulsory but when it is receptive to all the similitudes with which the ages issuing from it look back at it. I understood that the history of culture is a chain of equations in images which link in pairs each new unknown with something already known; whereby the known, constant for the whole series, is the legend set at the foundation of the tradition, and the unknown, new each time, is the actual moment in the flow of culture.

This is what interested me at that time, this is what I then understood and loved.

I loved the living essence of historical symbolism, in other words that instinct with whose help, like salangane swallows,[87] we have built the world: a vast nest, stuck together from earth and sky, life and death, and two kinds of time, present and absent. I understood that what prevents it from falling apart is the force of cohesion contained in the figurativeness permeating all its particles.

But I was young and did not know that this does not encompass the fate of a genius and his nature. I didn't know that his essence rests in the experiencing of an actual biography and not in a symbolism refracted in images. I didn't know that, as distinct from the Primitives, his roots lie in the coarse immediacy of moral sentience. One peculiarity of his is remarkable. Though all the flarings of the moral passion are acted out within the culture, it always seems to the rebel that his rebellion goes rolling along the street beyond its fence. I didn't know that the longest-lived images are left untouched by the iconoclast in those rare cases where he is not born with empty hands.

When Pope Julius II expressed displeasure at the chromatic poverty of the Sistine ceiling, Michelangelo, to justify himself, remarked with reference to the ceiling, which represents the creation of the world with appropriate figures: *"In those days* they did not dress up in gold. The people shown here were *not very rich."* Such is the thunderous and child-like language of this type.

Culture's boundary is reached by the person who hides within himself a tamed Savonarola. The untamed Savonarola destroys it.[88]

19

The evening before my departure there was a concert with illuminations on the piazza, such as were often held there. The façades enclosing it were decked from head to foot with the sharp points of light-bulbs. It was lit up on three sides by a black and white banner. The faces of the listeners under the open sky were steamed in a bath-like brightness as if in a closed, magnificently illumined hall. Suddenly from the ceiling of the imaginary ballroom a gentle rain began to fall. And suddenly stopped again, having hardly begun. The reflected glow of the illuminations seethed in a colourful haze above the square. Like a rocket of red marble the bell-tower of San Marco cut into the pink mist half clouding its summit. A little way off swirled a dark-olive steam and in it the five-headed frame of the cathedral was hidden like something in a fairy-tale. That end of the square was like an underwater kingdom. The cathedral door shone with the golden glitter of the four horses that had come galloping fast from ancient Greece and had halted there as on the edge of a precipice.

When the concert was over, a millstone of steady shuffling became audible; it had been revolving all the time round the circle of the galleries but until then had been muffled by the music. It was the ring of strollers, whose footsteps were resounding and merging together like the rustle of skates in the frozen bowl of an ice rink.

Among the strollers, women passed with rapid, angry gait, more menacing than seductive. They glanced over their shoulders as they walked, as if to repulse and annihilate. Curving their bodies challengingly, they quickly vanished beneath the porticoes. When they looked round, you were stared at by the mortally mascara'd face of a black Venetian head-scarf. Their quick gait in *allegro irato* time strangely corresponded to the black shivering of the illuminations among the white scratches of diamond lights.

Twice I have tried to express in verse the sensation that for me is forever connected with Venice.[89] In the night before my departure I was wakened in the hotel by an arpeggio on a guitar which broke off the moment I awoke. I hurried to the window, under which water was splashing, and peered intently into the distance of the night sky as if there might still be a trace of the instantly silenced sound. From the way I gazed, an observer would have said I was still half asleep and was looking to see whether some new constellation had arisen over Venice, having a dimly ready notion of it as the Constellation of the Guitar.

PART THREE

1

In the winters the chain of boulevards cut through Moscow behind a double curtain of blackened trees. Lights gleamed yellow in the houses like small star-shaped circles of lemons sliced through their centres. Blizzardy sky hung down low on the trees, and, all around, everything white was blue.

On the boulevards poorly dressed young people were hurrying along, bending as if they were going to butt. Some of them I was acquainted with, most of them I did not know, but all of them together were my coevals, that is to say the countless faces of my childhood.

They had just begun to be addressed by their patronymics,[90] endowed with rights and initiated into the secret of the words "possess", "profit", "acquire". They displayed a haste that is worthy of closer analysis.

In the world there is death and foreknowledge. The unknown is dear to us, the known in advance is terrifying, and every passion is a blind leap aside from the approaching inevitability. Living species would have nowhere to exist and repeat themselves if passion had nowhere to leap to off the common path along which rolls the common time, the time of the gradual demolition of the universe.

But life does have somewhere to live and passion somewhere to leap, because alongside the common time there exists an unceasing infinity of road-side arrangements, which are reproduced immortally, and every new generation is one of these.

Young people, bending as they ran, hurried through the blizzard, and although each one had his own reasons for haste they were spurred along by something they had in common more than by all their personal promptings, and that was—their historical wholeness, their surrender to the passion with which mankind, escaping from the common path and avoiding its end for yet one more innumerable time, had just sped into them.

And to screen from them the duality of their run through inevitability, and so that they should not go mad, abandon what they had begun and hang themselves, the whole earth's globe of them, a power kept watch behind the trees on all the boulevards, a much tested and terribly experienced power which accompanied them with its intelligent eyes. Behind the trees stood art, which understands us so splendidly that one always wonders from what non-historical worlds it has brought its ability to see history in silhouette. It stood behind the trees, terribly similar to life, and was endured in life because of this likeness, as portraits of wives and mothers are endured in the laboratories of scholars dedicated to natural science, that is to the gradual solution of death.

What kind of art, then, was it? It was the youthful art of Scriabin, Blok, Kommissarzhevskaia,[91] Belyi—advanced, gripping, original. And so astounding that not only did it not call up thoughts of replacing it but, just the contrary, one wanted to make it more stable by repeating it all from the foundation up, only more strongly, more hotly, more wholly. One wanted to re-say it all in a single breath, which was unthinkable without passion, but passion kept leaping aside, and in this way the new came into being. But the new did not come to take the place of the old, as is usually supposed—on the contrary, it arose in an enraptured reproduction of the model. That is the kind of art it was. And what kind of generation was it?

The boys close to me in age were thirteen years old in 1905,[92] and twenty-one just before the war. Their two critical periods coincided with two red-letter dates in our country's history. Their boyish maturity and their coming of call-up age straight away became welds for a transitional epoch. Our age is stitched through and through with their nerves and has been obligingly put by them at the disposal of old men and children.

To characterise them fully, however, one must bear in mind the state system whose air they breathed.

Nobody knew it was Charles Stuart or Louis XVI on the throne.[93] Why is it that final monarchs seem to be monarchs in the fullest sense of the word? There is evidently something tragic in the very essence of hereditary power.

A political autocrat takes up politics only in those rare cases where he is a Peter.[94] Such examples are exceptional and are remembered for thousands of years afterwards. More often nature limits the sovereign all the more firmly in that she is not parliament and the limits she sets are absolute. In the form of a centuries-hallowed rule, the name "hereditary monarch" is given to a person who is obliged to live through, ceremonially, one of the chapters of a dynasty's biography—that is all. Sacrificial custom survives in this, more starkly than in a bee-hive.

What happens then to people of this terrible vocation if they are not Caesars, if their experience does not boil over as politics, if they lack genius—the one thing that could free them from their life's fate in favour of a post-humous fate?

Instead of gliding they slip, instead of diving they sink, instead of living they accustom themselves to trivialities which reduce life to a mere decorative vegetating. At first these trivialities are hourly, then minute-by-minute; first they are genuine, then imaginary; first the accustoming takes place without external help, then with the help of table-turning.[95]

When they see a cauldron, they fear its gurgling. Ministers assure them it is all in the order of things and that the more perfect the cauldrons the more frightening they are. A technique of state reforms is expounded which consists in the conversion of heat energy into motor energy and which declares that states flourish only when they threaten explosion yet do not explode. Then, screwing up their eyes from fear, they take the handle of a whistle and, in all their innate gentleness, organise a Khodynka, a Kishinev pogrom, a Ninth of January,[96] and walk away shyly to their family and briefly interrupted diary.

Ministers clasp their hands to their heads. It finally becomes clear that vast territories are being governed by small minds. Explanations are vain, counsels do not reach their goal. The latitude of abstract truth is not once experienced by them. They are slaves of what is nearest to hand and most obvious, they draw conclusions from like to like. It is too late to re-educate them, the dénouement approaches. People submit to a notice of dismissal and leave them to its mercy.

They see its approach. They rush away from its threats and demands to whatever is most alarming and demanding in their home. The Henriettas, Marie-Antoinettes and Alexandras are given more and more of a voice in the terrible choir.[97] They estrange the progressive aristocracy from themselves, as though the market-place were interested in the life of the palace and were demanding that it reduce its comfort. They turn towards gardeners from Versailles, lance-corporals from Tsarskoe Selo, autodidacts from the common people, and then the Rasputins float to the surface and rapidly rise,[98] along with the monarchy's never-acknowledged capitulations to the people—which it thinks of as the "folk"—and concessions to the spirit of the time, wildly contrary to everything required of true concessions, for these concessions are made solely to their own detriment without the slightest benefit to anyone else; and usually it is this particular absurdity that lays bare the doomed nature of the terrible vocation and decides its fate, and—by the tokens of its weakness—itself gives the provoking signal for an uprising.

When I came back from abroad it was the centenary of the war of the Fatherland. The Brest line had been renamed the Alexandrovsky.[99] Stations were whitewashed, the guards who rang the bell were dressed in clean shirts. The Kubinka station building was stuck all over with flags, extra guards stood at the doors. An imperial inspection was taking place nearby and on account of this the platform shone with a vivid profusion of loose sand not yet trodden down everywhere.

For travellers this did not arouse recollections of the events being celebrated. In the jubilee decorations one sensed the reign's chief characteristic: indifference to its own history. If anything was affected by the festivities it was not the movement of people's thoughts but the movement of the train which was stopped at stations for longer than the timetable required and was held up in the countryside by signals oftener than usual.

I could not help thinking of Serov, who had died the previous winter, and his stories of the time when he was painting the Tsar's family; caricatures made by artists at the Iusupovs' sketching evenings; odd incidents that had accompanied the Kutepov edition of *The Tsar's Hunt*; and many trifles relevant to this moment and connected with the school of painting which was under the control of a Ministry of the Imperial Court and in whose building we had lived for some twenty years.[100] I might have recalled the year 1905 as well, the drama in the Kasatkin family[101] and my own half-baked revolutionism, which went no further than braving a Cossack whip and its lash on the back of a quilted overcoat. And finally, as for the guards, stations and flags, they too of course heralded a most serious drama and were not at all the innocent vaudeville act my shallow apoliticism saw in them.

The generation was apolitical, I might have said, were I not aware that the tiny part of it I came in contact with is not even enough to judge the whole intelligentsia. This was the side of itself, I shall say, that it turned towards me, but it was also the side that it turned towards the age when it came forth with its first declarations of a science, a philosophy and an art of its own.

2

But culture does not fall into the arms of the first comer. All the things I have listed had to be won by battle. The notion of love as a duel belongs here too. Art could pass across to the adolescent only as the result of a militant attraction experienced as a personal event in all its excitement. The literature of the beginners abounded in symptoms of this condition. The novices formed groups. The groups divided into epigonic and innovatory.[102] These were the parts—inconceivable in isolation—of that upsurge which had been so persistently subjected to guesswork that it already permeated everything with the atmosphere of a romance no longer merely expected but actually happening. The epigones represented an impetus without fire or gift, the innovators—a militancy moved solely by an emasculated hatred. These were the words and gestures of a serious conversation overheard by an ape[103] and spread in all directions, in bits, disjointed and verbatim, with no idea of what meaning inspired the storm.

Meanwhile the fate of the conjectural poet-elect already hung in the air. It was almost possible to say what kind of person he would be, though not yet possible to say who it would be. To judge by appearance, dozens of young people had the same restlessness, thought the same thoughts, made the same claims to originality. As a movement the innovators were distinguished by an apparent unanimity. But, as in movements of every age, this was the unanimity of lottery tickets whirling and swarming in the mixing drum. The fate of the movement was to remain forever as a movement, that is as a curious case of the mechanical shifting of chances, from the moment one of the tickets, coming away from the lottery wheel, would blaze up with the fire of winning, of conquest, of having a face and the significance of a name. The movement was called "futurism."

The conqueror and the justification of the draw was Mayakovsky.[104]

3

We became acquainted in the constrained circumstances of group prejudice. Long before this, Iulian Anisimov had shown me his poems in *A Trap for Judges*, the way one poet displays another. But that was in the epigonic circle, Lirika, for the epigones were not ashamed of their sympathies and in their circle Mayakovsky had been discovered as a phenomenon of great promise and imminence, like some huge bulk.[105]

But in the innovators' group, Centrifuga, of which I became a member shortly after, I learned (this was in the spring of 1914) that Shershenevich, Bolshakov and Mayakovsky were our enemies and that we were due to have a far from jocular confrontation with them.[106] The prospect of a quarrel with someone who had already made an impression on me and was attracting me more and more from the distance did not surprise me in the least. Here lay the whole originality of the innovators. The birth of Centrifuga had been accompanied all winter by interminable brawls. All winter I did nothing but play at group discipline, sacrificing to it conscience and taste. Now once again I got ready to betray whatever was required when the moment came. But this time I overestimated my strength.

It was a hot day at the end of May, and we were already sitting in the tea-room on the Arbat when the three I have mentioned came in noisily and youthfully from the street, handed their hats to the porter, and, without moderating the sonorousness of their talk, until then drowned out by trams and carts, made their way towards us with unforced dignity. They had beautiful voices. The later declamatory style in poetry had its beginning here. Their clothes were elegant, ours were slovenly. In all respects the enemy's position was superior.

While Bobrov[107] was having a wrangle with Shershenevich—the essence of which was that they had taunted us on one occasion and we had replied still more coarsely and an end had got to be put to all this—I was watching Mayakovsky, not taking my eyes off him. I think it was the first time I had seen him so closely.

The way he said "e" for "a", setting his diction rocking as with a piece of sheet-iron, was the trait of an actor. One could easily imagine his deliberate abruptness as the distinguishing characteristic of other professions and statuses. He was not the only one who was striking. Beside him sat his comrades. One of them acted the dandy like him, the other, like him, was a genuine poet. But all these similarities did not diminish Mayakovsky's exceptionalness, rather they underlined it. As distinct from playing a single role, he played everything at once; as opposed to the playing of roles, he played—life. This could be sensed at first glance, without the least thought of what his end would be. This was what was riveting about him, and frightening.

Although everyone, when they walk or stand, can be seen at their full height, yet this fact seemed a miracle when Mayakovsky made his appearance and it caused everyone to turn and look at him. The natural seemed in his case supernatural. The reason was not his height but another, more general and more elusive quality. More than other people are, he was wholly contained in his manifestation. There was as much expressed and definitive in him as there is little of it in the majority, who emerge rarely and only under some special shock from the murk of half-fermented intentions and unrealised suppositions. He existed as if on the day after an enormous spiritual life, lived on a large scale and stored up ready for all eventualities, and now everyone met him sheafed in its irreversible consequences. He sat in a chair as if it were the saddle of a motorcycle, he bent forward, cut and rapidly swallowed a Wiener schnitzel, he played cards with sidelong glances, not turning his head, he strolled majestically along the Kuznetsky, he droned out dully and nasally, like fragments of the liturgy, specially profound lines of his own and others' work: he scowled, grew, travelled, appeared in public, and in a depth behind all this, as behind the upright stance of a skater going at full speed, there was a perpetual dim image of the one day preceding all his days when the amazing initial run had been taken which had straightened him up so largely and uninhibitedly. Behind his way of behaving one sensed something like a decision once it has been acted on and its results can no longer be revoked. Such a decision was his own genius, the encounter with which had once so astonished him that it became for him a thematic prescription for all time and he gave himself up wholly to its embodiment without pity or hesitation.

But he was still young and the forms this theme was to take still lay ahead. However, the theme was insatiable and endured no putting off. Therefore, at the beginning, in order to please it, he was obliged to anticipate his future, and anticipation realised in the first person is posing.

From these poses, which are natural in the world of the highest self-expression, like the rules of propriety in everyday life, he selected the pose of an outward integrity, the hardest for an artist and the noblest in relation to friends and intimates. He kept up this pose with such perfection that it is now practically impossible to say what lay beneath it.

And yet the mainspring of his lack of shyness was a wild shyness, and under his pretended will-power lay hidden a phenomenally suspicious lack of will, an inclination to causeless gloom. The mechanism of his yellow blouse was just as deceptive.[108] With it he was fighting not the jackets of the bourgeoisie but the black velvet of the talent inside himself, whose cloying black-browed forms had begun to disturb him earlier than happens to less gifted people. For no one knew as he did all the vulgarity of the natural fire before it is roused to fury by gradual dousings with cold water; or knew as he did that the passion which suffices for the continuation of the race does not suffice for creation, and that this needs a passion sufficient to continue the race's *image*, one, that is, which inwardly resembles the Passion and whose newness inwardly resembles the Divine Promise.

The parley ended abruptly. The enemies we were supposed to annihilate went away untrampled. Rather, the peace terms arrived at were humiliating to us.

Meanwhile it had grown darker outside in the streets. It had started to drizzle. In our enemies' absence the tea-room seemed drearily empty. Flies became noticeable along with the half-eaten cakes and the glasses blinded with hot milk. But the thunderstorm did not take place. Lushly the sun struck at the pavement netted with little mauve spots. It was May of the year 1914. The vicissitudes of history were so near. But who thought of them? The crass town glowed with enamel and tinfoil, as in "The Golden Cockerel".[109] The poplars' lacquered green was glittering. For the last time, colours had that poisonous grassiness they were shortly to part with forever. I was crazy about Mayakovsky and already missing him. Do I need to add that the ones I betrayed were *not* the ones I had meant to?

4

Chance brought us together the following day under the awning of the Greek café. The large yellow boulevard lay flat, spreading between the Pushkin monument and Nikitsky Square. Lean dogs with long tongues lay yawning, stretching and laying their muzzles more comfortably on their front paws. Gossipy pairs of nannies were chattering away, continually bewailing something or other. Butterflies would fold their wings for a moment and melt away in the heat, then suddenly open out again, lured sideways by irregular waves of sultry heat. A small girl in white, who must have been wet through, hung in mid-air as she whipped her whole body by the heels with a skipping-rope's whistling circles.

I caught sight of Mayakovsky from a distance and pointed him out to Loks. He was playing heads or tails with Khodasevich.[110] At that moment Khodasevich got up, paid what he had lost, and, leaving the awning, went off in the direction of Strastnoi Boulevard. Mayakovsky remained at the table alone. We went in, greeted him, and got into conversation. After a while he offered to recite something.

The poplars were green, the lime trees a dryish grey. Driven out of all patience by fleas, the drowsy dogs kept jumping up on all four paws at once, calling Heaven to witness their moral impotence against brute force, then dropping to the sand again in a state of indignant sleepiness. Throaty whistles were uttered by engines on the Brest railway, now renamed the Alexandrovsky line, and all around us hair was being cut and whiskers shaved, baking and roasting were going on, people were selling things and moving about—and were wholly unaware.

It was the tragedy *Vladimir Mayakovsky*, which had just come out.[111] I listened with overwhelmed heart and held breath, oblivious. I had never heard anything like it before.

Everything was in it. Boulevard, dogs, poplars and butterflies. Hairdressers, bakers, tailors and steam engines. What is the use of quoting? We all remember this sultry, mysterious, summery text, now available to everyone in its tenth edition.

Far off, locomotives roared like great whales. The same unconditional distance as there was upon the earth was there in the throaty territory of his creation. This was that unfathomable spirituality without which there is no originality, that infinity which opens out in life from any point and in any direction and without which poetry is just a misunderstanding not yet cleared up.

And how simple it all was! Art was called a tragedy. Which is what it should be called. The tragedy was called *Vladimir Mayakovsky*. The title concealed a discovery which had the simplicity of genius: that the poet is not the author but the object of poetry that addresses the world in the first person. The title was not the name of the author but the surname of the content.

5

Actually I carried the whole of him with me that day from the boulevard into my life. But he was enormous; there was no holding on to him when apart from him. And I kept losing him. Then he would remind me of himself. With *A Cloud in Trousers, Backbone Flute, War and the Universe, Man*.[112] What was weathered away in the intervals was so huge that the reminders too had to be extraordinary. And such they were. Each of the stages I have mentioned found me unprepared.

At each one, he was grown out of all recognition and wholly reborn like the first time. It was impossible to get accustomed to him. So what was so unusual about him?

He possessed relatively constant qualities. My admiration too was comparatively stable. It was always ready for him. It would seem that under such conditions I could have grown used to him without having to make any leaps. Nonetheless, this was how matters stood.

While he existed creatively, I spent four years trying to get used to him but could not do it. Then I got used to him in the two and a quarter hours that were the time taken by the recital and discussion of his uncreative "150,000,000".[113] Then for more than ten years I carried the burden of being used to him. Then suddenly, in tears, I lost it all at once, when he gave a reminder of himself "at the top of his voice", as he had used to do, but now from beyond the grave.[114]

What one could not get used to was not so much him as the world which he held in his hands and which he would now set in motion, now bring to a halt, as the whim took him. I shall never understand what he gained from demagnetising the magnet when the horse-shoe which before had made every imagination rear up on end and had drawn to itself all possible weights "with the [oaken] feet of its lines",[115] now with no apparent change ceased to shift so much as a grain of sand. There can scarcely be another instance in history of someone going so far in a new experience and then—at the hour he himself had predicted, just when that experience, even if at a cost of discomforts, had become so vitally needed—rejecting it so completely. His place in the revolution, outwardly so logical, inwardly so forced and empty, will always be a mystery to me.

What one could not get used to was the Vladimir Mayakovsky of the tragedy, *the surname of its content,* the poet contained in the poetry from time immemorial, the potentiality which the strongest realise—and not the so-called "interesting person".

I had gone home from the boulevard charged with this unaccustomedness. I was renting a room with a window looking out on the Kremlin. From over the river, Nikolai Aseev was likely to turn up at any moment.[116] He would come from the S- sisters, a deeply and diversely gifted family. When he entered I would recognise in him a vivid, dishevelled imagination, an ability to transform frivolity into music, the sensitivity and the guile of a genuine artistic nature. I loved him. He was enthusiastic about Khlebnikov. I cannot understand what he found in me. From both art and life we were looking for different things.

6

The poplars were green, and reflections of gold and of white stone were running like lizards over the water of the river when I rode past the Kremlin to the Pokrovka on my way to the station and from there with the Baltrushaitises to the

Oka in the province of Tula. There, right next to us, lived Viacheslav Ivanov.[117] The other dachas too were occupied by people from the artistic world.

Lilac was still in bloom. It had run far out onto the road and had just arranged a lively welcome on the broad drive leading into the estate, lacking only the music and the bread-and-salt. Beyond it an empty yard, trodden down by cattle and overgrown with patchy grass, sloped down a long way towards the houses.

It promised to be a hot, rich summer. I was translating Kleist's comedy *The Broken Jug*[118] for the Chamber Theatre, which had then come into existence. There were a lot of snakes in the park. People talked about them every day. They talked about snakes while eating fish soup and while bathing. And whenever I was asked to say something about myself, I would start talking about Mayakovsky. This was no mistake. I had made a god of him. In him I personified my spiritual horizon. Viacheslav Ivanov was the first, as I remember, to compare him to the hyperbolism of Hugo.

7

When war was declared, the weather changed for the worse, it began to rain a good deal, the women's first tears began falling. The war was still new and quakingly terrible in its newness. People did not know what to do with it; they entered it like very cold water.

The passenger trains by which the local men travelled from the *volost'* to the assembly centres departed by the old timetable.[119] The train would set off and a surge of lamentation would roll in pursuit of it, banging its head against the rails and not resembling weeping at all, unnaturally tender and bitter like the rowanberry. Someone's arms would gather up an elderly woman warmly wrapped in unsummery clothes. And the relatives of the recruit would take her away, uttering short sounds of exhortation, under the arches of the station.

This keening, which was kept up only in the first months, was wider than the grief of the mothers and young wives that streamed forth in it. It was introduced all along the line like an emergency measure. Stationmasters touched their caps as it travelled past; telegraph poles made way for it. It transformed the region and was visible from every side in a pewter icon-setting of foul weather, because it was a thing of burning vividness which people had got unused to and had not touched since previous wars but had taken out of storage just the night before, brought to the train on horseback in the morning, and, when they had led it by the arms under the arches of the station, would take home again through the bitter mud of a country road.

But the soldiers who went in ready-formed marching units straight to the very heart of the terror were met and seen off without any wailing. In their tightly fitting clothes they jumped down onto the sand from the high goods trucks, not at all in the manner of peasants, ringing their spurs and trailing their crookedly flung-on greatcoats in the air. Others stood by the planks fixed across the truck doors and gave a few slaps to the horses digging into the filthy wood of the rotting floor with haughty hoof-blows. The platform was giving away no apples, had plenty of cheeky answers and grinned into the corners of tightly pinned kerchiefs, blushing crimson.

September was ending. Garbage-golden and burning in the hollows like the mud of a fire put out with water, a grove of hazels, all bent and broken by the winds and by climbers in search of nuts, made a chaotic image of ruin, twisted from all its joints by a stubborn resistance to disaster.

One noon in August the knives and plates on the terrace turned green, dusk fell on the flowerbeds and the birds went quiet. The sky began trying to tear from itself a bright net of night deceitfully thrown on it like a cloak of invisibility. The park had died out and was looking, sinisterly, obliquely upward at the humiliating enigma through which the earth, whose loud glory it had been drinking so proudly with all its roots, was being rendered unimportant. A hedgehog rolled out onto the path. A dead viper lay there in the shape of a knot, like an Egyptian hieroglyph. It shifted it, then suddenly stopped and froze. And again it broke and shed its dry bunch of needles, and first poked out, then hid, its pig-like muzzle. All the while that the eclipse lasted, that ball of prickly suspicion kept gathering itself, first in the shape of a small boot, then in that of a pine-cone, until a presage of renascent certainty drove it back into its lair.

8

In the winter one of the S—sisters, Z. M. M., came to live on Tverskoi Boulevard. People visited her. I. Dobrovein, a remarkable musician (with whom I was friends), used to drop in.[120] Mayakovsky sometimes came to her house. By then I was accustomed to seeing in him the leading poet of the generation. Time showed I was not mistaken.

It is true there was Khlebnikov with his subtle genuineness.[121] But part of his merit remains inaccessible to me even now, for poetry as I understand it proceeds in history, after all, and in collaboration with actual life.

There was Severianin too, a lyric poet who poured forth spontaneous stanzas, in ready forms like Lermontov's, and who, with all his untidiness and vulgarity, was impressive precisely because of this rare structure of his open, unfettered talent.[122]

But the peak of poetic destiny was Mayakovsky, and later this was confirmed. After this, every time the generation expressed itself dramatically by lending its voice to a poet, whether that poet was Esenin or Selvinsky or Tsvetaeva, an echo was heard of Mayakovsky's kindred note; it was heard in the very way they were bound to their generation—in the way they addressed the world from out of their own time. I am saying nothing about such masters as Tikhonov or Aseev because, both here and in the rest of what I shall say, I am confining myself to this dramatic line, which is closer to me, while they chose a different one.[123]

Mayakovsky rarely turned up alone. Usually his retinue consisted of futurists, men of the movement. In M-'s household at this time I saw the first primus stove of my life. This invention did not yet give off a stink, and who thought it would bring so much filth into our lives and come into such wide use?

Its clean roaring body threw out a high-pressure flame. Chops were fried on it one by one; the elbows of our hostess and her helpers got covered with a chocolate-coloured Caucasian tan. The cold little kitchen was transformed into a settlement in the Tierra del Fuego whenever we dropped in on the ladies from the dining-room and, as innocent of technology as wild Patagonians, we bent over the copper disk that embodied something bright and Archimedean. And—kept dashing out for beer and vodka.

A tall Christmas tree in the sitting room held out its paws towards the grand piano, secretly in league with the trees on the boulevard. It was still solemnly dark. The whole divan was piled with glittering tinsel, like heaps of sweets, some of it still inside cardboard boxes. Special invitations were issued for the decorating of the tree, in the morning if possible, which meant three in the afternoon.

Mayakovsky recited, made everyone laugh and ate his supper in haste, impatient for the game of cards. He was bitingly polite and with great skill hid his incessant agitation. Something was going on in him, some sort of crisis was taking place. His destiny had become clear to him. He was openly posing, but with such hidden anxiety and fever that on his posing stood drops of cold sweat.

9

But he was not always attended by the innovators. Often he would come in the company of a poet who had emerged with honour from the test usually set by his vicinity. Of the many people I had seen at his side Bolshakov was the only one I could see next to him without strain. It did not matter which of them spoke first, both could be listened to without violence to one's hearing. Like his later and even stronger union with his lifelong friend, Lilia Brik, this friendship was understandable, it was a natural one. One's heart didn't ache for Mayakovsky in Bolshakov's company, he was on his own level, was not lowering himself.

Usually, though, his sympathies aroused bewilderment. This poet with his overwhelmingly large self-awareness, who had gone further than anyone else in laying bare the essence of the lyrical and had, with medieval boldness, brought it close to a theme in whose vast design poetry began to speak almost in the language of sectarian identifications—took up just as hugely and broadly another, more local, tradition.

He saw beneath him a city which had gradually risen up to him from the depths of *The Bronze Horseman, Crime and Punishment* and *Petersburg*, a city in a haze which people called, with unnecessary vagueness, the problem of the Russian intelligentsia, but essentially a city in the haze of eternal divinations about the future, a precarious Russian city of the nineteenth and twentieth centuries.[124]

He could embrace such views, yet alongside these immense contemplations he was faithful, almost as if duty-bound, to all the dwarfish undertakings of his random, hastily assembled clique which was invariably mediocre to the point of indecency. This man with an almost animal craving for truth surrounded himself with petty, pernickety people of fictitious reputations and false, unjustified pretensions. Or—to come to the main point—right to the end he went on finding something in the veterans of a movement he himself had long since permanently discarded. Probably this was the consequence of a fatal loneliness which, once it is established, is then deliberately intensified with that pedantry with which the will sometimes moves in a direction it has recognised as inevitable.

10

But all this was to show itself later. At the time there were only faint signs of the strange things to come. Mayakovsky recited Akhmatova, Severianin and his own and Bolshakov's works about the war and the city, and the city we emerged into at night from the homes of friends was a city deep in the rear of the war.

Already we were failing in the matters always difficult for immense, spiritual Russia: transport and supplies. Already the new words—roster, medical kit, licensing, refrigeration—were hatching the first larvae of profiteering. While the profiteers were thinking in truck-loads, those same trucks were exporting large consignments of fresh indigenous population, night and day, in haste, with songs, in exchange for damaged batches coming back in the hospital trains. And the best of the girls and women were going as nurses.

The place of authentic positions was the front, and the rear would have fallen into a false one in any case, even if, on top of this, it had not excelled in voluntary falsehood. The city hid behind phrase-making like a cornered thief, although no one at the time was attempting to catch it. Like all hypocrites, Moscow lived an intensified external life and was vivid with the unnatural vividness of a flower-shop window in winter.

By night it seemed the very image of Mayakovsky's voice. What was happening in this city, and what was being heaped up and hurled to pieces by this voice, were as alike as two drops of water. This was not, though, the similarity dreamt of by naturalism, rather it was the link that combines anode and cathode, artist and life, the poet and the time.

Opposite M-'s house stood the house of the Moscow chief of police. There, in the course of several days that autumn I ran into Mayakovsky, and Bolshakov too, I think, at one of the formalities required for the registration of volunteers. We had been concealing this procedure from one another. I did not carry it through to the end, despite my father's sympathy. But, unless I am mistaken, nothing came of it in the case of my friends either.

Shestov's son, a handsome lieutenant, drew from me a solemn promise to give the idea up. Soberly and positively he told me what it was like at the front, warning me I would find there exactly the opposite of what I expected.[125] Soon after this he perished, in the first battle after his return to the front from that leave. Bolshakov entered the Tver Cavalry School, Mayakovsky was later called up when his turn came, but, following my release that summer just before the war, I was released again at all subsequent medical examinations.

A year later I went away to the Urals. Before that I spent a few days in Petersburg. The war was less perceptible there than in Moscow. Mayakovsky, who was called up by then, had been settled there for some time.

As always, the animated movement of the capital was tempered by the generosity of its dreamy spaces, which the needs of life could never exhaust. The very avenues were the colour of winter and dusk, and their impetuous silveriness did not need much lamplight and snow to send them dashing and sparkling into the distance.

I walked down Liteinyi Avenue with Mayakovsky; with sweeping strides he trampled miles of street, and I was amazed, as always, by the way he was able to be a kind of frame or edge to any landscape. In this he suited grey, sparkling Petrograd even better than Moscow.

This was the time of the *Backbone Flute* and the first drafts of *War and the Universe*. *A Cloud in Trousers* had come out as a little book with an orange cover. He told me about the new friends he was taking me to, about his acquaintance with Gorky, about how the social theme was taking an ever bigger place in his plans and allowing him to work in a new way, at definite times, in measured portions. And that was the first time I visited the Briks.[126]

Still more naturally than in the capital cities, my thoughts about him spread out into the semi-Asiatic wintry landscape of *The Captain's Daughter* in the Urals and in the Kama region of Pugachov.[127]

I returned to Moscow soon after the February revolution. Mayakovsky had come from Petrograd and was staying in Stoleshnikov Lane. In the morning I called on him at his hotel. He was getting up and, while dressing, he recited his new *War and the Universe* to me. I did not expatiate on the impression it made on me. He read it in my eyes. Besides, he knew well the extent of his effect upon me. I talked about futurism and said how marvellous it would be if he could now openly send all that to the devil. He laughed and almost agreed.

11*

Hitherto I have shown how I perceived Mayakovsky. But there is no love without scars and sacrifices. I have told what sort of person Mayakovsky was when he entered my life. How it was changed by him remains to be told. I shall now fill this gap.

When I came back from the boulevard that day, completely overwhelmed, I could not think what to do. I felt utterly untalented. This would not have mattered terribly. But I was aware of a kind of guilt towards him which I could not make sense of. Had I been younger, I would have given up literature. But my age prevented this. After all my metamorphoses, I could not decide to re-define myself a fourth time.

What happened was something else. The time and common influences made me similar to Mayakovsky. Some features coincided in us. I noticed them. I realised that if I did not do something to myself, they would occur more often in the future. I had to protect him from their banality. Although I could not have given it a name, I resolved to renounce what led to them. I renounced the romantic manner. This was how the unromantic style of *Over the Barriers* came into being.[128]

But the romantic manner which from then on I forbade myself contained a whole perception of life. This was the conception of life as the life of the poet. It had come to us from the symbolists, and the symbolists had adopted it from the romantics, principally the Germans.

Blok had been possessed by this idea for a certain period only. In the form in which it was natural to him it was not able to satisfy him. He had either to heighten it or to abandon it. He parted from the idea. Mayakovsky and Esenin heightened it.

In the poet who takes himself to be the measure of life and pays for this with his life, the romantic conception of life is overpoweringly vivid and is irrefutable in its symbols, that is, in everything that figuratively touches upon Orphism and Christianity. In this sense something non-transient is embodied in the life of Mayakovsky and in the fate of Esenin too, a fate that defies all epithets in the self-exterminatory way that it begs to become stories and recedes into them.

But outside the legend the romantic scheme is false. The poet who is set at its foundation is inconceivable without non-poets to bring him into relief, for this poet is not a living personality absorbed in moral cognition but a visual-biographical emblem which demands a background to make its contours visible. As distinct from the passion plays, which needed a Heaven in order to be heard, this drama needs the evil of mediocrity in order to be seen, as romanticism always needs philistinism and loses half its content with the disappearance of the petty-bourgeois outlook.

The conception of biography as spectacle was inherent in my time. I shared this conception with everyone else. I parted from it while it was mild and non-compulsory among the symbolists, before it presupposed heroism and before it smelt of blood. And, in the first place, I freed myself from it unconsciously, by rejecting the romantic devices for which it served as basis. In the second place, I avoided it consciously as well, as a brilliance unsuited to me because, having confined myself to my craft, I feared any kind of poetising that would place me in a false and unsuitable position.

But when *My Sister Life* appeared,[129] a book in which wholly uncontemporary aspects of poetry were expressed that had been revealed to me in the revolutionary summer, I became utterly indifferent as to the name of the power that had given the book, because it was immeasurably bigger than me and the poetic conceptions surrounding me.

12

From Sivtsev Vrazhek,[130] into a dining-room not cleared up for months, peered winter twilight, the terror, and the roofs and trees of the quarter round the Arbat. The apartment's owner, a bearded newspaperman of extreme absentmindedness and kindliness, gave the impression of being a bachelor, although he had a family in the province of Orenburg. Whenever he had any spare time he would rake up from the table a whole month's newspapers of every possible persuasion and carry them in armfuls into the kitchen, together with the petrified remains of breakfasts that used to accumulate between his morning readings in regular deposits of pork rinds and loaf ends. Until I lost my conscience, there would be a bright, loud, odorous flame in the stove on the thirtieth of every month, as in Dickens's Christmas tales of roast geese and counting-house clerks. With the approach of darkness, sentries on point duty would open inspired fire from their revolvers.[131] Sometimes whole bursts were fired and sometimes sparse separate shots like inquiries into the night, full of a piteous unanswered fatality, and as it was impossible for them to fall into rhythm and many died from stray bullets, one wanted, for safety's sake, to set metronomes from pianos along the side-streets instead of militiamen.

Sometimes their crackling changed to a barbarous wail. And, as often happened in those days, you could not tell at first whether it was in the street or the house. But it was the sole inhabitant of the study, a portable one with a plug, calling for someone to go to it, like moments of lucidity in a continuous delirium.

It was from here that I was invited by telephone to a private house in Trubnikovsky Lane for a gathering of all the poetic forces that could possibly be found at that moment in Moscow. On this same telephone, though a good deal earlier, before the Kornilov revolt, I had had a disagreement with Mayakovsky.[132]

Mayakovsky informed me that he had put me on his poster, alongside Bolshakov and Lipskerov,[133] but also along with the most faithful of the faithful, including, it seemed, one who could break thick planks with his forehead. I was almost pleased to have the opportunity to talk to my idol for the first time as if he were a stranger, and, getting more and more irritated, I parried his self-justifying arguments one by one. It was not so much his lack of ceremony that surprised me as the poverty of imagination it displayed, for, as I pointed out, this incident consisted not in his unbidden use of my name but in his annoying conviction that my two-year absence had altered neither my life nor my interests. He ought first to have inquired whether I was still alive and whether I had not given up literature for something better. To this he replied quite reasonably that we had already met since the Urals, one day in the spring. But in a most surprising way this piece of reasoning failed to get through to me. And with misplaced stubbornness I demanded that he publish a correction of the poster in the press, which was impracticable as the evening was so near, and, since I was quite unknown at that time, it was affected nonsense as well.

But although I was still hiding *My Sister Life* and concealing what was going on in me, I could not endure it when those around me assumed that everything was the same as before. Besides which, precisely that spring conversation Mayakovsky alluded to so unsuccessfully was doubtless dimly alive in me, and I was irritated by the inconsistency of this invitation after all that had been said then.

13

He reminded me of this telephone skirmish some months later, in the house of the amateur verse-writer A-. Present were Balmont, Khodasevich, Baltrushaitis, Ehrenburg, Vera Inber, Antokolsky, Kamensky, Burliuk, Mayakovsky, Andrei Belyi and Tsvetaeva.[134] I could not know, of course, what an incomparable poet Tsvetaeva was to develop into. But even without knowing her remarkable *Mileposts*,[135] written at that time, I instinctively set her apart from the others in the room because of her striking simplicity. I sensed something akin to me in her: a readiness to part at any moment with all privileges and habits if something lofty were to kindle her and move her to admiration. On this occasion, we exchanged a few sincere, friendly words. At that evening gathering, she was a living palladium for me against the people of two movements, the symbolists and futurists, who thronged the room.

The reading began. People read by seniority, with no perceptible success. When Mayakovsky's turn came, he stood up, put one arm round the edge of the empty shelf in which the back of the divan ended, and started reading *Man*. Like a *bas-relief*, as I have always seen him against the background of the age, he towered among the others who were sitting or standing, and, supporting his fine head with one hand or pressing his knee into the bolster of the divan, he recited a work of extraordinary depth, elation and inspiration.

Opposite him, with Margarita Sabashnikova, sat Andrei Belyi. He had spent the war in Switzerland. The revolution had brought him back to his own country. This was possibly the first time he had seen and heard Mayakovsky. He listened as if spellbound, and though he did nothing to betray his rapture his face was all the more eloquent. Astonished and grateful, it flew to meet the reader. Part of the audience was out of sight to me, including Tsvetaeva and Ehrenburg. I watched the others. Most kept within the boundaries of an enviable self-esteem. All felt themselves to be names, thought of themselves as poets. Belyi alone was listening with complete self-abandon, carried far, far away by the joy that regrets nothing because on the heights where it is at home there is nothing but sacrifice and the eternal readiness for it.

Chance was bringing together before my eyes two geniuses who justified two literary movements which had become exhausted, one after the other. In Belyi's vicinity, which I experienced with proud delight, I felt Mayakovsky's presence with double force. His essence was revealed to me in all the freshness of a first encounter. I experienced it that evening for the last time.

After this many years passed. One year passed and when I read the poems of *My Sister* to Mayakovsky before anyone else, I heard ten times more from him than I ever expected to hear from anyone. Another year passed. In a small group of friends he read his *150,000,000*. And for the first time I had nothing to say to him. Many years passed, during which we met at home and abroad, tried to be friends, tried to work together, and all the time I was understanding him less and less. Others will tell about this period, for in those years I came up against the limits of my understanding and it seemed they were not to be overcome. My memories of that time would be pale and would add nothing to what has been said already. And so I shall go straight on to what I still have to tell.

14

I shall tell of the strangeness which is repeated from age to age and may be called the last year of a poet.

All of a sudden an end is put to projects that have been resisting completion. Often nothing is added to their unfinished state except for a new certainty— hitherto unpermitted—that they are complete. And this certainty is conveyed to posterity.

Habits are changed, new plans are cherished, boasts are made of being endlessly in high spirits. And all of a sudden—the end, sometimes violent, more often natural, but very like suicide even then, through a lack of desire for self-defence. And then one is brought up short and one notices similarities. Plans had been cherished, *The Contemporary* was being edited, preparations were made to establish a peasant journal.[136] An exhibition of twenty years' work was being opened, steps were taken to obtain a foreign passport.[137]

But it turns out that others had seen them during those very same days depressed, complaining, weeping. Men who had spent whole decades in voluntary solitude were suddenly afraid of it like children frightened of a dark room and would seize the hands of chance visitors, clutching at their presence, only not to be left alone. Witnesses of these states of mind refused to believe their ears. Men who had received far more corroborations from life than it grants to others now talked as if they had not yet begun to live and had had no experience or support in the past.

But who will understand or believe that it was suddenly given to the Pushkin of 1836 to recognise himself as the Pushkin of any year, as the Pushkin, say, of 1936?[138] That a time comes when the responses long since coming from other hearts in answer to the beats of the main one, which is still alive and still pulsing, thinking and wanting to live, are suddenly fused into one reborn and expanded heart? That the irregular, constantly accelerating beats are coming at last so thick and fast that all at once they even out and, coinciding with the main heart's tremors, start to live one life with it, beating in unison with it from now on? That this is no allegory. That this is experienced. That this is a kind of age of life, impulsive, felt in the blood and real—only as yet unnamed. That this is a kind of non-human youth, but a youth that rends the continuity of one's preceding life with such abrupt joy that, because there exists no name for it and because comparisons are inevitable, its abruptness makes it, more than anything else, resemble death. That it resembles death. That it resembles death but—is *not* death, not death at all, and if only, if only people did not want complete resemblance.

And together with the heart, a displacement occurs between memories and works, works and hopes, the world of the created and the world of the yet to be created. What kind of personal life did he have?—people sometimes ask. You shall now be enlightened about his personal life. A huge region of utter contradiction contracts, concentrates, smooths itself out and, suddenly, shuddering with simultaneity in every part of its structure, begins to exist physically. It opens its eyes, takes a deep breath and flings off the last remnants of the pose that was given it as a temporary support.

And if one recalls that all this sleeps by night and wakes by day, walks on two feet and is called a human being, it is natural to expect corresponding phenomena in its behaviour.

A large, real, really existing city. Winter is in it. Darkness comes early in it, in it the working day goes by in the light of evening.

Once, long, long ago it was terrible. It had to be conquered, its refusal to give recognition had to be broken. Much water has flowed past since then.

Recognition has been wrung from it; its submission has become a habit. A great effort of memory is needed to imagine how it could once have inspired such agitation. Lamps twinkle in it, people cough into handkerchiefs and click their abacuses. It gets covered with snow.

Its uneasy immensity would have swept past unnoticed were it not for this new, wild impressionability. What is the shyness of adolescence beside the vulnerability of this new birth? And again, as in childhood, everything is noticed. Lamps, typists, door pulleys, galoshes, storm clouds, the crescent moon and the snow. Terrible world.[139]

It bristles with backs of fur-coats and sleighs, like a penny rolling across the floor it rolls on its edge along the rails, rolls away into the distance and tenderly falls off its rim into the mist, where a signal-woman in a sheepskin coat bends to pick it up. It rolls about and grows tiny and teems with fortuities. It is so easy to come across a slight want of attention in it. These are deliberately imagined annoyances. They are blown up consciously from nothing. But even when blown up they are still utterly trivial next to the wrongs one strode over so majestically only a short while ago. Yet that is just the point, that there can be no comparison, because it was in that previous life which was such a joy to tear up. Oh, if only this joy were more equable and more credible.

But it is incredible and incomparable, and yet nothing in life ever flung one so much from extreme to extreme as does this joy.

What lapses there are here into despondency. What repetition of the whole of Hans Christian Andersen and his unhappy duckling. What elephants are here made out of flies.[140]

But perhaps the inner voice is lying? Perhaps the terrible world is right? "No smoking." "Please state your business briefly." Are these not truths?

"Him?—What, hang himself? Don't you worry." "Love?—What, him?—Ha-ha-ha! He only loves himself."

A large, real, really existing city. Winter is in it, freezing cold is in it. Squeaking and willow-woven, the air, in its twenty degrees of frost, stands over the road as if on stilts hammered into the ground. Everything is misting over, rolling away and becoming lost in it. But can things be as sad as this when they are so joyful? So is this not a second birth? So is this death?

15

In public registry offices there is no apparatus for measuring truthfulness, no device for the X-raying of sincerity. For a record to be valid, nothing is needed but the firmness of somebody else's hand as it makes the entry. And then nobody has any doubts, nothing is debated.

He'll write a last message with his own hand, presenting his treasure to the world like something evident; he'll measure and X-ray his own sincerity by a rapid performance that allows of no alteration, and then all around people start discussing and doubting and making comparisons.

They compare her with her predecessors, whereas she is comparable only with him and the whole of his previous life.[141] They build up conjectures about his feeling, without knowing that it is possible to love not only in days, though it be forever, but also, though it be not for ever, with all the collected strength of past days.

But these words, genius and beautiful woman, have long since become identically banal. And how much they have in common.

From childhood she is constrained in her movements. She is lovely and she learns this early. The only one with whom she can be wholly herself is God's earth, as we call it, for with others she cannot take a step without hurting someone or getting hurt herself.

As a young girl she goes out beyond the gate. What is she going to do? Already she receives clandestine letters. She has let two or three friends into her secrets. She already has all this and let's say: she is going out to meet someone.

She goes out beyond the gate. She wants the evening to notice her, the air's heart to miss a beat for her, the stars to be able to pick up something about her. She wants the renown enjoyed by trees and fences and all things upon earth when they are not in the head but in the open air. Yet she would reply with a cheerful laugh if anyone ascribed such desires to her. She is not thinking anything of the sort. For that she has in the world a distant brother, a person of vast ordinariness, who is there to know her better than she knows herself and ultimately to answer for her. She has a healthy liking for healthy nature and is unaware that reliance on the universe's reciprocity never abandons her.

Spring, an evening in spring, little old women on benches, low fences, shaggy willows. A wine-green, weakly infused, mild, pallid sky, dust, homeland, dry splintery voices. Sounds as dry as chips of wood and a smooth hot silence all covered with their splinters.

Someone comes along the road towards her, the very one it was natural to meet. Overjoyed, she keeps saying she has come out to meet just him. To some extent she is right. Who is not to some extent dust and homeland and the quiet of a spring evening? She forgets why she has come out, but her feet remember. He and she walk on, they walk together, and the further they go the more people they come across. And as she loves her companion with all her heart, her feet distress her more than a little. But they carry her onward, he and she can scarcely keep pace with each other, but unexpectedly the road leads out to some wider place where there seem to be fewer people and they could pause for breath and look around, but often this is the very moment when her distant brother comes out, along his own path, and they meet, and nothing that happens now can make any difference: some utterly perfect "I am thou" binds them with all the bonds conceivable upon earth, and proudly, youthfully and wearily it stamps, as on a medal, profile upon profile.

16

The beginning of April found Moscow in a white stupor of renewed winter. On the seventh there started a second thaw, and on the fourteenth, when Mayakovsky shot himself, not everyone had got used to the newness of spring.

When I heard of the disaster I sent for Olga Sillova to come to the place of the event. Something told me this shock would be a release for her own grief.[142]

Between eleven and twelve the undulating circles generated by the shot were still rippling outward. The news rocked telephones, covering faces with pallor, sending people to the Lubiansky Passage, across the yard and into the house, where all the way up the staircase people from the town and from other parts of the house were already crowding, crying and pressing together, all of them hurled and splashed against the walls by the laminating force of the event. Cherniak and Romadin, the first to tell me of the disaster, came up to me. Zhenia was with them.[143] At the sight of her, my cheeks began twitching convulsively. Weeping, she told me to run upstairs, but at that moment the body was dragged downstairs on a stretcher, covered with something from head to foot. Everyone rushed down and dammed up the exit so that, by the time we managed to get out, the ambulance was already driving through the gate. We streamed along after it into Hendrikov Lane.

Outside the gates, life went on at its own pace, unconcerned, as people say mistakenly. The concern of the asphalt courtyard, eternal participant in dramas of this kind, remained behind.

Over rubbery mud the spring air was wandering on uncertain legs, as if learning to walk. Cockerels and children were announcing themselves for everyone to hear. In early spring their voices are strangely far-reaching, despite the busy rattle of the town.

The tram was clambering slowly up Shvivoi Hill. There is one spot there where first the right footpath and then the left one steals up so close to the tram's windows that, catching at the strap, you involuntarily bend over Moscow like over an old woman who has slipped—for she suddenly goes down on all fours, strips herself drearily of cobblers and clockmakers, raises and transfers certain roofs and bell-towers, then suddenly stands up and, shaking out her skirt, sends the tram speeding along a level and quite unremarkable street.

This time her movements were so manifestly an excerpt from the man who had just shot himself, that is, they so forcefully brought to mind something important in his being, that I began trembling all over and the famous telephone call from *A Cloud* thundered in me of its own accord, as if someone beside me had loudly recited it.[144] I was standing in the gangway next to Sillova, and I leaned towards her to remind her of those eight lines, but my lips, as they tried to form the words: "And I feel that 'I' is too small for me", were like gloved fingers, and in my agitation I could not utter a word.

Two empty cars stood by the gate at the end of Hendrikov Lane. They were surrounded by a group of inquisitive people.

In the hall and dining-room, people were standing or sitting, some with hats on and some bare-headed. He was lying further off, in his study. The door from the hall into Lilia's room was open, and on the threshold, pressing his head against the lintel, Aseev was weeping. In the depth of the room, by the window, Kirsanov, his head hunched between his shoulders, was convulsively shaking and sobbing without any sound.[145]

Even here the damp mist of lamentation kept being interrupted by anxious half-loud conversations, just as happens at the end of a requiem when, after a service thick as jam, the first whispered words are so dry that they seem to be spoken from under the floor and have a smell of mice. During one such interruption the caretaker cautiously entered the room with a chisel stuck in the top of his boot and, removing the winter window-frame, slowly and noiselessly opened the window. It was still shudderingly cold outside for anyone without a coat, and sparrows and children were cheering themselves on with shouts about nothing in particular.

Someone tiptoed from where the dead man lay and quietly asked whether a telegram had been sent to Lilia. L. A. G. replied that it had.[146] Zhenia took me aside to point out with what courage L. A. was bearing the terrible weight of this shattering event. She burst into tears. I pressed her hand warmly.

In through the window poured the apparent unconcern of the immeasurable world. Along the sky, as if between earth and sea, stood grey trees guarding the boundary. As I looked at the branches covered with excited buds, I tried to imagine far, far beyond them that improbable London where the telegram had been sent. There, soon, someone would cry out, stretch arms in our direction and fall down unconscious. My throat contracted. I decided to go back into his room and this time really cry my eyes out.

He was lying on his side, his face to the wall, sullen, tall, with a sheet drawn up to his chin and his mouth half-open like someone sleeping. He had proudly turned away from everyone and, even while lying down, even in this sleep, was striving to go somewhere, to get away. His face took one back to the time when he himself said that he was "handsome, twenty-two-year-old",[147] for death had set fast a facial expression that practically never falls into its clutches. It was the sort of expression with which one starts life, not ends it. He was sulking and indignant.

But now a movement occurred in the hall. Separately from her mother and elder sister, who were grieving inaudibly now among the crowd, the dead man's younger sister, Olga Vladimirovna, had arrived at the apartment. Her arrival was demanding and noisy. Her voice came sailing into the room in advance of her. As she came up the stairs alone, she was talking loudly to someone, evidently to her brother. Then she herself appeared and, walking past everyone as if stepping over rubbish, she reached her brother's door, threw her hands in the air, and stopped. "Volodia!" she shouted and her voice filled the house. A moment passed. "He won't speak!", she started to shout even more loudly. "He won't speak! He's not answering! Volodia! Volodia! Horrible!"[148]

She began to fall, people caught her and rushed to bring her round. Scarcely conscious, she went avidly to the body, sat at its feet and rapidly started up again her unquenchable dialogue. I burst into tears, in the way I had long been wanting to.

It had not been possible to cry like this at the scene of the event, where the gunshot freshness of the fact was speedily ousted by the herd spirit of drama. There, like saltpetre, the asphalt yard stank of the deification of the inevitable, that is, of the false urban fatalism that is founded on ape-like imitation and presents life as a chain of obediently imprinted sensational events. There too, people sobbed, but only because the shaken gullet reproduced with animal mediumism the convulsions of the apartment blocks, the fire escapes, the revolver case, and everything that makes one feel sick with despair and spew murder.

His sister was the first to weep for him by her own will and choice, as something great is wept for, and one could weep to her words insatiably, expansively, as to the roar of an organ.

And she didn't stop. *"The Bathhouse* for them!" raged Mayakovsky's own voice, strangely adapted to his sister's contralto.[149] "And make it funny! They kept laughing. Calling him out.—And look what was happening to him.—Why didn't you come to us, Volodia?" she wailed and sobbed, then quickly got control of herself and impetuously moved closer to him. "Remember, remember, Volodichka?"—she suddenly reminded him, almost as if he were alive, and she started declaiming:

And I feel that *I* is too small for me!
Someone is stubbornly breaking out of me.
Hallo!
Who is it?! Mother?
Mother! Your son is gloriously ill!
Mother! His heart is on fire.
Tell Liuda and Olia, his sisters,
He's got nowhere to go any more.

153

When I went there in the evening, he was already lying in his coffin. The faces that had filled the room during the day had been replaced by others. It was fairly quiet. There was almost no weeping now.

Suddenly, down below, under the window, I imagined his life, now utterly past. It led away at a slant from the window in the shape of some quiet tree-planted street, such as the Povarsky. And the first to stand upon it, right by the wall, was our State, our unprecedented, impossible State, bursting into the centuries and taken up into them forever. It stood there below, it could be called to and taken by the hand. In its palpable extraordinariness there was something resembling the dead man. So striking was the link between the two they could have seemed twins.

And then, just as spontaneously, I thought that this man had been practically the only citizen to have this citizenship. All the rest struggled, sacrificed their lives and built things up, or else endured, bewildered, but still they were natives of the previous epoch and its close kinsmen, despite their difference. He was the only one who had the newness of the times climatically in his blood. He was strange through and through with the strangenesses of the age which were as yet half-unrealised. I began calling to mind traits of his character, his independence which in many ways was utterly his own. All of them could be explained by his being accustomed to conditions which, though implicit in our time, had not yet come into their everyday force. From childhood he was spoiled by the future, which came to him quite early and, it seemed, without much effort.

Commentary on II
(A SAFE-CONDUCT, or "THE PRESERVATION CERTIFICATE")

The political moment

A Safe-Conduct is Pasternak's most significant prose work before *Doctor Zhivago* and, despite a few opaque passages, the most accomplished of all his works in prose. He himself felt it to be exceptionally important and wrote to his translator George Reavey in 1932 that, although he had previously not cared very much whether he was read in the West, he was greatly concerned that this one book should be translated. "I wrote it", he said, "not as one of many but as the only one . . . the most important of everything I have done. In this book I do not depict, I think and talk. In it I am not trying to be interesting, but to be exact."[150]

The exactitude is that of a poet, not of a conventional autobiographer. It has, moreover, been called Pasternak's one "real and original work of philosophy".[151] Here it will be discussed as a work containing a series of aesthetic ideas. But it is also a response to the political and literary-political situation in Soviet Russia, a forceful if (of necessity) cryptic statement of opposition to the views that had become influential. Implicitly it contradicts ideas both of "Lef" and of "RAPP". "Lef" (Left Front of the Arts), a group with roots in pre-revolutionary futurism, was reconstituted in 1923 with the declared purposes of getting art to serve the revolution while making use of the old avant-garde's formal innovations, of opposing everything metaphysical in literature and promoting a "literature of fact", and—in 1928, its last year—of requiring writers to respond to the "social demand" issued by the proletarian state. As Christopher Barnes notes, it is hard to fathom how Pasternak could have been a member of this group, yet for a short time he was, after which it seems he had only negative things to say about it.[152] *A Safe-Conduct*, both in its style and in the views it expresses about poetry, is entirely antipathetic to Lef ideology. A movement actually dangerous to Pasternak was RAPP, the Russian Association of Proletarian Writers (Russian for "writer" is *pisatel'*) which supported the official Party line on literature, and violent action against writers who did not actively implement it. Certain passages in *A Safe-Conduct* are veiled objections to the RAPP conception of literature.

For a politically informed reading of *A Safe-Conduct* one should turn to Fleishman's *Pasternak, The Poet and His Politics*, to *Pasternak, The Tragic Years* by Evgeny Pasternak, and to Barnes's *Boris Pasternak, A Literary Biography*.[153]

The present study will look at political aspects only where necessary, but it is important to bear in mind that Pasternak was working on Part Three of his book at the very time when persecution of intellectuals was escalating, a time of inquisitorial newspaper campaigns against "fellow-travelling" writers—of whom he was regarded as one. Also he was writing soon after an event by which he was personally shocked and distressed. This was the state execution, in secret and without any trial whatever, of V. Sillov, a gifted young writer whom he considered the one completely sincere and honourable member of Lef; the name of Sillov could never afterwards be mentioned in the Press. As Pasternak told Reavey (in the 1932 letter quoted above) "there were some questions which *could not be spoken about*." He found ways, however, of drawing attention to what could not be spoken of. A passage in *S-C* 3,1 ostensibly describing the last period of tsarism, can be read, as Fleishman has pointed out, as a statement of opposition; it was removed by the editor of the 1931 edition.[154] Even more pointedly, Pasternak draws attention to the Sillov incident by conspicuously stating in *S-C* 3,16 that he invited Sillov's widow, Olga (called "O.S." in the 1931 text), to join those who were weeping over Mayakovsky's dead body. And twice, earlier on in this work, he mentions the "lions' maw" slots once used in Venice for denunciations, tacitly referring (as has been shown by Michel Aucouturier) to the impossibility of speaking about what happened to Sillov. First, he observes in 2,16 that it became a sign of ill-breeding in sixteenth-century Venice to utter the name of anyone who had disappeared into those slots—and letters he wrote in 1929 show how heavily the similar Soviet situation weighed upon him; and secondly, in the following chapter, he evokes the all-surrounding "lions' maws" and "lions' roar"; that passage, too, was cut out by the editor.[155]

Rilke

A Safe-Conduct is dedicated to Rilke. Or rather, in Pasternak's words: "I myself received these reminiscences from him as a gift." (1,5) Not long before writing it, he said, in the sole letter he ever sent to Rilke: "I am indebted to you for the basic features of my character, for the make-up of my mental existence; they are your creations." Years later he said: "I had always thought that in all my artistic activity I did nothing else but translate or diversify his [Rilke's] motifs . . . I always swam in his sea."[156] In fact he had set out to make *A Safe-Conduct* a book about Rilke, until he found it becoming a book of thoughts about art.

There have been several studies of affinities between Rilke and Pasternak; the German poet's enormous importance to the Russian one is indisputable. Yet in this poetic memoir (which originally had an epilogue in the form of a long letter to Rilke),[157] Rilke is scarcely mentioned. This may be no surprise when we consider that, for Pasternak, a poet's life-story cannot be written because "his subconscious consists of everything that happens to his readers." In that idiosyncratic sense the whole of *A Safe-Conduct* is a contribution to Rilke's life-story.

Devices for removing attention from himself are paralleled by devices for removing attention from the real-life Rilke. At the very beginning of the book, the only time Rilke appears, the black cloak, silhouette, unfamiliar speech and the driving away of the carriage-and-pair with no longer any mention of Rilke (although his companions are mentioned)—turn his one appearance into a disappearance: after being half-seen in the book's second sentence, he vanishes. Rilke's subsequent absence from the entire three-part text (except for a brief recollection of him in 1,5) is in this way finely prefigured, as is the tacit distinction between him and Mayakovsky, who is later to loom forth so intently visible and physical. Not the adored great poet that he was, not someone to stare at, not even quite a person at all but a "fiction", Rilke merges into the very category of "art".

Some patterns

To look at *A Safe-Conduct* with the theme of artistic creativity in mind is to see that almost every detail in it is related to the origin of art in the artist's everyday-life experience. City streets, scent of narcissi, a professor lecturing or walking, Alps through a train window—all convey something of the randomness, freshness or sharp change that accompany creativity. Other themes are, of course, prominent. Love is central to each of the book's three parts. The fleeting glimpse of Rilke at the beginning signifies a love which informs the whole book; then there is the love for Scriabin in Part One, for Cohen and for "V-" (Ida Vysotskaia) in Part Two, for Mayakovsky in Part Three. Yet each of these is as much a narrative of incipient creativity as of love. Further, each of the three parts of the book is set in a city or in cities to which the author's emotional relation is, again, of paramount significance for his idea of art: Moscow, Marburg and Venice, and again Moscow.

But each part has one or more chapters where thoughts about the origin of poetry are drawn together and can be read as sketches towards a theory of creativity. Thus in Part One chapter six (1,6) there is the account of how poetry was born from the interaction of diverse experiences; Part Two chapter three (2,3) is a meditation on the contribution of sexuality to art; Part Two chapter seven (2,7) contains fundamental statements on inspiration and the nature of art; Part Two chapter seventeen (2,17) is a discourse on Venetian painting and on genius; in Part Three chapter eleven (3,11) comes Pasternak's explanation of his rejection of the "romantic manner" and the romantic "understanding of biography as spectacle". That rejection was made, of course, long before the writing of *A Safe-Conduct* and is related to the assertion in 1,5 that a poet cannot have a biography—a paradoxical assertion in a work that looks so much like a poet's autobiography. Each of these quasi-theoretical passages is marked in the text with an asterisk to indicate that it will be discussed in the present Commentary, 3,11 being discussed under the heading "Mayakovsky".

Almost from the beginning of *A Safe-Conduct* Pasternak speaks of two opposite ways of choosing one's fate. This is not the opposition between "lyrical" and "historical" outlined in *The Black Goblet* but is closer to that in *Doctor Zhivago* between gifted (gifted for *life*, as he insists) and ungifted. Some people, he says, prefer what is fixed, conventional and conformist; others welcome what is unique, unfixed and indefinable. Everyone is offered a chance of belonging to the second kind, a chance of uniqueness; most, inexplicably, do not take it. This distinction informs many motifs. On the one hand there are prefaces (mere preparations for living, as, later, Zhivago will say); on the other there is what they are prefaces *to*. On the one hand, the "tedious cooking" of life's ingredients; on the other, the discovery that real life starts when one "dines off the finished dish". There is the deadness of giving lessons to pupils who are merely aware of having to repeat the year, and the liveness of lessons to pupils trying to shift from the spot to which "life was preparing to nail them". Two ways of living—the one deadly and repetitious, the other vividly felt and new: this opposition is present in the whole structure of *A Safe-Conduct* and occurs at its most emphatic at the very end of the book when, at Mayakovsky's death, "worship of inevitability" is fiercely contrasted with the defiance in the poet's suicide and with the force of his sister's response to it.

But Pasternak dwells less on his horror of a dull acceptance of the inevitable than on the "moments of second birth" in his own life, moments when life leapt wholly out of its usual rut.[158] Such switches of direction, reminiscent of the fractures of fate he was once fascinated by in Kleist's life, are fundamental to his view of life and history altogether, as well as to his aesthetic theory in which art invariably arises from a complete change or renewal.

Part One, chapter six (1,6)

Pasternak's account of the "birth of poetry" in his life (paragraphs four to seven of this chapter) comes after a "deliberately random" list of his experiences as a student in Moscow. Random because poetry results not from particular things or particular moments but from the dynamic relations between things or moments—from their irregularities, interruptions and differences of speed. Poetry first enters his life in the form of a shift of attention at the midpoint of a fast run.

Everything in this short account is passionate, rapid, vivid and concentrated. A race is being run between "love" and "the sun". It is not so much a competition to see who will win, as a racing ahead which itself has value. The race appears to be a metaphor for life lived intensely. Meanwhile, the things not involved in it—forgotten times, inanimate objects—are pitiable for their non-involvement, so much so that the runner, becoming aware of them, seems to hear from them a yearning hiss (or whistle, *svist*). Up to the point at which the hiss is heard and a backward glance takes place, the narrative is concerned only with intensity of feeling and not yet with poetic inspiration. Only when the runner turns to look at the left-behind objects and facts does "that which is called inspiration" occur.

Something like this was sketched out twenty years previously in "Ordering a Drama", written at the very time which is being recalled in this part of *S-C*. There, the artist's material and mental environs—including not only the room's furniture but his remembered childhood (which is thought of as equally static because it is past)—are seen as "inanimate principles, demanding to be set in motion", and, that early text continues, "people would set off here at a run", some of them to become poets in the course of the run. In *A Safe-Conduct* 1,6 the idea is taken up again and developed, with, significantly, a progressive effacement of the poet as person; for the event of inspiration happens not so much in the mind as in the world. First, "love" seems to have engaged autonomously in the competition with the sun; then the "hiss of yearning" comes from outside the person; and in the all-important statement—"That which is called inspiration consisted in this backward glance"—there is a grammatical shift into the impersonal mode, as "this" has no antecedent (it has not been said that "I looked back, and in that look back . . . "); the ellipsis enacts a renunciation, or a disappearance, of the self. (This is discussed more generally in Introduction, 6.) A glance but no person glancing: "madness without a madman" comes to mind again from the 1913 lecture-synopsis. But the main concern is with how everyday phenomena are left out from human passions until "inspiration" attends to them. Captives of causality, doomed to destruction, helpless in their subjection to the definitions immobilising them, they can be saved from their condition only by art.

So Pasternak conceived of poetry as a reanimating of the inanimate, the rescue of past or everyday things from stasis, the shifting of them "from cold axles to hot ones", as he puts it here—setting "the outlived in motion, to pursue and catch up with life". This, not "depiction" (*izobrazhenie*), is art's purpose. If there had been a second universe, he oddly speculates, art would not have been needed, as we could have looked down from that second level to "lift reality out of the first"—thereby (presumably) giving movement to the lifeless objects. As there is no second level, we are obliged to make use of art and its symbols, and to try to give objects life by depicting them. The fact that depiction could mean "still-life" paintings (for which the Russian, used in this passage, is a transliteration of the French *nature morte*) shows that it is only a hopeful means and not the ultimate purpose. The purpose is to set everything moving. All the vocabulary of shifting, pursuing, catching up and changing to hot axles shows Pasternak at pains to insist that poetry is born from the onward movement in time. There is nowhere else it could emerge from, no eternal or unmoving other universe to look *down* from—you can only move on and look back. Positive acceptance of living in time distinguishes him from many other thinkers. In the same way, the non-fulfilment of the human desire for another level of existence is gladly accepted as a beneficial limitation, since it necessitates finding new ways of describing the universe we actually inhabit.

That concentrated narrative of inspiration in the first half of *S-C* 1,6 is followed by something different but closely related: a description of what it was like for him to live an urban life, young Pasternak's "sensation of the town" and of other people's lives in it. The opposition between two ways of living is now presented in the image of two opposite "poles" which focus his divided perception. The first pole, or mast, represents a sense of the town's habits and inhabitants as repeating ready-made, hackneyed old patterns (of wretchedness, self-indulgence, violence)—a scene of "stubborn crudeness", "turgid obviousness". The second is the "distant mast of genius", to which the first cries out its need for "some new Balzac". The urban—and, altogether, the existential—condition, then, is one of subjection to a "mass predestination" from which, once again, only art is the rescuer.

The first pole, as it sends its call to the second, provokes in the poet feverish impatience and anxiety. But (just as, much later, in 3,1, a new young generation, pursuing the path of "inevitability" and "demolition", will be seen as having innumerable opportunities for escape from that path through unique assertions of passion) "one had only to move a short way from the fatal rod for immediate tranquillity to set in". The short way leads to a "non-typical" lecturer (an enthusiast, not dealing in cliché), then to the non-typical students (mentioned above) seeking to leap out of their lives' stasis, and then straight on—as if to a culmination of those two encounters with authenticity—to the flower-merchant's cellar with which the chapter magnificently ends. This evocation of daffodils' scent and violets' colour does more than tell us what kind of place in Moscow saved Pasternak from agitation, it is oriented towards shifting us readers, too, sideways from the usual rush towards repetition and death, into art through powerful feeling.

Part Two, chapter three (2,3)

"All this is breathtakingly difficult", Pasternak says of the ideas he presents in this chapter. He might have said the same of his own manner of presenting them, for his style here is at its most dense and complex.

Once again, ideas about art's origin arise directly from life-experiences. The difficulty of coming to terms with bodily sexuality is, Pasternak claims, part of nature's plan for facilitating human evolution, the purpose of which is the promotion of feeling. So once again an existential limitation becomes a spur to creativity. "Holding to the philosophy that only the almost-impossible is real", Nature makes sexual love a daunting barrier to be surmounted, purposely arranging things so that "all the pedagogues' efforts to make it easier to be natural invariably make it more difficult, and *this is just how it should be.*" He goes on: "And there is art." The surmounting of the sexual barrier is related to the creating of art because, during the effortful transition from disgust to passion, an image of the human being will be engendered, and it "can be engendered only in motion," only in the movement from the one to the other. What is this engendering of an image? Presumably it means that, in the transition, we become aware of being human rather than animal, and capable of tenderness rather than mere obedience to instinct; above all, we become able to create or feel something new instead of staying fettered to repetition. We will then communicate our image of this change to others. Such images, created by people in love, contribute to the evolving image of humanity. Evolution of the image is bigger than us, going on all the time, *in* time, and always to our benefit—resembling a second universe though actually a transformation of the first one. Having started with an attempt to understand how adolescents cope with sexuality, the chapter thus ends with a vision of art "speaking about love through the centuries" and thereby developing its lyric images of humanity, to be preserved and increased by succeeding generations.

Pasternak is convinced of the absolute "rightness" of great art. He does not ascribe admirable personal powers to the artist or claim that the artist gets things right while other people get them wrong. Human beings get them wrong, and art (which is not concerned with people as such but with their image) gets them right.

Part Two, chapter seven (2,7)

This most theoretical and best known of Pasternak's statements about art links the story of his love for Ida Vysotskaia to the story of his beginning to devote himself to poetry. The new beginning centres on his discovery that the force of feeling alters the environment. After the rejection by Vysotskaia and his wild pursuit of her to Berlin, he found himself—so he writes in 2,5—"surrounded by changed things." That he does not write "I felt everything had changed" is no slip of the pen. Things themselves had changed—in the direction of "laconicism," "brotherhood" and "reliability." Back in Marburg, he finds the hill taller, the town thinner and blacker. Now he clears away his philosophy books and starts writing poems.

In describing the abandonment of one career for another, Pasternak is noticeably not interested (as many a less extraordinary autobiographer might be) in the psychology of choosing between intellect and feeling, or in asking how he could feel glad and positive at such an unhappy moment (a feeling brilliantly explored in the poem "Marburg"), any more than, previously, he was interested in what it would mean for him to be a musician rather than a philosopher or a poet. He is interested not in his own character but in the quality of the experienced change and its effect on everything around him.

The experience of changed things leads straight into the aesthetic theory with its central idea of a reality so changed that it is no longer recognizable and has no name: "We try to name it. The result is art." But Pasternak is not really formulating a theory. "If I were to decide to construct a creative aesthetics," he says, "I would show, would explain . . . " The hypothetical mode indicates that direct philosophical exposition would be in vain; his idea can only be pointed to. A further sign of the delicacy, not of art but of talk about it, is Pasternak's curious resort to a footnote, attached to the end of this chapter—the only one in the whole of his book. In it he makes yet another attempt to point to the main thing. Yes, of course, he concedes, art's separate images are visual, like anything else that we see, and of course its separate words are open to ordinary understanding. But his intention is not to say what a work of art is made of, or to talk about words and images. His intention is to speak of "the meaning of its appearance"—the meaning of art as something which, amazingly, appears in our life. Yes, of course, single words and images may be picked out, noted and handed round for discussion. But the word for the whole phenomenon of art (if there were such a word) cannot be quoted because it "consists in the movement of the allegory itself."

Why "movement"? Because inspiration does not remain: it strikes in, speeds by, vanishes. "Denn Bleiben ist nirgends" (For staying is nowhere), runs Rilke's existential lament in the first Duino Elegy. Pasternak could have used almost the same words, but his voice would have been full of amazement and applause. And why "symbolical"? ("Allegorical" [speaking otherwise, in other ways] and "symbolical" [throwing together, comparing—with something other] are used by him more or less interchangeably.) Because the language of symbols, figurative language (unlike clichés which stand still, to be used a thousand times), is also, as Pasternak sees it, always in movement.

The reality of the power comes across in his reference to the natural sciences. Art is their antithesis in being "interested in life at the moment when the ray of power *is passing through it*" (again there is the stress on movement). This "passing through" seems for a moment credibly physical—until the next statement reveals that the "power" is sometimes named "feeling". Nonetheless there remains a kind of balance between two insights: that the "power" which is sometimes (but not always) called "feeling" really *is* out there in nature like electricity and light; and that it only *seems* to be. This power "displaces" reality (or the poet's perception of it). The changed reality (or changed perception) is then art's sole content.

So art is both free and not free. It is not free to be about anything else, "not a telescope" to be directed here and there according to some whim or decision. Reference to a "telescope" undoubtedly encodes opposition to the Lef theory of "social command" and the RAPP assumption that artists can work to order,[159] and clearly Pasternak's view is that, in its *own* way of being unfree, art is not free to be unfree in *their* way. But the reference to a telescope also expresses his lifelong distrust of literary fantasies, poetic inventions and everything "romantic". When once, however, the "displacement" (or dislocation, *smeshchenie*) has happened, art is free to focus on absolutely anything: everything within range has become a sign of the displacement. In this sense, details are interchangeable with one another. As noted in the Introduction, the "interchangeability of images" is a phrase Pasternak laconically offers as a synonym for "art".

Part Two, chapter seventeen (2,17)

The third passage to give a concentrated account of "that which is called inspiration" comes as part of a meditation on Venetian painting. It opens with an unexpected comment on the date of writing *A Safe-Conduct* and an explanation that his thoughts will be given differently in 1930 from how he conceived them in Venice in 1912. All the same, "in my condensed conclusion I shall not move away from the truth." We are left to guess that his experience of the late Soviet 1920s is behind the announced difference. Much of 2,17 is motivated by anguish and anger, not encountered before in this work, and the whole chapter (even with restoral of the censored passage about "lions' maws . . . ") does give an impression of being abbreviated or "condensed". Its conclusion describes an artist of genius who starts to paint with unusual power only when he is seized by fury at the state's cruelties.

Three statements about Venetian painting are set up, one above the other like three rungs of a ladder, three stages in the creating of great art. The first is about "what first strikes the painterly instinct"; the second is about "syncretism"; the third, about moral fury. The first two represent cherished ideas of Pasternak's which he is here unexpectedly subordinating to a third idea.

What first strikes the painterly instinct is "what it is like for the visible when it begins to be seen". This extraordinary thought, that our perceiving of objects is an experience for the objects themselves, is presented with a minimum of highlighting—as was (in 1,6) "the hiss of a yearning" which "had not begun with me" but issued from motionless external objects. Pasternak reaffirms his intimation that the subjective agent in artistic creation is, in some sense, the visible world itself. Artists for whom this intimation suffices have nothing to do but to "carry" the somnolently passive visible world onto their canvases. Such is "depiction" (*izobrazhenie*), with its ring of "*mere* depiction" recalling the thought in 1,6 that depiction is a means to an end, not an end in itself.

The second statement is that artists may become totally fused with their work. Because of this fusion, named "syncretism",[160] it is impossible to say whether the performer (here, the painter), the performed (the painting) or the object of the performance (nature) is the most active on the canvas, and impossible to say for whose benefit and at whose expense the work is done. The age can thus believe it is raising art to its own (actually transitory) height. With disconcerting dismissiveness, Pasternak calls this stage "art". But now he proceeds to subordinate all of art, including these greatest Renaissance masters, to a third stage.

The third stage is an artist's revolt. Instead of the first stage's insights about subjectivity, and instead of the closed syncretism, or synthesis, of the second stage, he now conjures up an artist's anger against the injustice and terror inflicted by the state. Only to such an artist does he now give the name of "genius". Genius is attained through a "small, explosive" addition: the realisation that total absorption in one's work amounts to "indifference to the immediate truth"; and that there has got to be someone who will feel and see that truth. At this realisation, passion overwhelms craftsmanship: "a storm enters his canvas, cleansing the chaos of craftsmanship with defining blows of passion."

This is perhaps the point at which Pasternak joins the often invoked Russian tradition in which the great writer is one who, outside politics, tells the political truth; the tradition whereby only poet or novelist dare point out social iniquities, the holy fool alone blurts the truth to the guilty king. No calm reflective insight leads to this truth-telling. Instead, with a sudden sensation that the insult to the mass of the people is an insult to himself, the artist is overwhelmed by a "storm" and there comes a furious end to his absorption. In the work he now creates, everything will be changed by being set in motion.

Naming Tintoretto, Pasternak continues to conceal *himself* from the scene. But, although some factors suggest that by Tintoretto he means Mayakovsky, the genius of "the slap" (for the Venetian artist's feeling that he has received a "slap in the face" is bound to recall the futurists' famous 1912 manifesto, "A Slap in the Face of Public Taste"), it could also be said that Pasternak's own violent feeling is enciphered in Tintoretto's. The Venetian's rebellion would correspond to the Russian's helpless fury with the Soviet situation and would explain his readiness to demote his own hitherto valued theories. A particular clue to reading the "he" in this passage as an unspoken "I" is the word "defining". For it is Pasternak, rather than Tintoretto, who is working out a fresh definition of genius. Moreover, the paragraph is not only *about* passion, it is written *with* passion and is itself a "cleansing storm" entering the poet's work, entering, in fact, this very work, *A Safe-Conduct*. The "cleansing storm" recaptures, too, Pasternak's characteristic celebration of the way the old yields again and again to the new—in personal life, in history, and in art—whenever passion leaps off the predetermined path.

A related but different kind of celebration of the creative continuation of culture is then the theme of the following chapter (2,18), which reverts from veiled reference to the difficult year 1930 to a re-living of the 1912 stay in Venice and the insights gained there by Pasternak the young student. These culminate in a declaration which anticipates the view of history to be expounded in *Doctor Zhivago*:

> I loved the living essence of historical symbolism, in other words that instinct with whose help, like salangane swallows, we have built the world: a vast nest, stuck together from earth and sky, life and death, and two kinds of time, present and absent. I understood that what prevents it from falling apart is the force of cohesion contained in the figurativeness permeating all its particles.

Birds' nests made of pure saliva are evidently what interest Pasternak here. As certain swiftlets make their homes from a secretion of their bodies, so we humans make our symbolic universe from a secretion of our minds.[161] Pasternak must have known that many of the nests are sold to be eaten, though this is clearly not the point of his analogy. Was he leaving his reader to add to the rapturous account of our living in a home-made nest of history the darker thought that the nest is, in the end, destructible? Or is this a typical example of his attending to the positive aspect of something which, like life altogether, has also a negative one? Never mind that the nest is due for demolition, only *look* (his characteristic gesture) how wonderfully it has been constructed. The acknowledging of only two kinds of time—present and absent—reinforces his acclamation of the present and his refusal to be dismayed by past and future. These, then, are the thoughts he had in 1912, recalled in the changed circumstances of 1930.

Mayakovsky

In Part Three chapter eleven, Pasternak explains how he made a radical change of direction when he "renounced the romantic manner" and the view of life that went with it. The renunciation came directly out of his friendship with and adoration of Mayakovsky, although opposition to the "romantic", which from now on was an explicit theme, had long been implicit in his writing about art.

What he opposes is not, of course, Romanticism as a distinct literary period but any art that is a product of invention and fantasy (rather than of reality powerfully sensed and known), and, above all, the cult of the poet's personal self. "Life as the life of the poet", " the conception of biography as spectacle", making oneself into a "visual emblem" to be seen against an indispensable background of philistines, the adoption of a public pose (instead of "absorption in moral cognition")—these Pasternak saw in Mayakovsky and these he decided he must himself avoid at all costs. His own path was to be the opposite one: self-concealment, subordination to the nameless aesthetic power, devotion to craft. Yet emotionally he was overwhelmed by Mayakovsky, admiring in him, from the first moment of their meeting, the very features he would determine to avoid in himself.

In the later 1920s Mayakovsky was commonly seen as a "romantic" in his relation to the revolution ("it is my revolution", he said of October 1917),[162] while Pasternak's preference for the (non-romantic) process of moral cognition is evident in his own relation to the revolution—his painstaking attempts to understand, rather than any premature commitment for or against. As Tsvetaeva wrote (in 1922): "Pasternak's word about the revolution . . . is yet to come. In the summer of 1917, he walked in step with it, listening."[163]

The glimpse of the vanishing Rilke with which *S-C* opens could not be more different from the way the third and last part of the book is preoccupied with putting forward the physical and personal figure of Mayakovsky, "wholly contained in his manifestation" and doomed to self-destruction. In Pasternak's presentation, Mayakovsky is someone who tragically enacts his own life, and (after his death) seems the sole conceivable citizen of the new state. Yet he also embodies certain essential aspects of Pasternak's own conception of creativity. For one thing, Mayakovsky's personality is conveyed in terms of the utmost speed and dynamism: behind everything he did was "an image of the day preceding all his days when the amazing initial run had been taken which had straightened him up so largely and uninhibitedly" (3,3). In this he is closely related to Pasternak's sense of the authentic. For another, Mayakovsky's inner drama is the strange drama of art altogether: by knowing how to pour cold water gradually on to his "native fire" and rouse it to the "fury" of genius, he retraces the transition from sex to art which was described in 2,3—a transition from the passion which reproduces humankind to the passion which reproduces humankind's image. And Mayakovsky achieves the reality which Pasternak means by "only the almost-impossible is real", since, despite his choice of a life of posing, he avoids artificiality by being ready to pay for that choice with life itself—a payment he is soon to make.

Pasternak goes to great lengths to justify Mayakovsky's "posing" and playing. He explains that, having been shocked by the encounter with his own genius, the young Mayakovsky is acting out in advance the role that will later be his—of the revolution's "premier poet". When in 1914 Mayakovsky recites to him the "lyric tragedy" which bears his own name as its title, Pasternak praises (as "simple to the point of genius") its discovery that "the poet is not the author of the lyric work but is its subject (*predmet*)"—as if this were similar to the discovery he himself has made. Yet the difference is great. For Pasternak, "the poet is not the author" answers the question "what creates a poem?", while for Mayakovsky it answers the question "what am I?" Enraptured by *Vladimir Mayakovsky* no less than by Vladimir Mayakovsky, Pasternak gives the "lyric tragedy" huge prominence, while an instance of his own *non*-self-display is the slightness of reference to *My Sister Life*, the major volume of poems he himself produced three years later.

The effort of combining heartfelt praise of Mayakovsky (of the Mayakovsky, that is, who had not yet "demagnetised the magnet" or begun writing uninspired verse for the mass reader) with equally heartfelt rejection of the "romantic" features of his life, makes for what Fiona Björling calls a "tense and explosive text".[164] The phrase well indicates the paradox in Pasternak's relation to "romanticism". On the one hand, he objects to the romantic poet's need to be seen against a background of non-poets, yet on the other he shows, in his account of Mayakovsky's death, how "the impressive body of the poet" (to borrow a phrase from Peter France) is surrounded by ordinary, unimpressive things and people that show up, by contrast, its admirable extraordinariness. Similarly, in his poem of that same year, "Death of a Poet", Pasternak praises Mayakovsky's suicide shot as an "Etna among foothills", a courageous act surrounded by crowds of cowards.[165] Discussing both the poem and the *S-C* account, Peter France comments: "The fascinating thing is the degree to which . . . Pasternak uses the deathbed scene to give superb expression to the romantic conception he is at the same time repudiating."[166]

The title

The Russian title of this work—*Okhrannaia gramota*—means "a document guaranteeing that a person, or his property, stands under the special protection of state authority."[167] Its relevance to revolutionary and Soviet conditions is explained by Lazar Fleishman:

> This term went back to the vocabulary of the first years of the revolution, when the Soviet government issued documents confirming the inviolability of valuable private cultural collections and thus saved them from being plundered by mobs and from nationalization. By using this term, which at the end of the 1920s was already anachronistic, Pasternak was drawing an eloquent parallel between the first years of the revolution, when even under harsh conditions art had not been degraded, and the current situation, when art seemed defenseless before the attacks of Lef and RAPP.[168]

Recalling that, in the recent past, works of art required physical protection, the title thus hints that, at the end of the 1920s, with artists being forced to conform to politically motivated commands, they require protection in a new way.

It is unfortunate that most English translations bear the misleading title "Safe Conduct". Without a definite or an indefinite article, "conduct" means "behaviour" rather than "guidance", and the title suggests cautious behaviour. Such a mistaken reading, even if it takes place at the very back of the reader's mind, is damaging to Pasternak, who experienced art as danger and yet chose it, and most certainly did *not* spend his life trying to keep safe. Not wishing to replace the traditional translation of the title with an unrecognisable one, I am at least adding a hyphen and an article. There are two purposes to this. The first is to remove the harmful ambiguity. It must be said, though, that "A Safe-Conduct" is still incorrect as it implies a journey; neither journey nor guidance is implied by a "document of preservation" or, as Christopher Barnes suggests, "a preservation order". The second purpose is to enable it to refer to a concrete object, a document. Whereas "safe conduct" is an abstraction, "*gramota*" denotes a document and could be imagined as referring to the very book it entitles, suggesting, for example, that this written statement of its author's values implies that, by its means, he will avoid yielding to government or party pressures. I am therefore supplying a subtitle, "The Preservation Certificate".

In fact, although it was published—first in journals and then as a book in 1931—it was subjected to excisions by the censor and severely criticized both in the press and at RAPP meetings, was called the work of a "class enemy" and was not allowed to be reprinted for half a century. Not until 1982 was it published again and in full.

III

FIFTEEN
POEMS

FIFTEEN POEMS* / ПЯТНАДЦАТЬ СТИХОТВОРЕНИЙ

* See page 211.

FEBRUARY . . .

February. Get ink and weep!
To write and write of February
like bursting into sobs, with thundering
slush burning in black spring.

For half a rouble hire a cab,
ride through chimes of bells and wheels'
shrieks to where downpouring rain
drowns out tears and ink.

Where rooks like thousands of charred pears
will come tearing out of trees
straight into puddles, an avalanche:
dry grief to ground of eyes.

Under it blackening spots of thaw,
and all the wind is holed with shouts,
and poems—the randomer the truer—
take form as sobs burst out.

ФЕВРАЛЬ . . .

Февраль. Достать чернил и плакать!
Писать о феврале навзрыд.
Пока грохочущая слякоть
Весною черною горит.

Достать пролетку. За шесть гривен,
Чрез благовест, чрез клик колес
Перенестись туда, где ливень
Еще шумней чернил и слез.

Где, как обугленные груши,
С деревьев тысячи грачей
Сорвутся в лужи и обрушат
Сухую грусть на дно очей.

Под ней проталины чернеют,
И ветер криками изрыт,
И чем случайней, тем вернее
Слагаются стихи навзрыд.

SPRING

What hundreds of buds—gluey, blurry—
stuck on twigs like cigarette-butts!
April is kindled. The park sends out
a mood of maturity, woods shout back.

And the forest's neck is tightly noosed
by feathered throats—a buffalo netted,
groaning the way a cathedral organ,
steel gladiator, groans in sonatas.

Poetry! Be a Greek sponge with suckers—
I'll put you down on the damp green
plank of a garden bench beneath
all this sticky foliage—grow

lush frills and enormous fringes,
drink clouds in, absorb ravines,
and, poetry, at night I'll squeeze you out
to the health of thirsting paper.

ВЕСНА

Что почек, что клейких заплывших огарков
Налеплено к веткам! Затеплен
Апрель. Возмужалостью тянет из парка,
И реплики леса окрепли.

Лес стянут по горлу петлею пернатых
Гортаней, как буйвол арканом,
И стонет в сетях, как стенает в сонатах
Стальной гладиатор органа.

Поэзия! Греческой губкой в присосках
Будь ты, и меж зеленой клейкой
Тебя б положил я на мокрую доску
Зеленой садовой скамейкой.

Расти себе пышные брыжжи и фижмы,
Вбирай облака и овраги,
А ночью, поэзия, я тебя выжму
Во здравие жадной бумаги.

MARBURG

Trembling—I kept flaring up, then guttering—
shaking—I'd just—made a proposal—
late—lost my nerve—got a refusal.
How I pity her tears! I'm more blessed than a saint.

Out onto the square. I could be regarded
as someone reborn: every tiniest thing
was alive, every detail, completely ignoring
me, rose in its own valedictory form.

Paving-stones blazed, the street's brow
glowered, cobbles looked at the sky
with a quizzical look, while wind, a boatman,
rowed through the limes. All of this: likenesses.

Whatever it meant I avoided their glances,
didn't notice their signs of welcome
nor want to hear of their wealth, I was rushing
away—so as not to burst out howling.

That senile boring old toady, instinct,
—intolerable—crawled alongside me
thinking: "a childish crush—henceforth,
unfortunately, we must be more cautious".

"One step, then another", instinct insisted,
leading me wisely like some old scholar
through virginal reedbeds—impenetrable—
of warmed trees and lilac and passion.

"First learn to walk", it said, "then later
run". A new sun watched from the zenith
to see how walking is taught all over
again to a native of earth on a new star.

МАРБУРГ

Я вздрагивал. Я загорался и гас.
Я трясся. Я сделал сейчас предложение,—
Но поздно, я сдрейфил, и вот мне отказ.
Как жаль ее слез! Я святого блаженней.

Я вышел на площадь. Я мог быть сочтен
Вторично родившимся. Каждая малость
Жила и, не ставя меня ни во что,
В прощальном значеньи своем подымалась.

Плитняк раскалялся, и улицы лоб
Был смугл, и на небо глядел исподлобья
Булыжник, и ветер, как лодочник, греб
По липам. И все это были подобья.

Но, как бы то ни было, я избегал
Их взглядов. Я не замечал их приветствий.
Я знать ничего не хотел из богатств.
Я вон вырывался, чтоб не разреветься.

Инстинкт прирожденный, старик-подхалим,
Был невыносим мне. Он крался бок о бок
И думал: «Ребячья зазноба. За ним,
К несчастью, придется присматривать в оба».

«Шагни и еще раз»,—твердил мне инстинкт
И вел меня мудро, как старый схоластик,
Чрез девственный, непроходимый тростник
Нагретых деревьев, сирени и страсти.

«Научишься шагом, а после хоть в бег»,—
Твердил он, и новое солнце с зенита
Смотрело, как сызнова учат ходьбе
Туземца планеты на новой планиде.

177

Some things were dazzled by all this, others
thought it as dark as having no eyes.
Chicks were digging in dahlia bushes,
grasshoppers, dragonflies ticking like watches.

Tiles floated, noon stared
at roofs, unblinking. Someone in Marburg,
whistling loudly, was building a crossbow,
someone else quietly preparing for market.

Yellow sand gobbled clouds,
nascent thunder played with bushes'
eyebrows, sky curdled, stuck
on stalks of blood-stopping arnica.

That day, I carried you with me, from combs
to feet, like a tragic provincial actor
of Shakespeare, carried you everywhere, knew you
by heart as I roamed round the town, rehearsing.

The moment I fell down before you, grasping
this fog, this ice, this surface of things
(how lovely you are!), this stifling whirlwind—
What—? Be sensible! Gone. Rejected.

Luther lived here, Brothers Grimm—over there.
Roofs—like claws. Trees. Gravestones.
They all recall it. I'm drawn to them all.
And they're all alive. And it's all—likenesses.

No, I'll not go there tomorrow. Refusal's
more than farewell. It's clear. We're quits.
Not for us the commotion at stations.
Ancient flagstones, what's to become of me?

Everywhere fog will set out suitcases,
a moon will be put in each paired window.
Melancholy, a passenger, skims
volumes, sits down with a book on the sofa.

Одних это все ослепляло. Другим—
Той тьмою казалось, что глаз хоть выколи.
Копались цыплята в кустах георгин,
Сверчки и стрекозы, как часики, тикали.

Плыла черепица, и полдень смотрел,
Не смаргивая, на кровли. А в Марбурге
Кто, громко свища, мастерил самострел,
Кто молча готовился к Троицкой ярмарке.

Желтел, облака пожирая, песок,
Предгрозье играло бровями кустарника.
И небо спекалось, упав на кусок
Кровоостанавливающей арники.

В тот день всю тебя, от гребенок до ног,
Как трагик в провинции драму Шекспирову,
Носил я с собою и знал назубок,
Шатался по городу и репетировал.

Когда я упал пред тобой, охватив
Туман этот, лед этот, эту поверхность
(Как ты хороша!)—этот вихрь духоты . . .
О чем ты? Опомнись! Пропало . . . Отвергнут.

Тут жил Мартин Лютер. Там—братья Гримм.
Когтистые крыши. Деревья. Надгробья.
И все это помнит и тянется к ним.
Все—живо. И все это тоже—подобья.

Нет, я не пойду туда завтра. Отказ—
Полнее прощанья. Все ясно. Мы квиты.
Вокзальная сутолока не про нас.
Что будет со мною, старинные плиты?

Повсюду портпледы разложит туман,
И в обе оконницы вставят по месяцу.
Тоска пассажиркой скользнет по томам
И с книжкой на оттоманке поместится.

What am I scared of? I know, after all,
insomnia's grammar—we've a bond, it and I.
Why should I fear my habitual thoughts
coming back to me now like sleepwalkers?

For the nights sit down to play chess with me,
on a parquet floor lit up by the moon.
There's a scent of acacia, the window's wide open,
and passion, a witness, grows grey in the corner.

A poplar is king. I'm playing with insomnia.
A nightingale's queen. I reach for the nightingale.
And night is winning, the pieces make way.
I'll know the white dawn when I see its face.

Чего же я трушу? Ведь я, как грамматику,
Бессонницу знаю. У нас с ней союз.
Зачем же я, словно прихода лунатика,
Явления мыслей привычных боюсь?

Ведь ночи играть садятся в шахматы
Со мной на лунном паркетном полу,
Акацией пахнет, и окна распахнуты,
И страсть, как свидетель, седеет в углу.

И тополь—король. Я играю с бессонницей.
И ферзь—соловей. Я тянусь к соловью.
И ночь побеждает, фигуры сторонятся,
Я белое утро в лицо узнаю.

ABOUT THESE VERSES

I'll crush them on city paths,
mix with half sun, half glass,
show in the winter to damp
corners, reveal to rafters.

The attic will start declaiming,
bowing to winter and frames,
while up to the cornices leapfrog
lunacies, griefs, motifs.

The snow will go on for weeks,
burying beginnings and ends.
A sudden thought of sun—
and I'll see the light has changed.

Christmas will take a glance
quick as a jackdaw, cleared
skies will shed light on things
we two neither saw nor heard.

With muffler tied, face shielded,
I'll shout through a window-slot:
Hey, children, tell me, what
millennium's that outside?

Who trod a path to the door,
a hole heaped up with snow,
while I was having a smoke
with Byron, a drink with Poe?

While—let in as a friend—
I was dipping life, like the ferment
of Lérmontov—into the gorge
of Daryál, into arsenals, hell,
like dipping lips in vermouth.

ПРО ЭТИ СТИХИ

На тротуарах истолку
С стеклом и солнцем пополам.
Зимой открою потолку
И дам читать сырым углам.

Задекламирует чердак
С поклоном рамам и зиме,
К карнизам прянет чехарда
Чудачеств, бедствий и замет.

Буран не месяц будет месть,
Концы, начала заметет.
Внезапно вспомню: солнце есть;
Увижу: свет давно не тот.

Галчонком глянет Рождество,
И разгулявшийся денек
Прояснит много из того,
Что мне и милой невдомек.

В кашне, ладонью заслонясь,
Сквозь фортку кликну детворе:
Какое, милые, у нас
Тысячелетье на дворе?

Кто тропку к двери проторил,
К дыре, засыпанной крупой,
Пока я с Байроном курил,
Пока я пил с Эдгаром По?

Пока в Дарьял, как к другу, вхож,
Как в ад, в цейхгауз и в арсенал,
Я жизнь, как Лермонтова дрожь,
Как губы в вермут, окунал.

183

DEFINITION OF POETRY

It's a whistle, acutely full,
it's a crackle of squeezed ice,
it's night, freezing a leaf,
it's two nightingales in a duel.

It's the gone-wild sweetness of peas,
it's tears of the universe in pods,
it's Figaro hurtling like hail
from flutes and scores onto soil.

Everything night needs to find
at the bottom of deep bathing-pools,
and to carry a star to the pond
on slippery trembling hands.

Sultriness: flatter than boards in water.
Sky—overturned like a bowed alder.
It would suit those stars to laugh out loud,
but the universe—is without sound.

ОПРЕДЕЛЕНИЕ ПОЭЗИИ

Это—круто налившийся свист,
Это—щелканье сдавленных льдинок,
Это—ночь, леденящая лист,
Это—двух соловьев поединок.

Это—сладкий заглохший горох,
Это—слезы вселенной в лопатках,
Это—с пультов и флейт—Фигаро
Низвергается градом на грядку.

Все, что ночи так важно сыскать
На глубоких купаленных доньях,
И звезду донести до садка
На трепещущих мокрых ладонях.

Площе досок в воде—духота.
Небосвод завалился ольхою.
Этим звездам к лицу б хохотать,
Ан вселенная—место глухое.

DEFINITION OF CREATION

With shirt lapels wide open,
a wild-hair torso of Beethoven,
and one hand covering over—
like draughtsmen—night's darkness
and sleep and love and conscience,

it prepares one king-promoted
black piece, mad with yearning,
for the end of the world: above
pedestrian pawns—a horseman.

But out in the garden where stars
sweetly gasped from ice and cellar,
over Isolde's osier—rasp
of nightingale, chill of Tristan.

Gardens and ponds and fences,
the whole white-seething crying
cosmos—all of it's only
discharged passion the human
heart has accumulated.

ОПРЕДЕЛЕНИЕ ТВОРЧЕСТВА

Разметав отвороты рубашки,
Волосато, как торс у Бетховена,
Накрывает ладонью, как шашки,
Сон, и совесть, и ночь, и любовь оно.

И какую-то черную доведь,
И—с тоскою какою-то бешеной—
К преставлению света готовит,
Конноборцем над пешками пешими.

А в саду, где из погреба, со льду,
Звезды благоуханно разахались,
Соловьем над лозою Изольды
Захлебнулась Тристанова захолодь.

И сады, и пруды, и ограды,
И кипящее белыми воплями
Мирозданье—лишь страсти разряды,
Человеческим сердцем накопленной.

LET'S DROP WORDS . . .

Let's drop words as gardens
drop orange-peel and amber:
lavishly, diffusely,
and scarcely, scarcely.

No need to analyse
why with such ceremony
foliage is sprinkled
with madder and lemon—

who made needles tearful,
flooding between fences
to bookshelves and music
through venetian sluices—

who blackened the doormat
with rowan, with these hempen
lovely continuous
quivering italics.

Will you ask who orders
greatness for August,
to whom nothing's trivial,
who's plunged in trimming

each leaf of the maple,
and—since Ecclesiastes—
has stayed at his workbench
chiselling alabaster?

And lips of September's
dahlias and asters:
who says they must suffer?

ДАВАЙ РОНЯТЬ СЛОВА . . .

Давай ронять слова,
Как сад—янтарь и цедру;
Рассеянно и щедро,
Едва, едва, едва.

Не надо толковать,
Зачем так церемонно
Мареной и лимоном
Обрызнута листва.

Кто иглы заслезил
И хлынул через жерди
На ноты, к этажерке
Сквозь шлюзы жалюзы.

Кто коврик за дверьми
Рябиной иссурьмил,
Рядном сквозных, красивых
Трепещущих курсивов.

Ты спросишь, кто велит,
Чтоб август был велик,
Кому ничто не мелко,
Кто погружен в отделку

Кленового листа
И с дней экклезиаста
Не покидал поста
За теской алебастра?

Ты спросишь, кто велит,
Чтоб губы астр и далий
Сентябрьские страдали?

Or a small leaf of willow
must float from pilasters
down onto wet stone
of clinics in autumn?

You'll ask who ordains it?
The omnipotent god
of details, of love,
of Iagailos and Iadvigas.

I don't know if the riddle
of the grave is unravelled,
but life, like an autumn
stillness, is detailed.

Чтоб мелкий лист ракит
С седых кариатид
Слетал на сырость плит
Осенних госпиталей?

Ты спросишь, кто велит?
Всесильный бог деталей,
Всесильный бог любви,
Ягайлов и Ядвиг.

Не знаю, решена ль
Загадка зги загробной,
Но жизнь, как тишина
Осенняя,—подробна.

INSPIRATION

Embrasures run along fences,
breaches form in walls,
when night resounds with a van-load
of tales not known to the spring.

Crutches are torn from nooks, not
by pincers, pulled solely
by the roar of the van's approach—
far-off dust of completed paths.

This thundering's new to them.
Tomorrow I'll show you, tomorrow,
how roads sped out of gates,
flying on tracks of heat.

While in dewy, coniferous sadness
of a stream tar-sharp like morning,
buildings plunged their frames,
and a guard dipped his face.

Now everyone, even a lime-tree,
knows why the town is empty at dawn:
the last of mortals lies in a guarded
cart, underneath a poem.

Same morning, not trusting their ears,
no time to rub their eyes—
how many poor tortured pens
fly to windows from scribblers' hands!

ВДОХНОВЕНИЕ

По заборам бегут амбразуры,
Образуются бреши в стене,
Когда ночь оглашается фурой
Повестей, неизвестных весне.

Без клещей приближенье фургона
Вырывает из ниш костыли
Только гулом свершенных прогонов,
Подымающих пыль издали.

Этот грохот им слышен впервые.
Завтра, завтра понять я вам дам,
Как рвались из ворот мостовые,
Вылетая по жарким следам.

Как в росистую хвойную скорбкость
Скипидарной, как утро, струи
Погружали постройки свой корпус
И лицо окунал конвоир.

О, теперь и от лип не в секрете:
Город пуст по зарям оттого,
Что последний из смертных в карете
Под стихом и при нем часовой.

В то же утро, ушам не поверя,
Протереть не успевши очей,
Сколько бедных, истерзанных перьев
Рвется к окнам из рук рифмачей!

HERE'S THE BEGINNING . . .

Here's the beginning. Two years old—
tear from the wetnurse into a murk
of melodies, to whistle, chirp.
Words will appear by three years old.

Here's the beginning of understanding.
In the started turbine's boom
it seems your mother's not your mother,
you aren't you, home's not home.

What can the terrible loveliness
of lilac leaning low on a bench
do, unless it kidnaps children?
Here's the arising of suspicion.

Terrors grow. Can he allow
any star to elude his grasp
when he's Faust, a fantasist?
Here's the beginning of gipsydom.

This is how—soaring over fences
where there should be houses—seas
suddenly open out, like a sigh.
Here's the beginning of iambic verse.

Thus summer nights, falling face down
in oats to pray "oh be fulfilled",
set up a threat to the dawn: your eye.
Here's the beginning of feuds with the sun.

Here's the beginning of life in verse.

ТАК НАЧИНАЮТ . . .

Так начинают. Года в два
От мамки рвутся в тьму мелодий,
Щебечут, свищут,—а слова
Являются о третьем годе.

Так начинают понимать.
И в шуме пущенной турбины
Мерещится, что мать—не мать.
Что ты—не ты, что дом—чужбина.

Что делать страшной красоте
Присевшей на скамью сирени,
Когда и впрямь не красть детей?
Так возникают подозоренья.

Так зреют страхи. Как он даст
Звезде превысить досяганье,
Когда он—Фауст, когда—фантаст?
Так начинаются цыгане.

Так открываются, паря
Поверх плетней, где быть домам бы,
Внезапные, как вздох, моря.
Так будут начинаться ямбы.

Так ночи летние, ничком
Упав в овсы с мольбой: исполнься,
Грозят заре твоим зрачком,
Так затевают ссоры с солнцем.

Так начинают жить стихом.

SLANTED PICTURES . . .

Slanted pictures flying like storms
of rain from high-roads, blowing out candles,
tearing from hooks and walls into rhyme,
falling in metre—I cannot stop them.

Who cares if the entire world's masked?
Who cares if there's no latitude
whose mouths no one's provoked to plug
with putty against the winter?

But things tear their disguises off,
forfeit authority, drop their honour,
when there's a reason for singing,
or an excuse for a downpour.

КОСЫХ КАРТИН . . .

Косых картин, летящих ливмя
С шоссе, задувшего свечу,
С крюков и стен срываться к рифме
И падать в такт не отучу.

Что в том, что на вселенной—маска?
Что в том, что нет таких широт,
Которым на зиму замазкой
Зажать не вызвались бы рот?

Но вещи рвут с себя личину,
Теряют власть, роняют честь,
Когда у них есть петь причина,
Когда для ливня повод есть.

POETRY

Poetry, I will swear by you,
and my husky oath concludes:
you're no sweet-voiced performer,
you're a third-class seat in summer,
a suburb, not a tune.

Stifling as May, Iamskáia,
Shevardino's night redoubt,
where rain-clouds full of groaning
one by one loosen out.

They split at the rail's turn
—faubourg, no ritournelle—
to unravel home from stations,
struck dumb, no song at all.

Long before dawn the downpour's
shoots, in muddy clumps,
scrawl acrostics from roof-tops,
set bubbles off in rhyme.

Poetry, when beneath your tap
is a cliché, blank as a zinc pail,
the water even then won't spoil.
So here's a notebook—flow!

ПОЭЗИЯ

Поэзия, я буду клясться
Тобой и кончу, прохрипев:
Ты не осанка сладкогласца,
Ты—лето с местом в третьем классе,
Ты—пригород, а не припев.

Ты—душная, как май, Ямская,
Шевардина ночной редут,
Где тучи стоны испускают
И врозь по роспуске идут.

И в рельсовом витье двояся,—
Предместье, а не перепев,—
Ползут с вокзалов восвояси
Не с песней, а оторопев.

Отроски ливня грязнут в гроздьях
И долго, долго до зари
Кропают с кровель свой акростих,
Пуская в рифму пузыри.

Поэзия, когда под краном
Пустой, как цинк ведра, трюизм,
То и тогда струя сохранна,
Тетрадь подставлена—струись!

TO ANNA AKHMATOVA

It seems to me I'll pick out words that fit
Your nonpareil originality,
And if I get them wrong—so what?
I'll keep my errors, come what may.

I hear the murmuring speech of drenched roofs,
Silenced eclogues sunk in woodblock cobbles.
Manifest from the first lines, a town
Grows and resounds with every syllable.

Springtime around us, yet we can't go out.
Some miserly employer won't relent.
Hunched over her sewing, dawn burns,
Tears in her eyes from work by light of a lamp.

She'll breathe the smooth space of a great lake,
Speed to the water, soothe her own flagging.
But nothing's profited from such excursions.
Canals smell of mould of mildewed packaging.

Dipping along them like an empty nutshell,
Hot wind flicks the lashes
Of stars and branches, street-lamps and land-marks
And bridge with seamstress gazing into distance.

The sharpness of an eye will often vary,
Images can be apt in various ways.
But a potion of the most dread potency
Is night's distance under a white night's gaze.

АННЕ АХМАТОВОЙ

Мне кажется, я подберу слова,
Похожие на вашу первозданность.
А ошибусь,—мне это трын-трава,
Я все равно с ошибкой не расстанусь.

Я слышу мокрых кровель говорок,
Торцовых плит заглохшие эклоги.
Какой-то город, явный с первых строк,
Растет и отдается в каждом слоге.

Кругом весна, но за город нельзя.
Еще строга заказчица скупая.
Глаза шитьем за лампою слезя,
Горит заря, спины не разгибая.

Вдыхая дали ладожскую гладь,
Спешит к воде, смиряя сил упадок.
С таких гулянок ничего не взять.
Каналы пахнут затхлостью укладок.

По ним ныряет, как пустой орех,
Горячий ветер и колышет веки
Ветвей и звезд, и фонарей, и вех,
И с моста вдаль глядящей белошвейки.

Бывает глаз по-разному остер,
По-разному бывает образ точен.
Но самой страшной крепости раствор—
Ночная даль под взглядом белой ночи.

This is how I see your face, your look—
Not prompted by the pillar of salt you used
Five years ago to fasten on to verse
Your fear of looking back,

No, but beginning with your earliest books
And all their sharp-eyed grains of prose, your look
Makes everything that's in them pulse with past—
The way a wire makes sparks.

Таким я вижу облик ваш и взгляд.
Он мне внушен не тем столбом из соли,
Которым вы пять лет тому назад
Испуг оглядки к рифме прикололи.

Но, исходив из ваших первых книг,
Где крепли прозы пристальной крупицы,
Он и во всех, как искры проводник,
Событья былью заставляет биться.

TO MARINA TSVETAEVA

You're right to turn your pocket out
And say: go on, then, rummage round.
I don't care why the mist is damp.
Anything past is a morning in March.

Trees in soft coats of heavy cloth
Stand in a ground of gluey grey,
Though branches surely can't enjoy
The thick of so much coverage.

Dew makes every tendril shiver,
It flows like fine merino fleece,
And flees, and, like a hedgehog, quivers,
On its brow a dry sheaf.

I don't care whose the talking is
That floats from nowhere, overheard.
Anything past is a springtime yard
Muffled up with morning mist.

I don't care how the law's laid down
For styles of clothing in my time.
Anything past will be swept aside
Like sleep, the poet caulked up inside it.

He'll wreathe about in plumes and curls
And move like smoke
Out through a fateful age's holes
To another trackless cul-de-sac.

He'll pour out smoke, he'll tear his way
From crowds of pancake-flattened fates,
And his heirs will say, as in talk of peat,
"So-and-so's epoch is alight".

МАРИНЕ ЦВЕТАЕВОЙ

Ты вправе, вывернув карман,
Сказать: ищите, ройтесь, шарьте.
Мне все равно, чем сыр туман.
Любая быль—как утро в марте.

Деревья в мягких армяках
Стоят в грунту из гуммигута,
Хотя ветвям наверняка
Невмоготу среди закута.

Роса бросает ветки в дрожь,
Струясь, как шерсть на мериносе.
Роса бежит, тряся, как еж,
Сухой копной у переносья.

Мне все равно, чей разговор
Ловлю, плывущий ниоткуда.
Любая быль—как вешний двор,
Когда он дымкою окутан.

Мне все равно, какой фасон
Сужден при мне покрою платьев.
Любую быль сметут как сон,
Поэта в ней законопатив.

Клубясь во много рукавов,
Он двинется, подобно дыму,
Из дыр эпохи роковой
В иной тупик непроходимый.

Он вырвется, курясь, из прорв
Судеб, расплющенных в лепеху,
И внуки скажут, как про торф:
Горит такого-то эпоха.

LOVELY WOMAN . . .

Lovely woman, how your way of
being soothes and pleases, rushes
into music, pleads for rhyme.

But in rhyme, destiny disappears,
and into our small world, as truth,
comes a polyphony of worlds.

For rhyme's not just repeated vowels,
it's a cloakroom token for a seat
next to the columns in the after-
world's hum of wombs and roots.

In rhyme another love can grow
which can't be tolerated here—
they'd frown at it with wrinkled nose.

And rhyme's not merely echoed verse,
it's an entry, it's the right to pass
across a threshold, handing in
(like handing in your coat for a coin)
the weight of pain and stress, the fear
of being known, the fear of sin,
for the loud counterfoil of verse.

Lovely woman, how your way of
being pulls my breast and pulls
at me and pulls me into song.

Polycletus said prayers to you.
Your laws are written for all to see.
Your laws exist in distant time.
I've known you since antiquity.

КРАСАВИЦА МОЯ . . .

Красавица моя, вся стать,
Вся суть твоя мне по сердцу,
Вся рвется музыкою стать
И вся на рифмы просится.

А в рифмах умирает рок,
И правдой входит в наш мирок
Миров разноголосица.

И рифма не вторенье строк,
А гардеробный номерок,
Талон на место у колонн
В загробный гул корней и лон.

И в рифмах дышит та любовь,
Что тут с трудом выносится,
Перед которой хмурят бровь
И морщат переносицу.

И рифма не вторенье строк,
Но вход и пропуск за порог,
Чтоб сдать, как плащ за бляшкою,
Болезни тягость тяжкую,
Боязнь огласки и греха
За громкой бляшкою стиха.

Красавица моя, вся суть,
Вся стать твоя, красавица,
Спирает грудь и тянет в путь
И тянет петь и—нравится.

Тебе молился Поликлет.
Твои законы изданы.
Твои законы в далях лет.
Ты мне знакома издавна.

207

AGAIN CHOPIN . . .

Again Chopin—not seeking gain
but growing wings while on the wing—
constructs an exit all his own
from likelihood to certainty.

Backyards with gaps along the fences,
tow-caulked huts,
two maples—at the third, abrupt,
the neighbourhood of Reitar Street.

All day, the maples hear the children,
but when we light the lamps at night,
sewing motifs on leaves like napkins,
they crumble in a rain of fire.

Then after playing at piercing through
with white-pyramid bayonets,
in horse-chestnut tents across the road
music thunders out of windows.

Thundering, Chopin bursts from windows
while to his force, from down below,
straightening the chestnuts' candlesticks
last century looks at the stars.

Now how they pound in his sonata,
swinging a massive pendulum—
the hours of lessons and departures,
dreams with no death or stop in them.

Again? To come from underneath
acacias and be crushed beneath
Parisian carriages? Stagger, race
like life's unsteady *diligence*?

ОПЯТЬ ШОПЕН . . .

Опять Шопен не ищет выгод,
Но, окрыляясь на лету,
Один прокладывает выход
Из вероятья в правоту.

Задворки с выломанным лазом,
Хибарки с паклей по бортам.
Два клена в ряд, за третьим, разом—
Соседней Рейтарской квартал.

Весь день внимают клены детям,
Когда ж мы ночью лампу жжем
И листья, как салфетки метим,
Крошатся огненным дождем.

Тогда, насквозь проколобродив
Штыками белых пирамид,
В шатрах каштановых напротив
Из окон музыка гремит.

Гремит Шопен, из окон грянув,
А снизу, под его эффект
Прямя подсвечники каштанов,
На звезды смотрит прошлый век.

Как бьют тогда в его сонате,
Качая маятник громад,
Часы разъездов и занятий
И снов без смерти и фермат!

Итак, опять из-под акаций
Под экипажи парижан?
Опять бежать и спотыкаться,
Как жизни тряский дилижанс?

Again to chase, peal, clang, and flog
soft flesh to blood? Again
give birth to sobs, but never cry,
only not die, not die?

Again, one visit to the next
by mailcoach through the damp of night,
to hear funereal singing tones
in wheels, in leaves, in bones?

At last, like a recoiling girl,
to stop—by miracle—the press
of shouters in the dark—and freeze,
the grand-piano crucified?

After a hundred years—to catch
in self-defence at white flowers
and smash against apartment flagstones
the flagstones of winged certainty.

Again? And, offering up to petals
the piano's resonant ritual,
to fall, the whole nineteenth century,
down onto ancient cobbles.

Опять трубить, и гнать, и звякать,
И, мякоть в кровь поря,—опять
Рождать рыданье, но не плакать,
Не умирать, не умирать?

Опять в сырую ночь в мальпосте,
Проездом в гости из гостей,
Подслушать пенье на погосте
Колес, и листьев, и костей.

В конце ж, как женщина, отпрянув
И чудом сдерживая прыть
Впотьмах приставших горлопанов,
Распятьем фортепьян застыть?

А век спустя, в самозащите
Задев за белые цветы,
Разбить о плиты общежитий
Плиту крылатой правоты.

Опять? И, посвятив соцветьям
Рояля гулкий ритуал,
Всем девятнадцатым столетьем
Упасть на старый тротуар.

* "February. . ." (*Fevral'*. . .): published 1913; "Spring" (*Vesna*): published 1917; "Marburg": published 1917—these three poems are in PSS, 1, on pages 62, 90 and 110 respectively. The translation of "Marburg" given here follows the version in *Poverkh bar'erov* (1929), reprinted in *Stikhi* (Moscow: Khudozhestvennaia literatura, 1966). "Definition of Poetry" (*Opredelenie poezii*), "Definition of Creation" (*Opredelenie tvorchestva*), "Let's drop words . . ." (*Davai roniat' slova* . . .), and "About These Verses" (*Pro eti stikhi*)—all are from *"My Sister Life: Summer 1917"* (*Sestra moia—zhizn', leto 1917-go goda*), published 1922; PSS, 1, pages 131, 133, 156, 115 respectively. "Inspiration" (*Vdokhnovenie*), "Here's the beginning . . ." (*Tak nachinaiut* . . .), "Slanted pictures . . ." (*Kosykh kartin* . . . "), "Poetry" (*Poeziia*)—all are from "Themes and Variations" (*Temy i variatsii*), published 1923; PSS, 1, pages 164, 188, 190, 205 respectively. "To Anna Akhmatova" and "To Marina Tsvetaeva"—both first published in *Krasnaia nov'*, 5, 1929; PSS, 1, 212 and 214 respectively. "Lovely Woman . . ." (*Krasavitsa moia* . . .), and "Again Chopin . . ." (*Opiat' Shopen* . . .), first published in 1931 and included in the collection "Second Birth" (*Vtoroe rozhdenie*), published 1932; PSS, 2, pages 72 and 75 respectively.

Commentary on III
(FIFTEEN POEMS)

Of the selected poems, all written between 1912 and 1931, eleven are about the writing of poetry; one, "Marburg", is about an experience which led to such writing (it could be read in conjunction with *S-C* 2, 4/5); two are addressed to, and about, fellow-poets ("To Akhmatova" could be read with the two short reviews of her work in Part IV); and one, "Again Chopin . . . ", is about hearing music (and could be compared with the 1945 essay "Chopin").

My translation seeks to be faithful to vocabulary and meaning, and to imitate the original metres where possible. The originals' rhyme schemes are not adhered to. In a few stanzas the number of lines has been altered.

Inevitably, a great deal is lost in the translations. For a more vivid idea of the main qualities of Pasternak's early poetry, here are responses to it by three of his fellow-poets.[1]

In 1922, Tsvetaeva[2] (who had just received *My Sister Life*) wrote: "Downpour: the whole sky onto my head, plumb-down . . . A downpour of light." And: "Pasternak is all wide-open—eyes, nostrils, ears, lips, arms." And further: "The whole book is the affirmation 'I am!' And yet how little is said directly about himself. Unmindful of himself . . . "

A year later, Mandelstam[3] wrote: "When I read Pasternak's *My Sister Life* I experience the sheer joy of the vernacular, of the lay language freed from all extraneous influences, the common everyday language of Luther after strained and unnecessary Latin . . . This is the joy the Germans felt in their tiled houses when for the first time they opened their Gothic bibles still smelling of printer's ink." And: "To read poems by Pasternak is to get one's throat clear, to fortify one's breathing, to renovate one's lungs; such poems must be a cure for tuberculosis. At present we have no poetry healthier than this. This is *kumys* after tinned milk. I see *My Sister Life* as a collection of magnificent exercises in breathing . . . " (*Kumys*: fermented mare's or camel's milk, valued as highly nourishing.)

In 1936 Anna Akhmatova[4] wrote the poem "Boris Pasternak" which ends with the two stanzas given here in the translation by Donald Davie:

> *For likening smoke to the Laocoön,*
> *For celebrating cemetery thistles,*
> *For plenishing the world with a new accord*
> *In the new spaces of respondent stanzas,*

> *He is awarded a kind of age-long childhood,*
> *Such a profuseness and such keenness as*
> *The illustrious have, the earth all his, of which*
> *He makes all men the co-inheritors.*

Instead of a discursive Commentary, a few comments on individual poems:

"About these Verses". *My Sister Life* is dedicated to Mikhail Lermontov (1813–1841); Pasternak told his American translator, Eugene Kayden, in 1958: "I dedicated *My Sister Life* not to the memory of Lermontov but to the poet himself, as if he were still living among us, to his spirit, still active in our literature. You ask what he was for me in the summer of 1917? The personification of creative boldness and discoveries, the principle of free daily poetic affirmation of life."[5] Daryál is the Caucasian mountain gorge of Lermontov's poems.

"Definition of Poetry", "Definition of Creation". Pasternak wrote, in 1914, that "poetry cannot be defined, precisely because its definition is this: that, by the time you have named it, it has become something else".[6]

"Definition of Poetry". In stanza three of the original there is a non-sequitur, as there is in my translation ("to carry . . . ").

"Definition of Creation". Stanza two: Pasternak himself provided a note, saying that the unusual word *doved'* means a draughts piece which has been crowned upon reaching the opposite end of the board. Stanza three: "Tristan" and "Isolde" allude to Wagner's opera and the ancient legend it is based on, of illicit passion and death. Tristan calls to Isolde from the woods, imitating a nightingale; after their burial, a briar, or withe, grows from his tomb into hers. Last stanza: the word for "discharges" could alternatively be translated as "categories".

"Let's Drop Words". Stanza six: the Book of Ecclesiastes contains melancholy generalizations such as "Vanity of vanities; all is vanity . . . " and "There is no new thing under the sun" (Eccles. 1:2); despite these—the poem may be asserting—the world has continued to produce beauty. It also contains, as E.B. and E.V. Pasternak note,[7] cheerful statements such as "God made everything beautiful in his time" (3:11); with these the poem may be agreeing. Stanza eight: Iagailo and Iadviga (in Polish Jagieło and Jadwiga), the Lithuanian prince and Polish queen whose marriage in 1386 led to the long-lasting union of Poland and Lithuania.

"Inspiration". E.B. and E.V. Pasternak note that this poem was written during a night of revolutionary terror, the van being a cart carrying arrested persons, the guard also a sign of the time, and the scribblers at the end—official poem-writers for newspapers;[8] this would suggest that the poet lying in the cart with a guard standing over him is being punished by the new Bolshevik government for his unpolitical verse. But the poem also shows Pasternak merging his (pre-revolutionary) view of poetry's origin with imagery taken from current revolutionary terror.

"Poetry". Stanza two: Iamskaia street is part of a poor district in Moscow, fairly central but of inferior repute; Shevardino—the site of a battle near, but much less well known than, Borodino (where a major battle against the Napoleonic French was fought and lost in 1812).

"To Anna Akhmatova". Stanzas two and six: Leningrad (St Petersburg), with its white nights at the height of summer, is closely associated with Akhmatova. Stanza seven: "pillar of salt"—the poet, not feeling at home in the Soviet age, feared the grief of looking back to the past; her poem "Lot's Wife" is about the woman (in Book of Genesis) turned to salt for looking back at her devastated home town (Sodom). Last stanza: the word "past" translates the word *byl'* (discussed in Commentary to "On the Threshold of Inspiration"); "prose"— Pasternak often praised the "prose" of poetry, for instance in his review of Akhmatova's *Selected Works* and in his 1934 speech; see also his preference for Shakespeare's prose ("Remarks on Translations from Shakespeare") and his own desire to be a prose-writer.

"To Marina Tsvetaeva". In stanzas one, four and five, "past" is again *byl'*. For Pasternak's admiration of Tsvetaeva's poetry, one should read the two poets' correspondence: in translation—*Letters Summer 1926, Pasternak, Rilke, Tsvetayeva;** or in the original—their 1922–36 correspondence published as *Dushi nachinaiut videt'.**

"Lovely Woman . . . " Polycletus was a celebrated third-century-BC sculptor, one of whose works "was so nice and exact in all its proportions that it was looked upon as a perfect model, and accordingly called the Rule".[9]

"Again Chopin . . . " The setting is Reitarsky Street in Kiev. In stanzas one and eleven, "pravota" (rightness) has been translated as "certainty", for better rhythm and connotation. As in his later essay, the poet stresses that art contains and conveys reality, not fantasy.

IV

SPEECHES AND ARTICLES
1930s and 1940s

SPEECH AT THE FIRST ALL-UNION CONGRESS OF SOVIET WRITERS (1934)*

I have prepared my short speech[1] and have written it down and now I shall read it, but at the last moment I've remembered that discussions are going on amongst us and people may well look for allusions in what I say. Bear in mind that *in this respect* I am no fighter. Do not look in my speech for references to personalities. I am addressing it to people of my own age or younger than me in age and work. *[Applause followed these words.]*

Comrades, my appearance upon the platform is not my own doing. I was afraid you might think badly of me if I didn't appear.

For twelve days, from behind the presidium table, together with my comrades, I have been conducting a silent conversation with you all. We have exchanged glances, and tears of emotion, we have made ourselves understood through signs and have thrown flowers to one another. For twelve days we have been united by the overwhelming happiness of the fact that this grand poetic language is being born spontaneously in a conversation with the present age, in which people have torn away from the anchors of property and are freely soaring, floating and flying in the space of the biographically conceivable.

Some of those here are members with a deciding, consultative vote, others are guests and are here on tickets.

The poetic language I spoke of has sounded most strongly in the speeches of those with the most decisive vote—the guests without tickets, members of visiting delegations. In the case of all these, the poetic language has attained such strength that it has shifted the boundaries of reality and transported us into the realm of the possible, which in the socialist world is also the realm of what is to come about. Then the pioneers,[2] instead of being children in general, became your own children and you caught the modulations of your own voice in the words of the student Ilichev.[3] And when I instinctively tried to remove from the shoulder of a woman metro-construction worker a heavy ramming tool the name of which I do not know *[laughter from the audience]* but which was dragging her shoulders down, and a comrade from the presidium made fun of my

* *Vystuplenie na pervom vsesoiuznom kongresse sovetskikh pisatelei.* PSS, 5, 227–9. Eleven changes were introduced into this speech for its publication in *Pravda* of 31.8.1934 (see PSS, 5, 608–9); for two of these, see endnotes 5 and 6.

cultured sensitivity, how could he know that somehow, in the multiple steam and speed created by the situation, she was fleetingly my sister and I wanted to help her as someone close to me and long known to me?[4]

In the course of the Congress so much has been said, comrades, in this poetic language, and said with such force, that there is nothing to add. But as I am talking about this on the day for theoretical discussions of poetry, I will make use of all that has been said, to draw a conclusion about the essence of the object of our debates.

What is poetry, comrades, if we are seeing its birth before our very eyes? Poetry is prose, prose not in the sense of the aggregate of someone or other's prose works, but prose itself, the voice of prose; prose in action, not in literary narration. Poetry is the language of organic fact, that is to say of fact which has living consequences. And, like everything else in the world, it may of course be good or bad, depending on whether we preserve it undistorted or contrive to spoil it. In any case, comrades, precisely this—pure prose in its primal intensity—is poetry.

I'll end with some friendly wishes. When the Congress is over and the flow of all that's been heard, seen and felt is replaced by its ebb, my hope is that, in the quiet which uncovers the sea-bed before a new upsurge, only the essential and perfect shall remain in each one of us, while all the useless[5] and lightweight wordiness is washed, rinsed and swept away by our experiences at the Congress, by the very phenomenon of the Congress, by the speeches of the best of our comrades at the Congress. It's certainly our good fortune that there have been so many of them!

There exist norms of behaviour which make the artist's work easier. We must use them. Here is one of them:

If fortune smiles on one of us, we shall be prosperous, comrades, but may the kind of wealth that ruins people pass us by. "Do not lose contact with the masses", says the Party in such cases. I do not have the right to use its expressions. "Do not sacrifice your personality for the sake of your status", is what I shall say in exactly the same sense as the Party. Given the immense warmth with which nation and state are surrounding us, there is all too great a danger of becoming a socialist dignitary.[6] Keep away from such favour in the name of its direct sources, in the name of a great, active and fruitful love of country and of the greatest of its present-day people. *[Prolonged applause followed these words.]*

SPEECH AT THE INTERNATIONAL CONGRESS OF WRITERS FOR
THE DEFENCE OF CULTURE (1935)*

Poetry will always remain that celebrated height, higher than any Alps, which lies in the grass underfoot, so that all one has to do is bend down to see it and pick it up from the earth; it is something which will always be too simple to be able to be discussed at meetings; it will always remain an organic function of the happiness of the human being, who is filled full of the blessed gift of rational speech, and therefore the more happiness there is on earth the easier it will be to be an artist.[7]

SPEECH AT THE THIRD PLENUM OF THE BOARD OF
THE UNION OF SOVIET WRITERS (1936)**

Comrades, I too am in a state of excitement, like all those who have spoken before me.[8] I may say that Aseev's excitement most closely expressed mine— when he spoke of Belorussia and Belorussian poetry, and when he spoke of the joy that comes from the closeness of languages.

On my way here I was chiefly looking forward to meeting Iakub Kolas, Ianka Kupala, Aleksandrovich.[9] For the moment I'll confine myself to offering them my sincere gratitude for their existence, for their being so pure and genuine. *[Applause.]*

At the thought of them such names as Koltsov and Nikitin came to mind.[10] I thought of speaking about folk poetry in this connection. But I have listened so carefully and assiduously to the debates of these three days that, as I gradually got involved in them, I lost my initial zeal. However, some material has accumulated which it is useful to speak of, somewhat drily and with a certain lowering of my intended level.

When Italy started military action against Abyssinia, *Izvestiia* published excerpts from Tolstoy's diary of, it must have been, 1896, the time of Italy's first attack on Abyssinia.[11] I read those excerpts and was astonished by the similarity of Tolstoy's language to the language of Lenin on the same questions. I mention it because this similarity is dear to me, since even if it is deceptive and imaginary as regards content it is striking as regards tone, the simplicity with which Tolstoy dealt with the specious, generally accepted conventions of philistine civilization and imperialism. Mustangova prefaced her speech on

---

* *Vystuplenie na kongresse v zashchitu kul'tury. PSS, 5, 229.*
** *Vystuplenie na III plenume pravleniia Soiuza pisatelei SSSR. PSS, 5, 230–36.*

Mayakovsky with an extensive piece about the true precursors of our present-day poetry; she did this with theoretical thoroughness and from a more indisputable point of view.[12] Following her in a somewhat unexpected direction, I want to remind you that even our socialist realism could not have dropped from the sky ready-made, that even here there may be other roots in the past than merely those that are sufficiently studied and known to everyone. To me personally, for instance, it seems that the honour of being a herald in this respect is shared by Tolstoy with Maksim Gorky,[13] or, more precisely, shared by the storms of Tolstoy's unmaskings and bluntnesses. For me personally it is somewhere in this area that there lies the saving tradition in the light of which everything exaggerated, high-flown and rhetorical appears unfounded, useless, sometimes even morally suspect.

It seems to me that in recent years we with our literary banquets have deviated widely from that tradition, and that in our barristerial eloquence we seem to be waiting for some new Tolstoy, this time one brought up by the socialist revolution (Aleksei Tolstoy springs to one's lips at this point), who would represent us socialist realists at our plenum in the context of a new *Fruits of Enlightenment*.[14]

From this point of view I very much liked the talk by Surkov.[15] There was much less of that high-flown, trumpeting vulgarity which has become such a habit among us that it seems obligatory for everyone. The truth is, comrades: we ourselves are to blame for much of this. After all, not everything in the world is created deductively, from somewhere on high. Every level of society lives in its own way and is partly to blame for the kind of deposits it leaves behind. We keep putting extra fetters on ourselves which no one needs and no one has asked for. Action is wanted from us, yet we keep swearing oaths of loyalty. Svetlov[16] spoke very well about this.

Very few speakers, rare exceptions, spoke calmly, soberly, substantially. True, it's an unrealisable task—to discuss the very bases of art in the context of a plenary session, even if each speaker were to be given a whole hour. There are many inveterate prejudices and preconceived opinions. An analysis of these errors would take a lifetime, which in itself is not easy, yet the task has been made difficult in another way too. A great many false views have become dogmas just because whenever they are affirmed they are coupled with some other view which is irrefutable, even sacred, and part of the grace belonging to those absolutely indisputable matters seems to transfer to statements which are far from obligatory for all of us.

For example, Bezymensky began with such things as the revolution, the masses and Soviet society, and then, not without demagogy, he went on to make reproaches, accusing me—as if it were something unsoviet—of not "travelling about on poetry-reading tours" (his expression).[17] But what if the reason I do not do this is my respect for our age, which has grown to be capable of genuine, more serious forms? And what if I consider my merit to lie in the very thing Bezymensky finds incomprehensible? What if, for instance, I was once captivated by the way Pushkin and Tiutchev[18] travelled, and still do, through their books, what if I have given up all the strength of my heart to the difficulty of that sort of travelling, to the neglect of the easiness—so inordinately rooted among us—of stage-performance tours?

Comrades, long long ago, about the year twenty-two, I felt ashamed of the sybaritic accessibility of stage success. You only had to appear on a platform and applause would start up. I felt faced with the possibility of the birth of a second life, a false and artificial one, repulsive in its cheap brilliance, and this made me recoil from that path. I saw that my role lay in the rebirth of the book of poetry with pages that spoke by the force of their deafening muteness; I began to emulate higher models.

Comrades, if we put up with the depravity of stage readings, which have developed into a fairground entertainment and at times reach the point of sheer barbarism, then it is only because Mayakovsky, in this respect too, I mean as an *appearance* upon a stage, was such a living truth and gave such an amazing amount that he justified this field of activity for several generations ahead, as it were, redeeming the sins of many music-hall heroes to come.[19]

I have been very surprised to hear my own name repeated so often at this plenary session.

Comrades, I am not to blame for this, I do not understand these tendencies, I have not myself given occasion for these exaggerations. Like each one of you, I am something real, I am not transparent, I am a body in space. But we have many humorists among us with excessively histrionic imaginations. Not only I, but any subject, as soon as they start dealing with it, gets overgrown with a mountain of vulgarities; you yourselves have witnessed performances of this sort. Am I responsible for the fact that Bezymensky sees life, art, human destiny and his own role in it all, in this particular way and not some other way? Am I responsible for the elegance with which Vera Inber divided the history of mankind into two main parts and found the solution to all the troubles and griefs she considers unthinkable in our country in a geometric tracing on a frosty tram-window?

Even Utkin, who is far from being my idol and is not at all well disposed towards me, observed, when retorting to the critique of his verse undertaken by Vera Mikhailovna,[20] that she was not pleased with the way he kills off one of the characters in it and that she would have done it some other way.

It must be said in Vera Inber's defence that she is not alone in this. With few exceptions, everyone here has been analysing lines and stanzas as if they were real events, or as blunders due to some oversight, or, at best, as dull or vivid anecdotes. But, comrades, the *feuilleton* is but one genre of many, and, however prevalent it may be in our day we are not in the least obliged to accept it as a philosophical system.

In general, people have talked here about writing poetry as if they were talking about the working of a machine which is constantly in action, the output of which is directly proportional to the labour applied. I visualised a water pump which, despite all efforts, kept lagging behind general requirements. But everyone kept vowing: we'll apply ourselves, then obviously there will be more water and our minds can be at rest about our poetic future.

No, seriously, comrades, in many points I just do not understand some of the speakers—we don't talk the same language. For example, confident distinctions have been made between good poems and bad ones, as if it were a matter of machine parts accurately or inaccurately turned. Yet what were quoted as bad poems were not poems at all but simply models of bad taste, bad taste which, morally, is not accidental, and I have been convinced yet again that, generally speaking, there are not bad or good lines, but there are bad and good poets, that's to say whole systems of thinking which either are productive or else run idle. And the Stakhanovite promises from the latter kind can be very depressing in their contradictoriness.[21]

Those who spoke best about Stakhanovites, and spoke with a sincere and fruitful excitement, are the German poet Johannes Becher and Semion Kirsanov.[22] I should like to add one point to what they said: this unexpectedness is the greatest gift life can delight us with; in our sphere there ought to be more such unexpected things; at this plenum we ought to have spoken about the unexpected, and yet nothing has been said about it. In a moment you will see what I am leading up to by mentioning this.

Although I cast doubt just now on the expediency of dividing poems into good and bad, the latter sort, generally speaking, are conceivable in a somewhat different connection. Thus, comrades, a period of this sort has begun for me, and I am glad of it. For a while I am going to write badly—from my previous point of view—up to the moment when I get accustomed to the novelty of the themes and propositions I want to touch on. It will be bad in several respects, starting with the artistic, for this flight from one position to another will have to be accomplished in a space which has become rarefied through journalistic abstractions and is lacking in imagery and concreteness. It will also be bad as regards the aims for the sake of which it is being accomplished, because on these themes that are common to us all I shall not speak in the common tongue, I shall not repeat you, comrades, but shall argue with you, and as you are the majority, then once again it will be a fateful argument and its outcome will be in your favour. And although I don't flatter myself here with any hopes, I have no choice, all this is what I am living at the moment and I cannot do otherwise.

I have published two such poems in the January number of *Izvestiia*;[23] they were written in the heat of the moment, just anyhow, with an ease that is permissible in pure lyric poetry but inadmissible for such themes as those, which demand to be artistically thought through; but so it will be, I cannot alter it, for a while I shall write like a cobbler, forgive me.

Now, comrades, something else, which I have lightly touched upon already. There are consequences of gigantic upheavals, compared with which each one of us is just an insect. But we ourselves, as members of a corporation, atoms of a social fabric, are to blame for a certain aspect of our literary stagnation. And salvation is not to be expected from an increase in hard work, as people here have said it is. Art is unthinkable without risk and spiritual self-sacrifice; freedom and boldness of imagination have to be gained in practice, and it is *here* that the unexpected belongs which I spoke of earlier: do not expect a directive on this score. Only two people here have spoken in this spirit: Svetlov and Becher.

Is it the business of the Board of the Union to tell you to be more bold? It is the task of every one of us, it is our own task. Every one of us has been given a mind and a heart for this purpose. I do not recall any decree in our legislation forbidding us to be a genius—if there were, some of our leaders would have to prohibit themselves. This must mean we have just as much scope regarding the possibility of new ideas as we have in the refurbishing of old ones.

And now that I have used such a word as genius I shall dwell on this concept a little, to avoid misinterpretations. In my view the genius is akin to the ordinary man, and more than that: he is the greatest and rarest representative of this species, its immortal expression. These are the quantitative poles of qualitatively homogeneous models of humanity, but the distance between them does not lie empty. This gap is filled by those "interesting people", those non-ordinary persons who are always third persons, and who, to my mind, constitute the mass of so-called mediocrity. I expressed this conviction once before à propos of Mayakovsky in a book I would now write differently.[24] But there he was called a person of huge ordinariness.[25] Comrades, there is no ordinary person who is not a genius in rudiment, this is what unites us, it is on this correct observation that religion has erected its false superstructure about the immortality of the soul, and we are separated only by mediocrity which has invented long hair, violins and velvet jackets.

Solely in the understanding of this in-between area, solely, that is, in mediocrity's distorting mirror, does it appear that, if I write as I best know how, I am consequently obliged to do such and such, obliged, in particular, let us say, to reject Demian Bednyi.[26] I'll start with the fact that I prefer him to the majority of you, and I'll go on to say something else. Do you see, comrades, I am deeply indifferent as to the separate components of any integral form, so long as it is primal and genuine; that is, I am indifferent as to whether or not the artistic passion, either the kind described by Balzac in "Le Chef-d'oeuvre inconnu", or some other kind, is the source of an ample participation in life, so long as between author and expression there are no intrusive links of imitativeness, false attempts to be unusual, or bad taste: bad in the sense of being the taste of the mediocre. And I tell you, comrades, that Demian Bednyi is not just a historical figure of the revolution in its decisive moments of fronts and of war communism, for me he is and remains to this day the Hans Sachs of our popular movement,[27] and Mayakovsky, whose genius I was amazed at before many of you were and whom I loved to the point of adoration, cannot, in this field, enter any comparison with the naturalness of Demian's role. Where the one dissolves without remainder into the naturalness of the vocation that is right for him, the other finds a point of application for only a part of his immense strength. I am looking at this, comrades, from a historical point of view and not from the angle of aesthetic technique, and, to avoid further misinterpretations, I shall end here. *[Prolonged and tumultuous applause.]*

ON SHAKESPEARE*

The declaration of war tore me away from the first pages of *Romeo and Juliet*. I abandoned my translation and, while seeing off my son who was leaving for defence work, and dealing with other disturbing matters, I forgot about Shakespeare. Weeks followed when everything in the world, willy nilly, joined in the war. During the nights of bombardment I was on duty on the roof of a twelve-storey building—and in one of my duty periods I saw the building hit by two high-explosive bombs; I constructed a dug-out at my place outside town, and I attended military training courses which unexpectedly revealed me as a born marksman. My family was sent to the inner depths of the province. I was constantly trying to join them.

At the end of October I travelled to my wife and children; winter in a provincial town far from the railway, on a frozen river which served as the sole means of communication, cut me off from the outside world and sat me down for three months at the interrupted *Romeo*.

Shakespeare will always be the favourite of generations which are historically mature and have lived through a lot. Numerous ordeals teach people

* *O Shekspire*. PSS, 5, 44–45. Written at the request of the Soviet Bureau of Information. First published, as "My New Translations" (*Moi novye perevody*), in *Ogonek* 47 (1942), with alterations.

to value the voice of facts, actual knowledge and the art of realism, serious and full of content.

Shakespeare remains the ideal and high point of this trend. In no one else does knowledge of humanity attain such a level of rightness, and no one else has set out that knowledge so wilfully. At first sight these are contradictory qualities. But they are connected by a direct dependence on each other. The lawlessness of Shakespeare's style, which so irritated Voltaire and Tolstoy,[28] shows how volcanic is the structure of our much-praised artistic objectivity. For it is, in the first place, a miracle of objectivity. It is his famous characters, that gallery of types, ages and temperaments, all with their distinctive actions and individual modes of speech. And Shakespeare is not bothered if their conversations get interwoven with the effusions of his own genius. His aesthetics is constructed upon an alternation of self-forgetfulness and attentiveness, the lofty and the absurd, prose and verse.

In every respect he is a child of nature, whether we consider his unbridled form, his composition and manner of sculpting, or his psychology and the moral content of his dramas. The explosions of Shakespeare's imagery are quite exceptional. His analogies represent a limit beyond which the subjective principle in poetry has never gone. He set a deeper personal imprint on his works than anyone before or after him.

His presence is felt in them not only by virtue of their originality. When there is talk in them of good and evil, or falsehood and truth, there rises up before us an image inconceivable in a grovelling, servile situation. We hear the voice of a genius, of a king among kings and a judge over gods, the voice of the most recent western democracies, based as they are on the proud dignity of labourer and fighter.

For a long time I have wanted to work on Shakespeare's dramatic chronicles. Our age prompts a new interest in them. The two *Richards* are a veritable Bible for the historian. But in artistic work, as in all other kinds of work, one has to be guided by practical considerations.[29]

Two or three years ago I translated *Hamlet*, and last winter—*Romeo and Juliet*. What can I say about the principles behind my translations? The greatness of the original saves me from superfluous explanation. For Shakespeare nothing will do but perfect naturalness and mental freedom. For the first of these I had prepared myself as well as I could in the modest course of my own writings, my convictions prepared me for the second.

Again it is winter. Again I am about to join my family in a remote little town on the Kama and, if fate wills, shall start work translating *Antony and Cleopatra* for a production planned by the Moscow Arts Theatre.

A NEW COLLECTION OF WORK BY ANNA AKHMATOVA*

Recently a volume of poems by Anna Akhmatova came out in Tashkent with the publishing house "Soviet Writer".

Powerful, clear, profound poems which have long been loved, and which are effective no matter what selection is made; poems about Russian life, the agitations of youth, the vicissitudes of history and the beauties of nature. Among the many additions are new poems about the war which flow forth in a different way from the famous Akhmatova lines about 1914—headlong, gripping poems written by a great person with a great nature.

A new and rewarding occasion for making a fundamental restoration of this splendid writer's image, in her role as a bold renovator who counterbalances the gigantic, chaotically inspired effect of Blok the reformer with the traits of her own new realism, every last word of which is uttered here.

Two blood-shedding wars, their traces on almost every page, and amid them the well-known profile with proudly raised head—the life and activity of a staunch, unbending, straightforward daughter of the nation and of the age, hardened, accustomed to losses, courageously ready for the trials of immortality. What more can be added to this cursory list?

With satisfaction our eye seeks out records of recent years, of 1939, 1940 and 1941, amongst the delightfulness of the rest of the poems. Akhmatova's conciseness, fluency and freedom from coercion are qualities long known to us, qualities which were already, in her always masterly work, Pushkinian squared and cubed, and are from now on Pushkinian to an infinite degree.

SELECTED WORKS BY ANNA AKHMATOVA**

A selected "Akhmatova" has been published. It convinces us that this writer has never fallen silent but has, with short intervals, always responded to the demands of the age.

The book is three times more condensed than the recent collection *From Six Books*.[30] It is supplemented by a large amount of new material. These works, most of which recall the vivid and fascinating manner of Akhmatova's last book,

---

* *Novyi sbornik Anny Akhmatovoi.* PSS, 5, 46. Written for *Ogonek*, August 1943. First published in *Russian Literature Triquarterly* 9 (Ann Arbor, 1974). First published in Russia in *Zvezda* 6 (1989).

** *Izbrannoe Anny Akhmatovoi.* PSS, 5, 46–49. Written for *Literatura i iskusstvo,* Autumn 1943. First published in *Russian Literature Triquarterly* 9 (Ann Arbor, 1974). First published in Russia in *Zvezda* 6 (1989).

Willows, develop her characteristic style and doubtless point forward to her new contemporary *poema*, her central work which, although it has been read in public, has not yet been published by its exacting author.[31]

The book shows once again Akhmatova's main characteristic—equality in artistic value between her early and her later period. With no fear of their being stylistically incompatible, the compiler was able to put side by side poems from the 1910s and from the 1940s. Thus between the poem "The first long-range [weapon] in Leningrad", in which the sensation of enemy fire is described by means of a device belonging to Akhmatova of the present day:

> *How indifferently he brought*
> *Death to my child . . .*

and the poem "To the Memory of July 19th 1914" with its famous lines:

> *We aged a hundred years and this*
> *Took but a single hour . . .*

there is a gap of twenty-seven years. But that is a secret of their chronology. Just as these wars followed one upon the other in the history of Russian existence, so the thoughts contained in the two poems are spoken by the same voice and as if simultaneously.

Another poem of extraordinary power and with a similar title, "July 1914", is missing from this collection. Its absence, like the absence of a number of the best poems in *Rosary* and *White Flock*, such as "At Evening" or "The sky sows a thin rain", is upsetting and leaves us bewildered.

It would be strange to call Akhmatova a war poet. But the predominance of stormy elements in the century's atmosphere has given her work a tinge of civic significance. This patriotic note, especially valued at the moment, stands out in her work as a complete absence of pompousness or straining. Faith in her native sky and loyalty to her native earth break through of themselves with the naturalness of an innate way of walking.

To praise a great artist's personal virtues is to lower the worth of that artist's all-consuming gift. Akhmatova has given expression to the present war more vividly than to the previous one not as a consequence of the increased warmth and experience of her heart but because, as the greatest mirror of Russian life, she has reflected these wars in their actual historical differentness.

In the present war there is a brutality and a considered inhumanity which were not known in the last one. Fascism fights not against armies but against peoples and historical customs. A personal challenge is thrown to every individual. Bombing from the air has turned big cities into areas of the front line. There is nothing surprising in the fact that Akhmatova, a Leningrader, wrote to Londoners a poem as direct as a letter,[32] and that her lines about a Leningrad boy who was killed are full of heart-rending bitterness and seem written to the dictation of his mother, or of an old Sebastopol soldier's wife.

Along with the tone of national pride, we would say that the chief distinguishing feature of Akhmatova is her artistic realism.

So often the conventionally alive "you" of most poetic outpourings degenerates into an erotic abstraction: in opposition to this, Akhmatova used the voice of real feeling, full of the meaning of a real love-relationship. Such openness to life she shared with Blok, with the then still scarcely fledged Mayakovsky, and with Ibsen and Chekhov, Hamsun and Gorky, all of them already in full view with their concern for matters of clear importance and for people of strength. This gave her first books, *Evening* and *Rosary*, the narrative freshness and original dramatic quality of prose. There are specimens of poems of that kind in the present book—"Song of the Last Meeting", "I wrung my hands under my dark veil", "The beloved always asks for much", "Real tenderness cannot be confused". But there are few of them and there could well have been more.

These were the poems which became engraved in readers' memories and which, in the main, created a name for Akhmatova the lyric poet. At one time they had an enormous influence on ways of feeling, not to mention the literary school of their time. It is impossible to judge these verses without judging their imitators, and any account of this aspect of Akhmatova will say more about the degree of her fame and popularity than about the essence of her lyric Muse.

Nonetheless Akhmatova's words about the female heart would not be so warm or so striking if her eye did not have such astonishing sharpness and accuracy when she looks at the wider world of nature and history. All her descriptions, whether of a remote spot in a forest or of the noisy street life of the metropolis, are sustained by an uncommon flair for details. Her ability to make an inspired choice of them and to characterize them quickly and precisely saved her from the false, redundant imagery of many contemporaries. In her descriptions there are always features, particulars, which turn them into historical pictures of the age. For the way they illuminate the whole epoch they belong beside the visual authenticities of Bunin.

The compiler has selected valuable and long-praised material with due taste and understanding.

NOTES OF A TRANSLATOR*

1

Last year E.F. Knipovich, I.N. Rozanov and I brought to its finish the *Anthology of English Poetry* already compiled but not yet published by Goslitizdat.[33] As we looked through it, we revived certain thoughts we had had many times before. We will communicate them.

Compilers of foreign anthologies begin by making a selection of original texts, and then look for the required translations. Our compiler, A.I. Startsev, chose the opposite path, taking already achieved results as his starting point. The best Russian translations produced during the last century and a half, starting with Zhukovsky,[34] were made the basis of the anthology irrespective of whether these best witnesses to the Russian genius corresponded to the greatest successes of the English genius.

As it turned out, this kind of selection corroborated a conviction we had long held. Translations either have no meaning at all or else they have got to have a closer link with their originals than is usually accepted. Correspondence of text to text is too weak a link to guarantee that a translation achieves its aim. Such translations fail to justify their promise. The pale re-tellings they offer give no idea of the most important aspect of the thing they undertake to reflect— its power. To attain its purpose, a translation must be linked to its original by a more real dependence. The relation between an original and a translation must be that between a base and its derivative,[35] between a tree-trunk and a cutting from it. The translation must come from an author who has felt the effect of the original upon himself long before he starts work. It should be the original's fruit and historical consequence.

This is why imitations and borrowings, the phenomena of a school and instances of foreign influence lead more intimately into the world of European models than do direct transpositions of them. What the present anthology does is offer a picture of such influences. It portrays English poetry in respect of the power we have experienced from it. It shows English poetry in its Russian effect. This corresponds most profoundly to the very idea and purpose of translation.

As we have said, translations are essentially impossible because the main charm of a work of art lies in its unrepeatability. So how can a translation repeat it?

Translations are conceivable because ideally they too have to be works of art, and, by virtue of their own unrepeatability, must stand on the same level as the originals, while sharing their text. Translations are conceivable because,

---

* *Zametki perevodchika.* PSS, 5, 51–54. First published in *Znamia* 1 (1944), with four poems by Shelley in Pasternak's translation.

for centuries before our time, whole literatures translated one another, and translation is not so much a method of becoming acquainted with individual works as a medium for the age-old communion of cultures and peoples.

2

The possibilities of English metre are inexhaustible. The non-polysyllabic nature of the English language offers immense scope to English style. The compactness of the English phrase is a pledge of its richness in content, and richness in content is a guarantee of musicality, since the music of a word consists not in its sonority but in the correlation between sound and meaning. English versification is in this sense supremely musical.

At one time we vainly tried to explain Pushkin's and Lermontov's youthful anglomania as solely the influence of Byron's ideas. We always sensed that there was some other, elusive, foundation to their enthusiasm. Later, when we gained a modest acquaintance with Keats and Swinburne, we were arrested by the same enigma. The measure of our delight was not accounted for by the attraction they themselves exerted. Behind their effect on us we seemed to glimpse that same repeated, mysterious, additional something. For a long time we attributed this phenomenon to the enchantment of the English language itself and the advantages it offers to lyrical form. We were wrong. The secret additional something that gives an extra charm to every line is the invisible presence of Shakespeare and his influence in a multitude of the most active and typical English devices and turns of phrase.

Quite recently the editors of the *Anthology* came to believe its publication was hindered by the absence of translations from Shelley. They turned to Akhmatova, Zenkevich[36] and the present writer to fill this gap.

Despite editorial prejudice and opposition, we still think the Russian Shelley was and is the three-volume Balmont translation.[37] In its time this work was a discovery similar to those made by Zhukovsky. The neglect it has received is due to a misunderstanding. Balmont's work on Shelley coincided with the creative years of his youth, before his freshness and singularity were vitiated by his later watery artificiality. It is a great shame that the later Balmont uncrowns the earlier.

With extreme reluctance we addressed ourselves to a poet we had always found distant and abstract, foreseeing no joy from the task. Probably we were right and have failed. But we would never have completed the work had we retained our previous opinion of this great lyric poet. In order to come into contact with him, even at the price of failure, we had to look into him more closely. We reached an unexpected conclusion.

In this invoker of the elements, singer of revolutions, atheist and author of atheistic treatises, we discovered a precursor and harbinger of the urbanistic mysticism later to pervade Russian and European symbolism. As soon as we heard the future voices of Blok, Verhaeren and Rilke in Shelley's apostrophes to clouds and wind, everything in him took on flesh for us. Naturally, we still translated him as a classical poet. These remarks refer chiefly to "Ode to the West Wind".

PAUL-MARIE VERLAINE*

One hundred years ago, on 30 March 1844, in the town of Metz, was born the great lyric poet of France, Paul Verlaine. What is there about him that can interest us today, in these serious and ardent days of ours, in the light of our stupendous victory? He left a vivid record of things seen and experienced, similar in spirit and expression to the later work of Blok, Rilke, Ibsen, Chekhov and other recent writers, and linked by threads of deep kinship to the young impressionist painting of France, Russia and the Scandinavian countries.

Artists of this type were surrounded by a new urban reality, unlike that of Pushkin, Mérimé and Stendhal. The nineteenth century with its caprices, with the tyrannical stupidity of its industry, with financial tempests and a society consisting of the victimized and the pampered, was in its prime and was moving towards its end. The streets had just been covered with asphalt and lit by gas. Factories were settling on them and growing like mushrooms, just like the daily newspapers which were also multiplying inordinately. The railways had expanded to the utmost degree and had become a part of every child's existence, differing according to whether his childhood itself flew by train past a town at night or whether night trains flew past his poor suburban childhood.

On that street, with its new kind of lighting, shadows lay differently from those in Balzac's time; people walked along it in a new way, and one wanted to draw it in a new way, too, in accordance with the model. The chief novelty about the street, however, was not the lamps or the telegraph wires but the whirling of an egoistic elemental force[38] that rushed down it as distinctly as the autumn wind, chasing beggary, consumption, prostitution and other delights of the age down the pavements like leaves from the boulevards. This whirlwind leapt to everyone's eye and was the centre of the picture. The workers' movement entered its conscious phase in the blowing of this whirlwind. Its breathing particularly formed the new artists' angle of vision.

The reason they painted in smears and dots, in hints and half-tones, was not that they especially wanted to, or that they were symbolists. Reality itself was

* Pol'-Mari Verlen. PSS, 5, 54–58. Written for the centenary of the birth of Verlaine (1844–1896). First published in Literatura i iskusstvo, 1.4.1944.

the symbolist, for it was made up wholly of transitions and fermentations, the whole of it signified rather than constituted something, served as symptom and portent rather than gave satisfaction. Everything was displaced and transferred, the old and the new, church, village, city and national character. It was a rushing whirlpool of conventions, in between two absolutes, one left behind and one not yet attained, a distant presentiment of the most important matter of the age— socialism—and the event that would give it a face, the Russian revolution.

And as Blok the realist gave the best and most intimate picture of Petersburg in this flashing by of portents and signs, so Verlaine the realist acted too, when in his impermissibly personal confessions he assigned the main role to the historical time and circumstances amid which his downfalls and repentances took their course.

He was the son of a colonel who died young, he was the favourite of his mother and of the female servants, and as a boy he was sent from the provinces to a private boarding-school in Paris. There was something resembling the life of Lermontov in the dove-like purity which he derived from a circle of women, and in its consequent fate among dissolute companions in Paris. When he finished school he became a town council employee. The year 1870 found him in the National Guard in the fortifications of Paris. He married. The Insurrection broke out. He took part in the activities of the Commune,[39] working in the press. This had an effect on his fate. He was dismissed when order was re-established. Then fate sent him an evil genius in the form of that monster of talent, the riotous eccentric adolescent poet, Arthur Rimbaud.

To his cost he himself dug up this "beginner" somewhere in Charleroi and got him to join him in Paris. From the time when Rimbaud moved in with the Verlaines their normal life was finished. Verlaine's subsequent fate is flooded with the tears of his wife and child. Now began the wanderings of Rimbaud and Verlaine—who had left his family for good—along the highways of France and Belgium, their hard drinking together, their half-starving life in London, earning a pittance, the fight in Stuttgart, lock-ups and hospitals.

Once, in Brussels, after a serious quarrel, Verlaine dashed out after Rimbaud who was leaving him, shot at him twice and wounded him, and was arrested and sentenced by law to two years' confinement in the prison at Mons.

After this, Rimbaud set off for Africa to conquer new territories for Menelik, the Abyssinian whose service he had entered, while Verlaine wrote one of his best books in prison.

He died in the winter of 1896, having added nothing remarkable to his already long-established fame, and surrounded by the respectful attention of young people and imitators.

Verlaine had started writing early. The *Poèmes saturniens* of his first book were written at college. His deceptive poetics, as well as the titles of some of his books, such as *Romances sans paroles* (an audacious name for a work of literature) led to false conceptions. It might be thought that the scorn he proclaimed for considerations of style was prompted by an aspiration to the notorious "musicality" (understood by few), that he was sacrificing the semantic and graphic side of poetry in favour of the vocal. This is not so. Just the opposite is true. Like every great artist, he demanded "not words but action", action even from *the art of the word*—that is, he wanted poetry to contain what had been really experienced, what had been truly witnessed by the observer.

Here is what he says about this in the famous poem "Art Poétique", which has been mistakenly used as a manifesto of *zaum'* [40] and of "melodiousness":

> *Tu feras bien, en train d'énergie,*
> *De rendre un peu la Rime assagie.*

And further:

> *Que ton vers soit la chose envolée*
> *Qu'on sent qui fuit d'une âme en allée*
> *Vers d'autres cieux à d'autres amours,*
> *Que ton vers soit la bonne aventure*
> *Eparse au vent crispé du matin*
> *Qui va fleurant le menthe et le thym . . .*
> *Et tout le reste est littérature.* [41]

Verlaine had the right to speak like this. He knew how to imitate bells in his poems, he caught and made fast the smells of the chief flora of his native land, he successfully mimicked birds, and, in his work, ran through all the modulations of silence, both inner and outer, from the starry speechlessness of winter to the torpor of a hot sunny noon in summer. Like no one else, he expressed the long, gnawing, relentless pain of a lost possession, whether it was the loss of God, who had been and who had ceased to be, or of a woman who had changed her mind, or of a place dearer than life which one had to leave, or the loss of peace.

What sort of person must one be to imagine a great and accomplished artist as a medium-like nonentity, a depraved child who doesn't know what he is doing? Our ideas also undervalue the eagle-like sobriety of Blok, his historical tact, *his feeling of the rightness of being on the earth,* a feeling which is inseparable from genius. No, Verlaine had a splendid knowledge of what he had to do and what French poetry needed to convey the new whirlwind in the soul and the town that we have spoken of. And, whatever his degree of drunkenness or irresponsible scribbling, he broke down sensation to the desired limit, brought his thoughts to a supreme clarity, and gave to the language in which he wrote that boundless freedom which was his own discovery in lyric poetry and is found only in masters of prose dialogue in novel and drama. The Parisian idiom, in all its purity and enchanting aptness, flew in from the street and lay down whole in the line of verse, without the slightest constraint, as melodic material for the whole of the subsequent construction. Verlaine's chief fascination lies in this forward-moving spontaneity. For him, French turns of speech were indivisible. He wrote in entire phrases, not in separate words, he did not fragment them, did not re-arrange them.

Many, though not all, are both simple and natural, but they are simple in that initial degree where it is a matter of their conscience and where the only interesting question is whether they are sincerely simple or just pretending to be simple. That sort of simplicity is a non-creative quantity and bears no relation to art. But we are talking here about an ideal, infinite simplicity. This is the simplicity which Verlaine had. In comparison with de Musset's naturalness,[42] Verlaine's naturalness cannot be anticipated, he does not move from the spot, he is natural in a colloquial, supernatural way—that is, he is simple not because he wants to be believed but in order not to impede the voice of life that bursts forth from him.

This is essentially all we have allowed ourselves to say, given the limited time and space.

CHOPIN*

1

It is easy to be a realist in painting, an art which visually addresses the external world. But what does realism mean in music? Nowhere are conventionality and evasiveness so easily forgiven as they are in music, no other sphere of creativity is so haunted by the spirit of romanticism, that principle of arbitrariness, always successful because never verifiable. Yet even here everything is based on exceptions. There are a multitude of them, and they constitute the history of music. There are exceptions, however, even among the exceptions. There are two: Bach and Chopin.

These chief creators and pillars of instrumental music do not seem to us heroes of invention, figures of fantasy. They are personifications of authenticity,

---

* *Shopen.* PSS, 5, 61–65. First published (shortened) in the periodical *Leningrad,* 1945, nos. 15–16, pp. 22–3. For the fuller publication of this essay in 1945 in *Kuznica,* see Lazar Fleishman, "Pervaia publikatsiia pasternakovskoi stat'i 'O Shopene'" in *V krugu Zhivago, pasternakovskii sbornik,* ed. L. Fleishman (Stanford, 2000), 239–250.

wearing their own clothes. Their music abounds in details and produces the impression of a chronicle of their lives. In them more than in anyone else, reality comes out into the open through sound.

When we speak of realism in music, we certainly do not mean music as illustration, whether in opera or in programme music. But something quite different.[43]

Everywhere, in every art, realism, apparently, is not a distinct tendency but is a certain level of art, the highest degree of authorial exactitude. Realism is probably that decisive measure of creative attention to detail which neither the general rules of aesthetics nor contemporary listeners and spectators require of the artist. It is precisely here that the art of romanticism always stops short and is satisfied. How little is needed for it to thrive! At its disposal it has stilted pathos, false profundity and pretended sweetness; all forms of the artificial are at its service.

The realist artist is in a different position altogether. His work is his cross and his destiny. Not a shadow of liberty-taking, no trace of caprice. How should *he* play games and amuse himself when his future is playing with him, when he is its plaything!

And above all, this. What makes an artist a realist, what creates him? An early impressionability in childhood—we believe—and a timely conscientiousness in maturity. These two forces make him sit down to work, a kind of work the romantic artist does not know and is not compelled to do. His very own memories drive him into the area of technical discoveries necessary for reproducing them. Artistic realism, it seems to us, is the depth of the biographical imprint when it becomes the artist's main moving force and impels him into innovation and originality.

Chopin is a realist in just the same sense as Lev Tolstoy. His work is original through and through, not by its dissimilarity from the work of his rivals but by its similarity to the model from which he was drawing. It is always biographical, not out of egocentricity but because, like all other great realists, Chopin saw his own life as an instrument for the cognition of every life in the world, and he led exactly that sort of existence—extravagantly personal, improvidently solitary.

2

The main means of expression, the language in which Chopin set forth all he had to say, was his melody—the most powerful and unfeigned of all melody known to us. This is no matter of a short melodic motif in repeated couplets or the reiteration of an operatic aria endlessly performing one and the same thing through a voice; it is a gradually developing thought, which resembles the movement of an enthralling story or the content of a historically important event. It is powerful not only in the sense of its effect upon us. It is also powerful in that its despotic qualities were experienced by Chopin upon his own self when, as he harmonised and polished it, he traced out all the windings and subtleties of this demanding, subjugating process of formation.

For example, the theme of the third E major *étude* would have brought its author the fame of Schumann's best collections of *Lieder* even if he had used commoner, more moderate resolutions. But no! For Chopin this melody was a representative of reality; some actual image or occasion stood behind it. (Once, when his favourite pupil was playing this piece, Chopin raised his clenched hands in the air and exclaimed: "Oh, my country!") And look how he had to multiply to the point of exhaustion the passing notes and modulations, running through the seconds and thirds of the middle voice right down to the last semitone, so as to remain faithful to all the purlings and flowing hues of this urgent theme, this prototype; so as not to diverge from the truth.

Or, in the G sharp minor *étude*, the eighteenth, in thirds, with the winter journey (a content more often attributed to the seventh *étude*, in C major), the mood, which is like the elegiac in Schubert, could have been achieved at less expense. But no! It was not just the bumping of a sleigh into pot-holes that had to be expressed, but the arrow of the path being constantly crossed by white flakes floating at a slant, while being cut across from another angle by the black leaden horizon, and this busy pattern of parting could only be conveyed by precisely this chromatically fleeting minor, dying away with vanishings and numb sounds of ringing.

Or, in the barcarole, that impression recalling Mendelssohn's "Song of the Venetian Boatman" might have been attained by more modest means, in which case it would have had just that poetic approximacy that is usually associated with such titles. But no! the embankment's lights whirled and scattered oilily in the bending black water, there were collisions of waves, people, speeches and boats, and in order to make an engraving of this, the whole of the barcarole, just as it was, with all its arpeggios, trills and grace-notes, was obliged, like an entire pool of water, to go up and down, to fly upward and to fall with a thud on its pedal point, resonantly proclaimed by the major-minor shudderings of its harmonic element.

There is always some model before the eyes of the soul (which is what hearing is)—a model that has to be approached by careful listening, self-perfecting and selecting. This is why there is such a tapping of drops in the D major prelude; this is why, in the A major polonaise, a cavalry squadron gallops off the stage and right onto the listener, why waterfalls crash down onto the mountain path in the last part of the B minor sonata, and why, in the middle of the quiet, unrebellious F major nocturne, the window of a country estate is unexpectedly flung open during a storm at night.

Chopin travelled, gave concerts, lived half his life in Paris. Many people knew him. There are testimonies about him by such outstanding people as Heinrich Heine, Schumann, Georges Sand, Delacroix, Liszt and Berlioz. In these responses to him there is much that is valuable, yet there is even more talk of *undines*, Aeolian harps and amorous *peris*,[44] intended to give us an idea of Chopin's compositions, his manner of playing, his appearance and character. How perversely and incongruously human beings sometimes express their rapture! Nymphs and salamanders were what there was least of in this man—whereas, on the contrary, the *haut-monde* drawing-rooms teemed round him in a continuous swarm of romantic butterflies and elves when, getting up from the piano, he would walk through their parting ranks, phenomenally definite, a genius, curbing his mockery, and tired to death from writing at night and working with his pupils all day. It is said that after such evenings, to draw the company out of the stunned condition into which these improvisations had plunged them, Chopin would often creep up unnoticed to some mirror in the entrance-hall, set his tie and hair in disorder, return to the drawing-room with changed appearance and start doing comic turns with a text of his own composition—enacting a distinguished English traveller, an enraptured Parisienne, a poor old Jew. Clearly a great tragic gift is unthinkable without a sense of objectivity, and the sense of objectivity cannot do without a vein of mimicry.

It is remarkable that wherever Chopin leads us, whatever he shows us, we always yield to his inventions without any violence to our sense of what is appropriate, without any mental awkwardness. All his storms and dramas touch us closely, they are capable of taking place in the age of railways and the telegraph. Even when, in a fantasia or part of a polonaise or the ballades, a world of legend emerges that is partly linked in subject with Mickiewicz and Słowacki,[45] even then the threads of a certain verisimilitude still extend from him to the man of our own times.

The seal of this seriousness is especially strong in the most Chopin-like of Chopin—his *études*.

Chopin's *études* are called technical manuals, but they are more like pieces of research than textbooks. They are musically expounded investigations into the theory of childhood, individual chapters of a pianoforte introduction to death (how striking that half of them were written by a twenty-year-old), and they teach history or the structure of the universe or anything whatever that is more distant and general than how to play the piano. Chopin's significance is wider than music. His work seems to us a second discovery of it.

REMARKS ON TRANSLATIONS FROM SHAKESPEARE*

"General Aim of the Translations"

At different times I have translated the following plays by Shakespeare: *Hamlet, Romeo and Juliet, Antony and Cleopatra, Othello, Henry IV* (parts I and II), *Macbeth, King Lear.*

Theatres and readers have a great and perennial need for simple, readable translations. Everyone who has done any translating flatters himself with the hope that he has answered this need better than others have. I have not escaped this common hope.

Nor are my views on the nature and tasks of artistic translation exceptional. Like many others, I consider word-for-word accuracy and formal correspondence no guarantee of genuine closeness. Like a portrait's similarity to what it portrays, a translation's similarity to its original is achieved by vitality and naturalness of language. No less than an original writer, the translator must avoid a vocabulary which is not his own in everyday life and the literary pretence consisting in stylisation. Like the original, the translation must give an impression of life, not literariness.

"Shakespeare's Poetic Style"

Shakespeare's style is distinguished by three peculiarities. The spirit of his plays is deeply realistic. The parts written in prose, and the places where poetic dialogue is combined with action or movement, are colloquial and natural. In other places the floods of blank verse are highly metaphorical, sometimes unnecessarily so and to the detriment of verisimilitude.

Shakespeare's figurative speech is not uniform. Sometimes it is the highest poetry, demanding from us an appropriate response; at other times it is frankly rhetoric, piling up a dozen empty circumlocutions instead of the one word which is on the tip of the author's tongue and which in his hurry he fails to capture. All the same, Shakespeare's metaphorical language, in its insights and its rhetoric, at its peaks and in its troughs, is true to the chief quality of any genuine allegory.

Use of metaphor is the natural consequence of the shortness of man's life and the vastness of his tasks planned for a long time ahead. Because of this discrepancy he is obliged to look at things with eagle-eyed keenness and to explain himself in momentary, instantly understandable, flashes of illumination. This is what poetry *is*. The use of metaphor is the stenography of a great personality, the shorthand of its soul.

---

* *Zamechaniia k perevodam iz Shekspira.* PSS, 5, 72–90. Only the first four remarks (PSS, 5, 72–74) are translated here. (This is the only example in the present book of an excerpted text.) First published in *Literaturnaia Moskva* I (Moscow, 1956), 794–809. Originally intended as preface to the 1949 two-volume edition of Shakespeare in Pasternak's translation.

The tempestuous vitality of Rembrandt's, Michelangelo's, Titian's brush is not a result of deliberate choice. Assailed, each one of them, by a stormy, insatiable thirst to draw the entire universe, they had no time for other kinds of drawing. Impressionism has been characteristic of art since time immemorial. It is the voice of man's spiritual wealth, pouring out over the edge of his doom.

Shakespeare united in himself widely distant stylistic extremes. He combined so many that it is as if several authors were living inside him. His prose is finished and perfected. It is written by a genius of comedy and detail, who possessed the secret of compression and a gift for mimicking everything in the world that is curious and remarkable.

The realm of blank verse in Shakespeare is just the opposite of this. Voltaire and Tolstoy[46] were irritated by its inner and outer chaos.

Often, certain roles in Shakespeare go through several stages of completeness. A character will speak first in scenes that are written in verse, then will suddenly burst into prose. When this happens, the verse scenes seem to be preparatory, and the prose scenes final and conclusive.

Verse was Shakespeare's quickest, most direct form of expression. He had recourse to it for the fastest possible recording of ideas. This went so far that in many of his verse episodes we seem to discern rough drafts for prose.

The force of Shakespeare's poetry lies in its powerful way of being a free sketch that knows no restraint and tosses about wildly.

"Shakespeare's Rhythm"

The fundamental principle of Shakespeare's poetry is rhythm. Metre prompted some of his thoughts, some of his words. Rhythm is at the basis of his texts, rather than being their final framework. Some of his stylistic caprices can be explained as explosions of rhythm. In his dialogues the driving force of rhythm defines the sequence of questions and answers, the speed of their alternation, in his monologues it defines the length or brevity of sentences.

This rhythm reflects the enviable laconicism of English speech, which lets a single iambic line embrace a whole statement consisting of two or more propositions set off one against another. This is the rhythm of a free historical personality which erects no idol for itself and is thus sincere and sparing of words.

"Hamlet"

This rhythm is at its most manifest in *Hamlet*. It has a threefold purpose here. It is a way of characterizing individual *personae*; physically present as sound, it sustains the tragedy's dominant mood; and it ennobles and softens certain coarse scenes in the play.

The rhythmic characterization is vivid and prominent. Polonius, the king, Guildenstern and Rosencrantz—these speak in one way; Laertes, Ophelia, Horatio and the others—in another way. The queen's credulity shows not only in what she says but in her sing-song way of speaking, the way she draws out the vowels.

But the definition of Hamlet himself through rhythm is the sharpest of all. To us it is so strong that it seems to be concentrated in some rhythmic motif or figure apparently present and as if repeated whenever Hamlet enters, yet actually not existing at all. It is the pulse of his whole being which has, as it were, become palpable. The inconsistency of his movements, his decisive gait with its long stride, and his proud half-turns of the head—these are signs of that pulse, as are the leaping and flying of ideas in his soliloquies, the way he flings out mocking, haughty replies right and left to the courtiers rotating around him, and his gaze into the unknown distance from which his dead father's shade has already called to him once and might at any moment begin speaking again.

Likewise the general music of *Hamlet* resists quotation. No one discrete rhythmic instance of it can be quoted. Yet in spite of this incorporeality its presence grows so sinisterly and substantially into the general tissue of the drama that involuntarily one wants to call it—in relation to the plot—clairvoyant and Scandinavian. This music consists in a measured alternation of the solemn and the anxious. Through it the work's atmosphere is condensed and made extremely compact, so its main mood is all the more perceptible. What is this mood?

A long-established conviction of the critics is that *Hamlet* is a tragedy of will. This is correct. But in what sense? Weakness of will was not known in Shakespeare's time. People were not interested in this. Hamlet's cast of mind, delineated by Shakespeare in so much detail, is obvious and it does not fit with the notion of a nervous disorder. Hamlet, in Shakespeare's conception, is a prince of the blood who does not for a moment forget his rights to the throne, he is the spoilt child of an old court and—thanks to his talentedness—self-reliant, a born maverick. In the aggregate of features his author gives him there is no place for anything limp and flaccid, they make it impossible. Quite the contrary, the spectator is left to judge how great is Hamlet's sacrifice if with such expectations he gives up his privileges for the sake of a higher purpose.

From the moment of the ghost's appearance Hamlet renounces himself in order to "fulfil the will of the one who sent him". It is a drama not of characterlessness but of duty and self-denial. When he discovers that appearance and reality do not coincide but are divided by a chasm, what is important is not that this reminder of the world's falsity comes in supernatural form or that the ghost demands from him an act of revenge. Far more important is the fact that Hamlet is chosen by fate's will to be a judge of his time and the servant of something more remote. *Hamlet* is a drama of lofty sacrifice, of a commanded feat, an entrusted destiny.

The rhythmic principle compacts and makes tangible this general tone of the play. Yet that is not its sole application. The rhythm has a modifying effect on certain harshnesses which would be unthinkable without its harmonious effect. Here is an example.

In the scene where he sends Ophelia to a nunnery Hamlet is talking to a girl who loves him and whom he crushes with the mercilessness of a post-Byronic egoistic renegade. His irony is not justified even by his own love for Ophelia, which at this moment he is painfully suppressing. But note what introduces this heartless scene. It is preceded by the famous "To be or not to be," and the first words in verse that Hamlet and Ophelia say to each other at the beginning of the offensive scene are still steeped in the fresh music of the monologue which has only just fallen silent. In the bitter beauty and disorder of the perplexities bursting forth from Hamlet, which pursue and jostle one another before coming to a stop, the soliloquy resembles the sudden, and suddenly broken off, testing of an organ before a Requiem begins. These are the most quivering and most crazy lines ever written about the anguish of uncertainty on the threshold of death, and strong feeling raises them as high as the painful music of Gethsemane.

It is not surprising that the soliloquy is placed just before the brutality of the coming dénouement. It precedes it as a burial service precedes a burial. It could have been followed by any inevitable event whatsoever. Everything is redeemed, cleansed and elevated, not only by the thought in the soliloquy but by the passion and purity of the weeping heard in it.

Commentary on IV
(SPEECHES AND ARTICLES, 1930s and '40s)

This section presents statements by Pasternak from the 1930s and 1940s about literature and writers. Much of the interest of these statements lies in insights they afford into the consistency of his views on art even while he was modifying their expression in the changing, sometimes threatening circumstances and with his own altering position in Soviet society.

His reaction to the pressures upon creative writers in those years shows both an idiosyncratic resistance and an idiosyncratic will to adaptation. Although he was never arrested and even, for a long time, seemed to enjoy some mysterious protection, the growing official disapproval of his kind of writing and thinking obliged him to take up a defence of it. There could no longer be the same unchecked delight and spontaneity in exploring and explaining such concepts as genius or inspiration; it was now a matter of fighting to defend his values. At the same time he was not at all antipathetic to the declared ideals of the new regime.

It is remarkable that, despite being compelled to make appearances before large audiences, something he never liked doing, Pasternak continued to speak in his own way, neither adopting anything of the usual "trumpeting" obeisance to Soviet ideals nor using a style in any way infected by what he was countering. However, although his conception of the nature of art did not alter, some emphases within it did. His frequent references to "genius" are meant as reminders to people drowning in ideology that they could still breathe fresh air if they wished. There is an increased vigour in his asserted belief that great art does not serve the current age. He gives still more importance now to "realism", "seriousness", "simplicity" and the avoidance of rhetoric, although these sober virtues are bound up no less than before with an admiration for dynamism and with the imagery of speed and energy which always informed his writing on creativity.

In 1925, in response to a Communist Party resolution, Pasternak gave his view of the contemporary condition of literature. This response is not included in the present volume but will be briefly discussed as an indication of the special quality of his relation to the Soviet political and literary establishment.[47]

The 1925 "Resolution" appeared in the midst of much debate about the role of "fellow travellers", as Trotsky had labelled writers who neither supported nor opposed communism.[48] Such writers were attacked by various groups of "proletarian" writers who believed that only they themselves represented the interests of the revolution and that there could not be co-operation, or even co-existence, among different classes and interests; for them art was a means of expressing ideas and was to be evaluated according to which ideas were expressed. "Fellow-travellers" were also attacked by the neo-futurist group "Lef" which deplored the idea that art had anything to do with cognition, reflection and observation[49] and had developed an idea of it as "construction of life" and "production of things". In the early 1920s these groups (the proletarians and Lef) clashed violently in their speeches and publications, and a statement from the Party, which would be the first it had issued about literature, was awaited with anxiety. When it came, it turned out to be apparently tolerant of all groups, recommending caution and patience towards the "fellow-travellers"—at least in so far as they were prepared to move from their "interim" position in the direction of a communist one; they had, after all, their specialist skills, their literary experience, to offer. But the Resolution was also intolerant, both explicitly so with regard to those suspected of developing a "new bourgeois ideology" and its declaration of war on "counter-revolutionary manifestations in literature", and also implicitly so in its very assumption of a right to proclaim which writers were to be "tolerated" and which ones were not.

Almost all who sent in responses to the Resolution, including such independent thinkers as Belyi, Leonov and Shklovsky, welcomed it as a wonderful promise of freedom. Only the published replies of Aseev, Pilniak and Pasternak were at all critical, and only Pasternak's expressed any antipathy.[50]

After asking the authors of the Resolution not to seek "aesopic" notes in what he is about to say, and not to look for signs of his progressiveness or backwardness as a citizen—an "irritable" beginning, as he says himself—Pasternak starts his comment with words that could sound ironic but could alternatively be taken as merely thoughtful:

> Sometimes it seems to me that hopes may take the place of facts and that words spoken in good order will necessarily correspond to the true state of affairs. In one such moment—in the summer—I read the resolution on literature in the newspaper, and it produced a very powerful impression on me.

When invited to respond, he says, he looked at it more closely and was especially struck by three of its clauses. They stated: "We have entered a period of cultural revolution"; we must bear in mind the "basic fact that the working class has seized power" and there is now "a proletarian dictatorship in the country"; and: "everything makes us suppose that the [literary] style corresponding to the epoch will be created" (clauses 1, 5 and 13). Pasternak describes his sensation on first reading these clauses:

I felt the breath of history which these assertions seek to breathe . . . Behind the predictions I seemed to hear a conversation about how history shall be utterly history, and I—utterly a human being within it.

Moreover, he continues, the Resolution helped him to abstract himself from certain things which "become hateful the moment one starts to admire them", and he gives a curiously unelaborated list of these things: "my tribe, Russia's messianism, the peasant, the honour given to my calling, the numerousness of writers, their hypocritical simplicity", all indicating certain hackneyed approaches to Russian literature which were being as facilely clung to by Bolshevik writers as they had been by pre-revolutionary ones. Perhaps his list of wrong approaches could be paraphrased as follows: adherence to a particular race rather than to the human race; belief in a national rather than a universal destiny; idolizing of a particular social class, and of a particular professional class; and two mistaken ideas—that the more writers there are the better, and the more popular literature becomes the better. Now, he feels, all these may at last be displaced by something more real and more glorious, namely "history", the sense of something great actually coming about.

So his first response to the Resolution was positive: gratefully to free himself from former, smaller values, for he, too, longed to breathe the spacious historical air which *it* aspired to breathe. But now he swings out into criticism of it, although one is again not sure at first whether the manner is ironical or shows the sincere disappointment of someone who has started off wholly trustful.

In a tone of incredulity he explains that he next realised the Resolution had itself forgotten that you have to hate those listed things if you are going to love history. The very document which helped him lose his illusions had itself turned out prey to such illusions. Its "many cares and attachments"—he offers it this excuse—prevent it from feeling "the boldness, breadth and magnanimity without which any enthusiastic run-up into the epoch . . . is impossible." So the Resolution is a failure—it idealises the worker in the wrong way and it conceives of the epoch in the wrong way. From this sad discovery he proceeds to contradict the three selected clauses, one by one. No, we are not in a cultural revolution, we are in a cultural reaction. No, there is no proletarian dictatorship, or anyway not enough of one to tell upon culture. No, nothing leads us to suppose that a style corresponding to the epoch will be created.

His initial irritation finds expression. The "style of the epoch" (he revises his own remark) *has* been created, it is already there and it is rubbish: "of illusory and zero worth". In the bad, average style of the day, brought about by "the logic of large numbers", we treat the age as "an incarnate generalisation", instead of leaving the generalising about it to posterity. This premature generalising makes for the most dreary dullness; to suit the wide public, writers are obliged to be average, characterless, indistinguishable; "the philosophy of the *tirage* (print-run) is working together with the philosophy of acceptability"; and: "All my thoughts have become subsidiary to the one important thought: 'am I or am I not acceptable?'"

Although this is fierce criticism, an inexplicable indirectness haunts Pasternak's statement and, as if nothing has been said to upset his friendship with the Resolution's authors, his last paragraph takes up, in a confidential manner, the hopefulness and the sense of a true historical grandeur which he spoke of at the beginning. Somehow he constructs for himself the space in which he can say:

> I consider labour more intelligent and more noble than the human being, and that the artist can expect nothing good unless from his own imagination. If I thought otherwise I'd say we should abolish the censorship. But the main thing is that I am convinced art has got to be the high point of the epoch, not its median.

In spite of the pervading tinge of ambiguity it is clear he was defining himself as an eccentric but unyielding supporter of the ruling Party's own slipping ideals.

Pasternak saw revolutionary Russia as presenting him with a task which was not natural to him, yet which he accepted, like—much later—the actor in the poem "Hamlet" who prays for "the cup to pass" from him yet agrees to act his assigned role to its very end.[51] His feeling of having a task was certainly due in part to his conviction that he was living at a time of exceptional strangeness and greatness which must be responded to. As he wrote in *A Safe-Conduct*, art cannot be directed any way you wish "like a telescope", it has to focus on the *actual* transformed reality. He wrote to his cousin in 1928:

> I'll never move a step forward either in life or in work if I don't report to myself on this piece of time. To get round this obstacle by busying myself with something else would be, given all my inclinations and my character, to devalue in advance everything I have yet to experience. I could do that only if I knew I was going to live twice. Then I would put off this terrible, prickly task until the second, more comfortable life. But I have got to write about this.[52]

Two years later he wrote to the same cousin (Olga Freidenberg): "You know, as time goes on, I am, despite everything, more and more full of faith in all that is going on in our country. Many things strike us as wholly uncouth, yet sometimes quite astounding things happen . . . " Even as late as 1936, he wrote to his friend Titsian Tabidze, who was being threateningly criticised by the literary establishment: "Have faith in the revolution as a whole, in fate, in the heart's new impulses, in the pageant of life, and not in the construings of the Union of Writers."[53]

Far from being based on any position of "compromise" with the regime, these utterances show Pasternak working his way through a highly complex mixture of hope, anguish, responsibility and struggle to understand; and they are not irrelevant to his ideas about art, which in many ways also apply to contemporary history. The "changed world" and the "ceasing to recognise reality" that he spoke of in *A Safe-Conduct* (2,7) apply to his experience of the revolution as well as to the experience of artistic inspiration; often he comes close to saying that art and revolution are one and the same. Because of this he was able to see his book *My Sister Life*, written during 1917, as a revolutionary work, although all the poems in it are about weather, vegetation, love and personal happenings. After a conversation he had had in 1922 with Leon Trotsky, who asked why he "abstained" from responding to social themes, Pasternak wished he had told Trotsky (so he wrote in a letter to Briusov) that *My Sister Life* was

> revolutionary in the best sense of the word. That the phase of revolution closest to the heart and to poetry—the *morning* of revolution, and its outburst, when it returns man to the *nature* of man and looks at the state with the eyes of *natural* right . . . are expressed by this book in its very spirit.[54]

In his postscript to *A Safe-Conduct* he had written, referring to *My Sister Life*:

> I saw a summer on earth which seemed not to recognise itself—natural and prehistoric, as in a revelation. I left a book about it. In it I expressed all the most unprecedented and elusive things to be known about the revolution.[55]

The phrase "morning of revolution" expressed, as ever, his love of origins and new beginnings; so did the phrase "summer on earth", since the summer referred to was that between the February and October revolutions of 1917, the all-expectant, gestatory period of the Bolshevik revolution. In January 1918 Alexander Blok had told fellow-intellectuals that, if ever they had enjoyed music in the concert-hall, they ought now to acknowledge that the same musical force was sounding in the revolutionary events happening all around them.[56] More than anyone else, Pasternak rose to Blok's challenge, and the more readily since music—experienced in a similar way, as a surrounding and challenging force—was what had first set him on the path to creation.

"Speech at the first all-union congress of Soviet writers"

In August 1934 Pasternak sat on the platform in front of a vast audience at the first congress of the recently founded Writers' Union; at the end of the Congress he was elected to the Board of the Union.

A guiding purpose of the Congress was to promote "socialist realism", the literary method named in the Union's statutes as the only method to be used by its members, those "engineers of human souls". Most of the speeches praised this method, which required "depiction of life in its revolutionary development" and the "ideological remoulding" of everybody but was otherwise scarily vague. They spoke of the need for tendentiousness, attacked "capitalist" and "formalist" literature, and glorified Soviet literature, present and future. The age as an "incarnate generalisation", lamented by Pasternak in 1925, seemed coming into being. According to one memoirist, Pasternak's first reaction to the discussions was one of disappointment and depression. He had had very great hopes: "Pasternak expected speeches with a large philosophical content, he believed the Congress would turn into a gathering of Russian thinkers."[57] By the end of the year, however, he was again filled with hope and for a while felt himself to be "a particle of my age and of my state; its interests have become mine."[58]

His own short speech was delivered two days before the end of the Congress. It was the first time he had spoken to such a large audience. During the fortnight of meetings he had been criticised several times from the platform for not making the revolution fully the subject of his writings. But he had also received approval, notably in an important speech by the then still eminent Nikolai Bukharin, who called him, though an apolitical poet, one of "individual poetic character" and a "most remarkable craftsman of verse".[59]

The chief points in Pasternak's speech are the down-to-earth nature of poetry and the need for modesty on the part of poets. Doubtless he was remembering his assertion that poetry is "about its own birth" when he told his audience that poetry was being born around them at that very moment. When he also told them that "poetry is prose" he may have forgotten the distinction between these categories (two inseparable but opposite poles) in his *Propositions* of 1918. But the vital thing to him now was to counter the compulsory worshipping of conspicuous correct-thinking persons by insisting on the accessibility of greatness, and on that unity of the everyday and the miraculous which he had, after all, always felt to be the main impulse of good writing. Others were losing sight of such truths as they swerved away into a slovenly romanticising of the period they were living in and into what Iurii Zhivago would call "the spirit of noisy rhetoric dominant in our days". For he goes on, from a friendly and positive beginning, to broach the subject of the "useless and light-weight wordiness" indulged in by many writers, and to warn his listeners against this habit and the related temptation to become "socialist dignitaries".

It is interesting to note how, just as in his reply to the 1925 Resolution, Pasternak, semi-adapting his quiet voice to the loud voice of the time, contrives to leave his hearers uncertain whether he is being simple or sophisticated. At the end of the speech comes this:

Do not lose contact with the masses, says the Party /in cases where writers have become well-to-do/. I do not have the right to use its expressions. Do not sacrifice personality for the sake of status, is what I say in exactly the same sense as the Party.

Exactly the same sense? At first this could seem blinkered: talking from deep within himself, not noticing that the two things are different. Then it could seem sarcastic: sharply pointing to a better morality. But then at a third glance it could seem both forceful and trustful: I do say this in the same sense, it's merely that my positive value would be expressed not as "the masses" but as "personality" (*litso*) which means the same, since true personality must include contact with other people, and the word "masses" can decently only be used to mean other people.

"Speech at the international congress of writers in defence of culture"

Early in 1935 Pasternak fell ill with a nervous disorder connected with chronic insomnia. In June that year he was summarily instructed to leave his sickbed and travel abroad to attend a Congress in Paris. The French organisers of the Congress had been surprised not to find there the two most gifted and best known Soviet writers, Boris Pasternak and Isaak Babel, and the Soviet authorities belatedly agreed that these two should turn up.[60] Severely depressed, Pasternak appeared on the Congress platform and said what he could in a short speech the text of which is lost. Ilia Ehrenburg, according to his own report, had torn up the text Pasternak was intending to read out, justifying this by saying it was "written in an archaic French, French of the last century", and asked him instead to say a few words about poetry, without preparation. The paragraph which has been translated here was put together from his notes by the author Nikolai Tikhonov along with no other than Pasternak's beloved friend Marina Tsvetaeva (living in emigration in France). The chief statements they drew from the notes are that "poetry is happiness" and that "it cannot be discussed at conferences", both, of course, paradoxical, being spoken at a conference by a poet who was unhappy. When Pasternak was visited years later, however, by Isaiah Berlin, he told his visitor that what he had said at that Congress was this:

I realise that this is a congress of writers who have met to organise against fascism. I can say only one thing to you on this subject: Do not organise! Organisation is the death of art. Only personal independence matters. In 1789, 1848 and 1917 writers were not organised in the defence of anything or against anything. I implore you—do not organise![61]

As he makes Vedeniapin say, in *Doctor Zhivago*: "Herd-behaviour is always the refuge of the untalented."

"Speech at the third plenum of the board of the writers' union"

The Leader of the Communist Party in Leningrad, Sergei Kirov, was murdered in December 1934 and there were signs of imminent persecutions and arrests. Pasternak was shortly to fall out of favour. At this 1936 congress in Minsk, he received very hostile remarks but also a good deal of praise. Indeed, much of the debate at the congress was focussed on the question whether he or Mayakovsky was to be named the "premier" Soviet poet. It is all the more remarkable that in his own speech he expressed such strong criticism of the atmosphere of the congress and the habits of his literary contemporaries.

With no apology, he renews the accusations of useless rhetoric which he made at the congress in 1934 and berates fellow-writers for pomposity, dishonesty and mediocrity. The distinction drawn in *The Black Goblet*, twenty years earlier, between the metaphorical "speed" of creativity and the vulgar cult of *literal* speed may come to mind when we see him contrasting, in this speech, the way great nineteenth-century poets went metaphorically travelling in their books with the way Soviet poets were *literally* travelling around the country to indulge in banquets and "the depravity of stage readings". As Olga Hughes has aptly noted, "In the 1930s the bohemians of 'Letters from Tula' had become members of the Writers' Union, professional writers and critics. The false and pretentious style not only remained typical of the times but was proclaimed the official style and was being imposed from above."[62]

In tacit opposition to the views currently promulgated, Pasternak states that the greatest gift life can delight us with is "unexpectedness", and that "art is unthinkable without risk"; this recalls his thoughts about the need for risk expressed in *A Safe-Conduct* 1,4. Yet at the same time as vigorously objecting to the current demand for mechanical production of poetry as if it were water to be got from a pump, he does his best to seem obedient to certain other contemporary demands, such as that writers be accessible and write on the great themes of the time: from now on, he says, he *is* going to write in a new way and this will mean, for a while, writing badly, since his aims are a simplicity he is not practised in and subjects which are still alien to him. In certain points, then, he plans to adapt himself to the demands of the times. But by no means in all points, for he warns his listeners that "on these themes which are common to us all I shall not speak in the common tongue, I shall not repeat you, comrades, but shall argue with you."

When in the last part of the speech Pasternak declares that a genius is akin to the common man, the "rarest representative" of the same species, he is renewing his opposition to the swollen rhetoric heard everywhere around him. The chief thing hampering and corrupting art, Pasternak is convinced, is the noisy activity of the untalented who make their career and status out of it. Were they not there, filling the intermediate space, the kinship between genius and common man would leap to the eye. He is not suggesting that every proletarian can write novels but is stating that a highly gifted person, being in an important sense only a more intense version of an ordinary person, should not be set on a pedestal. By implication, what the genius and the ordinary person have in common is precisely their freedom from the pomposity, dishonesty and mediocrity of those in between people. For example, the genius Mayakovsky was a "man of huge ordinariness." The power of the complacently ungifted was to be one of the main themes of *Doctor Zhivago*.

The Minsk speech is described by Lazar Fleishman as "explosively polemical". In linking "socialist realism" with Tolstoy's "storms of unmaskings and blunt outbursts", and, even more riskily, in comparing Lenin's style to Tolstoy's, Pasternak repeats the idea of art as being essentially rebellious which he put forward in the Venice section of *A Safe-Conduct* (a book now banned by the censors).[63] He was even more explosive and polemical at the ominous writers' meetings which took place in Moscow almost immediately after the Minsk congress.

The purpose of this series of meetings was to discuss what came to be known as the "campaign against formalism", a "campaign" which had begun in anonymous articles published in *Pravda* and authorised by Stalin. Emptied of their usual meanings, and indeed emptied of virtually all meaning, the terms "formalism" and "naturalism" were used in the articles for the stark purpose of attacking and banning particular musicians (Shostakovich was the first to be attacked) as well as artists and writers, while forcing the rest into an intimidated obedience to the Party line. Pasternak, in a rare move of overt opposition, unexpectedly joined the "discussions" on the third day to make a courageous speech which introduced into them a wholly unforeseen rationality. Three days later he spoke there for a second time. Unlike the other speeches, his were not published in the Press; indeed the shorthand records of them were not published in the Soviet Union until the "perestroika" period of the 1980s initiated by Mikhail Gorbachev.[64]

In his first speech, as though from a position of natural common sense, while in fact well aware of the danger that was gathering to himself and to the arts altogether, Pasternak ridicules the repetitive, unthinking and aggressive use of "formalism" and "naturalism". *Why* adopt these insensitive clichés? Why put up with their clumsy ousting of ordinary judgments such as "bad" or "unsuccessful"? Why not just call bad poems "bad"? If "formalism" suggests impermissible concern with form, then suppose we were to start looking at the concern with form in, say, Gogol's prose, or in folklore? Would anything at all, in the end, turn out to be acceptable? Arguing directly against the current of what was happening, Pasternak shows how absurd and wrong is the government's desire to interfere with artistic life and compares a poet or artist to a woman giving birth: you cannot tell her what kind of child to produce, girl or boy. Art likewise needs respect and freedom—the very things it is now losing.

And why do all of you—he addresses his colleagues, all either representatives of the state or intimidated by it—why do all of you forever yell one and the same thing in one and the same voice: "If you must yell, can't you at least do so in different voices? Then you might be understood . . . " This attack on the central Stalinist principle of "unanimity" leads to a further sharp admonition: you criticise writers for not being clear, but haven't the readers of your own writings also a right to demand something clear and comprehensible, instead of "formalism, naturalism, naturalism, formalism . . . ?" Such truths were unacceptable in the circumstances of the time, and the next one even more so: "What is it that's terrible in these articles of yours? It is that I do not sense any love for art in them . . . And I do not know what will become of each of us in our encounters with editors and censors, who will have only one thing in mind: 'is this a formalist or a naturalist'? There is no love for art to be felt in any of this."

Pasternak was the only person to condemn the unfolding brutal campaign, nor would he afterwards retract any of his statements, despite pleas and threats. He did, however, agree to make a second speech. Much of the second speech, to judge by the uncorrected shorthand reports, is nervously wordy and apologetic, but again it contains strong passages, above all when he blames the inadequacy of Soviet literature on its tendency to treat everything "idyllically" and to neglect that which has always been a vital aspect of art: the tragic. Thus once again Pasternak mentions something which is at once obviously true and dangerously unmentionable. He explains (but it must have remained obscure to many listeners) that he himself cannot accept even a landscape without an element of the tragic in it [*bez tragizma*], cannot perceive even the world of vegetation without the sense of tragedy. Among other things, Pasternak is surely recalling here the philosophy of inspiration he presented seven years earlier in *A Safe-Conduct*: art originates in the artist's attention to the deprivation and yearning of the world of the inanimate. But now he goes on: "What, then, is to be said of the human world?"—that is, how can we possibly depict our human lives as rosily and optimistically as we do when there is so much material for tragedy in them?

Pasternak's intervention in the "anti-formalist" campaign was, Fleishman demonstrates, amazingly effective, partly, no doubt, because it coincided with the visit of André Malraux to the Soviet Union: the discussions "lost momentum . . . " [65] But all this was taking place on the threshold of the "purges" of 1936–38 and, moreover, in an atmosphere full of foreboding of European cataclysms. The question, "what, then, is to be said of the human world?", could seem unwittingly directed to the human tragedies of those years. Pasternak's passionately reasonable remarks in his first speech and his lament for the lost understanding of the tragic, in the second, stand out now as unparalleled moments of bravery and of normality.

"Articles on Anna Akhmatova"

In the early 1920s the great poet Anna Akhmatova was attacked by the critics for writing "intimate, personal lyrics"; from 1925 until 1940 she was banned altogether from publishing; when at last a new volume of her poems—*From Six Books*—came out, it too was banned after a few months. On the occasion of another slim volume of her poems coming out, Pasternak wrote these two pieces in the hope of showing her importance and, as E.B. and E.V. Pasternak note, "of dispersing the myth that this great poet was elitist and a salon poet".[66] Neither of his articles was published. In 1946 Akhmatova was one of the main targets of attacks by Andrei Zhdanov (Party Secretary for Ideology) which led to the devitalisation of Soviet literature for seven years.[67]

A desire to influence public and official opinion shows in the style of these two short articles, which is less idiosyncratic than Pasternak's former style and does not avoid cliché. But he was in any case working at developing a simpler style. His cherished values are as evident here as in his more intensely detail-attentive prose: he admires in Akhmatova's poems the "headlong" (*stremitel'nyi*) element, the "freedom from coercion", "complete absence of pompousness", an "openness to life", a "quality of prose", avoidance of "the false, redundant imagery of many contemporaries" and, above all, her "artistic realism".

"Articles on Translation and on Shakespeare"

In the question of translation Pasternak wrote to Michel Aucouturier in 1959:

> The space which lies, so to speak, between a poem and a translation of it is a wider, more undefined poetry than either of those things. In the gap between them is the very reality which they describe—full of meaning, but silent. To cross from one language into another is more than to travel from one country to its neighbour. It is, rather, a step out of a century which has never existed into another which has only been dreamed of.[68]

This makes the act of translating seem a difficult, strange engagement with geographical and historical expanses. His earlier notes on translation are more closely related to views he had expressed on the nature of inspiration.

A translation should be, he says, "the original's fruit and historical consequence". This accords with all his statements celebrating the linking of the generations, new readings of old texts, the speeding-onward nature of creativity. The true task of a literary translator, Pasternak considers, and this too accords with his earlier views, is to reproduce the force of the work he is translating—by which he does not mean some vague spirit or atmosphere but its definite power (*sila*). As advice for translators this takes for granted a measure of verbal fidelity. His own translations, while often extremely free and recreative, do depart from their originals with care and after all the words have been taken into consideration. Pasternak's translations of foreign poetry occupy 500 pages of the *Complete Collected Works* (PSS, 6).

In Shakespeare, Pasternak writes excitedly, there is not only "knowledge of humanity" but also a kind of "wilfulness". Always concerned to point to individuality and a certain wildness in the art he praises, he particularly wants to convey this to those in control of literature in his day, with their habitual respect towards Shakespeare yet their fear of individuality in their contemporaries. The figure of Hamlet as witness and judge of his time was to be important in *Doctor Zhivago*.

It is in talking of Shakespeare that Pasternak expresses the idea of metaphor as a shorthand forced upon us by life's brevity, an idea which lacks any nuance whatever of lamentation about transience; instead, characteristically, there is a tone of thanksgiving, since life's shortness forces us into poetry.

About Shakespeare Pasternak conducted a lifelong inner debate with Tolstoy, who perceived nothing poetic in Shakespeare's writing. Yet Pasternak himself writes critically of much of the verse dialogue, thereby betraying perceptibly Tolstoyan intonations, as E.B. and E.V. Pasternak point out. The tendency to simplification in his translations of the plays, they observe, may have been due in part to the influence of Tolstoy: in these translations

> he tried to convey the naturalness and smoothness of the living colloquial language, he removed from the dialogues the improbability which had jarred on Tolstoy, he emphasised justly perceived detail and lowered the loftiness of tone, making comprehensible what Tolstoy had found devoid of logic.[69]

Himself a superbly gifted poet who longed all his life to become a great prose writer, Pasternak notably preferred Shakespeare's prose to his verse.

"Verlaine"

In this essay, Pasternak again moves towards the central questions: what is art? what is genius?—wittingly leaving them still in need of being answered.

He presents Verlaine as a "realist" by grounding his famously musical poetry firmly in space and time and asserting that his work is all content (something perceived and felt), not form. Realism is associated with a sense of the "rightness of being upon the earth" (a phrase which interestingly echoes Mandelstam's commendation of the acmeist poets for being, unlike the symbolists, at home in the four dimensions of existence).[70]

The image of things flying in from the street through the poet's window and straight into his verse, combines the motif of fast movement, familiar from Pasternak's very first writings, with his later stress on response to the historical moment. Earlier window imagery had more to do with garden and sky; the airborne images of this essay have their origin in the urban street. Although Pasternak does speak of Verlaine as an individual, he takes the movement of urban traffic, and of the modern city altogether, as typical of what happens when any modern genius is at work. Exactly the same flying-in-at-the-window is repeated by him in descriptions of the work of other poets, notably of Blok and Pushkin.

E.B. and E.V. Pasternak record that an early draft of this essay shows Pasternak asking, as his main question: what is there in Verlaine that can interest the "huge new Russian city after the /military/ victory?"—and answering it: "the overwhelming power of his colloquial phrase in all its intactness; his poetry's contemporary quality and living syntax."[71]

"Chopin"

This essay Pasternak regarded as one of his most important. He told his sister Lidia in a letter of 1959 that "it contains all I wanted to say."[72]

Like Verlaine, Chopin too is unexpectedly called a realist. But how (as Pasternak asks) can "realism" apply to music? The epithets spelling out the concept in the course of the essay seem chosen to make its application to music as unlikely as possible: "definite, exact, verifiable; cognition, a developing thought, biography, actual experience." It is hard not to suppose he means: it is *as if* the cognitional content of music were verifiable and you *seem* to hear a rational idea developing in a piece of music and to be in contact with someone's actual experience. But he leaves out "seems" and "as if", perhaps to identify the force felt by us from the music with the force felt by the composer from reality.

Opposed to those epithets is a series of words associated by Pasternak with romanticism: "arbitrary; stilted pathos; false emotion; invention; fantasy; artificiality; amusement; conventional and evasive; nymphs and salamanders . . . " The usual meaning of "romantic" is narrowed and that of "realistic" is stretched. Here "romantic" means only one aspect of what it can mean, and that aspect is viewed with relentless antipathy, while "realistic" means "the highest degree of authorial exactitude", not normally expected of the artist and marking for Pasternak only the best works of art. Probably it is what Tsvetaeva, too, had in mind when she spoke of listening with the most rigorous concentration to hear the words of the poem she was about to write, to *get them right* and not have to pad the lines out with invented stuff.

The real—"biographical"—musician, dwelt on at the moment when he gets up from the piano "phenomenally definite", to face the material world "after music", is a vivid recapitulation of the piece about Shestikrylov in *Ordering a Drama*. But in Chopin's return to the recital room with tie disarrayed to perform a piece of mimic relief, the actor theme in the early stories and in *A Safe-Conduct* has turned carnivalesque: laughter at oneself now seems inseparable from the high sobriety of art. And a certain lightheartedness about the business of propounding definitions—a sense of the wild "interchangeability" of abstractions—characterises the essay's concluding statement. This states what Chopin's *études* are "about": they are an investigation into the "theory of childhood" and an introduction to "death", they teach "history or the structure of the universe or anything whatever that is more distant and more general than how to play the piano".

Part of the essay, at first surprisingly, relates to visual and tactile imagery supposedly lying behind some of Chopin's works. Is Pasternak's realism infected, after all, by the programme music he rejects? In his very thorough account of Pasternak's eccentric use of the concept "realism", Christopher Barnes notes that the poet's conscious application of "realistic" to Chopin's music, probably begun in the 1940s, reflected not only his own lifelong closeness to Chopin but his high regard for the composer's freedom from any "illustrative tendency", any inclination whatever towards "programme music". So these waterfalls, bumpy roads and snowfalls associated with the music are paradoxical, to say the least.[73] Here I would stress that, however carelessly he may be writing at this point, Pasternak's main concern is not with putting pictures to the musical pieces but with conveying Chopin's refusal to do anything easily. Like all art, the music arose from biographical reality, and to get right the relation between the two he had to work incredibly hard. The "mood could have been achieved at less expense", Pasternak says of one piece, and, of another: "the impression . . . might have been attained by more modest means . . . " "But no!"—the composer could not let himself use modest means, could not spare himself expense, he had unfailingly to achieve "the highest degree of authorial exactitude". It is in the course of thus arguing for Chopin's absolute loyalty to the real (and "only the almost-impossible is real" [*S-C* 3,3]) that Pasternak brings in the unfortunate waterfalls; they are merely material tokens of what constituted the real and could not have been meant to prevail over the other, so carefully indefinite, names given in the same essay to music's content. They are signs of the force which made the composer compose. Even when a "cavalry squadron gallops" down from the stage onto the audience this is, I contend, not supposed to be what the music represents, and is not even a picture it calls up;

it is a suggestion of the force by which it is called into being. In the poem of 1931, "Again Chopin . . . ", the music played similarly contains all Chopin's life-experiences yet in no way represents them.

Pasternak's essay is not a world away from Schopenhauer's comment on music: "whoever gives himself up entirely to the impression of a symphony seems to see all the possible events of life and the world take place in himself; yet, if he reflects, he can find no likeness between the music and the things that passed before his mind."[74] Just as, for Schopenhauer, music is at once wholly like and wholly unlike "events of life and the world", Pasternak ascribes to music images from life and our surroundings even while he is declaring it to be about "the structure of the universe and anything whatever that is more general".

$\mathcal{V}$

AN ESSAY ON
DOCTOR ZHIVAGO

1. "A NOVEL IN PROSE"

In *Doctor Zhivago* Pasternak is no less concerned with artistic inspiration and creation than he is in *A Safe-Conduct*. This concern is now expressed in the looser, simpler style of his later years and becomes part of a wide-ranging fictional work which contains discursive passages about the pattern of history and the meaning of existence. In sections one and two of this essay I shall look at the simpler style and its effects, in sections three and four at the overtly presented ideas; throughout there will be comparisons with *A Safe-Conduct*.

In his adolescence Pasternak admired Scriabin's highly eccentric conception of simplicity in music. His own subsequent aspiration was to a far more normal simplicity of style, a way of writing everyone would understand. In 1921 he told a friend that he had resolved, after 1917, to "make a sharp turn" away from the so-called originality of the literary milieu he was used to, the "sea of arbitrariness" lying behind its "neo-aestheticism", and to start "writing the way people write letters . . . , disclosing to the reader everything I think . . . , abstaining from technical effects fabricated beyond his field of vision."[1] Moves towards simplicity can be traced from the narrative poems of the 1920s and the poems of the 1931 volume *Second Birth* (one of which predicts the fall "into an unheard-of simplicity, as into a heresy") right up to the *Zhivago* poems and those which followed them. When the fictional poet Iurii Zhivago desires his originality to be "concealed under the cover of a commonplace and familiar form" and his style to be "unnoticeable", he is dreaming Pasternak's own dream.

The earlier prose (such as the texts in Parts I and II of the present book) had been very much the prose of a poet, outstandingly original, sometimes condensed and difficult to penetrate, frequently enthralling. But *Doctor Zhivago* was to be written in a straightforward, easily accessible prose. Very conscious of its prosaic quality, Pasternak referred to it as "a novel in prose".[2] The phrase brings to mind Pushkin's *Evgenii Onegin*, a "novel in verse", and the fact that Gogol put the subtitle "a Poem" to his one novel, *Dead Souls*—two works which in their different ways seek to speak about "the whole of Russia". It also implies a contrast with Pasternak's own "novel in verse", *Spektorsky*, and is a reminder that writing a novel is not easy when you are a poet.

For a long time Pasternak had felt that a new style was required of him by the age he lived in. A remark he made in the 1920s—"I consider epic to be prompted by the age, therefore in my book *1905* I am moving from lyric thinking to epic, though it is very difficult . . . " anticipates a remark in the 1950s: "I believe it is no longer possible for lyric poetry to express the immensity of our experience . . . We have acquired values best expressed in prose. I have tried to express them in my novel."[3] One value best expressed in prose was certainly that very "immensity". While still writing the novel, Pasternak confessed to his cousin Olga Freidenberg that prose was much harder to write than poems, and yet—

> only prose brings me close to the idea of the absolute which sustains me and contains in itself both my life and norms of behaviour etc etc, and which creates an inner mental structure on one of whose tiers verse-writing—otherwise meaningless and shameful—can be accommodated.[4]

This view of poetry half-echoes a sentence in *A Safe-Conduct* 3,5, where Mayakovsky's poem contains "that infinity which opens out in life from any point and in any direction, and without which poetry is just a misunderstanding not yet cleared up". Both sentences, the earlier and the later, claim that to make sense poetry needs something vast to exist within or beside—a sensation of the infinite, an idea of the absolute (or unconditional: *bezuslovnoe*).

Paradoxically, the "novel in prose" is a poetic novel and a novel about poetry. Its protagonist is a poet, its last chapter consists of twenty-five poems, it contains meditations on art and poetry, its style (when at its best) is manifestly that of a poet, and, among many other things, it is Pasternak's demonstration, in as understandable terms as he could manage, of his central experience, the emergence of poetry from ordinary life.

Numerous passages, for instance, seem designed to point out likenesses or, more often, proximities, of things to each other which could give rise to poetic similes, metaphors or rhythms. "The drooping sack-shapes of the curtains at the windows almost resembled the drooping sack-shapes of the trees in the yard . . . " (10,5); Iurii is gladdened by "the sameness of lighting in the house and outside it" (13,4); and there are conspicuously guiding authorial remarks such as: "something similar was happening in the moral and in the physical world, in things near and far, on earth and in the air" (6,8). Such passages, supported by the recurrent preoccupation with mimicry, imitation and the merging of one thing into another,[5] suggest a development—less strenuous and vivid—of *A Safe-Conduct*'s account of poetic creation in which "details lose independence of meaning" and "any one of them will serve as witness of the state that envelops the whole of transposed reality."

A number of assertions in *Doctor Zhivago* (made by author or by characters) seem parts of *A Safe-Conduct* re-written. Sometimes almost the same words are used. Mayakovsky—described (in 1930) as having taken "an amazing initial run" into life, and as seeming to have behind him "a decision after it has been acted on, when its results can no longer be revoked" (*S-C* 3,3)—re-appears in the novel's account of Lara, who moves and lives "as if, long ago in childhood, she had taken a general run towards life and now everything in her life came about from the impetus of the run, all by itself, with the ease of a logical consequence." (8,13) The form the run-into-life image takes in the novel is simpler than in *A Safe-Conduct*. Other rehearsals of former motifs also show simplification. This includes the many statements about art. A notable example is the re-writing of the often quoted sentence in *S-C*: "When we suppose that in *Tristan, Romeo and Juliet* and other memorable works a powerful passion is portrayed, we underestimate their content. Their theme is wider than this powerful theme. Their theme is the theme of power (*sila*)." This re-appears in the novel without the reference to "power": "Works of art speak in many ways: through their themes, propositions, subjects, heroes. But above all they speak through the presence of art in them. The presence of art on the pages of *Crime and Punishment* is more stirring than Raskolnikov's crime" (9,4). *A Safe-Conduct* tells us new works of art come about from a desire to "re-say" existing ones, whereby repetition is avoided through passion's "leaps aside"; *Doctor Zhivago* paraphrases the first part of this ("a step forward in art is made according to the law of attraction, from the desire to imitate, follow and worship well-loved precursors" [9,7]) leaving out any allusion to passion's leaps. The seminal piece in *A Safe-Conduct* (about poetry being born when a force competing with the sun glances back at everyday, past or static things) makes a simpler, more concrete re-appearance in the novel when after a funeral the young poet literally walks ahead of the others at the graveyard and, glancing back at them, thinks of composing a poem into which he will put random images of everyday, past and inanimate things, such as the dead woman's best features and a monastery washing-line (3,17). Meanwhile, the difficult notions of racing the sun and hearing a plea from left-behind objects no longer figure.

One might ask which is preferable: the ecstatic, sometimes esoteric, exactitude of the *Safe-Conduct* style, or the widely accessible, toned-down approximation of the *Zhivago* style; the fast flinging across of an insight in the very form it demands at its turbulent inception, or the novel's patient analysing of it into quieter parts; the ecstatic instant or the measured, reflective re-collection. There is an extraordinary generosity in the older Pasternak's attempt to pin down and exhibit his once so elusive flights of inspiration. Often, as he well knew, the attempt meant giving up flying for walking. Some of his remarks show that he was aware of a stylistic decline. The increasingly urgent "aspiration to write modestly, without special effects or stylistic coquetry", he said, "has probably taken me too far, into the realm of virtues which are opposed to art, and, giving up the strenuous, energetic kind of writing obligatory for an artist, I have adopted a loose watery circumstantiality that is ruining my best intentions."[6] Yet his chief motive was undoubtedly a wish to share the wealth he possessed—a lifelong acquaintance with inspiration and the consequent "happiness of existence"—with those who lacked it or did not know they possessed it. This was not just an instinctively humane gesture but also a way of being in "contact with the masses" and actually furthering the once genuine ideals of the revolution. It would not be understood as such, however, and he must have known it would not be, hopeful though he was about the book's publication. So he was throwing his talent at once upon the whole bright world and upon darkness.

2. WRITING POETRY

In the novel there is only one direct description of poetic inspiration: this comes in Part 14, chapter 8, "Again in Varykino". Here Zhivago, in briefly blissful circumstances, sits down to look through old poems and start writing new ones. There follows an account of the "approach of that which is called inspiration"— the last five words are practically identical to those used in *S-C* 1,6,[7] while the word "approach" (*priblizhenie*), an important one for Pasternak, is the same as in the poem "Inspiration" and in the 1910 letter to Olga Freidenberg (quoted in Introduction, 6).

> After two or three verses which poured out easily, and several comparisons which surprised even him, the work took hold of him and he felt the approach of that which is called inspiration. The relation between the forces which govern creation stands, as it were, on its head. Primacy goes not to the person and the state of soul for which he is seeking expression, but to the language with which he wants to express it. Language, the birthplace and repository of beauty and meaning, itself begins to speak and think for the person, and becomes all music, in respect not of its external, acoustic sounds but of the swiftness and power of its inner current. Then, like the rolling bulk of a river's current which by its very movement moulds the stones of its floor and turns the wheels of mills, the pouring speech, by the force of its laws, itself creates—along the way and in passing—metre and rhyme and thousands of other forms and formations still more important but as yet unrecognized, not taken into account, not named.
> At such moments Iurii Andreevich felt that the main part of the work was being accomplished not by himself but by that which was higher than him, which was situated above him and governed him, namely: the condition of world thought and poetry and what was destined for it in the future, the next sequential step it was to take in its historical development. And he felt himself only a pretext and a pivot, for it to start this movement.

In some respects this account of inspiration resembles the accounts in *A Safe-Conduct* and other early writings; in other respects it differs greatly. It is similar in presenting inspiration as a definite event, the approach of which is always recognised; similar also in that the main agent is not the poet as a person but something bigger which is characterized by swift, powerful movement. But it differs from those earlier narratives, firstly in that there is now not a single force, but two forces, and secondly in that the indescribable and elusive *sila* as to whose name the young Pasternak was "utterly indifferent" (*S-C* 3,11) is not one of them. One is the poet himself, as person, the other—now confidently described and named—is "language". It differs further in that the way language acquires primacy is asserted in a new, "simple", explanatory manner. Now the expected reader is one who has not read either *A Safe-Conduct* or, indeed, many another poet's report on inspiration, and who is likely to assume that the poet himself is the central actor in the drama of inspiration; this reader must be explicitly told that the poet as person is not the sole actor: "the relation between the forces which govern creation stands, as it were, on its head."

The sensation that something other than the poet is doing the work does indeed reflect Pasternak's old way of thinking. And yet, without the excited, demanding concepts of a "displacement of reality" and of a force or "feeling" as real as the forces studied by physics, one's attention does turn to the person of the poet. For to say "not the man uses language, but language uses the man" is still to keep the man in clear view; he it is who experiences the reversal of emphases and who, instead of using language as a tool, is being used by it.

Further, although later in the quoted passage language is described as something dynamic ("a river's current"), it first appears as something settled, almost monumental: "the birthplace and repository of beauty and meaning." In *S-C* 2,7 the link between inspiration and language was a link between two utterly fleeting things ("there is nothing but the mobile language of images for power to express itself by, the fact of power which lasts only for the moment of its occurrence . . . "), but now, with the sensed permanence of "birthplace" and "repository", such evanescence is forgotten. Even the subsequent river is rather heavily magnificent. Altogether the grand has ousted the precise. It seems that, writing now for a less receptive readership, Pasternak has slipped into more traditional, classical conceptions of art which really have nothing to do with his own. But—is it in fact slippage, or a deliberate change undertaken for the sake of at last being understood?

In the next paragraph, the governing force which takes the lead receives a second name: "that which was higher than him". This does not mean "God", as might briefly be supposed, but "world thought and poetry" and their, or (as is written here) its, historical development. Somehow on this level of vastness the poet becomes indispensable to history.

The focus is far wider than in the past. Instead of an intensely perceived transformation of immediate surroundings, this verson of inspiration embraces (as the whole novel does) universal and universally intelligible matters: the movement of history, the world's cultural condition, language conceived not as the molten or racing words of the present moment but as a general "repository" of meaning and the source of "thousands of forms". The shift to this larger scale of things involves Pasternak in the "loose" style he was aware of. One sign of that style is a lavish use of near-tautologies: "acoustic sounds", "along the way and in passing", "forms and formations", "higher than him and above him", "next sequential . . . " At the same time one may well wonder how a repository may begin to speak, how language can create *pre*-linguistic forms, how the (horizontal) river leads to the (vertical) dimension of "that which was higher", and why the water images of paragraph two disappear into the dry, abstract "state, step, pretext, pivot . . . " of paragraph three. A remarkable, if more esoterically dismaying, lapse is the allotting of the singular pronoun "it" (*ei, ona*) to the plural "thought and poetry" (it cannot apply to the neuter noun "condition"), which erases in a flash the strict distinction once drawn, in the essay on Kleist, between "philosophy" and "lyricism".

Nevertheless, the following chapter gives a compelling account of the composition of a poem. "Fable" (or Fairy Tale [*Skazka*]) is the thirteenth of the twenty-five poems and thus the central one. It has often been remarked that its hero, Saint George, not named in the poem, bears Zhivago's name, since Iurii is a form of "Georgii". Saint George as solitary, dedicated wanderer, dragon-slayer and maiden-rescuer, who, after his exploit, swoons and disappears into a chant of "years and centuries", parallels aspects of Zhivago's life story,[8] while the vigorous, laconic ballad-form indicates that the exploit which for a warrior-knight takes the form of a physical slaying and rescuing takes for the poet the form of writing the poem. With its rapidity of movement, sharp vision and intense force of feeling, the poem *is* his contribution to history. Here is the passage:

> In his drafts of the day before, he had wanted to express—by methods so simple it was almost a babbling and was close to the intimacy of a lullaby—his mixed mood of love, fear, yearning and courage which should pour forth all by itself, as if independently of the words.
> Now, looking through these attempts the next day, he found they lacked a thematic link to unite the fragmenting lines. Gradually crossing out what he had written, Iurii Andeevich began to set out the legend of George the Brave in the same lyrical manner. He started with a broad pentameter which gave a lot of space. A euphony belonging to the metre itself, independent of the content, irritated him with its conventional melodiousness. He abandoned the pompous metre with its caesura and compressed the lines into tetrameters, the way one fights verbosity in prose. Writing became harder and more alluring. The work grew more alive, but still an excessive garrulity was getting into it. He made himself shorten the lines still further. In the trimeter the words felt cramped, the last traces of sleepiness flew

from the writer, he woke up, caught fire; the narrowness of the lines' spaces itself suggested what to put in them. Objects scarcely named in words began to stand out in earnest in the frame of references. He caught the sound of the horse's movement as it stepped over the surface of the poem, just as a steed's irregular amble is heard in one of Chopin's *ballades*. George the Victorious was galloping on his steed over the boundless space of the steppe; watching from behind him, Iurii Andreevich saw him getting smaller as he went into the distance. Iurii Andreevich wrote with feverish haste, hardly managing to write down the words and lines which appeared just at the right place and the right moment. (14,9)

All this accords with the theory of inspiration sketched out in the previous chapter. There are indeed two forces—first the poet, then language; and we see the relation between them being overturned. At first the poet (the person) has the primacy, as he expresses moods, crosses out drafts, rejects pomposity, chooses a metre. Then comes the phase of inspiration ("he woke up, caught fire")—which, as in 14,8, commences not before the writing begins but after it has begun—and the primacy switches to language. Verbs of personal action ("he started . . . abandoned . . . ") yield to actions taken by the language itself ("the lines' narrowness suggested . . . "; "objects scarcely named in words began to stand out . . . "). This must be the moment where language "begins to speak and think for the person". It is the closest this prose-novelist will bring his reader to the enigma of creation. In the end the poet-as-person, with his name and patronymic now mentioned twice as if to reassure the reader that nothing superhuman is going on, regains equality with the force of language, just managing to get the words down.

Particularly interesting here is the release of strength when utterance is reduced to a minimum. Shortening the lines is the last word, as it were, in the novel's long argument against debilitating empty talk—symbolists' etherealities, journalists' clichés, politicians' pomposities, revolutionaries' slogans. All these are contrasted in the course of the book with voices of birds and cows, people "speaking in tongues" when stirred by great events, words of love, silences, poetry.

3. A MERGING OF CONCEPTS

Is there one universe, or are there two? *A Safe-Conduct* states that there is no "second universe" and even that its non-existence is the *raison d'être* of art:

since there was no second universe from which reality could have been lifted up out of the first . . . the manipulations /reality/ itself called for required a representation of it to be made, as in algebra which, in respect of magnitude, is constrained by a similar singleness of plane. (*S-C* 1,6)

But that kind of thrilling, opaque logic has now been placed out of bounds and in the novel a "second universe" is mentioned. It does not contradict the earlier statement, however, as at first it seems to. That earlier one alluded to an ethereal level not made by humans and, by implication, the opposite of artistic creation; there was no such other level, it asserted. The second universe said to exist in *Zhivago* is not the ethereal one negated in *A Safe-Conduct*; rather, it is a human-made one, moving onward in time and conceivable as a great work of art in the course of its creation.

The words "second universe" occur only once in the novel. Nikolai Vedeniapin (whose views coincide with the narrator's and are undoubtedly to be taken as Pasternak's own)[9] is said to be writing books about

> history as a second universe, which mankind was erecting in answer to the pheno-
> menon of death, with the help of the phenomena of time and memory. The soul
> of these books was a new understanding of Christianity, their direct result a new
> idea of art. (3,2)

The previous exact and exacting style for philosophical statements is exchanged here for a new style, less enraptured and more expository. Its special feature is that it repeatedly brings together certain abstract conceptions in such a way that they tend to overlap, to replace each other or to merge. For example, of the eleven or so major abstract nouns in the quotation three recur regularly, often together, in philosophical assertions throughout the novel. "History—Christianity—Art" becomes a single compound motif with the purpose, it seems, of focusing on all of reality at once. In the "new understanding" sought by Vedeniapin, ostensibly different conceptions turn out to be different names for one and the same thing; all of them in various ways overlap in meaning with "life". One could extend the list of all-important, quasi-magically reiterated concepts to include life, immortality, symbolism and parables, genius, Christ, happiness.

By the time of *Zhivago*, Christianity had become very important to Pasternak. Barnes writes of his "increasingly active religious belief in the post-war years". Fleishman says "it is no accident that Pasternak drew close to the church precisely when the regime's unfavourable attitude toward it was becoming more pronounced . . . The moral values cherished by the church formed . . . the sole alternative to the oppressive political atmosphere". Mikhail Polivanov observes, somewhat differently, that the Jewish Pasternak was drawn to Christianity since his childhood, his new relation to it in the novel suggesting some intense personal encounter in the 1940s: "Pasternak then entered Christianity," he writes, "like someone returning home."[10]

Home, or "at home", is the concluding motif of Vedeniapin's first main speech. Since Christ, human beings have been able to die, he says, " not under a fence but *at home in history*" (my italics—A.L.). Given that Christ is the starting-point, it is particularly noticeable that "at home in history" (rather than, say, "at home in God") is the culminating moment. Here is the speech, made, typically, to someone who cannot understand it (reminding us of Pasternak's own difficulty in getting his thought across to contemporary readers). Vedeniapin tells his unreceptive listener:

> it is possible to be an atheist, possible not to know whether God exists and what he is for, yet at the same time to know that man lives not in nature but in history, and that history, as we understand it today, is founded by Christ, that the Gospels are its basis. And what is history? It is the setting up, throughout the ages, of works that are consistently concerned with the solving of death and with overcoming it in the future. For this, mathematical infinity and electromagnetic waves are discovered, for this symphonies are composed. Without a certain elation no forward movement is possible in this direction. These discoveries need spiritual equipment. The things necessary for it are contained in the Gospels. This is what they are. First of all, love of one's neighbour, this highest form of live energy filling the human heart to the brim and demanding to be let out and lavished; and, secondly, the chief components of modern man, without which he is inconceivable, namely the idea of free personality and the idea of life as sacrifice. Bear in mind that all this is still extremely new. Among the ancients there was no history in this sense . . . Only after Christ did the centuries and generations begin to breathe freely. Only after him does life in one's posterity begin and man does not die in the road by a fence but at home in history, at the height of all the works dedicated to the overcoming of death; he dies while he is himself dedicated to this theme. (1,5)

As several commentators have noted, the idea of "overcoming death" calls to mind the philosopher Nikolai Fedorov, according to whose influential book *Philosophy of the Common Task* mankind's sole and concerted task ought to be precisely that: the overcoming of death.[11] Pasternak's "there will be no death" (Iurii's words to the dying Anna), though attributed to John the Divine, author of the Book of Revelation, may also appear to hint at Fedorov. But Fedorov meant a rational, physical conquest of death, something scientists would achieve. They would work out how to extend our lives for ever and, furthermore, how to bring about the bodily resurrection on earth of all deceased human beings. Pasternak's "overcoming of death" does not mean that.[12] He might agree with Fedorov that death is our chief problem and that an eternal after-life is no solution. But the solution, for him, is to build here and now the symbolical, mutable, never-completed "home" of "history".

This idea sounds abstract and difficult, but in the account of Iurii's thoughts after the funeral, an account which exactly exemplifies "work dedicated to the overcoming of death", it appears easy, natural and light-hearted.

Iurii was walking alone, getting ahead of the others with his fast walk, stopping now and then to wait for them. In response to the desolation death had produced in this company stepping slowly behind him, he felt—as invincibly as water twisting into funnels and streaming down to a depth—the wish to dream and think, to work hard at forms, to produce beauty. Now as never before, it was clear to him that art is unceasingly occupied with two things. It persistently meditates upon death and through this it persistently creates life. Genuine, great art—that which is called the Revelation of Saint John and that which goes on writing it. (3,17)

The last book of the New Testament is the starting-point for art to create history in this sense, both because it *is* the last and because of its announcement "death is finished"; nothing implies that the works which continue it are ones with a Christian orientation. Indeed, it could be said that death is already overcome in the passage just quoted, since it is death that gives rise to the wish to create something beautiful. As Schopenhauer said: "Death is the actually inspiring genius".[13]

Vedeniapin's is a highly special view of history. Not history as an attempted account of all that has happened, let alone "a written narrative constituting a continuous methodical record, in order of time, of important or public events" (O.E.D.); instead, history as a collective aspiration, a single, complex human creation, impelled by talent and love. It is indubitably temporal: operative phrases are "throughout the ages", "in the future", " forward movement". Time is welcomed, transience not in the least lamented, attainment of an end unnecessary; to die "at home in history" is already salvation. Moreover, "with the help of time and memory", we "live in our posterity"—that is, still in time. This is a larger, perhaps more intelligible, version of the human-built world which Pasternak once likened to a nest built by the birds known to him as "salangane swallows": "a vast nest, glued together from earth and sky, life and death, and two kinds of time, present and absent", prevented from falling apart by the "figurativeness permeating all its particles" (S-C 2,18).[14]

You do not need to be a Christian, says Vedeniapin/Pasternak, in order to think and feel in the way he is commending. An "atheist" can view history this way, even if it is a way made possible by energies derived from Christianity: love, self-sacrifice, symbolism. Just as Pasternak is concerned to make his experience of art available to everybody including the non-artistic, he is, I believe, concerned to make his experience of Christianity available to everybody including non-believers. The link between them is the second universe called "history", of which the essential component is art and its symbolical thinking.

Talking about the Gospels to a visiting Tolstoyan, Vedeniapin combines the concepts "life", "symbolical" and "immortal".

For me the chief thing /in the Gospels/ is that Christ speaks in parables from everyday life, elucidating the truth with the light of everyday occurrences. At the basis of this lies the thought that communication (*obshchenie*) between mortals is immortal and that life is symbolical because it is meaningful (2,10).

There is no perfect English word for *"obshchenie"*: the word used in the published translation, "communion", has spiritual connotations not present in the Russian word, which covers ordinary social intercourse and trivial as well as spiritual conversations; "relations" is better but covers too wide a field. I am using "communication", despite its sounding rather mechanical, while keeping "relations" in mind as well.

The second sentence in the quoted piece of speech presents two statements as a single thought: (1) "though individuals die, the communication between them does not", and (2) "life is symbolical". Their connection becomes clear if one adds (3) "communication is of meanings, through symbols" and (4) "to be symbolical is to be immortal". So: "although as individuals we are mortal, our communication (our life of everyday relations with one another) is meaningful, therefore symbolical, and therefore immortal." This is a softer (less rigorous, more accessible) form of a thought Pasternak has expressed before. Its formulation actually resembles that of a basic idea in *A Safe-Conduct*. What is immortal, he says here (in *DrZh* 2,10), is not the individual person but the *relations* between individuals, their communication; similarly, in *S-C* 1,6, poetry was born not from any individual episode or experience but from the *relations* between episodes and experiences—from their speeding ahead and lagging behind, their yearning to join one another—in a sense, then, from their communication.

The word "immortal" comes up again and again. Some time before the remark about parables, Vedeniapin opines that one of the few things that deserve loyalty is "immortality, that other, slightly strengthened, name for life." He adds: "we must preserve loyalty to immortality, we must be loyal to Christ!" Again, very large concepts—immortality, life, Christ—are placed in apposition, made virtually synonymous; and, if "life" means not my individual life but (as in the parables passage) everyday human relating and communicating, then this injunction about loyalty re-enacts the same thought: "human individuals die but human relationships do not." The paradox is emphasized by the direct equating of (mortal) "life" with "immortality". That Christ is part of the equation does not imply an expectation of after-death resurrection, as Pasternak has made it abundantly clear that he does not believe in an after-life. By "immortal" he surely means not "living for ever" but "deathless, without death", felt to be outside time. Whereas in the young Pasternak's long-ago lecture "Symbolism and Immortality" timelessness was a special experience of the inspired poet, now this is extended to lives in general: everyone can be free of time through communication (*obshchenie*) with others.

This thought is supported by a passage (in the narrator's own voice) which is also a supreme example of the carefully deliberate merging of concepts: the passage concludes with an unequivocal intimation that there really is only one thing, one essence, one complex moving and flowing event, one human home—merely given different names by different people:

> All the movements in the world, if taken separately, were deliberate and sober, but taken all together they were unaccountably drunk on the general flood of life that united them. People laboured and bustled, set in motion by the mechanism of their own concerns. But the mechanisms would not have worked if their main regulator were not the feeling of a higher and fundamental carefreeness. This carefreeness came from a sensation of the connectedness of human existences, a conviction that they flowed into one another, a feeling of happiness because everything that happens takes place not only upon the earth into which the dead are buried but also in something else, which some call Kingdom of God, others call history, and yet others name in some other way. (1,7)

The tone is carefree and the linked abstractions at the end repeat the robust vagueness which (like Keats's "Beauty is truth, truth, beauty . . . ") is found in other Pasternakian linkings, such as his calling Chopin's *études* lessons in history or in cosmic structure or in anything at all. Now "Kingdom of God" is offered as an alternative for "history", which can also be called something else. The third name could well be "art", or art's characteristic means, "symbolism".

Since the passage is of central significance, it is worth noting that the English translation published in London is misleading in two places. "On the earth which buries the dead" fails to record Pasternak's stress on the materiality of the earth *"into which* the dead are buried"; and instead of the original's carefully nondescript "in something else" the translation gives "on some other level", whereas Pasternak does not speak of "levels" here. His "second universe" is not another "level", but is right here with us, embedded, unispatial with our familiar first universe (of matter and facts), its symbolical equivalent. In the amended translation of the novel published in New York, these phrases are corrected to "in which . . . ", and "in some other region"; but "region" remains curiously unsatisfactory.[15]

As for Vedeniapin's celebration of dying in the midst of continuing history, it has a parallel, perhaps more musical than logical, in two other celebrations, not of dying but of being born in the midst of continuing reality. Both include reference to artistic work—genius, paintings, picture-galleries. One is Vedeniapin's brief vision of Christ's arrival:

And look, into this heap of marble and gold vulgarity, came that light one, clothed in radiance, emphatically human, intentionally provincial, Galilean, and from that moment nations and gods ceased and man began, man the carpenter, man the ploughman, man the shepherd amid his flock of sheep at sunset, man not sounding the least bit proud,[16] man gratefully dispersed through all the cradle-songs of mothers and all the picture galleries of the world.

In the progression from carpenter and ploughman to the suddenly pictorial "shepherd with flock of sheep", and from there to "all the picture galleries of the world", Christ, humanity and art overlap in meaning and almost merge.

The other celebration paralleling Vedeniapin's idea is of the two 1917 revolutions. Each, because of its bold optimistic suddenness, is said to have "genius"; once again a kinship with great art. Thus, speaking of the February revolution, Zhivago leaps in thought from "socialism" to "life", whereby he explicitly means *life transformed by art*:

Everyone has come alive, been reborn, in everyone there have been transfor-mations. It seems to me socialism is a sea of life—the life that can be seen in paintings, life changed by genius, creatively enriched. (5,8)

Speaking later of the October revolution, he evokes a surgeon-cum-artist—like himself and like the long-ago Shestikrylov in "Ordering a Drama"—and again connects the revolution with art and with "genius", by alluding to two great writers:

What magnificent surgery! To go and cut out the old stinking ulcers at once, artistically . . . There's something /in this/ of Pushkin's unequivocal radiance and Tolstoy's unswerving fidelity to the facts . . . This unprecedented thing, this miracle of history, this revelation, is sent slap into the very thick of everyday life as it goes along . . . not at the beginning but in the middle . . . on the first weekdays ready to hand, at the very busiest time for the trams plying about the town. This, above all, is genius. Only the very greatest is so out of place and out of time. (6,8)

Such are passion's "sideways leaps" off the common path of inevitability, to which Pasternak remained forever loyal. The intensity of his memory of that year did not alter, even though subsequent developments made him change his view of the revolutionaries.

That a name or theory should not fix feelings in an unchangeable mould was always of the highest importance to Pasternak. To a friend to whom he was posting the just-finished first part of his novel he wrote: "If it should seem to you that my manuscript sets out any dogmas, puts limits to anything or seeks to incline people towards something—it means the work is written very badly. Everything genuine should set people free, be liberating."[17] He himself certainly resisted being forced by anyone or any tradition into accepting ideas which were not his own, and he called the atmosphere of the novel his own Christianity. "The atmosphere of the work is my Christianity, somewhat differing in its breadth from the Quaker or Tolstoyan sort, and starting out from other aspects of the Gospel in addition to the moral aspects."[18] The relaxed tone of the assertion itself conveys a belief in mental freedom.

Historical change is compared to the work of artistic genius, and another name for kingdom of God is history. Pasternak wants to show that, just as an "atheist" can believe history started with Christ, a Christian can see that living in God may be called living in history; believer and non-believer can be united through symbolical thinking. Many motifs in the novel support such uniting, or bridging. To mention some instances from early in the book: Vedeniapin at once a priest and not a priest (unfrocked at his own request); his search for an idea at once "winged" and "material"; Lara "not religious" yet attending church for the sake of an "inward music"; music the force that raised man from the animals; the adolescent Iurii having "nothing like piousness" in his feeling of kinship with earth and sky (3,15); and his telling a dying woman that there is no death because "life fills the universe in innumerable combinations and transformations" and that our consciousness, which goes only outward, will not cease to be out there in it all. What does it matter, he asks (gesturing towards Pasternak's idea of alternative names for one essence)—if you will then be called a "memory"? There is no death and no after-life, there is only life, our miraculously evolving home in history. We cannot fall out of the universe we have made. To support his profoundly optimistic philosophy Iurii quotes from the New Testament. But the non-Christian reader will take heart from a report that (in 1958) Pasternak claimed to have put religious symbolism into his novel as one puts a stove into a house—to warm it up—and that he objected to the way "some people would like me to commit myself and climb into the stove".[19]

4. " . . . SOME MOVING ENTIRENESS"

Great common abstractions and images overlap: "Kingdom of God" is a way of saying "history"; "immortality" and "Christ" are names for "life"; symbolism merges with parable; "that which is called inspiration" (but could be called something else?) creates not only art but historical change, revolutions. If there are puzzles—such as "kingdom" sounding more static than "history"—this is (I suggest) because Pasternak's purpose is somehow to include *everything*: the potentially surveyable entirety, all versions of it there at once, yet also its internal, interminably mutable and mobile detail. In his account of "everything", analogies with artistic creativity are central.

It is of course not a systematic philosophy and the Pasternak speaking here is still the one who delighted in the "never-beginning of a synthesis", as he so aptly put it in 1911. As David Bethea writes: "he sought meaning not in a closed system but in life as openness, surprise, spontaneous revelation." [20] Nonetheless these ideas show a consistent pattern in their likening the universe, man-created as it is, to a work of art. Pasternak wrote to an English correspondent in February 1959, in his own English: "The objective world in my habitual, natural grasping is a vast inspiration, that sketches, erases, chooses, compares, and describes and composes itself". [21] In August of the same year, the year before his death, he wrote similarly, again using the word "inspiration", to another Englishman, the poet Stephen Spender (and again in English):

> there is an effort in the novel to represent the whole sequence of facts and beings and happenings like some moving entireness, like a developing, passing by, rolling and rushing inspiration, as if reality itself had freedom and choice, and was composing itself out of numberless variants and versions. [22]

I have dwelt largely on ideas about life and art expounded as such in the novel. Analysis of descriptions and structural forms has not been my purpose, nor is it needed now that so many and such varied discussions of the formal principles underlying the novel have been published. But I will say that among those discussions I have found Boris Gasparov's "Temporal Counterpoint as a Principle of Form in *Doctor Zhivago*" particularly illuminating. Recalling that Pasternak spent his youth as a musician, Gasparov suggests an analogy between the novel's structure and musical polyphony. "The whole of *Zhivago* is structured on the 'contrapuntal principle' of the irregular movement of time and the relativity of various events progressing at different speeds." [23] This principle is at work not only in the starting, finishing and interweaving of individual lives, in the evolution of ideas and forms of language, as well as in the spatial movements of trains and trams, it is at work in even the most insignificant happenings. For example (not Gasparov's example), Vedeniapin and his friend walk down a garden path:

> as they walked, the sparrows which teemed in the guelder rose bush kept flying out ahead of them in equal swarms and at equal intervals. This filled the bush with an even noise as though water were flowing through a pipe along the hedge in front of them. (1,5)

Two kinds of movement, a slow forward-walking and a quick outward-flying, sound together like two voices in a fugue, something like a slow bass and a more rapid alto. As the walkers repeatedly catch up with the sparrows, a single sound results from the two kinds of movement, as when one attends to the harmonies in a continuous polyphony. The pattern of flying ahead, interrupting and overtaking—like many other, both small- and large-scale, motifs in the novel—distantly recalls the irregular, interruptive movement of objects trying to catch up with the speeding-ahead poet in *A Safe-Conduct* 1,6.

The polyphony in *Doctor Zhivago* includes the minute and the cosmic. That he wished to describe "everything" Pasternak makes clear in the letters quoted above and makes even clearer in an earlier letter to Spender that same August, which expresses this wish in the extraordinary and memorable metaphor of "everything" as a sort of painting:

> To attain a true resemblance between the imitative efforts of art and the truly tasted and experienced order of life . . . I would pretend [surely meaning "claim"] to have seen nature and universe themselves not as a picture made or fastened on an immovable wall, but as a sort of painted canvas roof or curtain in the air, incessantly pulled and blown and flapped by a something of an immaterial unknown and unknowable wind.[24]

The image is developed further in a letter to Jacqueline de Proyart: the painting being buffeted is itself a depiction of turbulent movement, and the unknown wind has torn the painting off and is carrying it away.[25]

That all reality is a work of artistic genius, a painting depicting powerful movement while itself being powerfully moved: to demonstrate this was Pasternak's conscious purpose in writing *Doctor Zhivago*.

"Garden of Gethsemane" is the last of the twenty-five poems making up the novel's last chapter and is one of the nine on Christian themes. After closely following the Gospel of Saint Matthew for twelve quatrains, it ends with two that move into Pasternak's own imagery.

> *You see, the course of the ages is like a parable*
> *And can catch fire while in movement—*
> *In the name of its terrible greatness*
> *In voluntary torments I shall descend into the grave.*

> *I shall descend into the grave and rise on the third day,*
> *And, like rafts floating down a river,*
> *Like a convoy of barges, the centuries*
> *Will float to me for judgment, out of the dark.*

Ages, centuries . . . the concern is emphatically with time. But how is their course "like a parable" and how does it "catch fire"? Surely it is like a parable in that, as "history", it is a second universe co-spatial and co-temporal with the first, material, one, re-telling it in symbolical form. Then, "catching fire" is the same word (*zagoret'sia*) as in the account in 14,9 of what happens to the poet as he starts to write. So is not this the sudden kindling of inspiration (the "hot axles" in *A Safe-Conduct*)? Revolution breaking out like a conflagration in the midst of common nonchalant events? Our minds flaring up with an ecstatic awareness? And also the birth of Christ? Significantly, it catches fire when it is "in motion" (*na khodu*), the same phrase as in *S-C* 2,3: "The image of man can be engendered only in motion".

The poem—and the whole novel—ends with history moving to a bright destination. There Christ will give a judgment; the tone of the poem suggests that the judgment will be gentle. Less obvious from the translation is the fact that "its" in the third line refers not to "course", "fire" or "movement", but to "parable". Christ's suffering is undertaken "in the name of the greatness of the parable". It is for the parabolic, *the symbolic as such*, that this poem presents him as sacrificing his life. He dies for these very "rafts and barges", that is to say, for the fragile, shared, unlikely awareness which makes human beings able to write and paint figuratively and thus to create history and the whole habitable universe.

NOTES

Titles of works which are listed in the Bibliography are given here in shortened form and each is marked with an asterisk.

NOTES to Introduction

1. The character Igrek in "The Tale" (*Povest'*). PSS, 3, 137.
2. "People and Propositions" (*Liudi i polozheniia*). PSS, 3, 298.
3. Letter of 28.1.1917 to K.G. Loks. PSS, 7, 315.
4. "Tradition and the Individual Talent". *Selected Prose* (Harmondsworth: Penguin: 1953), 27–8.
5. The quoted letter—23.7.1910; PSS, 7, 49; "one commentator"—V.V. Abashev, "Pis'ma 'Nachal'noi pory' kak proekt poetiki Pasternaka", 6.*
6. Timothy Sergay links this passage with a theme of "kenotic self-dissemination" (*Boris Pasternak and the 'Christmas Myth of Blok'*).*
7. Letter of 20.4.1926 to Marina Tsvetaeva. PSS, 7, 662.
8. Timothy Clark, *The Theory of Inspiration*,* 238ff.
9. Maurice Blanchot, *The Space of Literature*,* 54–5.
10. Letter of 12.11.1922 to Tsvetaeva. PSS, 7, 409.
11. *Art in the Light of Conscience, Eight Essays on Poetry by Marina Tsvetaeva*,* 170.
12. "Utro akmeizma" (1913), *Sochineniia v dvukh tomakh** II 141–45.
13. See especially "How are Verses Made" (*Kak delat' stikhi*, 1926), translated by G.M. Hyde (Bristol: The Bristol Press, 1990).
14. "Epic and Lyric of Contemporary Russia. Vladimir Mayakovsky and Boris Pasternak" in *Art in the Light of Conscience, Eight Essays*,* 116 and 118.
15. Letter of 22.12.1959 to Jacqueline de Proyart. PSS, 10, 554.
16. "On Pasternak Soberly",* 205.
17. "an undertaking"—J.P. Stern, *On Realism* (London: Routledge & Kegan Paul, 1973), 32; "give an illusion"—M.H. Abrams, *A Glossary of Literary Terms* (New York, etc: Holt, Rinehart and Winston, 4th ed., 1981), 153.
18. *Opus Posthumous* (Faber and Faber: London, 1959), 166.
19. Letter of 25.3.1926. PSS, 7, 623.
20. Tiutchev—poem "Silentium", 1830; Schiller—*Gesammelte Werke in fünf Bänden*, ed. R. Netolitzky (Berlin, 1962) III 492.
21. Viktor Frank, "Realizm chetyrekh izmerenii",* 83ff. For useful discussion of the concept "nominalism" I am indebted to Fiona Hughes of the Philosophy Department, University of Essex.
22. "Pamiati Reisner", 1926. PSS, 1, 226.
23. Peter Kitson, ed., *Romantic Criticism, 1800–1825* (London: B.T.Batsford Ltd, 1989), 40.
24. "Volny". PSS, 2, 53.

NOTES to I
(Early Prose)

1. An idiom: "it is bound to give itself away".
2. Or capercaillie, a large bird (*tetrao urogallus*) which uses each year the same mating-ground, where it performs an elaborate courtship display. E.B. and E.V. Pasternak note

that, while staying in the Urals in 1916, Pasternak witnessed the hunting of capercaillies at their mating-time; the birds were so absorbed in their performance that they did not notice the hunters and let themselves be killed at a distance of two paces. PSS, 5, 523.

3. In the manuscript version this was followed by the words: "Art is doomed to give itself away by the smallest movement. This is the peculiarity of *the purest of consciences*." PSS, 5, 523.

4. *aktovyi zal:* large auditorium in school or college, where staff and students took the oath of allegiance to a new tsar.

5. Mary, Queen of Scots (1542–87).

6. From Pierre de Branthôme (1540–1614), *Mémoires*. PSS, 5, 524.

7. *Chastelard* (1865), the first of three plays by Swinburne about Mary Stuart. Pasternak translated this play in 1916 but the manuscript of the translation was lost. The correct order of Swinburne's first names is Algernon Charles.

8. "great man"—the printing pioneer Ivan Fedorov.

9. Addressing Reliquimini, the narrator uses the second person singular pronoun *"ty"* which, like French *"tu"*, implies a close relationship, but in his replies Reliquimini uses the second person plural *"vy"*, implying, like French *"vous"*, a more formal relationship.

10. Apparently from the Greek *"koinos"*: ordinary, shared, common to all.

11. Pythagoreanism—sixth-century BC development from Orphism (ancient cults involving belief in unity of all life, reincarnation of souls and importance of "enthusiasm"), adding number mysticism and belief that the soul can be purified by contemplating the divine order of the world.

12. "Aleksandr Makedonsky" sounds like a normal Russian name but is also Russian for "Alexander of Macedon", the conqueror Alexander the Great, 356–323 BC.

13. Most of the passages which the PSS editors put in brackets, to show that Pasternak deleted them, are omitted from the present text, but this one, from "so there was truth and untruth" to "a drawing set you as a task", is included despite its being bracketed, to make better sense of the words following.

14. German: "and one must put frames around the gods, and around love and around all frames which have become life . . . "

15. Shestikrylov: see Commentary.

16. The Russian word for "life" is of feminine gender.

17. Hylozoism—ancient theory that matter has life, or that life is a property of matter.

18. Reference to the German religious philosopher, Friedrich Schleiermacher (1768–1834); the name means "veil-maker".

19. "May everything be well-tempered"—like J.S. Bach's well-tempered clavier.

20. Up to 1902 the Pasternak family spent the summers in Odessa.

21. Kleist (1777–1811), major German writer of plays and stories. Among the stories, "Die Marquise von O", "Das Erdbeben in Chili", "Die Verlobung in St. Domingo", "Die heilige Cäcilie" and "Michael Kohlhaas" are especially important; among the plays—"Der Prinz von Homburg" and "Penthesilea".

22. Kleist tried numerous ways of spending his life (the army, music, philosophy, teaching, travel, administration, farming) before devoting himself to writing.

23. On 22.11.1811 Kleist carried out a joint suicide with the incurably ill Henriette Vogel, shooting both her and himself dead on the shore of the Wannsee near Berlin.

24. ἄσκησίς: exercise, practice, training.

25. Greek ῾ρόος: stream, flow.

26. Presumably the yearning felt by the poetic mind while self-exiled in the opposite kind of thinking (systematic, methodological).
27. The word *"nachinanie"*, used twice in this sentence, is first translated as "beginning", then as "enterprise".
28. See note 23.
29. This long sentence has no main finite verb.
30. Gospel according to Saint Matthew, 18:20.
31. past: *byl'*—for discussion of this word and its translation see Commentary.
32. *apeiron:* that which is boundless and indeterminate and, according to the Pythagoreans, lies at the basis of existence. E.B. and E.V. Pasternak note that "Aristotle develops the Orphic conception of *apeiron* as a productive cosmic chaos . . . " PSS, 3, 629.
33. *byl'* is a feminine noun, but as it consists of a single syllable it is necessarily stressed and therefore "masculine" according to the idea Pasternak introduces here.
34. At thirteen Pasternak began a study of music designed to lead to a career as a composer. See Introduction and *S-C* 1,4, for an account of his giving up music at the age of nineteen.
35. He had leapt onto a horse, one of a herd being ridden by peasant girls, and was thrown by it, getting a badly broken leg. See *S-C* 1,2.
36. That is: "at nineteen I put a stop to 'his' musical ambition, thus annihilating 'him-as 'composer'".
37. "falling-off": a fall (as from a horse) is in Russian *padenie*; decline, breakdown, collapse is *upadok*, translated here as "falling-off" to reflect Pasternak's repetition of the syllable *pad*.
38. The idea of defining the essence of creativity "with a brief line" suggests the 1915 story "The Mark—or Line—of Apelles" (*Apellesova cherta*).
39. "symbolists to wrap the heaped globe in the blue valleys of symbols"—apparently Pasternak's own formulation (*la globe comblée* should be *le globe comblé*).
40. Reference to the Marinetti-influenced conception of futurism, represented in Russia by, among others, Vadim Shershenevich whom Pasternak sharply criticized in "The Wassermann Reaction" (see Commentary).
41. Narzes: Byzantine general, 478–568 AD.
42. $\lim t = 0$: the limit of t is zero; t stands for the time of a cinema frame (sixteenth of a second), extremely fast as compared with the time of a lantern slide and imaginably close to zero.
43. Reference to a story by Hans Christian Andersen.
44. $V, d \ldots$: V stands for potential (electric, hydraulic, *etc.*), d for differential, in mathematical analyses of speed; *"anamnesis"*: reminiscence, particularly the Platonic concept of recollection in which the mind gains true knowledge by recalling the Ideas experienced by the soul in a previous existence.
45. River flowing through the town of Tula.
46. V.O. Kliuchevsky, Russian historian.
47. "Time of Troubles", the period of boyar feuds, pretenders to the throne, social unrest and warfare at the beginning of the seventeenth century, ending with the election of the first Romanov tsar in 1613. By 1611 Moscow and other Russian cities were occupied by Polish forces—hence the reference in this paragraph to "the Polish women".
48. Ivan Bolotnikov and Prince Peter led the uprising of 1606–7 against Tsar Vasilii Shuisky. Bolotnikov was defeated and captured at Tula in October 1607.

49. The small railway station where Tolstoy, fleeing from home at age 82, fell ill and died.

50. In his 1959 memoir, "People and Propositions", Pasternak wrote, of Tolstoy: "the main quality of this moralist, egalitarian and preacher of a lawfulness that would encompass everyone without exception was a unique and paradoxical originality." PSS, 3, 322.

51. V.A. Ozerov (1769–1816) and A.P. Sumarokov (1717–77), authors of classical tragedies on subjects from Russian history.

52. "Savvushka": diminutive of his first name, Savva.

53. M.K. Polivanov, "'Vtoraia vselennaia' u Pasternaka",* 138.

54. Translation of idiom *za kotorye stoiu goroi*": for which I stand like a mountain.

55. Letter of 23.5.1926. PSS, 7, 683.

56. Osip Mandelstam—"Zametki o poezii" in *Sochineniia v dvukh tomakh,*,* 210; translated as "Notes on Poetry" in Davie and Livingstone, eds, *Pasternak,*,* 71. Tsvetaeva—*Art in the Light of Conscience. Eight Essays*,* 51.

57. Letter of 11.5.1912 to his parents. PSS, 7, 91.

58. Letter of 25.7.1907 to P.D. Ettinger. PSS, 7, 32.

59. Wallace Stevens, "Another Weeping Woman." *Collected Poems* (London: Faber, 1984).

60. Lazar Fleishman, "Nakanune poezii: Marburg v zhizni i v 'Okhrannoi gramote' Pasternaka,"* 67.

61. PSS, 3, 539.

62. "Liniia i tsvet" in Isaak Babel', *Sochineniia* (Moscow: Khudozhestvennaia literatura, 1990) I 105–7. Translated by Walter Morison in *The Collected Stories* (Harmondsworth: Penguin, 1957).

63. Term introduced by Viktor Shklovsky in *"Iskusstvo kak priem"*(Art as Device), 1917.

64. Imagery of windows in Pasternak's work has been commented on by several critics, notably by A.K. Zholkovsky, "Mesto okna kak 'gotovogo predmeta' v poeticheskom mire Pasternaka", *Predvaritel'nye publikatsii Problemnoi gruppy po eksperimental'noi i prikladnoi lingvistiki* 61 (Moscow, 1974), 34–7.

65. Fleishman, *Poet and Politics,*,* 45.

66. For discussion of this Latin word I am indebted to the classicist Christine Spillane.

67. "comic device"—Anna Ljunggren, *Juvenilia Borisa Pasternaka,*,* 68; "laying bare"— Fleishman, *Poet and Politics,*,* 43; "deployment of irony"—L.L. Gorelik, *"Nachalo poleta"*,* 351.

68. "Nakanune poezii",* 59–74. Also Fleishman *et al*, eds, *Boris Pasternaks Lehrjahre,*,* in which see especially the Introduction, 11–138.

69. Letter of 23.7.1910 to Olga Freidenberg. PSS, 7, 53.

70. PSS, 5, 36–42.

71. In the Essay on Kleist, *byl'* is translated as "story of events" (2, penultimate paragraph) and "past happening" (4, fourth paragraph).

72. John Edward MacKinnon, "From Cold Axles to Hot",* 151.

73. PSS, 1, 141.

74. PSS, 5, 287–90 (*Mozhet byt', tema o bessmertii . . .*)

75. PSS, 3, 319.

76. "Vassermannova reaktsiia", PSS, 5, 6–11; quotation from page 11.

77. Aucouturier, "Poet i filosofiia"*, 268; Jakobson, "Marginal Notes on the Prose of the Poet Pasternak",* 135–151; Olga Hughes, *The Poetic World of Boris Pasternak,*,* 25.

78. Fleishman, *Poet and Politics,*,* 93–6.

79. The film was entitled *Baryshnia i khuligan* (The Young Lady and the Hooligan).

80. Boris Pasternak and his father were among those who went to the scene.
81. *Anna Karenina*, part 7, chapter 31.
82. *"Noch'."* For English translation by Michael Harari, see Pasternak, *Poems 1955–59* (London: Collins and Harvill, 1960), 59.
83. *"Apellesova cherta"; "Pis'ma iz Tuly"; "Detstvo Liuvers"; "Vozdushnye puti"; "Povest'"*. All are to be found in PSS, 3. For English translations see Pasternak, *Collected Short Prose,** *The Voice of Prose*, and *People and Propositions,** all three books edited by Christopher Barnes. "Istoriia odnoi kontroktavy," ed. E.V. Pasternak in *Izvestiia Akademii nauk SSSR. Seriia literatury i iazyka*, 33, 2 (Moscow: 1974), 150–61.
84. "The Image of Chopin" in Fleishman, ed. *A Century's Perspective,** 312.
85. Fiona Björling, "Child Perspective: Tradition and Experiment. An Analysis of 'Detstvo Liuvers' by Boris Pasternak." In *Studies in 20ᵗʰ Century Russian Prose*, ed. Nils Å. Nilsson. (Stockholm: Almqvist and Wiksell, 1982), 152.
86. Letter of 25.3.1926 to Tsvetaeva. PSS, 7, 623. Just how unfamiliar and difficult to take in is Pasternak's conception of "objectivity", can be seen in way the translators changed "revelation" to "revelations", producing a different meaning: "the revelations of objectivity" would mean things one can learn by being objective, but Pasternak spoke of the revelation to him *of* objectivity. *Letters Summer 1926,** 45.

NOTES to II
(A Safe-Conduct or The Preservation Certificate)

1. For discussion of the title see last section of Commentary to Part II.
2. The identity of "someone" is revealed at the end of section five.
3. On Lou Andreas-Salomé see Angela Livingstone, *Lou Andreas-Salomé, Her Life and Writings* (London: Gordon Fraser, 1984).
4. Town near Tolstoy's estate.
5. A small station or halt.
6. Tolstoy's wife (1844–1919).
7. Count Lev Nikolaevich Tolstoy (the novelist), 1828–1910.
8. Leonid Osipovich Pasternak (1862–1945).
9. Il'ia Repin (1844–1930), artist, associated with the "Itinerants" (*Peredvizhniki*).
10. Artist (1831–94).
11. A Russian folk dance, performed with wide-spread arms.
12. In his poem "Sixth Sense" (*Shestoe chuvstvo*) Nikolai Gumilev (1886–1921) suggests that human beings are evolving a new sense, of which their present inarticulate responses to beauty are a painful adumbration.
13. Carl Linnaeus (1707–78), Swedish botanist, pioneer in classification of plants and animals.
14. Alexander Scriabin (1871–1915), composer.
15. "Poème de l'Extase," orchestral work by Scriabin, first performed in Moscow on 21.2.1909.
16. During Lent only one bell chimes from each church.
17. Reinhold Glière (1876–1956).
18. Of Pasternak's compositions three have been preserved—two preludes and one sonata, all for piano. Recordings of these can be heard from the compact disk attached to PSS, 11.

19. A well-known, fashionable street in Moscow.
20. The boy Ganymede was taken up onto Mount Olympus by Zeus, and became the gods' cup-bearer.
21. Iulian Anisimov (1888–1940), poet, whose translation of Rilke's *Stundenbuch* was published in 1913. Richard Dehmel (1863–1920), German poet.
22. Volume of poems by Rilke.
23. An area of Moscow.
24. "this book", apparently Rilke's *Stundenbuch*. Pasternak's sole meeting with Rilke, in May 1900, is described at the beginning of *S-C*; Rilke was then making his second journey to Russia in the company of his friend and mistress Lou Andreas-Salomé.
25. A Moscow street.
26. Places in Moscow.
27. Alexander Blok (1880–1921) and Andrei Belyi (1880–1934), leading symbolist poets. Blok's first volume of verse, *Poems about the Beautiful Lady*, was published in 1904; his *poema* (long narrative poem) *The Twelve* (1918) was the first important response in poetry to the revolution. Belyi's first influential works were prose poems (1902–3) called "symphonies"; he is also author of important novels, especially *The Silver Dove* (c.1910) and *Petersburg* (1916).
28. A symbolist-oriented publishing enterprise.
29. The University of Marburg, Germany, was famous for its school of philosophy, of which Hermann Cohen (1842–1918) was Head, with Paul Natorp (1854–1924) a professor.
30. In Russian these words rhyme: *pogóda, priróda*.
31. Alexander Savin (1873–1923), professor of medieval and modern history. During the French revolution Maximilien de Robespierre dominated the Convention (the assembly through which political power was exercised) from October 1793 to July 1794.
32. Large central street in Moscow.
33. Paraffin lamps, so called after the firm which manufactured them.
34. A friend and writer (1886–1954).
35. For the later attitudes of these professors to the Soviet regime, see Fleishman, *Pasternak v dvadtsatye gody,** 231. For Pasternak's studies in Moscow see PSS, 3, 556.
36. Widespread movement for teaching literacy to the general population; see PSS, 3, 556f.
37. Henri Bergson (1859–1941) argued for intuitivism and the *élan vital*. Edmund Husserl (1859–1938), founder of the phenomenological approach, which made philosophy a strict discipline using the logic of the natural sciences. Sergei Trubetskoi (1862–1905), idealist philosopher, professor at Moscow University from 1900 until his death.
38. Dmitrii Samarin, friend of Pasternak at school and university, descendant of the well-known Slavophile Iurii Samarin; possibly a prototype for Iurii Zhivago.
39. Moscow University.
40. Tolstoy gave the name Nekhliudov to three of his fictional characters, all serious-minded; Pasternak doubtless has in mind the hero of the novel *Resurrection* (*Voskresenie*, 1899), who ruins a girl by seducing her, then works for the salvation of society, the girl and himself. In an earlier version of *S-C* 1,8 the last sentence of this paragraph was replaced by the following passage: "A mass *[klubok]* of loud and independent thoughts was transformed, in a moment, on the spot, with no superfluous adornments, into a mass of calm words, which were pronounced as if their sound alone sufficed for word to become deed. He thought aloud, that is, with such accuracy in the sequence

of thoughts that to the majority, for whom prejudice has become a second language, he was incomprehensible. Later, after losing sight of him, I involuntarily recalled him twice. Once, when I was re-reading Tolstoy and came across him again in Nekhliudov; then at the Ninth Congress of Soviets when I first heard Vladimir Il'ich [Lenin]. Of course I am talking of something utterly elusive, allowing myself one of those analogies on the basis of which comparisons are made with a crafty, thrifty little *muzhik* [peasant], and a multitude of other, less convincing, ones."

41. Konstantin Loks (1889–1956), a university friend, later a historian of literature.
42. Gottfried Wilhelm Leibniz (1646–1716), German Enlightenment philosopher and Pasternak's main interest in 1910–11, before his switch to the study of Cohen's philosophy. (Note by E.B and E.V Pasternak, PSS, 3, 557.)
43. German philosopher and historian of philosophy (1828–75); from 1872 professor at Marburg University where he introduced neo-Kantianism.
44. Swiss family of mathematicians, flourishing especially in the eighteenth century.
45. Goslar, ancient German mining town. "Terrible Vengeance": story by Gogol'.
46. Countess Elizabeth of Hungary (1207–31), famous for benevolence and almsgiving, canonised in 1235, patron saint of Marburg. "Mediator" (Posrednik), publishing house founded by Tolstoy to produce educational books for the people. Giordano Bruno (*c.* 1548–1600), Italian philosopher who travelled widely, teaching and writing, was arrested by the Inquisition and burned at the stake. Colin MacLaurin (1698–1746), leading Scottish mathematician. James Maxwell (1831–79), Scottish mathematical physicist.
47. Mikhail Lomonosov *(c.*1711–65), scientist and poet, father of modern Russian literature, called by Pushkin "a university in himself", instrumental in the founding of Moscow University; he was sent from Moscow to Marburg and Freiburg to study philosophy, physics and chemistry (1736 to 1741).
48. Hans Sachs (1494–1576), German poet and dramatist. The Thirty Years' War, 1618–48. Elend, Sorge ("poverty", "care")—names of settlements in the Wernigerode region of the Harz mountains, apparently describing the difficulty of cultivating the land there.
49. Jakob and Wilhelm Grimm (1785–1863 and 1786–1859), the collectors of folk tales, studied law at Marburg University.
50. M.P. Gorbunkov. G.E. Lants later wrote works on Husserl, Plotinus and Cohen (see Fleishman, *Pasternak v dvadtsatye gody,** 238).
51. At that time in Marburg there were a number of students from Spain, where Cohen had a considerable reputation; "recent . . . revolution", the Spanish revolution in the spring of 1930; the voice probably that of Fernando de los Rios (1879–1949), member of the Spanish Republican cabinet (see Fleishman, "Sredi filosofov. [Iz kommentariev k *Okhrannoi gramote* Pasternaka] in *Semiosis. Semiotics and the History of Culture. In Honorem Georgii Lotman.* Ann Arbor: Michigan Slavic Contributions, No. 10, 1984, 70–76; reprinted in Fleishman, *Ot Pushkina k Pasternaku. Izbrannye raboty po poetike i istorii russkoi literatury* (Moscow: Novoe literaturnoe obozrenie, 2006, 677–83). Rudolf Stammler, philosopher of law.
52. Nicolai Hartmann (1882–1950), professor at Marburg University; Kant's *Kritik der praktischen Vernunft* (1786) was lectured on by Hermann Cohen.
53. The Vysotsky sisters, from family of well-known Jewish millionaires (owners of what is now the "Wissotsky Tea Company" in Israel). Pasternak proposed to the elder sister, Ida, in Marburg, and dedicated some of his earliest verse to her.

54. Pierre Abelard (1079–1142), French philosopher and theologian; secretly married his pupil Héloise, incurring the anger of her uncle, whose hirelings attacked and mutilated him; withdrew to a monastery, was persecuted for heresy, died on his way to Rome to present his defence.

55. "magic stick": Pasternak has *palochka-ruchalochka,* a variant of *palochka-vyruchalochka,* a kind of hide-and-seek in which the child who "leads" covers his eyes while the others hide; if, when he looks up, he sees one of the others, he runs to grasp a stick which lies in an agreed place, saying "little stick, help me out" *(palochka-vyruchalochka, vyruchi menia);* if the child he caught sight of grasps it first, then that child becomes the leader and the game recommences.

56. These words were followed, in the manuscript and the 1931 typescript, by these sentences: "But love is insight (*prozrenie*). You suddenly discover, within time, that which you did not suspect was there. It is the presence of the future in the present, whereby the present is noticed for the first time. For it is the noticeability of the present that is the future, and the one cannot exist without the other." (Note by E.B. and E.V. Pasternak, PSS, 3, 561.)

57. Tolstoy's story "The Kreutzer Sonata" (*Kreitserova sonata,* 1890), had considerable impact. Its protagonist, having killed his wife from jealousy and rage against her as a sexual object, argues that all sexual intercourse is bad, even within marriage, and that self-control should be practised even if it leads to the extinction of the human race.

58. Frank Wedekind (1864–1918), author of the play *Frühlingserwachen* (Spring Awakening) about the ruin of young people's lives by the prevailing repressive attitudes to sex.

59. To make an elephant out of a fly: to make a mountain out of a molehill.

60. Instead of "it" (ono), which refers to "movement" in the preceding sentence, the manuscript has the word "nature" (priroda). PSS, 3, 561.

61. Russian has two words for "lie": one is *lgat';* the other, *vrat',* has an extra meaning of "to talk nonsense, tell stories, talk at random".

62. This experience is described in the poem "Marburg".

63. One in Hartmann's seminar, one (not mentioned) in Natorp's, two subsequent ones in Cohen's.

64. Two sentences following this in the manuscript were crossed out; they began: "This was a great triumph. For the first time my three-year romance with philosophy was illumined by a practical aim . . . " PSS, 3, 562.

65. Olga Freidenberg.

66. "In these words can be heard objections to the 'social command', the necessity of which was promoted in those years in Soviet literature." (Note by E.B. and E.V. Pasternak, PSS, 3, 563.)

67. "What is perception?"—that is, perception on basis of recognition.

68. *"Verse":* German for "verses".

69. Joachim Nettelbeck (1738–1824), Prussian patriot who helped defend Kolberg against the French in 1807.

70. Evgenii Borisovich Pasternak was born in 1923.

71. Gorbunkov maintained a sporadic friendship with Pasternak throughout the latter's life.

72. *uplotnitel':* "one who makes /the living space/ more compact"; this reflects the obligation at that time to make any unused space in one's home available to lodgers (the beginning of the later widespread "communal apartments").

73. *Narkompros: Narodnyi komissariat prosveshcheniia,* People's Commissariat of Education, established 1917 (later the Ministry of Education).

74. Evgeniia Vladimirovna Pasternak (1898–1965), his first wife.
75. St Gotthard: a high pass in the Swiss Alps..
76. The apostle Simon Peter fell asleep instead of keeping vigil for Jesus in Gethsemane (Mark, 14:37).
77. *"peremyvaia kostochki zemle"*.
78. Sculpture in the Medici chapel in Florence.
79. "Warehouse of the Turks! Warehouse of the Germans!"
80. Ancient patrician families who owned these palaces.
81. *à la Radetzki*: waxed and horizontally extended, like those of Josef Radetzki (1766–1858), governor-general of Austrian possessions in northern Italy.
82. Square of San Marco.
83. Byron, *Childe Harolde's Pilgrimage,* canto IV, stanza XIV, quoted here in English.
84. lion's mouth.
85. The passage from "All around are the lions' mouths . . . " to "more broadly" was omitted from the 1931 publication. E.B. and E.V. Pasternak note that, in the manuscript, the words "more broadly" were followed by "displacement (or dislocation, *smeshchenie*) of the power axes of objectivity". PSS, 3, 567.
86. On these ideas about art, see also Angela Livingstone, "Re-reading '*Okhrannaia gramota*': Reflections on Pasternak's use of visuality and his conception of inspiration" in Fleishman, ed., *Eternity's Hostage.**
87. The birds referred to are actually not swallows but small swifts (family *Apodidae*) known as swiftlets. While all swifts use saliva to bind the materials of their nests, some species of swiftlet build nests largely (even purely) of saliva. The latter are known as "swallows' nests" (in Russian *lastochkiny gnezda*) and are harvested, traded and used for food. Swiftlets are mainly to be found in South-East Asia and Polynesia. There are none in Russia but Pasternak doubtless heard of them as an interesting phenomenon. (Note based on information received with gratitude from Mike Wilson of the Department of Zoology, University of Oxford.)
88. Girolamo Savonarola (1452–98), Italian monk who preached against wickedness flourishing in Church and State; instrumental in getting citizens of Florence to drive out the Medici family; controlled the government there 1494–98; carried out a purge of vices and frivolities; was finally excommunicated and burned at the stake for heresy.
89. See Pasternak's poem "Venice" (Venetsiia), 1913, revised 1928.
90. Polite form of address to an adult Russian is first name plus patronymic.
91. Celebrated actress (1864–1910).
92. The first Russian revolutionary year.
93. Charles Stuart, king of England at time of the English revolution; executed 1649. Louis XVI, king of France at time of the French Revolution; executed 1793.
94. That is, Peter the Great.
95. "Table-turning" and (mentioned in the following three paragraphs) "diary," "notices of dismissal" and "estrangement" of the aristocracy, all refer to features of the last few years of Nicholas II's reign, which ended with the revolution in February 1917.
96. Khodynka: the day after Nicholas II's coronation in 1896, festivities in Khodynka meadow led to hundreds of deaths when spectators' stands collapsed. Kishinev pogrom: on Easter day 1903, a pogrom against Jews in the town of Kishinev was tolerated, perhaps organised, by the tsarist police, with many people killed. The 9th of January, 1905 (or, by the new calendar, the 22nd): "Bloody Sunday", when 150,000 people,

led by priest Father Gapon, marched peacefully to the Winter Palace with petitions to the tsar, to be met by a hail of bullets—this was prelude to the 1905 Russian revolution.

97. Queen Henrietta of England, Queen Marie-Antoinette of France, Empress Alexandra of Russia.

98. In the anxious last years of his reign, Nicholas II sought advice from everyone around him; the peasant priest Grigorii Rasputin (1872–1916) acquired enormous influence over the Empress.

99. After Alexander I, tsar at the time of the1812 Russian military defeat of Napoleon I.

100. Valentin Serov (1865–1911), artist and friend of Leonid Pasternak. The Iusupov family, one of the richest in Russia, was renowned for its patronage of the arts. Colonel N.I. Kutepov, in charge of the household management of the palace, published a book (in four volumes, 1896–1911), for which major Russian artists, including Leonid Pasternak, were commissioned to contribute on the subject of the Imperial Hunt.

101. Nikolai Kasatkin (1859–1930), artist and friend of Leonid; his son was imprisoned for four months in 1905.

102. "epigonic": of a succeeding and less distinguished generation, imitator.

103. This "ape" also appears in "The Black Goblet".

104. Vladimir Mayakovsky (1893–1930), leading futurist poet. An early autobiography is entitled "I Myself"; his famous and influential *poema, A Cloud in Trousers*, was published in 1915; after the revolution he devoted his talents to the new state.

105. "Trap for Judges" (or "Breeding-ground for Judges", *Sadok sudei*): of the two literary almanacs with this title (the first produced by the futurists in 1910, its publication marking their emergence as a group, and the second, more radical, published in February 1913) Pasternak probably refers to the second, in which Mayakovsky made one of his earliest published appearances. (See "Note on literary groups".)

106. Centrifuga, the innovatory futurist group which polemicised with Mayakovsky's cubo-futurists; it published Pasternak's poems until it ceased activity in 1917. Vadim Shershenevich (1893–1942) and Konstantin Bol'shakov (1895–1940), futurist poets.

107. Sergei Bobrov (1889–1971), poet, founder of Centrifuga.

108. Mayakovsky was notorious for the yellow blouse in which he strolled about Moscow.

109. Opera by Rimsky-Korsakov.

110. Vladislav Khodasevich (1886–1939), poet who represented the "epigonic" line in contemporary poetry, while Mayakovsky represented the "innovatory".

111. Published in 1914.

112. *Oblako v shtanakh,* 1915; *Fleita-pozvonochnik,* 1915; *Voina i mir,* 1915–16, *Chelovek,* 1916–17.

113. Written 1919–20, published 1921.

114. "At the Top of My Voice" (*Vo ves' golos*), title of Mayakovsky's last poetic work.

115. In the first draft of Mayakovsky's *"Vo ves' golos"*, these lines appear: "I know the strength of words, I know the tocsin of words, / They aren't the kind applauded by theatre-boxes, / From words like these, coffins tear themselves open / To go galloping on all four of their little oaken feet."

116. Nikolai Aseev (1889–1963), futurist poet, friend of Mayakovsky, member of Centrifuga; married one of the Siniakov sisters.

117. Jurgis Bal'trushaitis (1873–1945), symbolist poet of Lithuanian origin. Viacheslav Ivanov (1866–1949), symbolist poet and philosopher.

118. *Der zerbrochene Krug,* 1808.
119. *volost':* smallest administrative division of tsarist Russia.
120. Zinaida Mikhailovna Mamonova, eldest of the five Siniakov sisters. Isai Dobrovein (1890–1955), composer and conductor.
121. Velimir Khlebnikov(1885–1922), futurist poet.
122. Igor' Severianin (1887–1941), poet, member of the ego-futurist group; Mikhail Lermontov (1814–41), famous romantic poet.
123. Sergei Esenin (1895–1925), poet well known for writing about the Russian countryside, committed suicide in 1925; Il'ia Sel'vinsky (1899–1968), poet, member of the constructivist group; Marina Tsvetaeva (1892–1941), major poet (see note 135); Nikolai Tikhonov (1896–1979), poet and novelist; Aseev, see note 116.
124. "The Bronze Horseman" (*Mednyi vsadnik*), Pushkin's narrative *poema* of 1833, describes the 1824 flooding of the Neva in Petersburg; Dostoevsky's *Crime and Punishment* (*Prestuplenie i nakazanie,* 1866) is set in Petersburg; *Petersburg* (*Peterburg,* 1913)—novel by Andrei Belyi.
125. Son of the philosopher and literary critic Lev Shestov (1866–1938).
126. Osip Brik (1888–1945), prominent formalist critic; Mayakovsky's *ménage à trois* with Brik and his wife, Lilia, lasted several years.
127. *Kapitanskaia dochka,* 1836, Pushkin's only completed novel.
128. *Poverkh bar'erov,* volume of poems by Pasternak, published 1917.
129. *Sestra moia zhizn'* (My Sister Life): the volume of poems by Pasternak, mostly written in 1917 but not published until 1922, which won him his first considerable renown.
130. A Moscow street.
131. Pasternak describes the atmosphere in Moscow during the period following the October revolution of 1917. The word "terror" in the first sentence of chapter twelve was omitted in the 1931 publication.
132. In September 1917 General Kornilov marched on Petrograd (as St Petersburg was called in 1914–24) in an unsuccessful attempt to seize power from the Provisional Government. "I had had a disagreement . . . ": Pasternak refers to an evening of poetry organized by Mayakovsky under the heading "Bolsheviks of Art" (Moscow, 24.9.1917)—he was displeased to be put in this context (see Fleishman, "Pasternak i predrevoliutsionnyi futurism").*
133. K.A. Lipskerov (1889–1954), poet and translator.
134. Konstantin Bal'mont (1867–1943), symbolist poet; Khodasevich—see note 110; Bal'trushaitis—see note 117; Il'ia Erenburg (1891–1967), novelist and journalist; Vera Inber (1890–1972); Pavel Antokol'sky (1896–1978), poet; Vasilii Kamensky (1884–1961), futurist poet; David Burliuk (1882–1967), avant-garde poet and artist, founder of the Cubo-futurist group; Mayakovsky—see note 104 and *passim*; Belyi—note 27; Tsvetaeva—note 135.
135. *Versty,* volume of poems by Tsvetaeva, published 1922. Marina Tsvetaeva, a major poet and close friend of Pasternak, with whom she conducted an intense correspondence after her emigration from Russia (to Prague in 1922, thence to Paris in 1925); as well as a great deal of lyric verse, she wrote many *poemy,* pre-eminently *The Ratcatcher* (1925), as well as many very fine prose pieces; she returned to Russia in 1939 and committed suicide there in 1941.
136. *The Contemporary* (*Sovremennik*), literary periodical founded by Pushkin in 1836, the year before his death.

137. Mayakovsky's "Exhibition of Twenty Years' Work" opened on 1.2.1930 at the Moscow Club of Writers, where Mayakovsky first read his poem *"Vo ves' golos"*. He had been trying in vain, in this very period, to obtain permission to go abroad.

138. Mayakovsky (1893–1930) and Pushkin (1799–1837) died at the same age and both died violent deaths, Pushkin in a duel; their deaths are nearly a century apart; at the very ends of their lives both had seemed to be in the midst of new projects and activity; Mayakovsky mentions Pushkin in a number of his poems, and in one he writes of himself as equal and in some ways similar to Pushkin.

139. Blok's volume of poems *Terrible World* (*Strashnyi mir*) was published in 1916.

140. See note 59.

141. Veronika Polonskaia, young actress with whom Mayakovsky was in love at the time of his suicide.

142. Widow of Vladimir Sillov (Lef theorist executed shortly before the death of Mayakovsky); see first section of Commentary.

143. Iakov Cherniak (1898–1955), critic, literary scholar, editor; Nikolai Romadin, artist; Zhenia: Pasternak's first wife, Evgeniia Lur'e.

144. Passage from Mayakovsky's *A Cloud in Trousers (Oblako v shtanakh)*, quoted at end of chapter sixteen.

145. Semion Kirsanov (1906–72), poet and translator, member of Mayakovsky's Lef group.

146. Lilia Brik was then in London; L.A.G., Lev Aleksandrovich Grinkrug, lawyer, friend of Lilia and Osip Brik.

147. A well-known line in *Oblako v shtanakh*.

148. Volodia, Volodichka: diminutives of Vladimir.

149. Mayakovsky's play *The Bathhouse* (*Bania*) was performed at the Meyerhold Theatre in March and April 1930; he himself was at the performance on April 10th, four days before his suicide. The play was condemned by critics.

150. Letter of 20.11.1932 to George Reavey. PSS, 8, 629.

151. Michel Aucouturier, "Poet i filosofiia",* 264–65.

152. Barnes, *Biography** I 316.

153. As well as the works mentioned, see Fleishman, *Boris Pasternak i literaturnoe dvizhenie 1930-kh godov,** 28–46 and *passim*; and Aucouturier, "Ob odnom kliuche k *'Okhrannoi gramote'".**

154. The passage beginning "When they see a cauldron" and ending "to explode". This is pointed out by Fleishman, who calls the whole of *S-C* "allegorical" in this way. (Fleishman, *Boris Pasternak i literaturnoe dvizhenie 1930-kh godov,** 45.)

155. See note 85.

156. "Ich bin Ihnen mit dem Grundzuge des Charakters, mit der Art meines Geistesdaseins verpflichtet. Das sind Ihre Schöpfungen . . . "—from letter of 12.4.1926 to Rilke (written in German) published in C. Barnes, "Boris Pasternak and Rainer Maria Rilke: Some Missing Links", *Forum for Modern Language Studies*, 8,1 (January 1972), 67. (Translated into Russian in PSS, 7, 648.) "J'avais toujours pensé que . . . dans toute mon activité artistique je ne faisais que traduire ou diversifier ses motifs et que je nageais toujours dans ses eaux . . . "—from letter of 4.2.1959 to Michel Aucouturier (written in French), quoted in Aucouturier, *Pasternak par lui-même* (Paris: Editions du Seuil, 1963), 34.

157. For this Epilogue (*Posleslov'e*) see PSS, 3, 522–24.

158. As expressed by Aucouturier, in Aucouturier, ed., *Pasternak,** 338. Further on ideas of speed, change and dynamism, see Fiona Björling, "Speeding in Time: Philosophy

and Metaphor in a Presentation of *Okhrannaia gramota*", in Fleishman, ed. *Eternity's Hostage.**

159. On Pasternak and RAPP see Fleishman, *Poet and Politics** and Fleishman, *Pasternak v dvadtsatye gody.**

160. Fleishman points out that the reference to syncretism suggests a criticism of early twentieth-century aspirations to a synthesis of all the arts.

161. See note 87.

162. See Fleishman, *Poet and Politics,** 159.

163. Tsvetaeva, "Downpour of Light" in *Art in the Light of Conscience, Eight Essays,** 32.

164. Björling, "The Complicated Mix of the Private and the Public",* 258.

165. The poem "Death of a Poet" (PSS, 2, 63) is translated by Peter France in his "An Etna Among Foothills",* as well as in Boris Pasternak, *Selected Poems*, translated by Jon Stallworthy and Peter France (London: Allen Lane, 1983).

166. Peter France, "An Etna Among Foothills",* 16.

167. *Slovar' russkogo iazyka*, Moscow: Akademiia nauk SSSR, 1981.

168. Fleishman, "Poet and Politics",* 158. See also PSS, 3, 552–53.

NOTES to III
(Fifteen Poems)

1. The prose quotations are from Marina Tsvetaeva, "A Downpour of Light" in Davie and Livingstone (eds), *Pasternak,** pages 43, 46, 63, and Osip Mandelstam, "Notes on Poetry" in the same book, pages 69–71. Donald Davie's translation of Anna Akhmatova's poem "Boris Pasternak" is to be found on page 153 of the same book.

2. Tsvetaeva, see note 135 to Part II.

3. Mandelstam (1891–1938), one of the great poets of the twentieth century, starting as an "acmeist" with *Stone* (*Kamen'*, 1913) and *Tristia* (1922), and producing many more volumes of poetry; also author of great works of prose: *The Noise of Time* (*Shum vremeni*), *The Egyptian Stamp* (*Egipetskaia marka*), *Journey to Armenia* (*Puteshestvie v Armyniiu*) and *Conversation about Dante* (*Razgovor o Dante*); he suffered persecution and exile under Stalin; was arrested in 1938 and died in a far-eastern prison camp.

4. Akhmatova, see note 30 to Part IV.

5. PSS, 1, 454.

6. Letter of 12/13.7.1914 to his parents. PSS, 7, 185–6.

7. PSS, 1, 475.

8. PSS, 1, 480.

9. *Lemprière's Classical Dictionary* (London: Bracken, 1984), 546.

NOTES to IV
(Speeches and Articles, 1930s and '40s)

1. The first Congress of the Union of Soviet Writers opened in Moscow on 17.8.1934 and lasted fifteen days. Pasternak made his speech on August 29th.

2. Communist Party organization for children.

3. Il'ichev spoke in the name of sections of the Moscow garrison.

4. Pasternak had caused amusement by rising from his seat on the platform with an impulsive offer of help to a woman carrying a heavy work-instrument, although she was part of a delegation of workers proudly bearing the tools of their trade.

5. In the *Pravda* version, "useless" was replaced by "superfluous, unknown", and "the phenomenon of the Congress" was replaced by "opinions at the congress".

6. In *Pravda*, "socialist" was replaced by "literary".

7. The congress was held in Paris 21–25.6.1935. Pasternak spoke on June 24th.

8. The plenum was held in Minsk 10–24.2.1936. Pasternak spoke on the 16th.
   In their notes (PSS, 5, 611–15), E. B. and E.V. Pasternak cite different versions of many of the sentences from the stenographic record of the plenum. In *Literaturnaia gazeta* of 24.2.1936 the speech bore the title "On Modesty and Daring" (*O skromnosti i smelosti*). The stenographic record has been published, with commentary, by Christopher Barnes in *Slavica Hierosolymitana* IV (1979): 294–303.

9. Ianka Kupala (1882–1942), Iakub Kolas (1882–1956), Andrei Aleksandrovich (1906–63), Belorussian writers.

10. Aleksei Kol'tsov (1809–1842), peasant poet; Ivan Nikitin (1824–61), peasant poet whose main subject was the misery of the poor.

11. Italy's military action started on 3 October 1935. Christopher Barnes points out that it was not from Tolstoy's diary that *Izvestiia* published excerpts but from his (then) unpublished article "*K ital'iantsam*", and notes that "the political naiveté of comparing Tolstoy with Lenin was later unfavourably commented on at the plenum". See note 8.

12. E. Ia. Mustangova, writer; supportive of Pasternak.

13. Maksim Gorky (1868–1936), first president of Union of Soviet Writers (founded 1934).

14. "literary banquets": on their journey to Minsk and during their stay there, the participant writers indulged in luxurious banqueting. Aleksei Tolstoy (1882–1945), poet, novelist and dramatist (distant relative of Lev Tolstoy); *Fruits of Enlightenment* (*Plody prosveshcheniia*), play by Lev Tolstoy satirising high society and spiritualism, published 1889, first performed 1892.

15. Aleksei Surkov (1899–1982), poet.

16. Mikhail Svetlov (1903–64), poet.

17. Aleksandr Bezymensky (1898–1973), Komsomol poet; "poetry-reading tours": it had become common for Soviet poets to tour the country reciting their verse to large audiences.

18. Fiodor Tiutchev (1803–73), major poet.

19. See Pasternak's account of Mayakovsky in *S-C*, 3.

20. Iosif Utkin (1903–44), poet; Vera Mikhailovna is Vera Inber (1890–1972), poet and writer; the reference is to her speech at the Congress.

21. Reference to the practice of rewarding workers for unusually high output.

22. Johannes Becher (1891–1958), German poet, novelist and critic who lived in exile in the USSR from 1935 to 1945; admired by Pasternak. Kirsanov: see note 145 to Part II.

23. Pasternak refers to his poems "*Mne po dushe stroptivyi norov*" and "*Ia ponial: vse zhivo*"; in both poems (written at the request of Nikolai Bukharin, editor-in-chief of the newspaper *Izvestiia*) Stalin is either mentioned or alluded to.

24. *A Safe-Conduct.*

25. In *S-C* Pasternak describes Mayakovsky as "*chelovek ogromnogo obyknoveniia*" (a person of vast ordinariness); here he remembers calling him "*chelovek krupnogo obyknoveniia*" (a person of huge ordinariness).

26. Dem'ian Bednyi (1883–1945), the most highly recognised Soviet poet in the 1920s, but in disgrace in the 1930s; wrote popular, "folksy" poems and songs.

27. Hans Sachs, see note 48 to Part II; a cobbler by trade.

28. The words from "The lawlessness" to "Tolstoy" were omitted in the journal publication. Reference is to Tolstoy, "Shakespeare and the Drama", *c.* 1903 (described by E.J. Simmons as "one of Tolstoy's characteristically cross-grained efforts at literary criticism" [*Leo Tolstoy,* London, 1949, page 689]) and to works by Voltaire, including his "Essay on Epic Poetry" of 1728.

29. "practical considerations": the publisher refused to publish translations of Richard II and Richard III (though these had not then been translated into Russian); E.B. and E.V. Pasternak note: "Shakespeare's interpretation of the tyranny of Richard III is close to events of the time of Stalin's repressions". PSS, 5, 538.

30. Anna Akhmatova (1889–1966), major poet; her first volume of verse was *Evening* (*Vecher,* 1912); later famous for *Requiem* (written 1935–40) and for *Poem Without a Hero* (*Poema bez geroia,* written 1940). *From Six Books* (*Iz shesti knig*) had appeared in 1940.

31. "Poem Without a Hero", the first version of which Akhmatova read to Pasternak in 1940.

32. Her poem "To Londoners" (*Londontsam*) was written in summer 1940 and refers to German air attacks on London that summer (when the Soviet Union was Hitler's ally). The poem has eleven lines, of which a rough translation goes: "The twenty-fourth drama of Shakespeare / Is written by time with passionless hand. / Ourselves participants in the terrible feast / We'll do better to read, over the leaden river, / Hamlet, Julius Caesar, Lear, / Better today to accompany dear Juliet / To the grave with singing and torchlight, / Better to look in at Macbeth's window / And tremble with the hired murderer. / Only not this one, not this one, not this one—/ This one we have not the strength to read."

33. Evgeniia Knippovich (1898–1988), Ivan Rozanov (1874–1959), literary critics. Goslitizdat, State Literary Publishers.

34. Vasilii Zhukovsky (1783–1852), Romantic poet and translator of poetry.

35. *osnovanie i proizvodnoe.*

36. Mikhail Zenkevich (1891–1973), translator and poet.

37. Konstantin Bal'mont (1867–1942), symbolist poet, translated all Shelley's poems.

38. *stikhiia.*

39. The Paris Commune: committee formed of revolutionary insurrectionists which held power in Paris from March to May 1871.

40. "trans-rational language": a concept important to certain futurists which meant "freeing" the word from meaning and creating new meanings from invented words.

41. Pasternak quotes not from the French but from his own Russian version of "Art poétique" (first published in *Krasnaia nov',* 8, 1938; it differs greatly from the original and translates into English as follows: "O, if in a revolt against rules / You would add conscience to rhymes! // In your rushing verse / May another sky and love / Shine in transfigured distance. / Let it blurt out without thought / All that the dawn foretells to it / Wonder-working, in the dark. / Everything else is—literature."

42. Alfred de Musset (1810–57), French poet, playwright and novelist.

43. On Pasternak's use of "realism" see Barnes, "The Image of Chopin . . . "* in Fleishman, ed. *A Century's Perspective.**

44. *undine:* nymph, female water-sprite; *peri:* fairy.

45. Adam Mickiewicz (1798–1855) and Julius Słowacki (1809–49), Polish Romantic poets; Mickiewicz is author of the national epic *Pan Tadeusz;* Pasternak translated Słowacki's drama *Marija Stuart.*

46. See note 28.

47. For the translated text of Pasternak's reply to the 1925 Resolution—that is, to "O politike partii v oblasti khudozhestvennoi literatury. Rezoliutsiia TsK ot 18 Iiunia 1925"—see "A Propos of the Central Committee's Resolution on Literature", in Barnes, ed. *Boris Pasternak, Collected Short Prose,* * 263–5. (I quote here from my own translation of parts of his reply—A.L.) For the original Russian of Pasternak's reply see PSS, 5, 211–13.

48. Leon Trotsky, *Literature and Revolution* (*Literatura i revoliutsiia* [Moscow, 1924]), 44–5. Here the work of the "fellow-travellers" is called "a transitional art more or less organically connected with the Revolution, yet at the same time not the art of the Revolution."

49. "cognition . . . " belonged to the idea of art put forward by Aleksandr Voronsky (1884–1943), leading Marxist critic of the 1920s and editor of the periodical *Krasnaia nov'* which published the work of many fellow travellers and held to a policy of tolerance; Voronsky was successful until the emergence of RAPP (Russian Association of Proletarian Writers) in 1923; dismissed from his position in 1927 because of his affiliation with Trotsky (Trotskyism being defeated in 1927) and sent into internal exile; he returned to Moscow in the 1930s, was arrested and executed in 1937.

50. Andrei Belyi, 1880–1934, symbolist poet and novelist: see note 27 to Part II; Leonid Leonov, 1899–1994, Soviet novelist; Viktor Shklovsky, 1893–1984, formalist critic and writer; Nikolai Aseev, poet and friend of Pasternak; Boris Pil'niak, 1894–1937, novelist and friend of Pasternak, arrested and shot in October 1937.

51. "Hamlet" (*Gamlet*, 1946), first of the poems constituting the final chapter of *Doctor Zhivago*.

52. Letter of 10.5.1928 to Olga Freidenberg, in *Correspondence of Boris Pasternak and Olga Freidenberg 1910–1954** (*Perepiska s Ol'goi Freidenberg**); also PSS, 8, 207.

53. "You know . . . "—from letter of 3.4.1935 to Olga Freidenberg, *Correspondence,** 153, also PSS, 9, 21; "Have faith . . . "—from letter of 8.4.1936 to T. Tabidze, published in *Voprosy literatury* 1 (1966), 178–9, also PSS, 9, 76.

54. Letter of 15.8.1922 to V. Briusov, quoted by Fleishman in *Pasternak v dvadtsatye gody,** 14–15; also PSS, 7, 398.

55. See note 157 to part II.

56. A. Blok, "Intelligentsiia i revolutsiia", essay of 1918.

57. Em. Mindlin, *Neobyknovennye sobesedniki. Kniga vospominanii.* Moscow, 1968. Quoted by Lazar Fleishman in *Boris Pasternak i literaturnoe dvizhenie tridtsatykh godov,** 269.

58. Letter of 25.12.1934 to his parents. PSS, 8, 758.

59. Nikolai Bukharin (1888–1938), leading member of the Communist Party, influential in the early Soviet years; in disgrace from the late 1920s; subjected to a show trial (as "wrecker of Soviet military power") and executed.

60. Isaak Babel', 1894–1941, major short-story writer, arrested and disappeared in 1937.

61. Isaiah Berlin, *Personal Impressions* (London: Hogarth Press, 1980), 172.

62. Olga R. Hughes, *The Poetic World of Boris Pasternak,** 137.

63. Lazar Fleishman, *Pasternak, Poet and Politics,** 198. Discussed in detail in his *Pasternak i literaturnoe dvizhenie 30-kh godov,** 426–28.

64. "Na diskussii o formalizme". PSS, 5, 445–51. Quotations are from 449ff.

65. *Pasternak, Poet and Politics,** 199–201; see also *Pasternak i literaturnoe dvizhenie 30-kh godov,** 442ff and 481. Malraux's visit was to promote the cause of the international organization of writers against fascism; the halting of the anti-formalist meetings was no doubt due to a direct order from Stalin.

66. " . . . of dispersing the myth"—PSS, 5, 538.

67. Andrei Zhdanov (1869–1948), secretary of the Central Committee of the Communist Party, led a campaign (1946–48) against "cosmopolitanism" in the arts, with a decree attacking two leading Leningrad periodicals for "servility towards the bourgeois culture of the west" and, in particular, for publishing work by Zoshchenko and Akhmatova.
68. PSS, 10, 427.
69. PSS, 5, 556.
70. Mandelstam (see note 1 to Part III), "The Morning of Acmeism" ("Utro akmeizma") in *Sochineniia v dvukh tomakh** II 143.
71. PSS, 5, 543.
72. Boris Pasternak, *Pis'ma k roditeliam i sestram** II 313. This letter was written by Pasternak in English.
73. See note 43.
74. Artur Schopenhauer, *Die Welt als Wille und Vorstellung* II 52; this translation is by R.B. Haldane and J. Kemp, *The World as Will and Idea* (London, 1907), 339.

NOTES to V
(An Essay on *Doctor Zhivago*)

1. Letter of Summer 1921 to V.P. Polonsky. PSS, 7, 371.
2. For example, in letters of 13.10.1946 and 24.1.1947 to Olga Freidenberg (PSS, 9, 472 and 484) and in a letter of 21.5.1948 to V.D. Avdeev (PSS, 9, 519).
3. "I consider…"—from statement published by the journal *Na literaturnom postu* 4 (1927), see PSS, 5, 215; "I believe"—from Olga Carlisle, *Poets on Street Corners,** 88–9.
4. Letter of 20. 3.1954 to Olga Freidenberg. PSS, 10, 22.
5. See, for example, chapter four of Susanna Witt, *Creating Creation.**
6. Letter of 28.4.1955 to N.P. Smirnov. PSS, 10, 80.
7. In *S-C* 1,6—"to, chto *zovetsia* vdokhnoven'em"; in *DrZh* 14,8—"to, chto *nazyvaetsia* vdokhnoveniem [sic]" (my italics—A.L.).
8. See Rosette Lamont, "Yuri Zhivago's 'Fairy Tale': A Dream Poem",* 517–21.
9. On the view that the main characters in *DrZh* express the author's own opinions, M.K. Polivanov writes: "You could write out whole pages of /Vedeniapin's/ thoughts in *DrZh* and be convinced that their content is practically identical with Pasternak's ideas about a 'second universe'", in "'Vtoraia vselennaia' u Pasternaka",* 145; and D.S. Likhachev writes: "The poet writes as if not about himself and at the same time is writing about himself," in "Razmyshleniia nad romanom Borisa Pasternaka", *Novyi mir* 1 (1988), 6.
10. Barnes, *Biography** II 244; Aucouturier, "Poet i filosofiia",*272; Polivanov, as in note 9, 144.
11. Nikolai Fedorov, *Sobranie sochinenii v chetyrekh tomakh,* ed. A.G. Gacheva and S.G. Semenova (Moscow: "Progress/Traditsiia" (1995–2000); and *What was Man Created For? The Philosophy of the Common Task,* selections translated and abridged by Elisabeth Koutaissoff and Marilyn Minto (London: "Honeyglen/L'Age de l'Homme"), 1990.
12. Several writers have discussed Pasternak's relation to and divergence from Fedorov; for instance, David M. Bethea in *The Shape of Apocalypse in Modern Russian Fiction.** Timothy Sergay, in "Death is not our Bailiwick", in his *Boris Pasternak and the "Christmas Myth" of Blok,** shows that Vedeniapin's "historiosophy" is close to Nikolai Berdiaev's form of the idea of overcoming death (an idea which was widespread in the early twentieth century), and that in *DrZh* Pasternak is arguing *against* Fedorov without mentioning him.

13. Schopenhauer, "Der Tod ist der eigentlich inspirirende Genius" in *Die Welt als Wille und Vorstellung* (*The World as Will and Idea*) II chapter XLI.
14. See note 87 to Part II.
15. Boris Pasternak, *Doctor Zhivago*,* (London publication, p. 22; New York, p. 13).
16. Reference to Maxim Gorky's "Man: that sounds proud" in his play *The Lower Depths (Na dne)*.
17. Letter of 20.11.1949 to O.I. Aleksandrova. PSS, 9, 584.
18. Letter of 13.10.1946 to O.M. Freidenberg. PSS, 9, 473.
19. Olga Carlisle, *Poets on Street Corners,** 84.
20. David M. Bethea, as in note 12,* 237.
21. Letter of 8.2.1959 to John Harris, reprinted in Clowes, ed. *Zhivago,* *149.
22. Letter of 22.8.1959 to Stephen Spender, *Encounter* 83 (August 1960), 3–6; reprinted in Clowes* (see note 21), 155.
23. Boris Gasparov, "*Temporal Counterpoint as a Principle of Formation in* Doctor Zhivago". Clowes, ed. *Zhivago,** 92.
24. Letter to Spender (see note 22), 154.
25. Letter of 20.5.1959 to Jacqueline de Proyart, in *Lettres á mes amies françaises,** 174–5.

SELECTIVE BIBLIOGRAPHY

[Titles of frequently cited works are followed by their abbreviated titles in square brackets]

Abashev, V.V. "Pis'ma "Nachal'noi pory" kak proekt poetiki Pasternaka." In *Pasternakovskie chteniia. Materialy mezhvuzovskoi konferentsii*. Perm': Permskii gosudarstvennyi univer-sitet, 1990.

Abrams, M.H. *A Glossary of Literary Terms*, seventh edition. New York, etc: Heinle and Heinle, 1999.

Abrams, M.H. *The Mirror and the Lamp. Romantic Theory and the Critical Tradition*. London, Oxford, New York: Oxford University Press, 1953.

Al'fonsov, V. *Poeziia Borisa Pasternaka*. Leningrad: Sovetskii pisatel', 1990.

Aucouturier, Michel. "Poet i filosofiia (Boris Pasternak)." In *Literaturovedenie kak literatura. Sbornik v chest' S.G. Bocharova*. Moscow: Iazyki slavianskoi kul'tury, 2004.

Aucouturier, Michel. "Pol i "poshlost'": tema pola u Pasternaka." In *Pasternakovskie chteniia 2*. Moscow: Nasledie, 1998.

Aucouturier, Michel. "Ob odnom kliuche k 'Okhrannoi gramote'." In Aucouturier, ed. *Pasternak*.

Aucouturier, Michel. "The Metonymous Hero or the Beginnings of Pasternak the Novelist." In Erlich, ed. *Pasternak*.

Aucouturier, Michel. "The Legend of the Poet and the Image of the Actor in the Short Stories of Pasternak". In Davie & Livingstone, eds. *Pasternak*.

Aucouturier, Michel, ed. *Boris Pasternak, 1890–1960 (Colloque de Cerisy-la-Salle, 1975)*. Paris: Institut d'Etudes slaves, 1979. [Aucouturier, ed. *Pasternak*]

Azadovsky, Konstantin. "Boris Pasternak i Rainer Mariia Ril'ke." In Dorzweiler & Harder, eds. *Beiträge*.

Barnes, Christopher. "The Image of Chopin (à propos of Pasternak's article on Fryderyk Chopin)." In Fleishman & McLean, *A Century's Perspective*.

Barnes, Christopher. *Boris Pasternak, A Literary Biography*, volume I—*1890–1928*; volume II—*1928–1960*. Cambridge, New York, etc: Cambridge University Press, 1989 and 1998. [Barnes, *Biography*]

Berlin, Isaiah. "Meetings with Russian Writers in 1945 and 1956." In his *Personal Impressions*. London: Hogarth Press, 1980.

Bethea, David M. "Doctor Zhivago: The Revolution and the Red Crosse Knight." In his *The Shape of Apocalypse in Modern Russian Fiction*. Princeton: Princeton University Press, 1989.

Björling, Fiona. "Blind Leaps of Passion and other strategies to outwit inevitability. On Pasternak and the legacy from the turn of the 19th to the 20th century." In *On the Verge. Russian Thought Between the 19th and the 20th Centuries*, edited by Fiona Björling. Lund: Lund University, 2001.

Björling, Fiona. "The Complicated Mix of the Private and the Public. Pasternak's Obituary for Mayakovsky in *Safe Conduct* Part Three." In *Severnii sbornik*, Proceedings of the NorFa Network in Russian Literature 1995–2000, edited by Peter Alberg Jensen and Ingunn Lunde. Stockholm: Almqvist and Wiksell International, 2000.

Blanchot, Maurice. *The Space of Literature* (*L'espace littéraire*, 1955), translated by Ann Smock. Lincoln, London: University of Nebraska Press, 1982.

Bodin, Per Arne. "Pasternak and Christian Art." In *Boris Pasternak. Essays.* Edited by Nils Åke Nilsson. Stockholm: Almqvist and Wiksell International, 1976.

Carlisle, Olga. *Poets on Street Corners. Portraits of Fifteen Russian Poets.* New York: Vintage Books, Random House, 1970.

Clark, Timothy. *The Theory of Inspiration (Composition as a crisis of subjectivity in Romantic and post-Romantic Writing).* Manchester and New York: Manchester University Press, 1997.

Clowes, Edith W., ed. *Doctor Zhivago: A Critical Companion.* Evanston: Northwestern University Press, 1995. [Clowes, ed. *Zhivago*]

Davie, Donald, and Angela Livingstone, eds. *Pasternak. Modern Judgments.* London: Macmillan, 1969. [Davie & Livingstone, eds. *Pasternak*]

Döring, J.R. *Die Lyrik Pasternaks in den Jahren 1928–1934.* München: Verlag Otto Sagner, 1973.

Dorzweiler, Sergey, and Hans-Bernd Harder, eds. *Beiträge zum Internationalen Pasternak-Kongress 1991 in Marburg.* München: Verlag Otto Sagner, 1993. [Dorzweiler & Harder, eds. *Beiträge*]

Eliot, T.S. "Tradition and the Individual Talent." In his *Selected Prose,* edited by John Hayward. Harmondsworth: Penguin Books in association with Faber and Faber, 1953.

Erlich, Victor, ed. *Pasternak. A Collection of Critical Essays.* Englewood Cliffs, N.J.: Prentice-Hall, Inc., 1978. [Erlich, ed. *Pasternak*]

Evans-Romaine, Karen. *Boris Pasternak and the Tradition of German Romanticism.* München: Otto Sagner, 1997.

Fleishman, Lazar. *Boris Pasternak i literaturnoe dvizhenie 1930-kh godov.* St Petersburg: Akademicheskii proekt, 2005.

Fleishman, Lazar. "Pasternak i predrevoliutsionnyi futurism." In *Pasternakovskie chteniia 2.* Moscow: Nasledie, 1998.

Fleishman, Lazar. *Boris Pasternak, The Poet and his Politics.* Cambridge, Mass. and London: Harvard University Press, 1990. [Fleishman, *Poet and Politics*]

Fleishman, Lazar. "Nakanune poezii: Marburg v zhizni i v 'Okhrannoi gramote' Pasternaka." In Dorzweiler & Harder, *Beiträge.*

Fleishman, Lazar. "In Search of the Word: an Analysis of Pasternak's Poem 'Tak nachinajut . . .'" In *Filologia Rosyjska. Poetika Pasternaka,* edited by Anna Majmieskułow. Bydgoszcz: University of Bydgoszcz, 1990.

Fleishman, Lazar. *Boris Pasternak v tridtsatye gody.* Jerusalem: Magnes Press, The Hebrew University, 1984.

Fleishman, Lazar. *Boris Pasternak v dvadtsatye gody.* München: Wilhelm Fink Verlag, 1980.

Fleishman, Lazar. *Stat'i o Pasternake.* Bremen: K-Presse, 1977.

Fleishman, Lazar. "Neizvestnyi avtograf Borisa Pasternaka." In *Materialy XXVI nauchnoi studencheskoi konferentsii.* Tartu: Tartu State University, 1971.

Fleishman, Lazar, ed. *Eternity's Hostage. Selected Papers from the Stanford International Conference on Boris Pasternak, May, 2004. In Honor of Evgeny Pasternak and Elena Pasternak.* Stanford: Stanford University Press, 2006. [Fleishman, ed. *Eternity's Hostage.*]

Fleishman, Lazar, and Hugh McLean, eds. *A Century's Perspective. Essays on Russian Literature in Honor of Olga Raevsky Hughes and Robert P. Hughes.* Stanford: Stanford University Press, 2006. [Fleishman & McLean, eds. *Century's Perspective.*]

Fleishman, Lazar, Joan Delaney Grossman, Robert P. Hughes, Simon Karlinsky, John E. Malm-stad, and Olga Raevsky-Hughes, eds. *Boris Pasternak and his Times. Selected Papers from the Second International Symposium on Pasternak*. Berkeley: Berkeley Slavic Specialties, 1989. [Fleishman *et al*, eds. Pasternak and His Times]

Fleishman, Lazar, Sergei Dorzweiler and Hans-Bernd Harder. *Boris Pasternaks Lehrjahre: Neopub-likovannye filosofskie konspekty i zametki Borisa Pasternaka*. In two volumes. Stanford: Stanford University Press, 1996.

France, Peter. "An Etna Among Foothills: the Death of Mayakovsky." In *Dying Words. The Last Moments of Writers and Philosophers*, edited by Martin Crowley. Amsterdam: Rodopi, 2000.

Frank, Viktor. "Realizm chetyrekh izmerenii." In his *Izbrannye stat'i*. London: Overseas Publications Interchange, 1974.

Gasparov, Boris. "Vremennoi kontrapunkt kak formoobrazuiushchii printsip romana Pasternaka 'Doktor Zhivago'." In Fleishman *et al.*, eds. *BP and His Times*. Translated (a shortened version) as "Temporal Counterpoint as Principle of Formation in 'Doctor Zhivago'" in Clowes ed. *Zhivago*.

Gasparov, M.L. and I.Iu. Podgaetskaia. "Chetyre stikhotvoreniia iz *Sestry moei—zhizni*: sverka ponimaniia." In *Poetry and Revolution. Boris Pasternak's "My Sister Life"*, edited by Lazar Fleishman. Stanford: Stanford University Press, 1999.

Gerard, Alexander. *An Essay on Genius*. London, 1774.

Ghiselin, Brewster, ed. *The Creative Process: A Symposium*. Berkeley: University of California Press, 1952.

Gorelik, L.L. "*Nachalo poleta: Tema vozdushnogo puti v proze Pasternaka 1910-ogo goda.*" In *Studia Russica XIX*. Budapest: Budapest University, 2001.

Harding, Rosamund. *An Anatomy of Inspiration*. Cambridge: W.Heffer and Sons, 1940.

Hughes, Olga. "O samoubiistve Maiakovskogo v 'Okhrannoi gramote'." In Fleishman *et al*, eds. *BP and His Times*.

Hughes, Olga. *The Poetic World of Boris Pasternak*. Princeton: Princeton U.P., 1974.

Jakobson, Roman. "Randbemerkungen zur Prosa des Dichters Pasternak." In *Slavische Rundschau* 6 (1935): 357–374. Translated as "Marginal Notes on the Prose of the Poet Pasternak" in Davie & Livingstone, eds. *Pasternak*.

Jensen, Peter Alberg. "Boris Pasternak's 'Opredelenie poezii'." In *Text and Context. Essays to Honor Nils Åke Nilsson*. Stockholm: Almqvist and Wiksell International, 1980.

Lamont, Rosette. "Yuri Zhivago's 'Fairy Tale': A Dream Poem." In *World Literature Today* LI (1977), 517–21.

Likhachev, D.S. "Razmyshleniia nad romanom Borisa Pasternaka *Doktor Zhivago*." *Novyi mir* 1 (1988): 5–10.

Livingstone, Angela. "Re-reading *Okhrannaia gramota*: Pasternak's Use of Visuality and his Conception of Inspiration." In Fleishman, ed. *Eternity's Hostage*.

Livingstone, Angela. "How to Translate the Title '*Okhrannaia gramota*'." In Fleishman, ed. *Eternity's Hostage*.

Livingstone, Angela. "Unexpected Affinities between *Doctor Zhivago* and *Chevengur*." In *V krugu Zhivago. Pasternakovskii sbornik*, edited by Lazar Fleishman. Stanford: Stanford U.P., 2000.

Livingstone, Angela. *Pasternak, Doctor Zhivago (Landmarks of World Literature)*. Cambridge, New York, etc: Cambridge University Press, 1989.

Livingstone, Angela. "'Integral Errors': remarks on the writing of *Doctor Zhivago*." In *Essays in Poetics* 13, 2 (1988) 83–94.

Livingstone, Angela. "At Home in History: Pasternak and Popper." In *Slavica Hierosolymitana* 4 (1979): 131–45.

Livingstone, Angela. "Pasternak's Last Poetry." In Erlich, Victor, ed. *Pasternak*.

Livingstone, Angela. "Allegory and Christianity in *Doctor Zhivago*." In *Melbourne Slavonic Studies* 5–6 (1971), 24–33.

Ljunggren, Anna. *Juvenilia Pasternaka. Shest' fragmentov o Relikvimini*. Stockholm: Almqvist and Wiksell International, 1984.

Lotman, Yury. "Stikhotvoreniia rannego Pasternaka." In *Trudy po znakovym sistemam* IV (1969), 470–77.

Lotman, Yury. "Language and Reality in the Early Pasternak." In Erlich, Victor, ed. *Pasternak*.

MacKinnon, John Edward. "From Cold Axles to Hot: Boris Pasternak's Theory of Art". *British Journal of Aesthetics* 28, 2 (Spring 1988), 145–161.

Mandel'shtam, Osip. "Notes on Poetry." In Davie & Livingstone, eds, *Pasternak*.

Mandel'shtam, Osip. *Sochineniia v dvukh tomakh*, edited by S.S. Averintsev and P.M. Nerler. Moscow: Khudozhestvennaia literatura, 1998.

Masing-Delic, Irene. *Abolishing Death: a Salvation Myth of Russian 20th-Century Literature*. Stanford: Stanford University Press, 1992.

Miłosz, Czesław. "On Pasternak Soberly." *Books Abroad* 44, 2 (1970), 200–09.

O'Connor, Katherine. *Boris Pasternak's 'My Sister- Life'. The Illusion of Narrative*. Ann Arbor: Ardis. 1988.

Pasternak, Boris. *Polnoe sobranie sochinenii s prilozheniiami, v odinnadtsati tomakh* [Complete Collected Works with Appendices, in Eleven Volumes]. Chief editor: D.V. Tevekelian. Compiled and provided with commentaries by E.B. Pasternak and E.V. Pasternak. Introduction by Lazar Fleishman. Moscow: Slovo, 2003–05. [PSS]

Pasternak, Boris. *Sobranie sochinenii v piati tomakh*. Edited by A.A. Voznesensky, D.S. Likhachev, D.F. Mamleev, A.A. Mikhailov, Evgenii Borisovich Pasternak. Commentaries by E.V. Pasternak and K.M. Polivanov. Introduction by D.S. Likhachev. Moscow: Khudozhestvennaia literatura, 1989–1992.

Pasternak, Boris. *Doctor Zhivago*. Translated by Max Hayward and Manya Harari. London: Collins and Harvill Press, 1958; New York: Pantheon Books, 1958.

Pasternak, Boris. *Collected Short Prose*, edited by Christopher Barnes. New York: Praeger Publishers, 1977.

Pasternak, Boris. *The Voice of Prose:* volume I—*Early Prose and Autobiography*, volume II—*People and Propositions*. Edited by Christopher Barnes. Edinburgh: Polygon, 1986 and 1990.

Pasternak, E. *Boris Pasternak. Biografiia*. Moscow: Tsitadel', 1997.

Pasternak, Evgeny. Boris Pasternak. *The Tragic Years 1930–60*. Translated by Michael Duncan, poetry translated by Ann Pasternak Slater and Craig Raine. London: Collins Harvill, 1990.

Pasternak, E. *Materialy dlia biografii*. Moscow: Sovetskii pisatel', 1989.

Pasternak, Yevgeny, Yelena Pasternak, K.M. Azadovsky, eds. *Letters Summer 1926. Pasternak. Tsvetayeva. Rilke*. Translated by Margaret Wettlin and Walter Arndt. London: Jonathan Cape, 1986.

Pasternak, Boris. *Perepiska s Ol'goi Freidenberg*. Edited by Elliott Mossman. New York and London: Harcourt Brace Jovanovich, 1981. Translated by Elliott Mossman and Margaret Wettlin as *The Correspondence of Boris Pasternak and Olga Freidenberg 1910–1954*, edited by Elliott Mossman. London: Secker and Warburg, *c.* 1982.

Pasternak, Boris. *Pis'ma k roditeliam i sestram,* edited by E.B. and E.V. Pasternak. Stanford: Stanford University and Berkeley Slavic Specialties, 1998.

Pasternak, Boris. *Lettres à mes amies françaises 1956–60.* Introduction and Notes by Jacqueline de Proyart. Paris: Gallimard, 1994.

Pasternak, E.B. and E.V., eds, *Boris Pasternak ob isskustve.* Moscow: Iskusstvo, 1990.

Pasternak, E.V. "Iz rannikh prozaicheskikh opytov Borisa Pasternaka." In *Pamiatniki kul'tury.* Moscow: Nauka (1977), 106–18.

Pasternak, Evgeny, "Pamiat' i zabvenie kak osnova 'Vtoroi vselennoi' v tvorchestve i filosofii Borisa Pasternaka." In *Themes and Variations. In Honor of Lazar Fleishman,* edited by Konstantin Polivanov, Irina Shevelenko, Andrey Ustinov. Stanford: Stanford University Press, 1994.

Podgaetskaia, Irina. "Pasternak i Verlen." In Dorzweiler & Harder, eds. *Beiträge.*

Polivanov, Mikhail. "'Vtoraia vselennaia' u Pasternaka." In Dorzweiler & Harder, eds. *Beiträge.*

Pomorska, Krystyna. "Music as theme and constituent of Pasternak's poems." In *Slavic Poetics. Essays in Honor of Kiril Taranovsky.* Edited by Roman Jakobson, C.H. van Schooneveld and Dean S. Worth. The Hague, Paris: Mouton, 1973.

Rashkovskaia, M.A. "Pasternak o Maiakovskom." In *Pasternakovskie chteniia,* Moscow: Nasledie, 1998. (Speech by Pasternak in April 1933, with introductory note.)

Sergay, Timothy. "Death is not our Bailiwick," in his *Boris Pasternak and the "Christmas Myth" of Blok,* dissertation in progress for Yale University.

Smirnov, Igor'. *Roman tain, Doktor Zhivago.* Moscow: Novoe literaturnoe obozrenie, 1996.

Terras, Victor (ed.). *Handbook of Russian Literature.* New Haven and London: Yale University Press, 1985.

Tsvetaeva, Marina. "A Downpour of Light." In Davie & Livingstone, eds. *Pasternak.*

Tsvetaeva, Marina. *Art in the Light of Conscience. Eight Essays on Poetry.* Translated and edited by Angela Livingstone. Bristol: Bristol Classical Press, 1992.

Tsvetaeva, Marina. *Izbrannaia proza 1917–1937 v dvukh tomakh,* edited by Alexander Sumerkin. New York: Russica Publishers Inc., 1979.

Tsvetaeva, Marina and Boris Pasternak. *Dushi nachinaiut videt'. Pis'ma 1922–1936 godov.* Edited by E.B. Korkina and I.D. Shevelenko. Moscow: Vagrius, 2004.

Witt, Susanna. *Creating Creation, Readings of Pasternak's 'Doctor Zhivago'.* Stockholm: Almqvist and Wiksell International, 2000.

Zelinsky, Bodo. "Selbstdefinitionen der Poesie bei Pasternak." In *Zeitschrift für Slavische Philologie* 38 (1975), 268–78.

INDEX

1. REFERENCES TO WORKS BY BORIS PASTERNAK

2. REFERENCES TO PERSONS

CPSIA information can be obtained at www.ICGtesting.com
Printed in the USA
BVOW06s1913060815

412089BV00003B/16/P